ATS-21c   ADMISSION TEST SERIES

This is your
PASSBOOK for...

Scholastic Aptitude Test (SAT) - Math

Test Preparation Study Guide
Questions & Answers

COPYRIGHT NOTICE

This book is SOLELY intended for, is sold ONLY to, and its use is RESTRICTED to individual, bona fide applicants or candidates who qualify by virtue of having seriously filed applications for appropriate license, certificate, professional and/or promotional advancement, higher school matriculation, scholarship, or other legitimate requirements of education and/or governmental authorities.

This book is NOT intended for use, class instruction, tutoring, training, duplication, copying, reprinting, excerption, or adaptation, etc., by:

1) Other publishers
2) Proprietors and/or Instructors of "Coaching" and/or Preparatory Courses
3) Personnel and/or Training Divisions of commercial, industrial, and governmental organizations
4) Schools, colleges, or universities and/or their departments and staffs, including teachers and other personnel
5) Testing Agencies or Bureaus
6) Study groups which seek by the purchase of a single volume to copy and/or duplicate and/or adapt this material for use by the group as a whole without having purchased individual volumes for each of the members of the group
7) Et al.

Such persons would be in violation of appropriate Federal and State statutes.

PROVISION OF LICENSING AGREEMENTS – Recognized educational, commercial, industrial, and governmental institutions and organizations, and others legitimately engaged in educational pursuits, including training, testing, and measurement activities, may address request for a licensing agreement to the copyright owners, who will determine whether, and under what conditions, including fees and charges, the materials in this book may be used them. In other words, a licensing facility exists for the legitimate use of the material in this book on other than an individual basis. However, it is asseverated and affirmed here that the material in this book CANNOT be used without the receipt of the express permission of such a licensing agreement from the Publishers. Inquiries re licensing should be addressed to the company, attention rights and permissions department.

All rights reserved, including the right of reproduction in whole or in part, in any form or by any means, electronic or mechanical, including photocopying, recording, or by any information storage and retrieval system, without permission in writing from the Publisher.

Copyright © 2025 by
National Learning Corporation

212 Michael Drive, Syosset, NY 11791
(516) 921-8888 • www.passbooks.com
E-mail: info@passbooks.com

PASSBOOK® SERIES

THE *PASSBOOK® SERIES* has been created to prepare applicants and candidates for the ultimate academic battlefield – the examination room.

At some time in our lives, each and every one of us may be required to take an examination – for validation, matriculation, admission, qualification, registration, certification, or licensure.

Based on the assumption that every applicant or candidate has met the basic formal educational standards, has taken the required number of courses, and read the necessary texts, the *PASSBOOK® SERIES* furnishes the one special preparation which may assure passing with confidence, instead of failing with insecurity. Examination questions – together with answers – are furnished as the basic vehicle for study so that the mysteries of the examination and its compounding difficulties may be eliminated or diminished by a sure method.

This book is meant to help you pass your examination provided that you qualify and are serious in your objective.

The entire field is reviewed through the huge store of content information which is succinctly presented through a provocative and challenging approach – the question-and-answer method.

A climate of success is established by furnishing the correct answers at the end of each test.

You soon learn to recognize types of questions, forms of questions, and patterns of questioning. You may even begin to anticipate expected outcomes.

You perceive that many questions are repeated or adapted so that you can gain acute insights, which may enable you to score many sure points.

You learn how to confront new questions, or types of questions, and to attack them confidently and work out the correct answers.

You note objectives and emphases, and recognize pitfalls and dangers, so that you may make positive educational adjustments.

Moreover, you are kept fully informed in relation to new concepts, methods, practices, and directions in the field.

You discover that you are actually taking the examination all the time: you are preparing for the examination by "taking" an examination, not by reading extraneous and/or supererogatory textbooks.

In short, this PASSBOOK®, used directedly, should be an important factor in helping you to pass your test.

SCHOLASTIC APTITUDE TEST

Reading Test

In the Reading Test, students will encounter questions like those asked in a lively, thoughtful, evidence-based discussion.

The Reading Test focuses on the skills and knowledge at the heart of education: what you've been learning in high school and what you'll need to succeed in college. It's about how you take in, think about, and use information.

- All Reading Test questions are multiple choices and based on passages.
- Some passages are paired with other passages.
- Informational graphics, such as tables, graphs, and charts, accompany some passages—but no math is required.
- Prior topic-specific knowledge is not tested.
- The Reading Test is part of the Evidence-Based Reading and Writing section.

When you take the Reading Test, you'll read passages and interpret informational graphics. Then you'll use what you've read to answer questions.

Some questions ask you to locate a piece of information or an idea stated directly. But you'll also need to understand what the author's words imply. In other words, you have to read between the lines.

To succeed in college and a career, you'll need to apply reading skills in all sorts of subjects. Not coincidentally, you'll also need those skills to do well on the Reading Test.
The Reading Test always includes

- One passage from a classic or contemporary work of U.S. or world literature.
- One passage or a pair of passages from either a U.S. founding document or a text in the Great Global Conversation they inspired. The U.S. Constitution or a speech.
- A selection about economics, psychology, sociology, or some other social science.
- Two science passages (or one passage and one passage pair) that examine foundational concepts and developments in Earth science, biology, chemistry, or physics.

A lot more goes into reading than you might realize—and the Reading Test measures a range of reading skills.

Some questions ask you to:
- Find evidence in a passage (or pair of passages) that best supports the answer to a previous question or serves as the basis for a reasonable conclusion.
- Identify how authors use evidence to support their claims.
- Find a relationship between an informational graphic and the passage it's paired with.

From the official announcement for educational purposes

Many questions focus on important, widely used words and phrases that you'll find in texts in many different subjects. The words are ones that you'll use in college and the workplace long after test day.

The SAT focuses on your ability to:

- Use contextual clues in a passage to figure out which meaning of a word or phrase is being used.
- Decide how an author's word choice shapes meaning, style, and tone.

The Reading Test includes passages in the fields of history, social studies, and science. You'll be asked questions that require you to draw on the reading skills needed most to succeed in those subjects. For instance, you might read about an experiment then see questions that ask you to:
- Examine hypotheses.
- Interpret data.
- Consider implications.

Answers are based only on the content stated in or implied by the passage.

Writing and Language Test

The SAT Writing and Language Test asks you to be an editor and improve passages that were written especially for the test—and that include deliberate errors.

When you take the Writing and Language Test, you'll do three things that people do all the time when they write and edit:

1. Read.
2. Find mistakes and weaknesses.
3. Fix them.

- All questions are multiple choices and based on passages.
- Some passages are accompanied by informational graphics, such as tables, graphs, and charts—but no math is required.
- Prior topic knowledge is never tested.
- The Writing and Language Test is part of the Evidence-Based Reading and Writing section.

To answer some questions, you'll need to look closely at a single sentence. Others require reading the entire piece and interpreting a graphic. For instance, you might be asked to choose a sentence that corrects a misinterpretation of a scientific chart or that better explains the importance of the data.

The passages you improve will range from arguments to nonfiction narratives and will be about careers, history, social studies, the humanities, and science.

Questions on the Writing and Language Test measure a range of skills.

Questions that test command of evidence ask you to improve the way passages develop information and ideas. For instance, you might choose an answer that sharpens an argumentative claim or adds a relevant supporting detail.

Some questions ask you to improve word choice. You'll need to choose the best words to use based on the text surrounding them. Your goal will be to make a passage more precise or concise, or to improve syntax, style, or tone.

Analysis in History/Social Studies and in Science

You'll be asked to read passages about topics in history, social studies, and science with a critical eye and make editorial decisions that improve them.

Some questions ask about a passage's organization and its impact. For instance, you will be asked which words or structural changes improve how well it makes its point and how well its sentences and paragraphs work together.

This is about the building blocks of writing: sentence structure, usage, and punctuation. You'll be asked to change words, clauses, sentences, and punctuation. Some topics covered include verb tense, parallel construction, subject-verb agreement, and comma use.

Math Test

The SAT Math Test covers a range of math practices, with an emphasis on problem solving, modeling, using tools strategically, and using algebraic structure.

Instead of testing you on every math topic there is, the SAT asks you to use the math that you'll rely on most in all sorts of situations. Questions on the Math Test are designed to mirror the problem solving and modeling you'll do in:

- College math, science, and social science courses
- The jobs that you hold
- Your personal life

For instance, to answer some questions you'll need to use several steps—because in the real world a single calculation is rarely enough to get the job done.

- Most math questions will be multiple choices, but some—called grid-ins—ask you to come up with the answer rather than select the answer.
- The Math Test is divided into two portions: Math Test–Calculator and Math Test–No Calculator.
- Some parts of the test include several questions about a single scenario.

The Math Test will focus in depth on the three areas of math that play the biggest role in a wide range of college majors and careers:

- Heart of Algebra, which focuses on the mastery of linear equations and systems.
- Problem Solving and Data Analysis, which is about being quantitatively literate.
- Passport to Advanced Math, which features questions that require the manipulation of complex equations.

The Math Test also draws on Additional Topics in Math, including the geometry and trigonometry most relevant to college and career readiness.
The Math Test is a chance to show that you:

- Carry out procedures flexibly, accurately, efficiently, and strategically.
- Solve problems quickly by identifying and using the most efficient solution approaches. This might involve solving a problem by inspection, finding a shortcut, or reorganizing the information you've been given.

You'll demonstrate your grasp of math concepts, operations, and relations. For instance, you might be asked to make connections between properties of linear equations, their graphs, and the contexts they represent.

These real-world problems ask you to analyze a situation, determine the essential elements required to solve the problem, represent the problem mathematically, and carry out a solution.

Calculators are important tools, and to succeed after high school, you'll need to know how—and when—to use them. In the Math Test–Calculator portion of the test, you'll be able to focus on complex modeling and reasoning because your calculator can save you time.

However, the calculator is, like any tool, only as smart as the person using it. The Math Test includes some questions where it's better not to use a calculator, even though you're allowed to. In these cases, students who make use of structure or their ability to reason will probably finish before students who use a calculator.

The Math Test–No Calculator portion of the test makes it easier to assess your fluency in math and your understanding of some math concepts. It also tests well-learned technique and number sense.

Although most of the questions on the Math Test are multiple choices, 22 percent are student-produced response questions, also known as grid-ins. Instead of choosing a correct answer from a list of options, you'll need to solve problems and enter your answers in the grids provided on the answer sheet.

SAT Essay

The redesigned SAT Essay asks you to use your reading, analysis, and writing skills.

The SAT Essay is a lot like a typical college writing assignment in which you're asked to analyze a text. Take the SAT with Essay and show colleges that you're ready to come to campus and write.

- Read a passage.
- Explain how the author builds an argument to persuade an audience.
- Support your explanation with evidence from the passage.

The prompt (question) shown below, or a nearly identical one, is used every time the SAT is given.

As you read the passage below, consider how [the author] uses evidence, such as facts or examples, to support claims.

- evidence, such as facts or examples, to support claims.
- reasoning to develop ideas and to connect claims and evidence.
- stylistic or persuasive elements, such as word choice or appeals to emotion, to add power to the ideas expressed.

Write an essay in which you explain how [the author] builds an argument to persuade [his/her] audience that [author's claim]. In your essay, analyze how [the author] uses one or more of the features listed above (or features of your own choice) to strengthen the logic and persuasiveness of [his/her] argument. Be sure that your analysis focuses on the most relevant features of the passage. Your essay should not explain whether you agree with [the author's] claims, but rather explain how the author builds an argument to persuade [his/her] audience.

You can count on seeing the same prompt no matter when you take the SAT with Essay, but the passage will be different every time.

All passages have these things in common:

- Written for a broad audience
- Argue a point
- Express subtle views on complex subjects
- Use logical reasoning and evidence to support claims
- Examine ideas, debates, or trends in the arts and sciences, or civic, cultural, or political life
- Always taken from published works

All the information you need to write your essay will be included in the passage or in notes about it.

The SAT Essay shows how well you understand the passage and use it as the basis for a well-written, thought-out discussion. The two people who score your essay will each award between 1 and 4 points in each of these three categories:

Reading: A successful essay shows that you understood the passage, including the interplay of central ideas and important details. It also shows an effective use of textual evidence.

Analysis: A successful essay shows your understanding of how the author builds an argument by:
- Examining the author's use of evidence, reasoning, and other stylistic and persuasive techniques
- Supporting and developing claims with well-chosen evidence from the passage

Writing: A successful essay is focused, organized, and precise, with an appropriate style and tone that varies sentence structure and follows the conventions of standard written English.

You don't have to take the SAT with Essay, but if you do, you'll be able to apply to schools that require it. Find out which schools require or recommend the SAT Essay.

Key Content Features

Many questions on the SAT focus on important, widely used words and phrases found in texts in many different subjects. Some questions ask you to figure out a word's meaning based on context. The words are ones that you will probably encounter in college or in the workplace long after test day.

The Evidence-Based Reading and Writing section and the SAT Essay ask you to interpret, synthesize, and use evidence found in a wide range of sources. These sources include informational graphics, such as tables, charts, and graphs, as well as multiparagraph passages in the areas of literature and literary nonfiction, the humanities, science, history and social studies, and on topics about work and career.

For every passage or pair of passages you'll see during the Reading Test, at least one question will ask you to identify which part of the text best supports the answer to the previous question. In other instances, you'll be asked to find the best answer to a question by pulling together information conveyed in words and graphics.

The Writing and Language Test also focuses on command of evidence. It asks you to do things like analyze a series of sentences or paragraphs and decide if it makes sense. Other questions ask you to interpret graphics and to edit a part of the accompanying passage so that it clearly and accurately communicates the information in the graphics.

The SAT Essay also tests command of evidence. After reading a passage, you'll be asked to determine how the author builds an argument to persuade an audience through the use of evidence, reasoning, and/or stylistic and persuasive devices. Scorers look for cogent, clear analyses supported by critical reasoning and evidence drawn from the text provided.

The redesigned SAT Essay asks you to read a passage and explain how an author builds an argument to persuade an audience. This task closely mirrors college writing assignments because it is asking you to analyze how the author used evidence, reasoning, and stylistic and persuasive elements.

The new Essay is designed to support high school students and teachers as they cultivate close reading, careful analysis, and clear writing. It will promote the practice of reading a wide variety of arguments and analyzing how authors do their work as writers.

The essay prompt will be the same every time the SAT is offered, but the source material students are asked to write about will be different each time.

Not all students will take the SAT with Essay, but some school districts and colleges require it. The SAT is the only assessment in the SAT Suite that includes the Essay.

The Math Test focuses in-depth on three essential areas of math: Problem Solving and Data Analysis, Heart of Algebra, and Passport to Advanced Math.

Problem Solving and Data Analysis is about being quantitatively literate. It includes using ratios, percentages, and proportional reasoning to solve problems in science, social science, and career contexts.

The Heart of Algebra focuses on the mastery of linear equations and systems, which help students develop key powers of abstraction.

Passport to Advanced Math focuses on more complex equations and the manipulation they require.

Current research shows that these areas are used disproportionately in a wide range of majors and careers. The redesigned SAT also includes questions on other topics in math, including the kinds of geometric and trigonometric skills summary that are most relevant to college and careers.

SUMMARY

Throughout the SAT, you'll be asked questions grounded in the real world, directly related to work performed in college and career.

The Evidence-Based Reading and Writing section includes questions on literature and literary nonfiction, but also features charts, graphs, and passages like the ones students are likely to encounter in science, social science, and other majors and careers.

Questions on the Writing and Language Test ask you to do more than correct errors; they ask you to edit, revise, and improve texts from the humanities, history, social science, science, and career contexts.

The Math section features multistep applications to solve problems in science, social science, career scenarios, and other real-life situations. The test sets up a scenario and asks several questions that give you the opportunity to dig in and model it mathematically.

The redesigned SAT asks you to apply your reading, writing, language, and math knowledge and skills to answer questions in science, history, and social studies contexts. In this way, the assessments call on the same sorts of knowledge and skills that you'll use in college, at work, and throughout your life to make sense of recent discoveries, political developments, global events, and health and environmental issues.

The redesigned SAT includes a range of challenging texts and informational graphics that address these sorts of issues and topics in the Evidence-Based Reading and Writing section and the Math section. Questions will require you to read and understand texts, revise texts to be consistent with data presented in graphics, synthesize information presented through texts and graphics, and solve problems that are grounded in science and social science.

When you take the SAT, you'll be asked to read a passage from U.S. founding documents or the global conversation they inspired.

The U.S. founding documents, including the Declaration of Independence, the Bill of Rights, and the Federalist Papers, have been inspired by and have helped to inspire a conversation that continues to this day about the nature of civic life.

The SAT includes texts from this global conversation. The goal is to inspire a close reading of these rich, meaningful, often profound texts, not only as a way to develop valuable college and career readiness skills but also as an opportunity to reflect on and deeply engage with issues and concerns central to informed citizenship.

HOW TO TAKE A TEST

You have studied long, hard and conscientiously.

With your official admission card in hand, and your heart pounding, you have been admitted to the examination room.

You note that there are several hundred other applicants in the examination room waiting to take the same test.

They all appear to be equally well prepared.

You know that nothing but your best effort will suffice. The "moment of truth" is at hand: you now have to demonstrate objectively, in writing, your knowledge of content and your understanding of subject matter.

You are fighting the most important battle of your life—to pass and/or score high on an examination which will determine your career and provide the economic basis for your livelihood.

What extra, special things should you know and should you do in taking the examination?

I. YOU MUST PASS AN EXAMINATION

A. WHAT EVERY CANDIDATE SHOULD KNOW
Examination applicants often ask us for help in preparing for the written test. What can I study in advance? What kinds of questions will be asked? How will the test be given? How will the papers be graded?

B. HOW ARE EXAMS DEVELOPED?
Examinations are carefully written by trained technicians who are specialists in the field known as "psychological measurement," in consultation with recognized authorities in the field of work that the test will cover. These experts recommend the subject matter areas or skills to be tested; only those knowledges or skills important to your success on the job are included. The most reliable books and source materials available are used as references. Together, the experts and technicians judge the difficulty level of the questions.
Test technicians know how to phrase questions so that the problem is clearly stated. Their ethics do not permit "trick" or "catch" questions. Questions may have been tried out on sample groups, or subjected to statistical analysis, to determine their usefulness.
Written tests are often used in combination with performance tests, ratings of training and experience, and oral interviews. All of these measures combine to form the best-known means of finding the right person for the right job.

II. HOW TO PASS THE WRITTEN TEST

A. BASIC STEPS

1) Study the announcement

How, then, can you know what subjects to study? Our best answer is: "Learn as much as possible about the class of positions for which you've applied." The exam will test the knowledge, skills and abilities needed to do the work.

Your most valuable source of information about the position you want is the official exam announcement. This announcement lists the training and experience qualifications. Check these standards and apply only if you come reasonably close to meeting them. Many jurisdictions preview the written test in the exam announcement by including a section called "Knowledge and Abilities Required," "Scope of the Examination," or some similar heading. Here you will find out specifically what fields will be tested.

2) Choose appropriate study materials

If the position for which you are applying is technical or advanced, you will read more advanced, specialized material. If you are already familiar with the basic principles of your field, elementary textbooks would waste your time. Concentrate on advanced textbooks and technical periodicals. Think through the concepts and review difficult problems in your field.

These are all general sources. You can get more ideas on your own initiative, following these leads. For example, training manuals and publications of the government agency which employs workers in your field can be useful, particularly for technical and professional positions. A letter or visit to the government department involved may result in more specific study suggestions, and certainly will provide you with a more definite idea of the exact nature of the position you are seeking.

3) Study this book!

III. KINDS OF TESTS

Tests are used for purposes other than measuring knowledge and ability to perform specified duties. For some positions, it is equally important to test ability to make adjustments to new situations or to profit from training. In others, basic mental abilities not dependent on information are essential. Questions which test these things may not appear as pertinent to the duties of the position as those which test for knowledge and information. Yet they are often highly important parts of a fair examination. For very general questions, it is almost impossible to help you direct your study efforts. What we can do is to point out some of the more common of these general abilities needed in public service positions and describe some typical questions.

1) General information

Broad, general information has been found useful for predicting job success in some kinds of work. This is tested in a variety of ways, from vocabulary lists to questions about current events. Basic background in some field of work, such as sociology or economics, may be sampled in a group of questions. Often these are principles which have become familiar to most persons through exposure rather than through formal training. It is difficult to advise you how to study for these questions; being alert to the world around you is our best suggestion.

2) Verbal ability

An example of an ability needed in many positions is verbal or language ability. Verbal ability is, in brief, the ability to use and understand words. Vocabulary and grammar tests are typical measures of this ability. Reading comprehension or paragraph interpretation questions are common in many kinds of civil service tests. You are given a paragraph of written material and asked to find its central meaning.

IV. KINDS OF QUESTIONS

1. Multiple-choice Questions

Most popular of the short-answer questions is the "multiple choice" or "best answer" question. It can be used, for example, to test for factual knowledge, ability to solve problems or judgment in meeting situations found at work.

A multiple-choice question is normally one of three types:
- It can begin with an incomplete statement followed by several possible endings. You are to find the one ending which best completes the statement, although some of the others may not be entirely wrong.
- It can also be a complete statement in the form of a question which is answered by choosing one of the statements listed.
- It can be in the form of a problem – again you select the best answer.

Here is an example of a multiple-choice question with a discussion which should give you some clues as to the method for choosing the right answer:

When an employee has a complaint about his assignment, the action which will best help him overcome his difficulty is to
- A. discuss his difficulty with his coworkers
- B. take the problem to the head of the organization
- C. take the problem to the person who gave him the assignment
- D. say nothing to anyone about his complaint

In answering this question, you should study each of the choices to find which is best. Consider choice "A" – Certainly an employee may discuss his complaint with fellow employees, but no change or improvement can result, and the complaint remains unresolved. Choice "B" is a poor choice since the head of the organization probably does not know what assignment you have been given, and taking your problem to him is known as "going over the head" of the supervisor. The supervisor, or person who made the assignment, is the person who can clarify it or correct any injustice. Choice "C" is, therefore, correct. To say nothing, as in choice "D," is unwise. Supervisors have and interest in knowing the problems employees are facing, and the employee is seeking a solution to his problem.

2. True/False

3. Matching Questions

Matching an answer from a column of choices within another column.

V. RECORDING YOUR ANSWERS

Computer terminals are used more and more today for many different kinds of exams.

For an examination with very few applicants, you may be told to record your answers in the test booklet itself. Separate answer sheets are much more common. If this separate answer sheet is to be scored by machine – and this is often the case – it is highly important that you mark your answers correctly in order to get credit.

VI. BEFORE THE TEST

YOUR PHYSICAL CONDITION IS IMPORTANT

If you are not well, you can't do your best work on tests. If you are half asleep, you can't do your best either. Here are some tips:

1) Get about the same amount of sleep you usually get. Don't stay up all night before the test, either partying or worrying—DON'T DO IT!
2) If you wear glasses, be sure to wear them when you go to take the test. This goes for hearing aids, too.
3) If you have any physical problems that may keep you from doing your best, be sure to tell the person giving the test. If you are sick or in poor health, you relay cannot do your best on any test. You can always come back and take the test some other time.

Common sense will help you find procedures to follow to get ready for an examination. Too many of us, however, overlook these sensible measures. Indeed, nervousness and fatigue have been found to be the most serious reasons why applicants fail to do their best on civil service tests. Here is a list of reminders:

- Begin your preparation early – Don't wait until the last minute to go scurrying around for books and materials or to find out what the position is all about.
- Prepare continuously – An hour a night for a week is better than an all-night cram session. This has been definitely established. What is more, a night a week for a month will return better dividends than crowding your study into a shorter period of time.
- Locate the place of the exam – You have been sent a notice telling you when and where to report for the examination. If the location is in a different town or otherwise unfamiliar to you, it would be well to inquire the best route and learn something about the building.
- Relax the night before the test – Allow your mind to rest. Do not study at all that night. Plan some mild recreation or diversion; then go to bed early and get a good night's sleep.
- Get up early enough to make a leisurely trip to the place for the test – This way unforeseen events, traffic snarls, unfamiliar buildings, etc. will not upset you.
- Dress comfortably – A written test is not a fashion show. You will be known by number and not by name, so wear something comfortable.
- Leave excess paraphernalia at home – Shopping bags and odd bundles will get in your way. You need bring only the items mentioned in the official notice you received; usually everything you need is provided. Do not bring reference books to the exam. They will only confuse those last minutes and be taken away from you when in the test room.

- Arrive somewhat ahead of time – If because of transportation schedules you must get there very early, bring a newspaper or magazine to take your mind off yourself while waiting.
- Locate the examination room – When you have found the proper room, you will be directed to the seat or part of the room where you will sit. Sometimes you are given a sheet of instructions to read while you are waiting. Do not fill out any forms until you are told to do so; just read them and be prepared.
- Relax and prepare to listen to the instructions
- If you have any physical problem that may keep you from doing your best, be sure to tell the test administrator. If you are sick or in poor health, you really cannot do your best on the exam. You can come back and take the test some other time.

VII. AT THE TEST

The day of the test is here and you have the test booklet in your hand. The temptation to get going is very strong. Caution! There is more to success than knowing the right answers. You must know how to identify your papers and understand variations in the type of short-answer question used in this particular examination. Follow these suggestions for maximum results from your efforts:

1) Cooperate with the monitor

The test administrator has a duty to create a situation in which you can be as much at ease as possible. He will give instructions, tell you when to begin, check to see that you are marking your answer sheet correctly, and so on. He is not there to guard you, although he will see that your competitors do not take unfair advantage. He wants to help you do your best.

2) Listen to all instructions

Don't jump the gun! Wait until you understand all directions. In most civil service tests you get more time than you need to answer the questions. So don't be in a hurry. Read each word of instructions until you clearly understand the meaning. Study the examples, listen to all announcements and follow directions. Ask questions if you do not understand what to do.

3) Identify your papers

Civil service exams are usually identified by number only. You will be assigned a number; you must not put your name on your test papers. Be sure to copy your number correctly. Since more than one exam may be given, copy your exact examination title.

4) Plan your time

Unless you are told that a test is a "speed" or "rate of work" test, speed itself is usually not important. Time enough to answer all the questions will be provided, but this does not mean that you have all day. An overall time limit has been set. Divide the total time (in minutes) by the number of questions to determine the approximate time you have for each question.

5) Do not linger over difficult questions

If you come across a difficult question, mark it with a paper clip (useful to have along) and come back to it when you have been through the booklet. One caution if you do this – be sure to skip a number on your answer sheet as well. Check often to be sure that you have not lost your place and that you are marking in the row numbered the same as the question you are answering.

6) Read the questions
Be sure you know what the question asks! Many capable people are unsuccessful because they failed to read the questions correctly.

7) Answer all questions
Unless you have been instructed that a penalty will be deducted for incorrect answers, it is better to guess than to omit a question.

8) Speed tests
It is often better NOT to guess on speed tests. It has been found that on timed tests people are tempted to spend the last few seconds before time is called in marking answers at random – without even reading them – in the hope of picking up a few extra points. To discourage this practice, the instructions may warn you that your score will be "corrected" for guessing. That is, a penalty will be applied. The incorrect answers will be deducted from the correct ones, or some other penalty formula will be used.

9) Review your answers
If you finish before time is called, go back to the questions you guessed or omitted to give them further thought. Review other answers if you have time.

10) Return your test materials
If you are ready to leave before others have finished or time is called, take ALL your materials to the monitor and leave quietly. Never take any test material with you. The monitor can discover whose papers are not complete, and taking a test booklet may be grounds for disqualification.

VIII. EXAMINATION TECHNIQUES

1) Read the general instructions carefully. These are usually printed on the first page of the exam booklet. As a rule, these instructions refer to the timing of the examination; the fact that you should not start work until the signal and must stop work at a signal, etc. If there are any special instructions, such as a choice of questions to be answered, make sure that you note this instruction carefully.

2) When you are ready to start work on the examination, that is as soon as the signal has been given, read the instructions to each question booklet, underline any key words or phrases, such as least, best, outline, describe and the like. In this way you will tend to answer as requested rather than discover on reviewing your paper that you listed without describing, that you selected the worst choice rather than the best choice, etc.

3) If the examination is of the objective or multiple-choice type – that is, each question will also give a series of possible answers: A, B, C or D, and you are called upon to select the best answer and write the letter next to that answer on your answer paper – it is advisable to start answering each question in turn. There may be anywhere from 50 to 100 such questions in the three or four hours allotted and you can see how much time would be taken if you read through all the questions before beginning to answer any. Furthermore, if you

come across a question or group of questions which you know would be difficult to answer, it would undoubtedly affect your handling of all the other questions.

4) If the examination is of the essay type and contains but a few questions, it is a moot point as to whether you should read all the questions before starting to answer any one. Of course, if you are given a choice – say five out of seven and the like – then it is essential to read all the questions so you can eliminate the two that are most difficult. If, however, you are asked to answer all the questions, there may be danger in trying to answer the easiest one first because you may find that you will spend too much time on it. The best technique is to answer the first question, then proceed to the second, etc.

5) Time your answers. Before the exam begins, write down the time it started, then add the time allowed for the examination and write down the time it must be completed, then divide the time available somewhat as follows:
    - If 3-1/2 hours are allowed, that would be 210 minutes. If you have 80 objective-type questions, that would be an average of 2-1/2 minutes per question. Allow yourself no more than 2 minutes per question, or a total of 160 minutes, which will permit about 50 minutes to review.
    - If for the time allotment of 210 minutes there are 7 essay questions to answer, that would average about 30 minutes a question. Give yourself only 25 minutes per question so that you have about 35 minutes to review.

6) The most important instruction is to read each question and make sure you know what is wanted. The second most important instruction is to time yourself properly so that you answer every question. The third most important instruction is to answer every question. Guess if you have to but include something for each question. Remember that you will receive no credit for a blank and will probably receive some credit if you write something in answer to an essay question. If you guess a letter – say "B" for a multiple-choice question – you may have guessed right. If you leave a blank as an answer to a multiple-choice question, the examiners may respect your feelings but it will not add a point to your score. Some exams may penalize you for wrong answers, so in such cases only, you may not want to guess unless you have some basis for your answer.

7) Suggestions
   a. Objective-type questions
      1. Examine the question booklet for proper sequence of pages and questions
      2. Read all instructions carefully
      3. Skip any question which seems too difficult; return to it after all other questions have been answered
      4. Apportion your time properly; do not spend too much time on any single question or group of questions
      5. Note and underline key words – all, most, fewest, least, best, worst, same, opposite, etc.
      6. Pay particular attention to negatives
      7. Note unusual option, e.g., unduly long, short, complex, different or similar in content to the body of the question
      8. Observe the use of "hedging" words – probably, may, most likely, etc.

9. Make sure that your answer is put next to the same number as the question
10. Do not second-guess unless you have good reason to believe the second answer is definitely more correct
11. Cross out original answer if you decide another answer is more accurate; do not erase until you are ready to hand your paper in
12. Answer all questions; guess unless instructed otherwise
13. Leave time for review

b. Essay questions
1. Read each question carefully
2. Determine exactly what is wanted. Underline key words or phrases.
3. Decide on outline or paragraph answer
4. Include many different points and elements unless asked to develop any one or two points or elements
5. Show impartiality by giving pros and cons unless directed to select one side only
6. Make and write down any assumptions you find necessary to answer the questions
7. Watch your English, grammar, punctuation and choice of words
8. Time your answers; don't crowd material

8) Answering the essay question

Most essay questions can be answered by framing the specific response around several key words or ideas. Here are a few such key words or ideas:

M's: manpower, materials, methods, money, management
P's: purpose, program, policy, plan, procedure, practice, problems, pitfalls, personnel, public relations

a. Six basic steps in handling problems:
1. Preliminary plan and background development
2. Collect information, data and facts
3. Analyze and interpret information, data and facts
4. Analyze and develop solutions as well as make recommendations
5. Prepare report and sell recommendations
6. Install recommendations and follow up effectiveness

b. Pitfalls to avoid
1. Taking things for granted – A statement of the situation does not necessarily imply that each of the elements is necessarily true; for example, a complaint may be invalid and biased so that all that can be taken for granted is that a complaint has been registered
2. Considering only one side of a situation – Wherever possible, indicate several alternatives and then point out the reasons you selected the best one
3. Failing to indicate follow up – Whenever your answer indicates action on your part, make certain that you will take proper follow-up action to see how successful your recommendations, procedures or actions turn out to be
4. Taking too long in answering any single question – Remember to time your answers properly

EXAMINATION SECTION

EXAMINATION SECTION
TEST 1

DIRECTIONS: Each question or incomplete statement is followed by several suggested answers or completions. Select the one that BEST answers the question or completes the statement. *PRINT THE LETTER OF THE CORRECT ANSWER IN THE SPACE AT THE RIGHT.*

Questions 1-13.

DIRECTIONS: In solving Questions 1 through 13, the use of a calculator is NOT permitted.

1. Two new energy drinks, Able and Bolder, have been developed. One glass of Able contains 25 mg of iron, while two glasses of Bolder contain 28 mg of iron. Doctors recommend that a person should drink no more than 150 mg of iron per day.
   Which one of the following inequalities represents the number of allowable daily mg of iron from these two drinks when taking x glasses of Able and y glasses of Bolder?
   A. $25/x + 14/y \geq 150$
   B. $25/x + 28/y \geq 150$
   C. $25x + 14y \leq 150$
   D. $25x + 28y \leq 150$

   1.____

2. Suppose every tenth customer entering a shopping mall is asked which is their favorite clothing store.
   This would represent which type of sampling?
   A. Random
   B. Cluster
   C. Stratified
   D. Systematic

   2.____

3. Julie is staying at a local motel that charges $75 per night plus a 6% tax. Also, a one-time parking fee of $8 is charged. The parking fee is not taxed.
   Which one of the following represents Julie's total charges, in dollars, at this motel if she stays for x nights?
   A. $(75)(1.06)(x) + 8$
   B. $(75+1.06)(x) + 8$
   C. $[(75)(1.06) + 8][x]$
   D. $(75x+8)(1.06)$

   3.____

4. The graph of a system of three equations is shown at the right, namely $x^2 + y^2 = 4$, $x + y = 2$, and $y = 2x + 2$.
   How many solutions does this system have?
   A. 3
   B. 2
   C. 1
   D. 0

   4.____

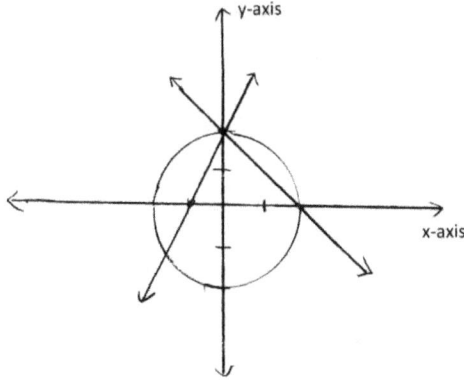

5. In a group of 15- and 16-year-old students, the number of 15-year olds is greater than the number of 16-year olds. The mean weight for all these students is 145 pounds and the mean weight for a the 15-year olds is 135 pounds.
If n represents the mean weight of all the 16-year olds, which one of the following inequalities CORRECTLY describes the value of n, in pounds?
   A. $n < 155$
   B. $n > 155$
   C. $135 < n < 145$
   D. $145 < n < 155$

6. In a certain region of Africa, the population of coyotes was 200 in the year 2010. It was predicted that this population of coyotes would grow by 20% every 3 years. Let Q represent the population of coyotes x years after the year 2010.
If this prediction were correct, which one of the following equations would represent the equation for Q?
   A. $Q = 200x + 3$
   B. $Q = (200)(1.2)^x$
   C. $Q = (20)(1.2)^{x/3}$
   D. $Q = 200 + 3x$

7. In the diagram shown at the right, $\overline{JK}$ is perpendicular to $\overline{KM}$ and $\overline{LN}$ is perpendicular to $\overline{LM}$. The points K, L, and M are collinear.
Which one of the following statements MUST be true?
   A. $KL = LM$
   B. $MN/LM = JM/KL$
   C. $JK/NL = JM/NM$
   D. $KL/NL = KM/JK$

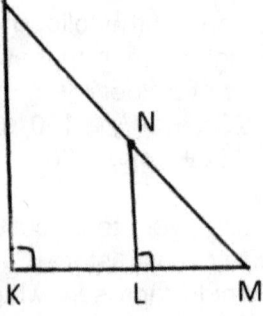

8. Jennifer buys apples and bananas at her local market. Apples cost $0.65 apiece and bananas cost $0.40 apiece. The total number of apples and bananas bought is 12 and the total amount spent is $6.80.
If Jennifer buys x apples and y bananas, which one of the following pairs of equations would be solved to determine the number of apples and the number of bananas that she buys?
   A. $x - y = 12$ and $0.65x - 0.40y = 6.80$
   B. $x + y = 12$ and $0.65x + 0.40y = 680$
   C. $x + y = 6.80$ and $0.65x + 0.40y = 12$
   D. $x + y = 6.80/12$ and $0.65x + 0.40y = 6.80$

9. If *k* is a negative number, which one of the following could represent the graph of y + 9 = kx?

A.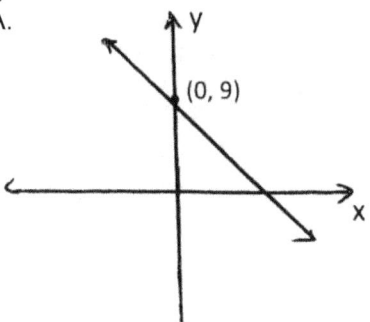

B.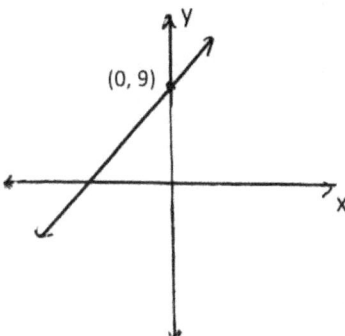

C.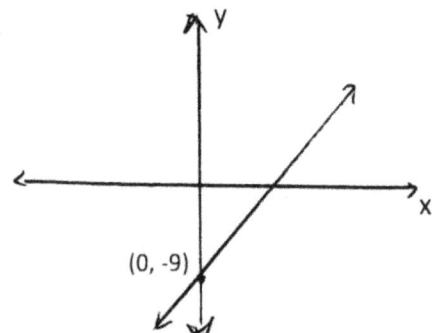

D.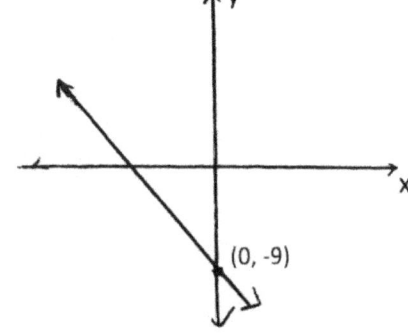

10. If the expression (3x+ 6.5)/(2x+1) is written as 5/(2x+1) + M, what is the value of M?
    A. 3
    B. 2
    C. 3/2
    D.

11. A real estate agent was comparing the prices of one-bedroom and two-bedroom apartments for six different apartment complexes. He determined that the equation of the line of best fit was y = 1.2x + 400, where *y* represents the dollar cost of a two-bedroom apartment and *x* represents the dollar cost of a one-bedroom apartment.
    What is the BEST interpretation for the number 1.2?
    A. For every dollar increase in y, there is a 1.2 dollar increase in x.
    B. For every dollar increase in x, there is a 1.2 dollar increase in y.
    C. A one-bedroom apartment costs 1.2 times that of a two-bedroom apartment.
    D. A two-bedroom apartment costs 1.2 times that of a one-bedroom apartment.

12. You are given the equations three lines: y = 2x + 1, y = -2x – 4, and y = (1/2)x – 5.
    Which two of these lines are perpendicular to each other?
    A. y = 2x + 1 and y = (1/2)x + 5
    B. y = -2x – 4 and y = 2x + 1
    C. y = - 2x – 4 and y = (1/2)x + 5
    D. No two of these lines are perpendicular to each other

13. Marie has Z dollars in her savings account. She needs to withdraw 10% of the Z dollars in January, then 10% of her remaining amount in February, then 10% of her remaining amount in March.
If she continues this pattern through June, which one of the following expressions represents the amount in her savings account after her June withdrawal?
    A. $.90Z^6$ B. $(Z)(.10^6)$ C. $.10Z^6$ D. $(Z)(.90^6)$

13._____

Questions 14-40.

DIRECTIONS: In solving Questions 14 through 40, the use of a calculator is permitted.

14. The following table classifies the number of students by grade and by the sport in which they participate at a local high school. Each student participates in only one sport.

	Basketball	Baseball	Football
9th Grade	30	23	15
10th Grade	28	17	42
11th Grade	32	29	33
12th Grade	40	21	20

What fraction, in LOWEST terms, of all basketball players are 10th graders?

14._____

15. Using the table shown in Question 14, what fraction, in LOWEST terms, of all 12th graders who play in these sports is involved in baseball.

15._____

16. Given that 54 < 12t + 8 < 65, what is one possible integer value for 3t + 2?

16._____

17. The Apex Company makes chainsaws, which it sells for $20 apiece. The cost, C, in dollars, to make n chainsaws is given by the equation C = 13n + 420.
Which one of the following inequalities represents all values of n for which the company makes a profit?
    A. n < 50   B. n < 60   C. n > 50   D. n > 60

17._____

18. Jason is planning to drive his car a distance of 200 miles. He will travel at 40 miles per hour for the first two hours.
If x represents his rate in miles per hour for the remainder of the trip, which one of the following represents his rate for the remainder of the trip in terms of his time in hours, t?
    A. x = t/120   B. x = 120/t   C. x = 120t   D. x = t/(120+t)

18._____

19. Each of 20 people on a group bus trip to Atlantic City will pay the same amount and will also contribute $2 as a tip to the bus driver.
If T represents the total amount in dollars charged for this bus trip (not counting the tip) and C represents the cost in dollars per person, which one of the following equations is CORRECT?
    A. C = (T+2)/20
    B. C = 20/T+2
    C. C = 20/(T+2)
    D. C = T/20+2

19._____

20. At a depth of 8 feet below the surface of the Atlantic Ocean, the water pressure is 17.5 pounds per square foot. This pressure increases linearly so that at a depth of 20 feet below the surface of this body of water, the pressure is 27.1 pounds per square foot.
Which one of the following equations is the CORRECT model for the pressure in pounds per square foot (P) in terms of the depth below the surface in feet (D)?
   A. P = 1.25D + 7.5
   B. P = 1.25D − 2.1
   C. P = 0.8D + 11.1
   D. P = 0.8D − 9.6

20._____

21. You are given the system of equations $x^2 + y^2 = 34$ and $y = x + 2$.
If (x,y) is a solution to this system, what is one possible value of $3x^2$?
   A. 75   B. 60   C. 30   D. 15

21._____

22. Phil wishes to use his international credit card when he travels to Mexico, where the currency is given in pesos. Phil makes several purchases at a gift shop in Tijuana that totals 70 pesos. After his bank converts his purchase to U.S. dollars and adds a 5% fee, this amount becomes $102.90.
What is the value of one peso in U.S. dollars?

22._____

23. The function $g(x) = x^3 + 5x^2 − 22x − 56$ intersects the x-axis at (a,0), (b,0), and (c,0).
What is the value of a + b + c?
   A. -15   B. -5   C. 5   D. 15

23._____

24. The function $f(x) = 3x^4 + cx + d$ has a y-intercept of 7.
If the point (-2,1) lies on the graph of this function, what is the value of c?

24._____

25. In the triangle shown at the right, ∠A = 90°.
What is the value of sine(x)?
   A. 3/5
   B. 4/5
   C. 5/4
   D. 5/3

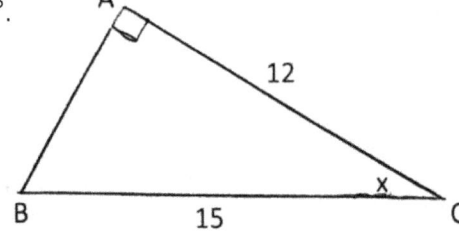

25._____

26. If 6t − 5 > 18, what is the smallest integer value of 4t?
   A.

26._____

27. A small village had a population of 300 in the year 1970. This population grew by 30% every four years after 1970.
What is the BEST approximation to its population in the year 1982?
   A. 420   B. 532   C. 659   D. 857

27._____

Questions 28-29.

DIRECTIONS: Questions 28 and 29 are to be answered on the basis of the following chart, that shows the number of gold, silver, and bronze medals won by the United States, Russia, China, and Sweden during the 1960 Olympics.

	Gold	Silver	Bronze
United States	40	35	42
Russia	32	28	10
China	20	19	15
Sweden	18	8	13

28. What fraction of the silver medals won by these four countries was won by China?
    A. 27/140   B. 19/90   C. 27/113   D. 19/71

29. What fraction of all the medals won by Sweden was in the gold category?
    A. 9/55   B. 9/46   C. 6/13   d. 9/11

30. Given the system of equations $4x - y = 17$ and $5x + 2y = 57$, what is the value of $y^2 - x^2$?
    A. 72   B. 66   C. 54   D. 40

31. In triangle MNP shown at the right, $\angle N = 90°$, and points N, P, Q are collinear.
    To the nearest tenth, what is the length of $\overline{NP}$?
    A. 9.8
    B. 10.4
    C. 11.2
    D. 12.6

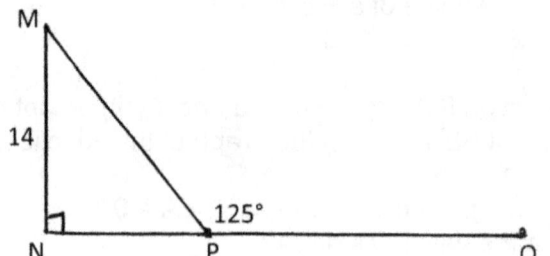

32. Given that s and t are integers such that $17 < 3s < 32$ and $21 < 4t < 51$, what is the LARGEST possible value of st?

33. Karen drove her car at 35 miles per hour for 4 hours. In her return trip she took a different route so she drove 10 miles further and required 5 hours. What was her average rate on the entire trip?
    A. $28.\overline{6}$ B. 29.8   C. 31.5   D. $32.\overline{2}$

34. Given the system $x^2 - y^2 = 119$ and $x + y^2 = 37$, if (x,y) represents a solution, what is one possible value of $x^2/3$?
    A. 36   B. 48   C. 52.3   D. 64.5

35. Mike wanted to use his credit card when traveling to France, where 1 franc is worth $0.60. He made several purchases and when the number of francs he spends were converted to U.S. dollars, his bank added an 8% fee.
If his purchases including the bank fee were $55.08, what was the amount of his purchases in francs?
   A. $71.80   B. $78.40   C. $85.00   D. $91.60

35.____

36. Twenty percent more than 90 is equivalent to 10% less than a number represented by N + 5. What is the value of N?
   A. 130   B. 125   C. 120   D. 115

36.____

37. Between the numbers 20 and 59, inclusive, how many numbers contain either the digit 3 or the digit 5, but not both a 3 and a 5?
   A. 14   B. 18   C. 22   D. 30

37.____

38. Walter has between 110 and 180 marbles. When he arranges the marbles into groups of 5, he has three left over. When he arranges the marbles into groups of 7, he has the same number of marbles left over.
How many marbles does he have?

38.____

39. The following chart classifies the number of cars in an auto dealer's lot by make and by color.

	White	Blue	Gray	Red
Chevrolet	17	10	15	26
Ford	12	6	20	16
Hyundai	7	14	13	8

How much larger, in lowest terms, is the fraction of Hyundais that are white than the fraction of Fords that are blue

39.____

40. Given the numbers 2, 9, 8, 5, 9, 9, how much larger is the median than the mean?
   A. 0.5   B. 1   C. 1.5   D. 2

40.____

SOLUTIONS WITH CORRECT ANSWERS

1. CORRECT ANSWER: C
   The expression "no more than" indicates the less than or equals symbol, which is ≤. Then x glasses of Able will yield 25x mg of iron. Since two glasses of Bolder yields 28 mg of iron, one glass of Bolder will yield 28/2 = 14 mg of iron. This means that y glasses of Bolder will yield 14y mg of iron.

2. CORRECT ANSWER: D
   Systematic sampling is obtained by selecting every kth subject, which k is an integer. Random sampling is without any system. Cluster sampling involves selecting a few groups of the population (such as all individuals who are wearing hats and all individuals who have a beard), then sampling each member of those groups. Stratified sampling involves dividing the entire population into groups (such as male and female), then sampling just a few members of those groups.

3. CORRECT ANSWER: A
   The number of nights she stays will cost $75 plus a 6% tax, which becomes (75)(1.06)(x). Since the parking fee of $8 is only one time and it is not taxed, it will be added to the quantity (75)(1.06)(x). Choice B is wrong because the 1.06 is added rather than multiplied by $75. Choice C is wrong because the $8 parking fee is being taxed at 6%. Choice D is wrong because the $8 fee is being applied to each of the x nights that Julie stays at the motel.

4. CORRECT ANSWER: C
   The solution is determined by the number of points at which all graphs intersect simultaneously. For this system, the only common point of intersection is (0,2).

5. CORRECT ANSWER: B
   Since there are a greater number of 15-year olds than 16-year olds, the mean weight for all the students should be closer to the mean weight of the 15-year olds than it is to the 16-year olds. Since 145 – 135 = 10, the mean weight for the 16-year olds should be more than 10 pounds higher than 145 pounds. Thus, n > 155. As a check, suppose there were 20 15-year olds and 10 16-year olds. Then the total weight for the 15-year olds is (20)(135) = 2700 pounds. Since the mean weight for all 30 students is 145 pounds, the total weight for all the students is (30)(145) = 4350 pounds. Now, the total weight for the 16-year olds is 4350 – 2700 = 1650 pounds. Thus, the mean weight for the 16-year olds is 1650/10 = 165 pounds, which is larger than 155 pounds.

6. CORRECT ANSWER: C
   A growth of 20% occurs every 3 years, so after a period of x years, this 20% growth occurs x/3 times. A growth of 20% is shown by the decimal 1.2, so the expression $Q = (200)(1.2)^{x/3}$ shows the value of Q after x years when the initial value is 200.

7. **CORRECT ANSWER: C**
Triangle JKM is similar to triangle NLM because they each contain ∠M and is a right triangle. The triangles are similar by the Angle-Angle Postulate. Thus, the ratio of corresponding sides must be equal. Each of $\overline{JK}$ and $\overline{NL}$ is the side opposite ∠M, and each of JM and NM is a hypotenuse. Choice A is wrong because L is not necessarily the midpoint of $\overline{KM}$ and N is not necessarily the midpoint of JM. Choice B is wrong because KL should be KM. Choice D is wrong because KL should be LM.

8. **CORRECT ANSWER: B**
Buying a total of 12 apples and bananas means x + y = 12. The cost of the x apples is $0.65x and the cost of the y bananas is $0.40y, so 0.65x + 0.40y = 6.80.

9. **CORRECT ANSWER: D**
Rewrite the original equation as y = kx − 9. The number -9 represents the y-intercept, so it corresponds to the point (0,-9). The letter k represents the slope, which we know is negative. This means that the graph of this line must stretch from the upper left quadrant to the lower right quadrant, as seen in choice D.

10. **CORRECT ANSWER: C**
Subtract 5/(2x+1) from each side of the equation to get (3x+6.5-5)/(2x+1) = M. Simplify the numerator of the fraction and multiply each side by 2x + 1 to get 3x + 1.5 = 2xM + M, so M = 3/2.

11. **CORRECT ANSWER: B**
In the equation y = 1.2x + 400, x is the independent variable and y is the dependent variable. The number 1.2 represents the slope of the line, which is defined as follows: for every unit change in x, there is a 1.2 unit change in y.

12. **CORRECT ANSWER: C**
When two lines are perpendicular to each other, their slopes are negative reciprocals of each other. The slopes of y = -2x -4 and y = (½)x + 5 are -2 and ½, respectively. The numbers -2 and ½ are negative reciprocals of each other.

13. **CORRECT ANSWER: D**
After withdrawing 10% of Z during January, Marie will have .90Z left in her account. After her February withdrawal of 10%, she will have $(.90)(.90Z) = (Z)(.90^2)$. By continuing this pattern, after 6 months she will have $(Z)(.90^6)$ dollars in her savings account.

14. **CORRECT ANSWER: 14.65**
The number of basketball players in all four grades is 30 + 28 + 32 + 40 = 130. There are 28 10th grade basketball players. Then the required fraction is 28/130, which must be reduced to 14/65.

15. **CORRECT ANSWER: 7/27**
The number of 12th graders in all three sports is 40 + 21 + 20 = 81. There are 21 12th graders who play baseball. Then the required fraction is 21/81, which must be reduced to 7/27.

16. CORRECT ANSWER: Any one of 14, 15, or 16.
Divide the original inequality by 4 to get 13.5 < 3t + 2 < 16.25. The only integer values between 13.5 and 16.25 are 14, 15, and 16.

17. CORRECT ANSWER: D
The gross sales that the company makes in selling n chainsaws is 20n. In order to make a profit, the value of 20n must exceed 13n + 420. Then 13n + 420 < 20n. So, 420 < 7n, which becomes n > 60.

18. CORRECT ANSWER: B
Jason will have traveled (40)(2) = 80 miles in the first two hours. Then the remaining distance is 200 – 80 = 120 miles. Since rate equals distance divided by time, x = 120/t.

19. CORRECT ANSWER: D
Not counting the tip to the bus driver, each person would have to pay the total amount divided by 20, which is T/20. Then the tip of $2 must be added to T/20.

20. CORRECT ANSWER: C
The initial equation is P = mD + c, where m and c are constants. The letter m represents the slope of the line where P represents the vertical distance and D represents the horizontal distance. So, m = (27.1 – 17.50)/(20-8) = 9.6/12 = 0.8. This means that P = 0.8D + c. To find c, we make the following substitution: 27.1 = (0.8)(20) + c. Then, 27.1 = 16 + c, so c = 11.1. Note that we could have also found c using the substitution 17.5 = (0.8)(8) + c.

21. CORRECT ANSWER: A
Since y = x + 2, we can rewrite $x^2 + y^2 = 34$ as $x^2 + (x+2)^2 = 34$. Then, $2x^2 + 4x + 4 = 34$, which leads to $x^2 + 2x - 15 = 0$. By factoring, we get (x+5)(x-3) = 0, so x = -5 or x = 3. If x = -5, then $3x^2 = (3)(-5)^2 = 75$. Note that the other possible value for $3x^2$ is $(3)(3)^2 = 27$, but this number is not one of the four choices.

22. CORRECT ANSWER: $1.40
Let x represent the total cost in U.S. dollars without the 5% fee. Then, 1.05x = $102,49m so x = $102.40/1.05 = $98. Since $98 is worth 70 pesos, we can determine the U.S. dollar amount of one peso by dividing $98 by 70, which is $1.40.

23. CORRECT ANSWER: B
We note that $g(-2) = (-2)^3 + 5(-2)^2 - (22)(-2) - 56 = -8 + 20 + 44 - 56 = 0$. This means that (x+2) is a factor of $x^3 + 5x^2 - 22x - 56$. Then, $(x^3+5x^2-22x-56)$ divided by (x+2) = $x^2 + 3x - 28$. Since $x^2 + 3x - 28$ factors as (x-4)(x+7), we can write g(x) = $x^3 + 5x^2 - 22x - 56$ = (x+2)(x-4)(x+7). Thus, the three x-intercepts, identified as (a,0), (b,0), and (c,0), are -2, 4, and -7. Their sum is -5.

24. CORRECT ANSWER: 27
The letter d has a value of 7 because the definition of a y-intercept is the value of y when x = 0. We note that $f(0) = 3(0)^4 + c(0) + d = 7$, so d = 7. By substituting (-2,1), we have 1 = $3(-2)^4 - 2c + 7$. Then, 1 = 48 – 2c + 7, which simplifies to -54 = -2c. Thus, c = 27.

25. CORRECT ANSWER: A
    By definition, the sine of an angle equals the opposite side divided by the hypotenuse. By the Pythagorean Theorem, AB = $\sqrt{15^2 - 12^2}$ = $\sqrt{81}$ = 9. Thus, sine (x) = 9/15 = 3/5.

26. CORRECT ANSWER: 16
    Add 5 to both sides of the inequality to get 6t > 23. Then, t > 23/6. This means that 4t > (4)(23/6) = 92/6 = 15.333, so that the smallest integer value of 4t is the next integer after 15.333.

27. CORRECT ANSWER: C
    We use the formula A + P(1+R)^n, where A represents the final population, P represents the initial population, R represents the rate of growth, and n represents the number of growth periods. The growth rate is 0.30 and the number of growth periods is (1982-1970)/4 = 3. Thus, A = (300)(1+.30)^3 = (300)(2.197) = 659.1.

28. CORRECT ANSWER: B
    There were a total of 90 silver medals for these four countries. Since China won 19 silver medals, the correct fraction is 19/90.

29. CORRECT ANSWER: C
    Sweden won a total of 39 medals, of which 18 were in the gold category. Thus, the correct fraction is 18/39, which reduces to 6/13.

30. CORRECT ANSWER: A
    Multiply the first equation by 2 to get 8x − 2y = 34. Now add this to the second equation to get 13x = 91, so x = 7. We can substitute this value into the original first equation to get (4)(7) − y = 17 to find that y = 11. Thus, y^2 − x^2 = 11^2 − 7^2 = 121 − 49 = 72.

31. CORRECT ANSWER: A
    ∠MPN = 180° - 125° = 55°. Then, tan 55° = 14/NP, which leads to NP = 14/tan 55° ≈ 14/1.428 ≈ 9.8. (Note that the length of PQ has no bearing on the solution.)

32. CORRECT ANSWER: 120
    We can rewrite each inequality as follows: 17/3 < s < 32/3 and 21/4 < t < 51/4. The largest possible value of s is 10, and the largest possible value of t is 12. Thus, the maximum value of st is (10)(12) = 120.

33. CORRECT ANSWER: D
    Initially, Karen traveled (35)(4) = 140 miles. On her return trip, she drove 150 miles and required 5 hours. Average rate is defined as total distance divided by total time, which becomes (140+150)/(4+5) = 290/9 = 32.2 miles per hour.

34. CORRECT ANSWER: B
    By adding the equations, we get x^2 + x = 156, which can be written as x^2 + x − 156 = 0. Then, (x+13)(x-12) = 0, so x = -13 or 12. If x = -13, then x^2/3 = 169/3 = 56.3, which is not one of the answer choices. However, when x = 12, x^2/3 = 144/3 = 48.

35. CORRECT ANSWER: C
His purchases in dollars without the bank fee was $55.08/1.08 = $51.00. Since 1 franc is worth $0.60, this means that $51.00 is worth $51.00/$0.60 = $85.00

36. CORRECT ANSWER: D
We first compute (90)(1.20) = 108. Now, 108 is 10% less than another number. This means that 108 represents 90% of this other number, which is 108/0.90 = 120. Finally, N + 5 = 120, so N = 115.

37. CORRECT ANSWER: C
From 20 thru 29, there are two numbers; from 30 thru 39, there are nine numbers; from 40 to 49, there are two numbers; from 50 to 59, there are nine numbers. The total is 2 + 9 + 2 + 9 = 22. Note that we cannot count the numbers 35 and 53 because they contain both a 3 and a 5. Here is the actual list of numbers: 23, 25, 30, 31, 32, 33, 34, 36, 37, 38, 39, 43, 45, 50, 51, 52, 54, 55, 56, 57, 58, 59.

38. CORRECT ANSWER: Either one of 143 or 178.
The least common multiple of 5 and 7 is 35. We need a number that is 3 more than a multiple of 35. Note that $110/35 \approx 3.14$ and $180/35 \approx 5.14$. This means that we can use either 4 or 5 as a number to multiply by 35. Then, (35)(4) + 3 = 143 and (35)(5) + 3 = 178.

39. CORRECT ANSWER: 1/18
There are 42 Hyundais, of which 7 are white. So the required fraction is 7/42 = 1/6. There are 54 Fords, of which 6 are blue. So the required fraction is 6/54 = 1/9. Finally, 1/6 – 1/9 = 1/18.

40. CORRECT ANSWER: C
First arrange the numbers as 2, 5, 8, 9, 9, 9. The median is the average of the third and fourth numbers, which is (8+9)/2 = 8.5. The sum of these six numbers is 42, so the mean is 42/6 = 7. Thus, the median is 8.5 – 7 = 1.5 larger than the mean.

EXAMINATION SECTION

TEST 1

DIRECTIONS: Each question or incomplete statement is followed by several suggested answers or completions. Select the one that BEST answers the question or completes the statement. *PRINT THE LETTER OF THE CORRECT ANSWER IN THE SPACE AT THE RIGHT.*

Questions 1-15.

DIRECTIONS: In solving Questions 1 through 15, the use of a calculator is NOT permitted.

1. The newest vitamins in pill form on the market are Y-Try and Z-Wow. Three pills of Y-Try contain 54 mg of zinc, while four pills of Z-Wow contain 48 mg of zinc. A medical specialist recommends that a person take at least 80 mg of zinc per week.
If a person takes c pills of Y-try and d pills of Z-Wow per week, which one of the following inequalities represents the recommended weekly dosage of zinc from these two pills?
    A. $18c + 12d \geq 80$
    B. $18/c + 12/d \geq 80$
    C. $54c + 48d \geq 80$
    D. $54/c + 48/d \geq 80$

1.____

2.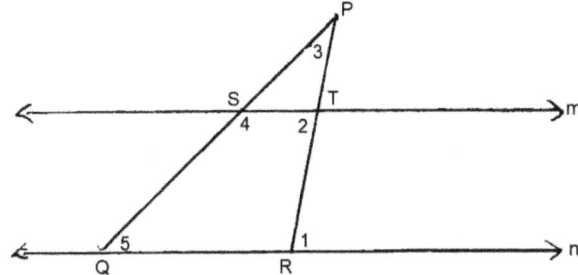

    In the above diagram, line m is parallel to line n. Points P, Q, and S are collinear. Points P, T, and R are collinear.
    Which one of the following MUST be true?
    A. $\angle 1 = \angle 2$
    B. $\angle 1 = \angle 3 + \angle 5$
    C. $\angle 2 + \angle 5 + \angle 4 = 180°$
    D. $\angle 1 + \angle 5 = \angle 2 + \angle 4$

2.____

3. Jack had $3,000 in his checking account at the end of January. He deposited x dollars at the end of each month, beginning with February.
Which one of the following expressions represents the amount of dollars in his checking account after his July deposit?
    A. $3,000 + 6x$ B. $3,000 + 7x$ C. $3,000x + 6$ D. $3,000x + 7$

3.____

Questions 4-5.

DIRECTIONS: Questions 4 and 5 are to be answered on the basis of the following chart which shows the number of races plus the number of first, second, and third place finishes for each of three specific horses at a local racetrack.

NAME OF HORSE	NUMBER OF RACES	FIRST PLACE	SECOND PLACE	THIRD PLACE
Able Arlene	56	15	9	18
Bold Bob	36	10	14	4
Cautious Carol	30	8	2	14

4. Which one of the following fractions represents the ratio of Bold Bob's combined first and second place finishes to the total number of races that Bold Bob ran?
   A. ½   B. ²/₃   C. ⁵/₇   D. ⁷/₉

5. The number 36% represents which one of the following?
   A. The ratio of Cautious Carol's third place finishes to the combined first place finishes of all three horses.
   B. The ratio of Cautious Carol's combined first and second place finishes to this horse's number of races.
   C. The ratio of Able Arlene's third place finishes to this horse's number of races.
   D. The ratio of Able Arlene's second place finishes to the combined number of second place finishes of all three horses.

6. At a certain national conference of educators, a survey was conducted regarding teaching methods for only those educators from New Jersey and Pennsylvania. What type of sampling is this survey?
   A. Cluster   B. Random   C. Stratified   D. Systematic

7. Given that $y = kx^2 + w^3$, which one of the following is the equivalent expression for x?
   A. $\sqrt{(y+w^3)/k}$
   B. $\sqrt{(y-w^3)}/k$
   C. $\sqrt{(y-w^3)/k}$
   D. $\sqrt{(y+w^3)}/k$

8. What is the simplified form of $(a^5 b^6 c^{-2})(a^{-5} b^2 c^4)$?
   A. $(a^{10} b^4)/c^6$ B. $(a^{10} b^3)/c^2$ C. $b^3/(a^{10} c^6)$ D. $b^4/(a^{10} c^2)$

9. What is the remainder when $x^3 - 6$ is divided by x-3?
   A. 2   B. 9   C. 16   D. 21

10. In the small town of Tinyville, there are eight traffic lights. At the intersection of each traffic light, one of the crossroads is a state-numbered road. The following chart shows the number of the state road, the speed limit in miles per hour (mph) on the state road, and the number of seconds that the light is green for the state road.

STATE ROAD NUMBER	SPEED LIMIT	NUMBER OF SECONDS FOR GREEN LIGHT
10	35 mph	20
12	45 mph	22
15	50 mph	18
18	40 mph	24
20	60 mph	30
24	40 mph	32
29	35 mph	36
32	55 mph	40

Which one of the following BEST describes the pattern that exists between speed limits and the number of seconds for a green light for these eight traffic lights?
A. Positive correlation B. Negative correlation
C. No correlation D. Identity correlation

11. If $ab^2 + b^2c = 9ad^4 + 9cd^4$, which one of the following is equivalent to b^3?   11.____
A. $27d^6$ B. $9d^3$ C. $3d^6$ D. d^3

12. If $k < 0$, which one of the following could be the graph of $y = kx^2 - 9x + 6$?   12.____

A.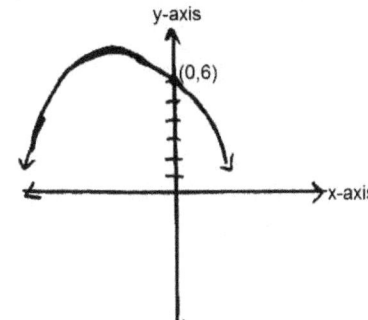

B.

C.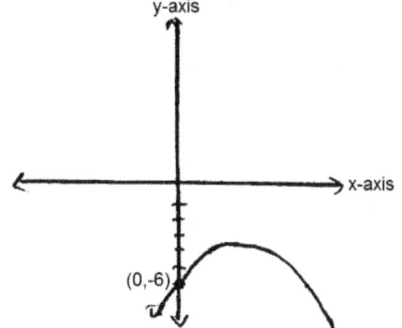

D.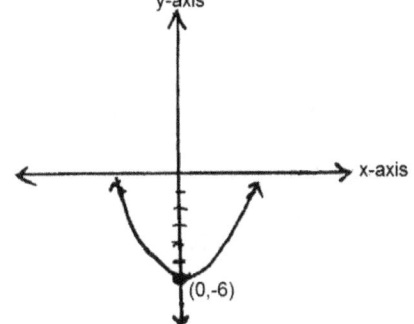

13. At a certain health club, there are *m* male members and *f* female members. The mean weight of the male members is 180 pounds and the total weight of the female members is *z* pounds.
    What is the mean weight of all the members?
    A. (180m + fz)/(m+f)
    B. (180m + fz)/(mf)
    C. (180m + z)/(m+f)
    D. (180m + z)/(mf)

14. Which one of the following is equivalent to $\log(a^2 b^{-4}/c^3)$?
    A. $(2 \log a)(-4 \log b) - 3 \log c$
    B. $2 \log a - 4 \log b - 3 \log c$
    C. $2 \log a + 4 \log b + 3 \log c$
    D. $(2 \log a)(4 \log b)/(3 \log c)$

15. The expression $x^2 + px - 40$ is factored as $(x+m)(x-n)$.
    What is the value of m-n-p?
    A. 0
    B. 1
    C. 5
    D. 10

Questions 16-40.

DIRECTIONS: In solving Questions 16 through 40, the use of a calculator is permitted.

16. Given that y = 16.2x + 8 is the line of best fit for a given set of points in the xy coordinate plane, which one of the following points lies closest to this line when measured vertically?
    A. (1, 25)
    B. (2, 41)
    C. (3, 57)
    D. (4, 73)

17. The fraction M/60 is greater than 3/7 but less than 5/11.
    If M is an integer, what is one possible value of M?

18. Given that $Z = 3^W + 100$, what is the SMALLEST integer value of W so that the value of Z exceeds 1,000?

19. Given that $x + 3y^2 = 19$ and $3x + y^2 + 25$, what is one possible value of $x^2 + y$?

20. Melissa stays at a hotel that charges *y* dollars per day, plus a tax rate of 6%. If she stays for more than five days, her daily rate is discounted by 10% for each additional day. However, the tax rate of 6% is still applied to the discounted rate.
    Which one of the following expressions represents her total cost (including tax) in dollars if she stays for nine days?
    A. 9.90y
    B. 9.726y
    C. 9.36y
    D. 9.116y

21. In the diagram shown at the right, points C, E, and H are collinear. Each of angles C and E are right angles. AC = 30, AE = 34, CH = 36, and GH = 25.
What is the length of $\overline{EG}$?
   A. 15
   B. 18
   C. 20
   D. 24

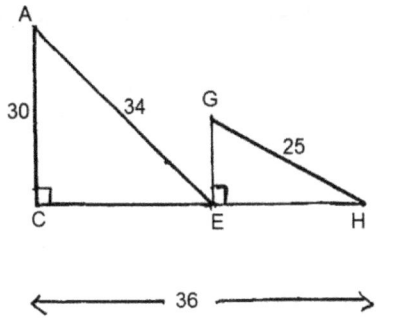

NOTE: DIAGRAM NOT DRAWN TO SCALE

22. A mattress company sells two types of mattresses, standard size and queen size. Although prices for these mattresses vary from region to region, a company statistician has determined that y = 1.4x + 60 is the line of best fit. In this equation, y represents the cost in dollars of a queen size mattress and x represents the cost in dollars of a standard size mattress. In one particular company store, the total cost of 15 standard size mattresses is $4,875. What would be the BEST approximation to the cost of this store's 20 queen size mattresses?
   A. $7,000   B. $10,000   C. $12,000   D. $15,000

23. In the diagram shown at the right, MN = MP, $\overline{MQ}$ is perpendicular to $\overline{NP}$, NP = 28, and MQ = 12.
What is the measure of ∠n, to the nearest degree?
   A. 59°
   B. 47°
   C. 41°
   D. 31°

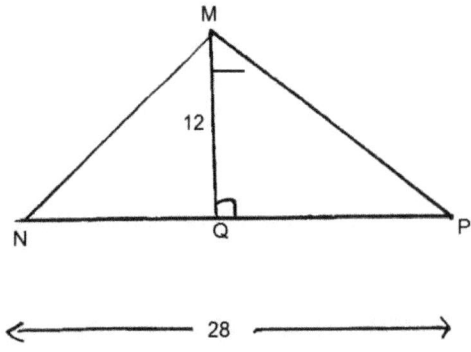

NOTE: DIAGRAM NOT DRAWN TO SCALE

24. Look at the following chart of x,y values.

x	0.4	0.9	1.2
y	0.016	0.081	m

If y varies directly as the square of x, what is the value of m?
   A. 0.048   B. 0.108   C. 0.144   D. 0.146

25. The mean value of 9, 16, x, 22, and 30 is 19. What is the value of x/3?
   A. 18   B. 13   C. 9   D. 7

26. What is the value of x in the equation $\sqrt{3x-26} = 11$?

27. In the circle shown at the right, point P is the center. Points Q and R are on the circle. PQ = 9 and ∠QPR = 135°. What is the length of minor arc QR?
    A. 9π/4
    B. 9π/2
    C. 27π/4
    D. 27π/2

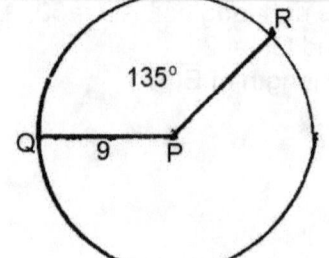

28. A parabolic curve contains the points (3,33) and (-3,3). If this curve has a minimum y-value, which one of the following could represent the equation of this curve?
    A. y = 2x² + 5x
    B. y = -x² + 42
    C. y = 2x² + 5x
    y = 4x² = 2x + 3

29. Which one of the following points satisfies the graphs of y > (1/2)(x) – 2 and x – 6y > 1?
    A. (5, 3/5)   B. (4, ¾)   C. (3, -2/3)   D. (2, -7/6)

30. In the diagram shown at the right, PQR is a right triangle and QRST is a rectangle. PQ = 9, PR = 41, and the perimeter of QRST is 128. To the nearest degree, what is the measure of the angle represented by x?
    A. 45°
    B. 54°
    C. 59°
    D. 78°

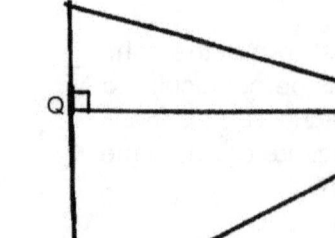

NOTE: DIAGRAM IS NOT DRAWN TO SCALE

31. Henry has only pennies, nickels, and dimes in his coin collection. The ratio of pennies to nickels is 2:7 and the ratio of nickels to dimes is 3:5. If he has 21 nickels, how many pennies and dimes combined does he have?
    A. 31   B. 41   C. 52   D. 62

Questions 32-34.

DIRECTIONS: Questions 32 through 34 are to be answered on the basis of the following chart, which shows the number of strikeouts, base on balls (walks), and home runs given up by three specific pitchers thus far for this season.

PITCHER	STRIKEOUTS	BASE ON BALLS	HOME RUNS
Ace Woodman	27	11	15
Bart Rader	20	7	12
Cap Tanner	23	9	19

32. What fraction represents the ratio of number of base on balls given up by Bart Rader to the total number of base on balls given up by the other two pitchers?

33. The fraction $3/14$ represents which one of the following?
    A. The ratio of home runs given up by Bart Rader to the total number of strike-outs, base on balls, and home runs for Cap Tanner.
    B. The ratio of base on balls given up by Cap Tanner to the total number of base on balls for all three pitchers.
    C. The combined number of base on balls given up by Ace Woodman and Bart Rader to the total number of base on balls for all three pitchers.
    D. The ratio of home runs given up by Ace Woodman to the total number of strike-outs for all three pitchers.

34. Assume that Cap Tanner will pitch in another game this season, but Ace Woodman and Bart Rader will not.
    If Cap Tanner gives up two more base on balls and no home runs, what is the minimum number of strike-outs he will need in order to exceed Bart Rader's ratio of strike-outs to base on balls?
    A. 9   B. 7   C. 5   D. 3

35. The height, in feet, of an object thrown vertically is given by the equation $h = -t^2 + 6t + 11$, where h represents feet and t represents time in seconds. What is the MAXIMUM height, in feet, of this object?
    A. 6   B. 11   C. 17   D. 20

36. The radius of a cylinder is 3 feet and is being rolled on its side at the rate of 5 feet per second. What is the MINIMUM number of integer seconds that this wheel must be rolled on its side in order to exceed 10 revolutions?
    A. 36   B. 38   C. 40   D. 42

37. Rochelle recently traveled to Israel, where one shekel is worth $0.28 in U.S. money. She made a purchase of 25 shekels at a grocery store and another purchase using shekels at a clothing store. When her purchases were converted to U.S. dollars, her bank added a 5% fee.
    If the total of her purchases for these two stores was $33.81 (including the bank fee), how many shekels did she spend at the clothing store?
    A. 96   B. 93   C. 90   D. 87

38. Walter traveled to Montreal, Canada, where a Canadian dollar is worth $0.75 in U.S. dollars. He spent 156 Canadian dollars in a gift shop and when his purchase was converted to U.S. dollars, his bank used a two-tier method for attaching a fee. The bank added an x% fee to the first 50 U.S. dollars and a (2x)% fee for the remaining amount of the purchase in U.S. dollars.
If the total amount of his purchase was $133.56 in U.S. dollars (including the bank fees), what is the value of x?

38.____

39. The deer population in a certain town in the year 2000 was P. This population grew by 8% every three years so that the deer population in the year 2018 was 380. Rounded off to the nearest ten, what is the value of P?
    A. 150   B. 180   C. 210   D. 240

39.____

40. From an ordinary deck of 52 playing cards, Fred selects three cards, one at a time with replacement of each card before selecting the next card.
What is the probability that he selects exactly two clubs?
    A. 3/256   B. 9/256   C. 3/64   D. 9/64

40.____

SOLUTIONS WITH CORRECT ANSWERS

1. CORRECT ANSWER: A
   Each Y-Try pill contains 54/3 = 18 mg of zinc and each Z-Wow pill contains 48/4 = 12 mg of zinc. Therefore, c pills of Y-Try and d pills of Z-Wow contain $18c + 12d$ mg of zinc. This sum must be greater than or equal to 80 mg of zinc.

2. CORRECT ANSWER: B
   For triangle PQR, ∠1 is an exterior angle and its two remote interior angles are ∠3 and ∠5. A theorem in geometry states that the measure of any exterior angle of a triangle is equal to the sum of the measures of the two remote interior angles. Choice A is wrong because interior angles on the same side of a transversal (TR) are supplementary, not necessarily equal. Choice C is wrong because the sum of the measures of ∠4 and ∠5 is 180°. Choice D is wrong because ∠1 + ∠2 = 180° and ∠4 + ∠5 = 180°; however, there is no required relationship between the value of ∠1 + ∠5 and the value of ∠2 + ∠4.

3. CORRECT ANSWER: A
   From February through July, Jack will have made 6 deposits of x dollars each. This amount of 6x dollars must be added to his initial amount of $3,000 that he had at the end of January.

4. CORRECT ANSWER: B
   The combined number of first and second place finishes is 10 + 14 = 24. The required ratio is 24/36 = 2/3.

5. CORRECT ANSWER: D
   Able Arlene had 9 second place finishes and the combined number of second place finishes for all three horses was 9 + 14 + 2 = 25. The indicated ratio is 9/25 = 36%. The ratio for each of choices A, B, and C are 42%, 33%, and 32%, respectively.

6. CORRECT ANSWER: A
   Cluster sampling involves selecting a few groups of the population and then sampling each member of these groups. In this case, the two groups are the educators from New Jersey and Pennsylvania. Choice B is wrong because random sampling involves no system. Choice C is wrong because stratified sampling involves sampling selected members from each subgroup of the entire population. In this case, the subgroups would be each of the states that are represented. Choice D is wrong because systematic sampling involves selecting every kth person from the entire population.

7. CORRECT ANSWER: C
   By subtracting w^3 from each side of the equation, we get $y - w^3 = kx^2$. Next, divide each side by k to get $x^2 = (y-w^3)/k$. Finally, take the square root of each side to get $x = \sqrt{(y - w^3)/k}$.

8. CORRECT ANSWER: A
   Using the basic rule of subtracting exponents of like bases when dividing, we get $a^{5-(-5)}b^{6-2}c^{-2-4} = a^{10}b^4c^{-6}$, which becomes $(a^{10}b^4)/c^6$.

9. **CORRECT ANSWER: D**
The remainder will be the value of $x^3 - 6$ when $x = 3$. Thus, the remainder is $3^3 - 6 = 27 - 6 = 21$.

10. **CORRECT ANSWER: C**
In some cases, an increased speed limit corresponds to an increase in the number of seconds for the green light. But in other cases, a lower speed limit corresponds to an increase in the number of seconds for the green light. Thus, there is no correlation between these two quantities. Note that there is no such item as identity correlation.

11. **CORRECT ANSWER: A**
We can write this equation as $b^2(a+c) = 9d^4(a+c)$. Then, $b^2 = 9d^4$, so $b = 3d^2$. Finally, $b^3 = (3d^2)^3 = 27d^6$.

12. **CORRECT ANSWER: B**
When $k < 0$, the graph of any parabola with a term of kx^2 will have a maximum value. This means that only answer choices B and C are possible. But for the graph of $y = kx^2 - 9x + 6$, the y-intercept is $(0,6)$. Thus, only answer choice B satisfies the given requirement.

13. **CORRECT ANSWER: C**
The total weight of the male members is $180m$ and the total weight of the female members is z. The total number of members is $m + f$. The mean weight of all the members is the total weight of all the members divided by the total number of members, which is $(180m+z)/(m+f)$.

14. **CORRECT ANSWER: B**
Using the rules of logarithms, $\log(a^2 b^{-4}/c^3) = \log a^2 b^{-4} - \log c^3 = \log a^2 + \log b^{-4} - \log c^3 = 2 \log a - 4 \log b - 3 \log c$. Recall these three rules of logarithms, namely, $\log(ab) = \log a + \log b$, $\log(a/b) = \log a - \log b$, and $\log(a)^b = (b)(\log a)$.

15. **CORRECT ANSWER: A**
$(x+m)(x-n) = x^2 + mx - nx - mn = x^2 + (m-n)(x) - mn$. This means that $m - n = p$, so $m - n - p = 0$. (Note that $mn = -40$, but this information is not needed to solve for $m - n - p$.)

16. **CORRECT ANSWER: A**
When $x = 2$, $y = (16.2)(1) + 8 = 24.2$; when $x = 2$, $y = (16.2)(2) + 8 = 40.4$; when $x = 3$, $y = (16.2)(3) + 8 = 56.6$; when $x = 4$, $y = (16.2)(4) + 8 = 72.8$. Then the vertical distances from each of the four given points listed in choices A thru D to the line of best fit are 0.8, 0.6, 0.4, and 0.2, respectively. These values are determined by evaluating the absolute value of the difference between the given y values of the four points and the obtained y values from the line of best fit.

17. **CORRECT ANSWER: 26 or 27**
Since $M/60 > 3/7$, we get $7M > 180$. Then, $M > 25.71$. Since $M/60 < 5/11$, $11M < 300$. Then, $M < 27.27$. The only two integers that satisfy both inequalities are 26 and 27.

18. CORRECT ANSWER: 7
We have $3^W + 100 > 1000$, which simplifies to $3^W > 900$. Taking the common log of each side, we get $(W)(\log 3) > \log 900$. Finally, $W > \log 900/\log 3 \approx 6.19$. Thus, the minimum integer value becomes 7.

19. CORRECT ANSWER: 47 or 51
Multiply the second equation by 3 to get $9x + 3y^2 = 75$. Now subtract the first equation to get $8x = 56$, so $x = 7$. By substitution into the first equation, we get $7 + 3y^2 = 19$. Then $y^2 = (19-7)/3 = 4$, which leads to $y = -2$ or 2. If $x = 7$ and $y = -2$, $x^2 + y = 7^2 - 2 = 47$. If $x = 7$ and $y = 2$, $x^2 + y = 7^2 + 2 = 51$.

20. CORRECT ANSWER: D
For each of the first five days, the cost is 1.06y; for each of the additional four days, the cost is (0.90y)(1.06) = 0.954y. Thus, the total cost in dollars for Melissa's stay of nine days is (5)(1.06y) + (4)(0.954y) = 9.116y.

21. CORRECT ANSWER: A
$CE = \sqrt{34^2 - 30^2} = \sqrt{256} = 16$. $EH = CH - CE = 20$. Finally, $EG = \sqrt{25^2 - 20^2} = \sqrt{225} = 15$

22. CORRECT ANSWER: B
The mean cost of a standard mattress is $4875/15 = $325. Then the mean cost of a queen size mattress can be best approximated as (1.4)($515) = $10,300. The closest of the answer choices is $10,000.

23. CORRECT ANSWER: C
Since MNP is an isosceles triangle, $\overline{MQ}$ not only is perpendicular to $\overline{NP}$, it also bisects $\overline{NP}$. Then $NQ = (1/2)(NP) = 14$. Thus, in triangle MNQ, tan ∠N = MQ/NQ = 12/14 ≈ 0.857. Finally, ∠N = arctan 0.857 = 40.6°. The closest of the answer choices is 41°.

24. CORRECT ANSWER: C
The equation $y = kx^2$, where k is a constant, expresses the relationship that y varies directly as the square of x. Substituting the first pair of x,y values, we get $0.016 = (k)(0.4)^2$, which becomes 0.016 = 0.016 = 016k. Then, k = 0.016/0.16 = 0.1. This means that $y = 0.1x^2$. Now substitute 1.2 for x so that $m = (0.1)(1.2)^2 = 0.144$. Note that we could have substituted the second pair of x,y values to obtain the same value of k.

25. CORRECT ANSWER: D
We note that the sum of the five numbers must be (19)(5) = 95. Then 9 + 16 + x + 22 + 30 = 95. This equation simplifies to 77 + x = 95, so x = 18. Thus, x/3 = 6.

26. CORRECT ANSWER: 49
Square both sides of the equation to get $3x - 26 = 121$. Next, add 26 to each side to get $3x = 147$. Thus, $x = 147/3 = 49$.

27. CORRECT ANSWER: C
PQ represents the radius of the circle, so the circumference of the circle is $(2\pi)(9) = 18\pi$. Thus, the length of minor arc QR is $(135°/360°)(18\pi) = 27\pi/4$.

28. **CORRECT ANSWER: C**
For the graph of $y = ax^2 + bx + c$ to have a minimum y-value, the number represented by a must be positive. This means that only choices C and D are possible. For answer choice C, we note that $33 = (2)(3)^2 + (5)(3)$ and $3 = (2)(-3)^2 + (5)(-3)$. Answer choice D is wrong because although the point (3,33) satisfies $y = 4x^2 - 2x + 3$, the point (-3,3) does not. We note that $3 \neq (4)(-3)^2 - (2)(-3) + 3$, which is 45.

29. **CORRECT ANSWER: A**
By substitution, $3/5 > (1/2)(5) - 2 = ½$ and $5 - (6)(3/5) = 7/5 > 1$. Answer choice B is wrong because by substitution into the second inequality, $4 - (6)(3/4) = -1/2$, which is not greater than 1. Answer choice C is wrong because by substitution into the first inequality, -2/3 is not greater than $(1/2)(3) - 2$, which is equal to -1/2. Answer choice D is wrong because by substitution into the first inequality, -7/6 is not greater than $(1/2)(2) - 2$, which is -1.

30. **CORRECT ANSWER: C**
By the Pythagorean Theorem, $QR = \sqrt{41^2 - 9^2} = \sqrt{1681 - 81} = \sqrt{1600} = 40$. Let $y = QT$. Then, $2y + 40 + 40 = 128$, which leads to $2y = 48$. So, $y = 24$. Finally, $\tan x = QR/QT = 40/24 \approx 1.67$ and the arctan $1.67 \approx 59°$.

31. **CORRECT ANSWER: B**
First, let x represent the number of pennies. Then $2/7 = x/21$. Cross-multiply to get $7x = 42$, so $x = 6$. Now let y represent the number of dimes. Then, $3/5 = 21/y$. Cross-multiply to get $3y = 105$, so $y = 35$. Thus, the total of pennies and dimes is $6 + 35 = 41$.

32. **CORRECT ANSWER: 7/20**
Bart Rader has given up 7 base on balls, whereas the combined total of base on balls for the other two pitchers is $11 + 9 = 20$.

33. **CORRECT ANSWER: D**
The number of home runs given up by Ace Woodman is 15. The total number of strikeouts for all three pitchers is $27 + 20 + 23 = 70$. The required fraction is 15/70, which reduces to 3/14. The ratios for A, B, and C are 12/51, 9/27, and 18/27, respectively. None of these fractions reduces to 3/14.

34. **CORRECT ANSWER: A**
The ratio for Bart Rader's strikeouts to base on balls is 20/7. Cap Tanner already has 23 strikeouts and will have 11 base on balls after the next game he pitches. Let x represent the minimum number of strikeouts needed. Then we want $(23+x)/11 > 20/7$. Cross-multiply to get $161 + 7x > 220$. Then, $x > (220-161)/7 \approx 8.42$. This means that the minimum value of x is 9.

35. **CORRECT ANSWER: D**
We can rewrite this equation as $h = (t^2-6t+9) + 11 + 9$, which can then be written as $h = -(t-3)^2 + 20$. In this format, we deduce that the maximum height is 20 feet and it occurs at $t = 3$ seconds.

36. **CORRECT ANSWER: B**
The circumference of this wheel is $(2)(\pi)(3) \approx 18.85$ feet. Then, 10 revolutions corresponds to approximately 188.5 feet. Finally, $188.5/5 = 37.7$, which must be rounded up to 38 seconds.

37. **CORRECT ANSWER: C**
Let x represent the number of shekels Rochelle spent at the clothing store. Then, $[(25)(0.28)+(x)(0.28)][1.05] = 33.81$. We can rewrite this equation as $(25+x)(0.28)(1.05) = 33.81$. Then, $(25+x)(0.294) = 33.81$, so $25 + x = 115$. Thus, $x = 90$.

38. **CORRECT ANSWER: 9**
First note that 156 Canadian dollars = $(156)(\$0.75) = \$117$ U.S. dollars. The first $50 will be assessed an x% fee and the remaining $67 will be assessed a (2x)% fee. Then, $(50)(1+x/100)+(67)(1+\{2x\}/100) = 133.56$. Simplifying this equation, we get $50 + (1/2)(x) + 67 + (67/50)(x) = 133.56$. Now, $(92/50)(x) = 133.56 - 50 - 67$, which becomes $(46/25)(x) = 16.56$. Finally, $x = (16.56)(25/46) = 9$.

39. **CORRECT ANSWER: D**
We use the equation $A = P(1+R)^t$, where A is the final value, P is the initial value, R is the rate of increase, and t is the number of time periods associated with the rate. For this example, $A = 380$, $R = 0.08$, and $t = (2018-2000)/3 = 6$. Then, $380 = P(1.08)^6$. Taking the common logarithm of each side, we get $\log 380 = \log P + (6)(\log 1.08)$, which becomes $2.58 = \log P + (6)(0.033)$. Then, $\log P = 2.58 - 0.198 = 2.382$. Thus, $P = (10)^{2.382} \approx 241$. rounded off to the nearest ten, we have $P = 240$.

40. **CORRECT ANSWER: D**
The probability for selecting a club is $13/52 = 1/4$ because there are 13 clubs in the deck. The expression to use for selecting exactly two clubs from three cards with replacement is $[C(3,2)][1/4]^2[3/4] = (3)(1/16)(3/4) = 9/64$. Note that $C(3,2)$ means the number of combinations of three items taken two at a time, which is $(3)(2)/[(2)(1)] = 6/2 = 3$.

EXAMINATION SECTION
TEST 1

DIRECTIONS: Each question or incomplete statement is followed by several suggested answers or completions. Select the one that BEST answers the question or completes the statement. *PRINT THE LETTER OF THE CORRECT ANSWER IN THE SPACE AT THE RIGHT.*

1. If $5(n+3) = 30$, which of the following is TRUE? 1.____

   A. $n + 3 = 25$
   B. $n + 15 = 30$
   C. $5n + 3 = 30$
   D. $5n + 15 = 30$
   E. $5n + 15 = 150$

2. According to the graph shown at the right, approximately how many years did it take Maine's population to double from what it was in 1840? 2.____

   A. 25
   B. 40
   C. 70
   D. 115
   E. 130

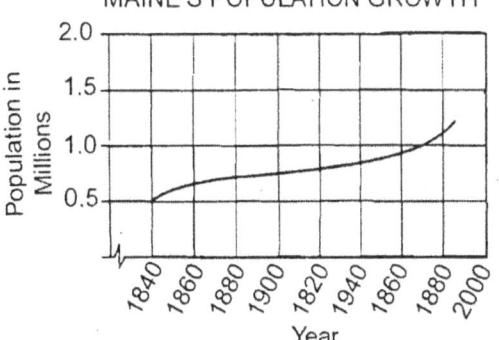

3. $-1, 0, 1, -1, 0, 1,...$ 3.____
   The numbers -1, 0 and 1 repeat in a sequence, as shown above. If this pattern continues, what will be the sum of the 12th and 16th numbers in the sequence?

   A. -2   B. -1   C. 0   D. 1   E. 2

4. In the figure shown at the right, the polygon with center O is equilateral and equiangular. 4.____
   The combined areas of the shaded regions represent what fraction of the total area of the polygon?

   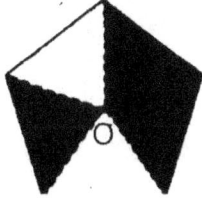

   A. 2/5
   B. 1/2
   C. 3/5
   D. 2/3
   E. 3/4

5. If $x - 8 = 8 - x$, then $x =$ 5.____

   A. -16   B. -8   C. 0   D. 8   E. 16

6. Tickets numbered from 1 to 40, inclusive, are placed in a bowl and one ticket is to be selected at random. What is the probability that the ticket selected will have a single-digit number on it? 6.____

   A. 1/40   B. 9/40   C. 1/4   D. 1/2   E. 3/4

7. Four straight lines that lie in the same plane intersect each other at point P. Which of the following is the sum of the measures of the non-overlapping angles formed?

   A. 60°   B. 90°   C. 180°   D. 320°   E. 360°

8. The difference between 2 times a number n and 7 is 81. Which of the following equations could be used to express the relationship in the above statement?

   A. $2n - 7 = 81$
   B. $2n + 7 = 81$
   C. $2(n-7) = 81$
   D. $n - 2(7) = 81$
   E. $n - 2 + 7 = 81$

9. An integer is divisible by 20, is a multiple of 30, and has 40 as a factor. What is the LEAST positive integer that satisfies these conditions?

   A. 10   B. 60   C. 120   D. 240   E. 360

10. If ab = 15, what is the value of the ratio of a to b?

    A. 1 to 15   B. 3 to 5   C. 5 to 3   D. 15 to 1
    E. It cannot be determined from the information given

11. If $a + 2a + 3a = 8$, what is the value of $3a + 4a + 5a$?

    A. 10   B. 12   C. 16   D. 20   E. 24

12. In the figure shown at the right, if BC is extended to the left to point A (not shown) so that B is the midpoint of AC, and if the length of AC is 2x, what is the length of CD in terms of x?

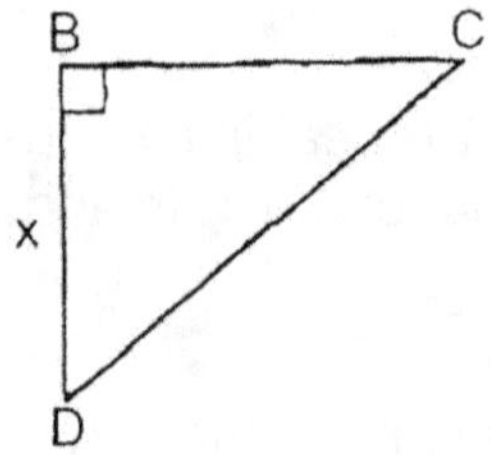

    A. $\sqrt{2}x$
    B. $\sqrt{3}x$
    C. $\sqrt{5}x$
    D. 1.5x
    E. 2x

    Note: Figure not drawn to scale.

13. For which of the following pairs of numbers is the second number 5 more than twice the first number?

    A. 5 and 30
    B. 5 and 35
    C. 10 and 40
    D. 20 and 50
    E. 25 and 55

14. The line that passes through (-3, 5) and (0, 4) also passes through which of the following points?

    A. (1, 7)   B. (3, 3)   C. (3, 5)   D. (5, 3)   E. (7, 1)

15. The average (arithmetic mean) of 5 test scores is 81. If 3 of the scores are 92, 83, and 78, which of the following could NOT be the other 2 scores?

    A. 73 and 79
    B. 72 and 80
    C. 69 and 83
    D. 64 and 86
    E. 59 and 93

16.
```
   2G
   H7
   4H
 + 38
  ───
  164
```
If the sum of the four two-digit numbers shown above equals 164, what is digit G?

A. 8 B. 7 C. 6 D. 5 E. 4

17. Each face of the solid cube shown at the right is to be completely covered with 2-inch-wide strips of tape that do not overlap. What is the TOTAL length of the tape that is needed to cover the cube?

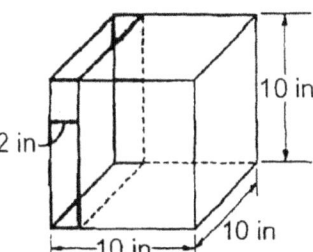

A. 300 in.
B. 450 in.
C. 600 in.
D. 900 in.
E. 1,000 in.

18. If $r = x + y + z$, $x = 2y$ and $2z = 3y$, what is the value of r in terms of y?

A. $\frac{7}{2}y$ B. $\frac{9}{2}y$ C. $5y$ D. $\frac{11}{2}y$ E. $6y$

19. In the figure shown at the right, if the area of △OPT equals the area of △TRS, what are the coordinates of P?

A. (0, 2)
B. (0, 5/2)
C. (0, 3)
D. (0, 4)
E. (0, 5)

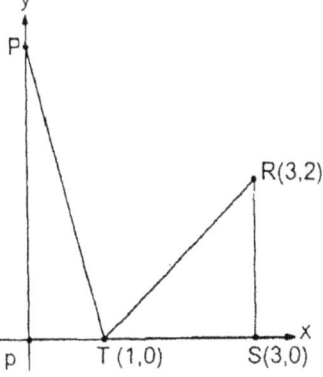

Note: Figure not drawn to scale.

20. If n>1, which of the following numbers will always be greater than 1?

I. $\frac{n}{n+1}$

II. $(n-1)^2$

III. $\frac{2n-1}{n}$

The CORRECT answer is:

A. None of the above   B. II only
C. III only   D. I and III
E. II and III

21. A square is inscribed in a circle of radius 10 centimeters, as shown in the figure at the right.
What is the area, in square centimeters, of the square?

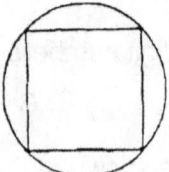

- A. 225
- B. 200
- C. $125\sqrt{2}$
- D. 169
- E. 100

22. All tickets to a certain concert are equally priced. A survey showed that increasing the price of these concert tickets by 5 percent would decrease the number of tickets sold by 20 percent.
By what percent would this decrease the amount of money received from the sale of concert tickets?

- A. 84%
- B. 80%
- C. 20%
- D. 16%
- E. 15%

23. $4^x + 4^x + 4^x + 4^x =$

- A. 4^{x+1}
- B. 4^{x+2}
- C. 4^{x+4}
- D. 4^{4x}
- E. $4x^4$

24. The numbers on the meter shown at the right are spaced at equal intervals along its circumference. If the hand is turned clockwise from its present position for 3,466 intervals and then turned counterclockwise for 7,934 intervals, at which number will the hand then be pointing?

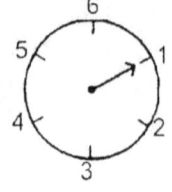

- A. 2
- B. 3
- C. 4
- D. 5
- E. 6

25. During 100 minutes of playing time, each of 5 teams plays each of the other 4 teams exactly once. Only 2 teams play at any given time.
If the total playing time for each team is the same, what is the TOTAL number of minutes that each team plays?

- A. 50
- B. 40
- C. 36
- D. 30
- E. 20

KEY (CORRECT ANSWERS)

1.	D	11.	C
2.	E	12.	A
3.	C	13.	E
4.	C	14.	B
5.	D	15.	D
6.	B	16.	E
7.	E	17.	A
8.	A	18.	B
9.	C	19.	D
10.	E	20.	C

21. B
22. D
23. A
24. B
25. B

ANSWERS GRIDDED

1. D
2. E
3. B
4. C
5. D
6. B
7. D
8. A
9. B
10. E

11. C
12. A
13. E
14. B
15. E
16. E
17. A
18. B
19. D
20. C

21. B
22. D
23. A
24. B
25. B

TEST 2

DIRECTIONS: Each question or incomplete statement is followed by several suggested answers or completions. Select the one that BEST answers the question or completes the statement. *PRINT THE LETTER OF THE CORRECT ANSWER IN THE SPACE AT THE RIGHT.*

Questions 1-15.

DIRECTIONS: Questions 1 through 15 each consist of two quantities in boxes, one in Column A and one in Column B. You are to compare the two quantities and mark your answer:
- A. if the quantity in Column A is greater;
- B. if the quantity in Column B is greater;
- C. if the two quantities are equal;
- D. if the relationship cannot be determined from the information given.

Notes:
1. In some questions, information is given about one or both of the quantities to be compared. In such cases, the given information is centered above the two columns and is not boxed.
2. In a given question, a symbol that appears in both columns represents the same thing in Column A as it does in Column B.
3. Letters such as x, n, and k stand for real numbers.

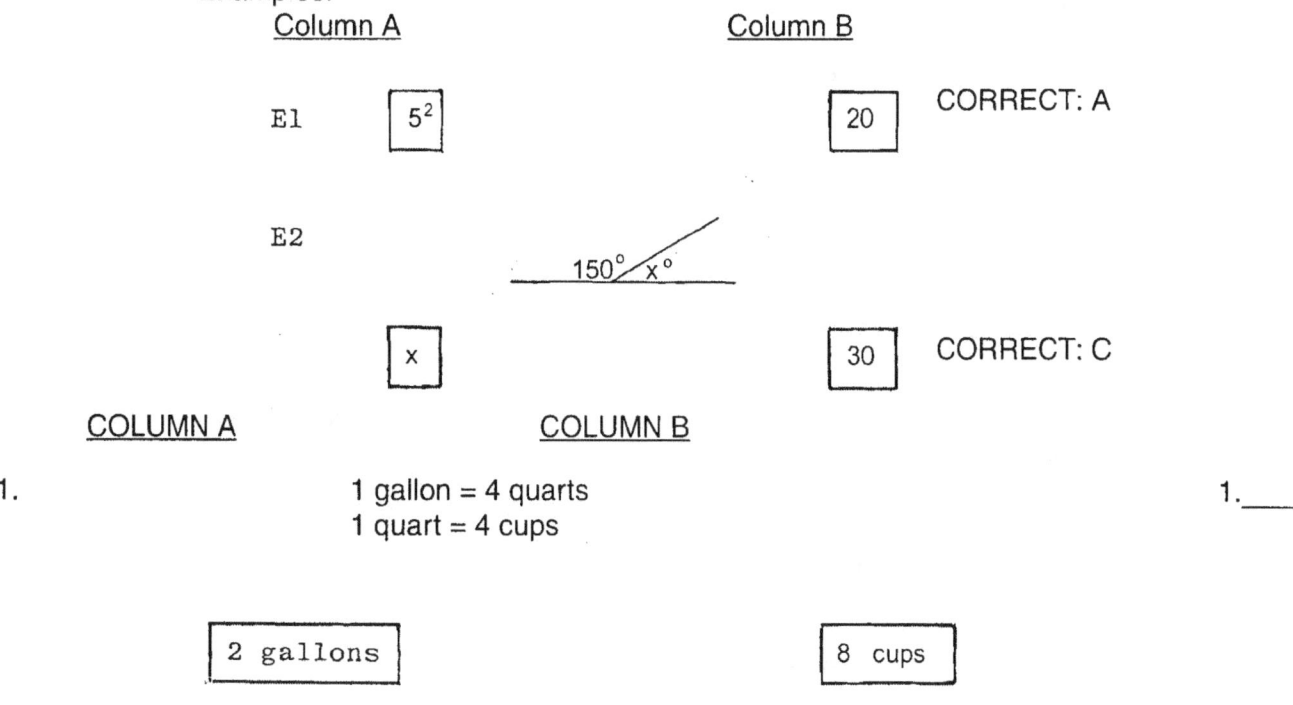

COLUMN A   COLUMN B

1. 1 gallon = 4 quarts
    1 quart = 4 cups

    [2 gallons]   [8 cups]

1.____

33

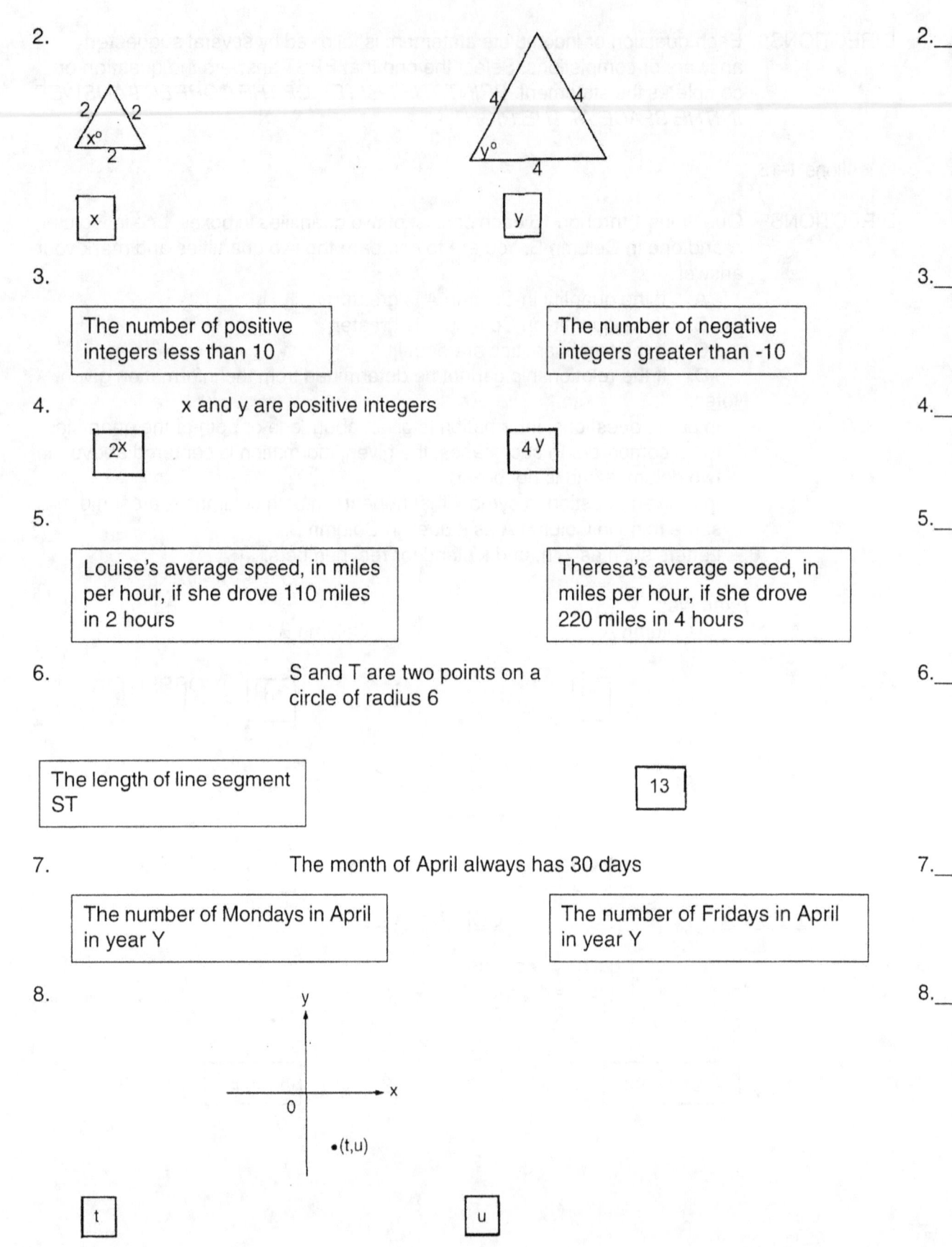

3 (#2)

9. $2n = -3q$ 9._____

     | n | | q |

10. The lengths of the sides of a triangle are 5, 5, and t   10._____

     | 5 | | t |

11. $3x > 15$ 11._____
        $4 - y > 5$

     | x | | y |

12. Lines *l* and *m* lies in a plane and are neither parallel nor perpendicular to each other.   12._____

     | The degree measure of the smaller angle formed by *l* and *m* | | 90 |

13. For all integers x and y, let $x \blacksquare y$ be defined as $x \blacksquare y = xy^2$.   13._____

     | (3 ■ 2) − (2 ■ 3) | | 0 |

14. $x + 3 = y$ 14._____
        $x + y = 10$

     | 2x + 3 | | 10 |

15. r and s are two different positive integers. r/s is an integer.   15._____

     | The number of integers that divide r with remainder zero | | The number of integers that divide s with remainder zero |

Questions 16-25.

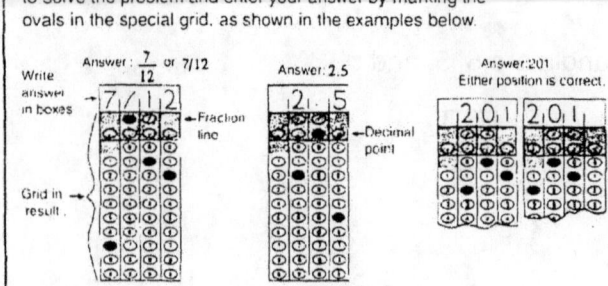

16. If $\dfrac{k}{10}+\dfrac{k}{10}+\dfrac{k}{10}=3$ what is the value of k?

17. Set S consists of all multiples of 3 between 10 and 25. Set T consists of all multiples of 4 between 10 and 25. What is one possible number that is in set S but NOT in set T?

18. -980, -76, -54, 0, 1, 2, 3, 54, 76, 980
    What is the average (arithmetic mean) of the 10 numbers in the list above?

19. If $(3x+1)(4x+3) = ax^2 + bx + c$ for all values of x, what is the value of b?

20. What is the perimeter of the eight-sided figure shown at the right?

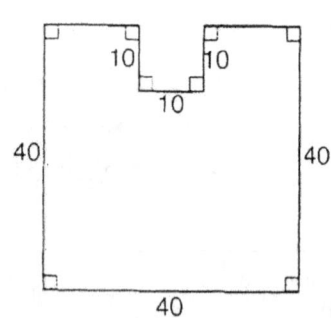

21. If 3s + 7t = 22 and s and t are positive integers, what is the value of s?

22. A cubic foot of a certain material weighs 4 pounds. How much will 216 cubic inches of this material weigh, in pounds? (1 cubic foot = 1,728 cubic inches)

23. In a certain factory, 0.2 percent of a batch of micro-chips are defective. If this batch contains 4 defective microchips, how many microchips are in the batch?

24. If $3/y^3 = 81$, what is the value of y?

25. Points P, Q, R, and S are the centers of four of the faces of the cube shown in the figure at the right.
What is the area of quadrilateral PQRS?

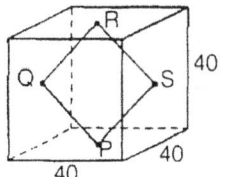

KEY (CORRECT ANSWERS)

1. A
2. C
3. C
4. D
5. C

6. B
7. D
8. A
9. D
10. D

11. A
12. B
13. B
14. C
15. A

16. 10
17. 15, 18, or 21
18. .6 or 3/5
19. 13
20. 180

21. 5
22. 1/2 or .5
23. 2000
24. 1/3 or .333
25. 800

ANSWERS GRIDDED

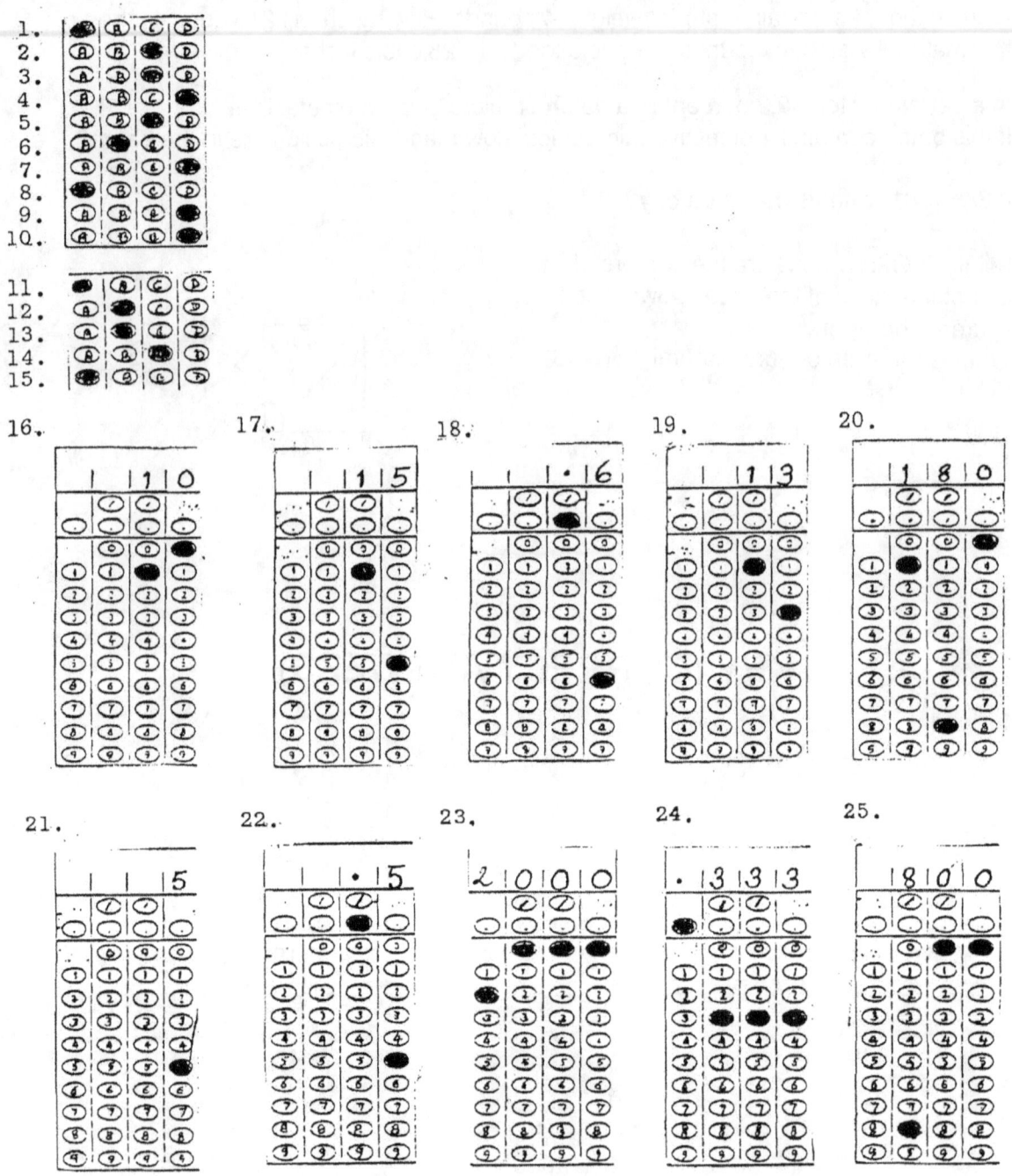

EXAMINATION SECTION
TEST 1

DIRECTIONS: Each question or incomplete statement is followed by several suggested answers or completions. Select the one that BEST answers the question or completes the statement. *PRINT THE LETTER OF THE CORRECT ANSWER IN THE SPACE AT THE RIGHT.*

1. Which of the following fractions is the GREATEST? 1.____
   A. 16/17   B. 8/9   C. 14/15   D. 9/10   E. 11/12

2. Sue ate $1/3$ of a sandwich at noon and then ½ of the remainder at supper. What part of the sandwich remained uneaten? 2.____
   A. $1/6$ B. $1/5$ C. $1/3$ D. ½   E. $2/3$

3. In a certain class of 30 students, 18 are girls. If $2/3$ of the girls are 16 years old or younger, what fractional part of the class is girls over 16? 3.____
   A. $2/16$ B. $1/5$ C. $1/3$ D. $2/5$ E. ½

4. In a certain factory, ¾ of the workers are married and ¾ of these married workers have children. What fraction of the workers in the factory are married without children? 4.____
   A. $1/16$ B. $3/16$ C. ¼   D. ½   E. $9/16$

5. Every student who studies art in a certain school receives exactly one of the grades A, B, C, or D. If $1/5$ of the students receive A's, ¼ receive B's, ½ receive C's, and 10 students receive D's, how many students in the school study art? 5.____
   A. 50   B. 60   C. 90   D. 100   E. 200

6. The gauge of a gas tank shows $1/8$ full. After 12 gallons are added, the tank is $7/8$ full. What is the capacity, in gallons, of the tank? 6.____
   A. 14   B. 15   C. 16   D. 17   E. 18

7. If x ranges in value from 0.0001 to 0.01 and y ranges in value from 0.001 to 0.1, what is the MAXIMUM value of x/y? 7.____
   A. 0.001   B. 0.1   C. 1   D. 10   E. 1,000

8. Sally used ¼ of her inheritance to pay her tuition and $2/3$ of the remainder to buy a new car. How much money was left from her original inheritance of $60,000? 8.____
   A. $12,000   B. $15,000   C. $18,000   D. $20,000   E. $24,000

Questions 9-10.

DIRECTIONS: Questions 9 and 10 consist of two quantities, one in Column A and one in Column B. You are to compare the two quantities and in the space at the right write:
- A. if the quantity in Column A is greater;
- B. if the quantity in Column B is greater;
- C. if the two quantities are equal;
- D. if the relationship cannot be determined from the information given;

An E response will not be scored.

9. x = {0.98, 0.098, 0.09}
   y = {0.089, 0.89, 0.9}

Column A	Column B
The greatest number in set x.	The greatest number in set y.

10.
Column A	Column B
$\dfrac{\frac{2}{3}}{\frac{3}{2}}$	1

Questions 11-16.

DIRECTIONS: Questions 11 through 16 are problems involving percents.

11. In a senior class, there are 200 boys and 300 girls. If 40 percent of the senior boys and 50 percent of the senior girls bought class rings, how many seniors bought class rings?
   A. 200   B. 225   C. 230   D. 250   E. 275

12. If 10 is 5 percent of N, then N =
   A. 2   B. 5   C. 20   D. 50   E. 200

13. In a basket of 120 apples, exactly 6 were rotten. What percent of the apples were rotten?
   A. 5%   B. 6%   C. 10%   D. 20%   E. 25%

14. In the rectangle shown at the right, PQ = x and QR = 2x. What percent of the perimeter of the rectangle is the sum PQ + QR + RS?
   A. 50%
   B. 66 2/3%
   C. 75%
   D. 80%
   E. 83 2/3%

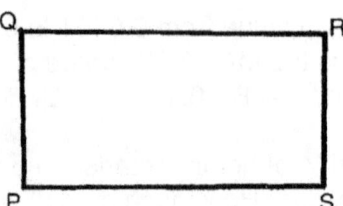

15. If the length and width of rectangle A are 10 percent less and 30 percent less, respectively, than the length and width of rectangle B, the area of A is equal to what percent of the area of B?
    A. 63%   B. 60%   C. 40%   D. 6%   E. 3%

16. The population of Norson, the largest city in Transitania, is 50 percent of the rest of the population of Transitania.
    The population of Norson is what percent of the entire population of Transitania?
    A. 20%   B. 25%   C. 30%   D. $33\frac{1}{3}\%$ E. 50%

Questions 17-20.

DIRECTIONS: Questions 17 through 20 consist of two quantities, one in Column A and one in Column B. You are to compare the two quantities and in the space at the right write:
    A. if the quantity in Column A is greater;
    B. if the quantity in Column B is greater;
    C. if the two quantities are equal;
    D. if the relationship cannot be determined from the information given;
    An E response will not be scored.

17. A coat that was priced at $36.50 is sold at 30 percent discount.
    Column A   Column B
    Price of coat after discount $25.55

18. On a certain day, 80 percent of the girls and 75 percent of the boys were present in a mathematics class.
    Column A   Column B
    The number of girls absent   The number of boys absent

19. x is 10% of y
    Column A   Column B
    The percent that y is of x   100%

20. x percent of y is z.
    Column A   Column B
    100   xy/z

21. A grocer has 100 apples, 100 oranges, and 100 pears.
    If he packs 1 apple, 2 oranges, and 1 pear in a bag, then the MAXIMUM number of bags he can fill in this manner is
    A. 20   B. 25   C. 50   D. 75   E. 100

22. Which of the following conditions will make x – y a positive number?
    A. 0<x   B. y<x   C. x<0   D. x<y   E. x=y

4 (#1)

23. If xy is positive, which of the following CANNOT be true about x and y?   23.____
    A. x<y<0   B. y<x<0   C. x<0<y   D. 0<x<y   E. 0<y<x

24. The area of a living room is 465 square feet. If this area were increased by   24.____
    25 square feet, the enlarged area would be twice the area of the adjoining
    dining room.
    What is the area, in square feet, of the dining room?
    A. 245   B. 240   C. 235   D. 230   E. 220

25. If the two middle digits of 4,579 are interchanged, the resulting number is   25.____
    A. 18 less than 4,579   B. 180 less than 4,579
    C. equal to 4,579   D. 18 more than 4,579
    E. 180 more than 4,579

KEY (CORRECT ANSWERS)

1.	A		11.	C
2.	C		12.	E
3.	B		13.	A
4.	B		14.	B
5.	E		15.	A
6.	C		16.	D
7.	D		17.	C
8.	B		18.	D
9.	A		19.	A
10.	B		20.	C

21. C
22. B
23. C
24. A
25. E

SOLUTIONS TO PROBLEMS

1. (A). Converting each fraction to a decimal, we have (rounded to the nearest hundredth) 16/17 = 0.94, 8/9 = 0.89, 14/15 = 0.93, 9/10 = 0.90, 11/12 = 0.92. Thus, 16/17 is the largest of these.

2. (C). After eating 1/3 of her sandwich, Sue had 1 – 1/3 = 2/3 of her sandwich left. She ate 1/2 of this 2/3 portion at supper, which represents (2/3)(1/2) = 1/3 of the entire sandwich. Thus, the part of the sandwich that remained uneaten is 1 – 1/3 – 1/3 = 1/3.

3. (B). The number of girls who are 16 years old or younger is (2/3)(18) = 12. This means that the number of girls who are over 16 years old is 18 – 12 = 6. Thus, 6/30 = 1/5 represents the fractional part of the class of girls who are over 16 years old.

4. (B). The fraction of workers who are both married and have children is (3/4)(3/4) = 9/16. Since 3/4 of all the workers are married, the fraction of married workers who do not have children is 3/4 –9/16 = 12/16 – 9/16 = 3/16.

5. (E). The fraction of students who receive a D grade is 1 – 1/5 – 1/4 – 1/2 = 20/20 – 4/20 – 5/20 – 10/20 = 1/20. Since 1/20 represents 10 students, the total number of students is 10 / (1/20) = 200.

6. (C). The amount of 12 gallons represents 7/8 – 1/8 = 6/8 = 3/4 of a tank of gas. Therefore, the capacity of the gas tank is 12 / (3/4) = (12)(4/3) = 16 gallons.

7. (D). In order to maximize any fraction, we maximize the numerator and minimize the denominator. In this case, the maximum value of x is 0.01 and the minimum value of y is 0.001. Thus, the maximum value of x/y is 0.01 / 0.001 = 10.

8. (B). Sally used (1/4)($60,000) = $15,000 to pay her tuition. She then had $60,000 – $15,000 = $45,000 left over. From this $45,000, she used 2/3 of this amount, which is (2/3)($45,000) = $30,000 to buy a new car. Thus, after paying her tuition and buying a new car, she had $60,000 – $15,000 –$30,000 = $15,000 left over from her original inheritance.

9. (A). The greatest number in set x is 0.98 and the greatest number in set y is 0.9. We note that 0.98 > 0.9.

10. (B). (2/3)/ (3/2) = (2/3)(2/3) = 4/9. We note that 1 > 4/9.

11. (C). The number of seniors who bought class rings is (200)(0.40) + (300)(0.50) = 80 + 150 = 230.

12. (E). We can write 10 = 0.05N. Then N = 10 / 0.05 = 200.

13. (A). The percent of rotten apples is (6/120)(100) = 5%.

14. (B). Opposite sides of a rectangle are equal, so RS = x and PS = $2x$. Then PQ + QR + RS = $x + 2x + x = 4x$. The perimeter of the rectangle is $x + 2x + x + 2x = 6x$. Finally, $4x / 6x = 2/3$ = 66 2/3 %.

15. (A). Let x and y represent the length and width, respectively, of rectangle B. Then $0.9x$ and $0.7y$ represent the length and width, respectively, of rectangle A. The area of rectangle B is xy, whereas the area of rectangle A is $(0.9x)(0.7y) = 0.63xy$. This means that the area of rectangle A is 63% of the area of rectangle B.

16. (D). Let x represent the population of Norson, so that $2x$ represents the population of the rest of Transitania. Then the entire population of Transitania can be represented by $3x$. Therefore, $x / 3x = 1/3 = 33\ 1/3\%$.

17. (C). The price of the coat after discount is $\$36.50 - (0.30)(\$36.50) = \$36.50 - \$10.95 = \$25.55$. This matches the amount in column B.

18. (D). We cannot determine how many girls or how many boys were absent unless we are given the number of girls and boys in the class. For example, if the class had 15 girls and 24 boys, the number of girls who are absent would be $(0.20)(15) = 3$. The number of boys who are absent would be $(0.25)(24) = 6$. In this case, there would be more boys absent than girls. But suppose that there are 25 girls and 12 boys in the class. Then the number of girls absent is $(0.20)(25) = 5$ and the number of boys absent is $(0.25)(12) = 3$; in this case, there are more girls absent than boys.

19. (A). If x is 10% of y, then $x = 0.10y$. Solving for y, we get $y = 1/(0.10) = 10x = 1000\%$ of x. Note that 1000% > 100%.

20. (C). x percent of y is z can be written as $(x/100)(y) = z$. Multiply this equation by 100 to get $xy = 100z$, which becomes $xy/z = 100$. The amounts in columns A and B match.

21. (C). The maximum number of bags that can be filled is determined by the number of oranges in each bag, which is $100 / 2 = 50$.

22. (B). Given $y < x$, subtract y from each side to get $0 < x - y$. This inequality means that $x - y$ represents a positive number.

23. (C). If $x < 0 < y$, then x must be negative and y must be positive. This would force xy to be a negative number because the product of a negative and a positive is a negative.

24. (A). The enlarged area of the living room would be $465 + 25 = 490$ square feet. Thus, the area of the adjoining dining room is $(1/2)(490) = 245$ square feet.

25. (E). By interchanging the middle digits, we get the number 4759. This number is 180 more than 4579.

TEST 2

DIRECTIONS: Each question or incomplete statement is followed by several suggested answers or completions. Select the one that BEST answers the question or completes the statement. *PRINT THE LETTER OF THE CORRECT ANSWER IN THE SPACE AT THE RIGHT.*

1. What is the difference between the greatest and least of all three-digit positive integers, each of whose digits is a different non-zero multiple of 3?
   A. 324 B. 540 C. 567 D. 594 E. 604

   1.____

2. A two-digit number has a tens' digit x and a units' digit y.
   What is the product of this number and the number 5, in terms of x and y?
   A. 5x + y   B. 5x + 5y   C. 5x + 50y
   D. 50x + 50y   E. 50x + 5y

   2.____

3. An arithmetic progression is a sequence of numbers for which each new number is found by adding a given number n to the previous number. In the arithmetic progression below, only two numbers are known:

   __, __, 3, __, __, __, 19, __, X, Y
   What is the sum of x and y?
   A. 52 B. 54 C. 55 D. 56 E. 58

   3.____

4. Jack begins reading at the top of page N and finishes at the bottom of page R. If the pages are numbered and read consecutively and if there are no blank pages, how many pages has he read?
   A. R-N+1 B. N-R+1 C. N-R-1 D. R-N E. N-R

   4.____

5. If a, b, c, d, and e are whole numbers, the expression a(b(c+d)+e) will be an even number whenever which of the following is even?
   A. a B. b C. c D. d E. e

   5.____

Questions 6-11.

DIRECTIONS: Questions 6 through 11 are student-produced response questions.

6. A chemist has 80 pints of a 20% iodine solution.
   How many pints of iodine must be added to produce a solution that is 33 1/3% iodine?
   A. 15 B. 16 C. 20 D. 32

   6.____

7. A model for a certain battery-driven car will provide 30 hours of driving time at 50 miles per hour without recharging the batteries.
   The present distance that the car can travel at 50 miles per hour is how many miles less than the design goal of 2,000 miles?
   A. 500 B. 600 C. 750 D. 1500

   7.____

45

8. What is the sum of 5 consecutive integers if the middle one is 70?
   A. 300   B. 350   C. 450   D. 500

9. If 45 cards can be copied in 30 minutes, how many hours will it take to copy 540 such cards at the same rate?
   A. 6   B. 9   C. 12   D. 15

10. If 3 persons who work at the same rate can do a job together in 5 days, what fractional part of that job can one of these persons do in 1 day?
    A. 1/9   B. 1/12   C. 1/14   D. 1/15

11. If $m^2 = 16$ and $n^2 = 36$, then the difference between the greatest possible value of m – n and the least possible value of m – n is
    A. 20   B. 24   C. 26   D. 30

12. For which of the following pairs of numbers is the square of one of the numbers the reciprocal of the other number?
    I. .25, 2   II. 1, 1   III. 0.5, 4
    The CORRECT answer is:
    A. I only   B. II only   C. III only
    D. I and II only   E. I, II, III

Questions 13-15.

DIRECTIONS: Questions 13 through 15 consist of two quantities, one in Column A and one in Column B. You are to compare the two quantities and in the space at the right write:
   A. if the quantity in Column A is greater;
   B. if the quantity in Column B is greater;
   C. if the two quantities are equal;
   D. if the relationship cannot be determined from the information given;
   An E response will not be scored.

13. $-1 < x < 1$
    $x \neq 0$
    Column A   Column B
    1/x   x

14. x and y are points on the number line

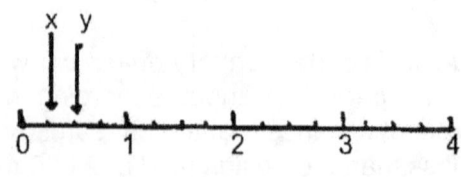

    Column A   Column B
    (x)(y)(2)(3)(4)   4

15. Column A   Column B   15._____
    Remainder when 731^{500} is   1
    divided by 10.

16. If 6.363 = 63k, what does k equal?   16._____
    A. .001   B. .002   C. .101   D. .103

17. In a certain country, a Q-type coin is equivalent to 25 cents and a D-type   17._____
    coin is equivalent to 10 cents.
    How many D-type coins have a total value equal to the value of 30 Q-type
    coins?
    A. 15   B. 25   C. 35   D. 75

18. Square ABCD shown at the right is   18._____
    divided into 16 equal squares.
    The total area of the shaded regions is
    what fraction of the area of ABCD?
    A. $1/5$ or .2
    B. ¼ or .25
    C. $1/3$ or .33
    D. ½ or .5

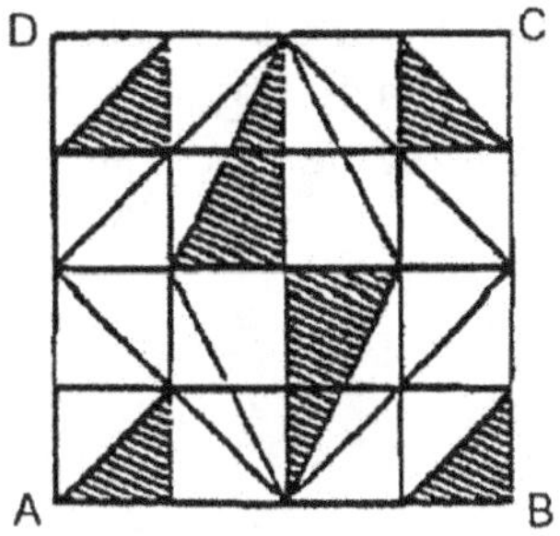

19. If x = 2, what is the value of $\dfrac{2(x-2)^2}{x+2}$?   19._____

    A. -2   B. -1   C. 0   D. 2

20. In the last step of a series of computations, a student divided by 2 when he   20._____
    should have multiplied by 2.
    If his incorrect answer was 0.25 and he made no other errors, what was the
    CORRECT answer?
    A. 0   B. 1   C. 2   D. 4

21. In the triangle shown at the right, what is   21._____
    the value of 4x?
    A. 45
    B. 66
    C. 70
    D. 72

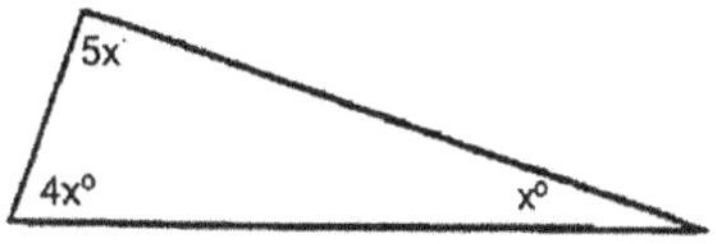

22. Four cake pans are graduated in size so that the capacity of each pan is   22._____
    twice that of the next smaller one.
    If the capacity of the smallest pan is $1/3$ cup, what is the capacity, in cups, of the
    largest pan?
    A. $8/3$ or 2.67   B. 3   C. $10/3$ or 3.33   D. 4

23. Set S contains all integers from 100 to 200, inclusive.   23._____
    If x is a number in S that is an integer multiple of both 6 and 10, what is one possible value of x?
    A. 100   B. 150   C. 160   D. 170

24. In the figure shown at the right, if PQ is a diameter of the circle with center O, and OR and RQ are of equal length, what is the value of y/3?   24._____
    A. 20
    B. 30
    C. 35
    D. 40

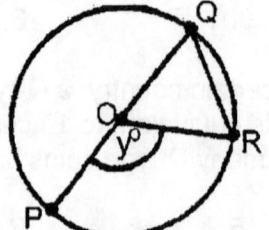

25. A discount store offers a calculator listed at $60 for $48.   25._____
    What would be the selling price, in dollars, of a model listed at $150 if it were discounted at 1½ times the percent discount on the $60 model?
    A. 65   B. 75   C. 100   D. 105

KEY (CORRECT ANSWERS)

1. D	11. A
2. E	12. E
3. E	13. D
4. A	14. B
5. A	15. C
6. B	16. C
7. A	17. D
8. B	18. B
9. A	19. C
10. D	20. B

21. D
22. A
23. B
24. D
25. D

5 (#2)

SOLUTIONS TO PROBLEMS

1. (D). The two numbers in question are 963 (greatest) and 369 (least). Then 963 − 369 = 594,

2. (E). The value of the given number is $10x + y$. Then $(5)(10x + y) = 50x + 5y$.

3. (E). Since the third number is 3 and the seventh number is 19, the difference between consecutive numbers is $(19 − 3)/4 = 4$. Then X = 19 + (2)(4) = 27 and Y = 27 + 4 = 31. Thus, X + Y = 27 + 31 = 58. (The entire sequence is − 5, − 1, 3, 7, 11, 15, 19, 23, 27, 31).

4. (A). The number of pages read is one added to the difference between the two page numbers, which is R − N + 1. As an example, if Jack began reading at the top of page 5 and finished reading at the bottom of page 20, he would have read 20 − 5 + 1 = 16 pages.

5. (A). When the values of a, b, c, d, and e are used, the last step would be the product of a and the value of $b(c + d) + e$. Regardless of whether $b(c + d) + e$ is even or odd, when this expression is multiplied by an even number, the result must be even.

6. (B). Let x represent the number of pints of iodine that must be added. The number of pints of iodine in the original solution is (0.20)(80) = 16. The number of pints in the final solution is (1/3)(80 + x). Then 16 + x = (1/3)(80 + x). Multiply this equation by 3 to get 48 + 3x = 80 + x. Then 2x = 32. Thus, x = 16.

7. (A). The present distance that the battery-driven car can travel is (50)(30) = 1500 miles. Thus, this distance is short of the design goal distance by 2000 − 1500 = 500 miles.

8. (B). The five consecutive numbers must have an average of 70, so their sum must be (5)(70) = 350. An alternative method is to identify the five numbers as 68, 69, 70, 71, 72. The sum of these numbers is 350.

9. (A). 540 / 45 = 12. Since we want the number of hours to copy 540 cards, we convert 30 minutes to 1/2 hour. Then (12)(1/2) = 6 hours.

10. (D). Let x represent the (common) number of hours each of the three people would need to do the entire job alone. Then $5/x + 5/x + 5/x = 1$. This equation simplifies to $15/x = 1$, so x = 15. Since each person would require 15 hours alone to do the job, the fraction of the job one person can do in 1 day is 1/15.

11. (A). $m = \pm\sqrt{16} = 4$ or −4, whereas $n = \pm\sqrt{36} = 6$ or − 6. The greatest possible value of $m − n$ is 6 − (−4) = 10. The least possible value of $m − n$ is − 4 − 6 = −10. Thus, the required difference is 10 − (−10) = 20.

12. (E). For item I, $2^2 = 4 = 1/0.25$. For item II, $1^2 = 1/1$. For item III, $(0.5)^2 = 0.25 = 1/4$.

13. (D). If $0 < x < 1$, then $1/x > x$. For example, let x = 1/2. Then 1/(1/2) = 2 > 1/2. But if −1 < x < 0, then $1/x > x$. For example, let x = −1/2. Then 1/(−1/2) = −2 < −1/2.

14. (B). The values of x and y are .25 and .5. Thus, $(x)(y)(2)(3)(4) = (.25)(.5)(2)(3)(4) = 3$, which is less than 4.

15. (C). The number 731^{500} must end in 1. Whenever a number has a units digit of 1 and is multiplied by itself any given number of times, the units digit must remain 1. Thus, when 731^{500} is divided by 10, the remainder is 1.

16. (C). $k = 6.363/63 = .101$

17. (D). 30 Q-type coins is worth $(30)(25) = 750$ cents. Since a D-type coin is worth 10 cents, we need $750/10 = 75$ D-type coins to be worth 750 cents.

18. (B). The four shaded areas nearest the points A, B, C, D are each worth 1/2 box, so their total area is equivalent to $(4)(1/2) = 2$ boxes. Each of the two triangular central shaded areas is worth $(1/2)(1)(2) = 1$ box, so their total area is $(2)(1) = 2$ boxes. There are a total of $(4)(4) = 16$ boxes, so the shaded areas comprise $4/16 = 1/4$ (or .25) of the total area of ABCD.

19. (C). The computed value is $(2)(2-2)^2/(2+2) = (2)(0)/4 = 0$.

20. (B). The next-to-last step must have been 0.50. Then the student mistakenly divided 0.50 by 2 to get 0.25. Therefore, the student should have multiplied 0.50 by 2 to get the correct answer of 1.

21. (D). The sum of the angles of a triangle is 180 □, so $5x + 4x + x = 180$. Then $10x = 180$, so $x = 18$. Thus, $4x = (4)(18) = 72$.

22. (A). The second pan is $(2)(1/3) = 2/3$ cup. The third pan is $(2)(2/3) = 4/3$ cup. Finally, the fourth pan is $(2)(4/3) = 8/3$ cup.

23. (B). In order for a number to be a multiple of both 6 and 10, it must be a multiple of 30. The multiples of 30 that lie between 100 and 200 are 120, 150, and 180. Only answer choice (B) has one of these three numbers.

24. (D). Since OR = OQ and OQ = OR (they are radii), each angle of triangle OQR must equal 60 □. Then $y = 180 - \angle QOR = 180 - 60 = 120$, so $y/3 = 40$.

25. (D). The percent discount for the $60 model is $(12/60)(100) = 20\%$. Then $(1.5)(20) = 30$. Thus, a 30% discount on a model listed at $150 would result in a selling price of $150 - (.30)(\$150) = \$105$.

TEST 3

DIRECTIONS: Each question or incomplete statement is followed by several suggested answers or completions. Select the one that BEST answers the question or completes the statement. *PRINT THE LETTER OF THE CORRECT ANSWER IN THE SPACE AT THE RIGHT.*

1. | | 2 | 3 | 5 | 8 | | | ▨ |

   The boxes above show part of a sequence of numbers in which each number after 3 is the sum of the two numbers immediately to the left of it.
   If one number goes in each box, what number goes in the shaded box?
   A. 13   B. 21   C. 31   D. 34   E. 65

2. All the boxes in the strip above are equal size.
   When the strip is folded together along the dotted line, point P is MOST likely to coincide with point
   A. A   B. B   C. C   D. D   E. E

3. In the figure above, six segments intersect line *l*.
   Which of the degree measures, a, b, c, d, or e, is equal to x?

4. If the center of a number is defined to be ½ of the number, then what number is the center of itself?
   A. -1   B. 0   C. 1   D. 2   E. 10

5. In a certain language, a *word* is defined as any 5-letter combination in which the position of at least one letter in the *word* is in the same position in which it is found in the English alphabet. For example, *dbacc* is a word because of the placement of the letter *b*, but *bdaac* is not.
   Which of the following is a word in this language?
   A. cddcd   B. cdddc   C. ccdcc   D. dcdcc   E. dddcd

6. For any sentence J, the expression N(J) is defined to mean the number of times the letter t appears in J.
   If J is the sentence *All cats are good luck*, then N(J) =
   A. 0   B. 1   C. 2   D. 3   E. 4

7. After Jane gave Bill $4, she then had $12 more than Bill.
   How much more money than Bill did Jane have originally?
   A. $4   B. $8   C. $12   D. $16   E. $20

8.

2	X	14	y
X	14	y	2
14	y	2	X
y	2	X	14

In the figure above, the sums of the numbers in each row, column, and main diagonals are the same.
What is the value of x?
   A. 2   B. 8   C. 12   D. 14   E. 16

9.

	Event I	Event II	Event III
First Place 5 pt.	School A	School B	
Second Place 3 pt.		School C	
Third Place 1 pt.			

Shown above is a partially completed score card for an athletic contest among schools A, B, and C.
If each school entered one contestant in each of these events and there were no ties, what is the LOWEST possible total score that any one of these schools could achieve for all three events?
   A. 3   B. 4   C. 5   D. 6   E. 7

10. If the odometer of an automobile registers 62,222 miles, what is the FEWEST number of miles that the automobile must travel before the odometer again shows four of the five digits the same?
   A. 99   B. 444   C. 555   D. 999   E. 1,111

11. If half the people in a room leave at the end of every five-minute interval and at the end of twenty minutes the next to the last person leaves, how many people were in the room to start with? (Assume that no one enters the room once the process begins.)
   A. 32   B. 28   C. 16   D. 12   E. 8

12. In the correctly computed multiplication problem shown at the right, if $\triangle$ and 🍎 are different digits, then $\triangle$ =

$$\begin{array}{r} 5\,\triangle\,2 \\ \times\ \ 9 \\ \hline 5{,}2\,🍎\,8 \end{array}$$

   A. 1   B. 5   C. 6   D. 7   E. 8

13. In the addition problem shown at the right, 🍎 represents the same digit in each number.
What must 🍎 represent in order to make the answer correct?

　🍎4
　3🍎
　🍎3
　5🍎
　🍎1
　15🍎

A. 8
B. 6
C. 5
D. 4
E. 2

13.____

14. If the road distances between any two points are as indicated on the map shown at the right, what is the SHORTEST road distance from P to R?

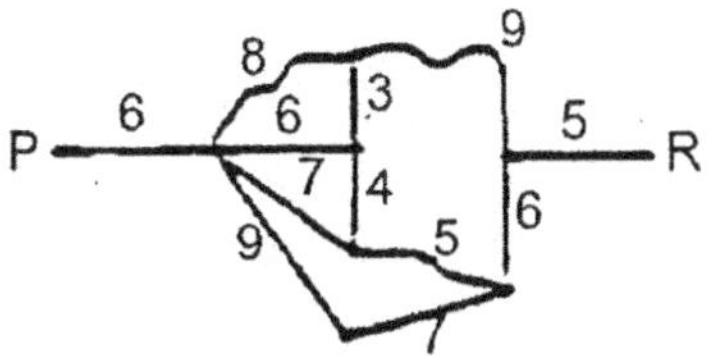

A. 27　　B. 28　　C. 29　　D. 30　　E. 33

14.____

15. In the figure shown at the right, the pattern is repeated every 15 symbols.
Which of the following, when placed below the arrows in the design, will continue the pattern of the design?

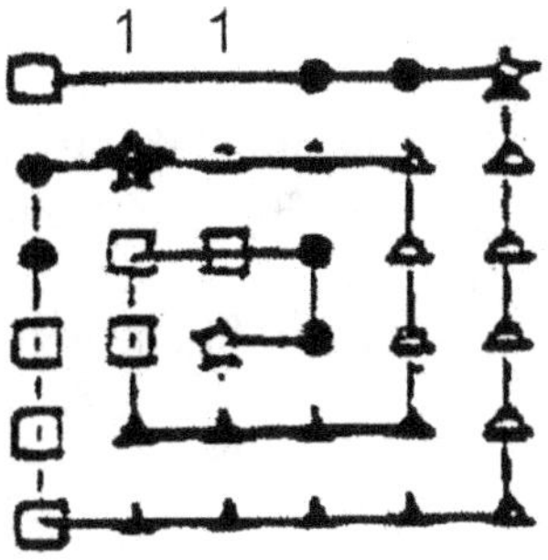

A. 🍎🍎
B. ••
C. ▲▲
D. *▵
E. ▵*

15.____

16. A machine began knitting a row of 100 stitches by making 3 knit stitches and 2 purl stitches and repeated the same pattern thereafter.
What is the order in which it knitted the 77th, 78th, 79th, and 80th stitches in the row?

A. 2 knit, 2 purl
B. 1 knit, 2 purl, 1 knit
C. 3 knit, 1 purl
D. 2 purl, 2 knit
E. 1 purl, 2 knit, 1 purl

16.____

17. It is now 4:00 P.M. Saturday; in 253 hours from now what time and day will it be? (Assume no daylight savings time changes in the period.)

A. 5:00 A.M. Saturday
B. 1:00 A.M. Sunday
C. 5:00 P.M. Tuesday
D. 1:00 A.M. Wednesday
E. 5:00 A.M. Wednesday

17.____

18. If the figure at the right is the mirror image of an accurate clock, what time will it be 15 minutes after the time shown?

A. 1:50
B. 1:40
C. 1:10
D. 10:40
E. 10:05

18.____

19. The twelve-hour digital clock shown at the right shows one example of a time at which the number representing the hour is equal to the number is equal to the number representing the minutes. What is the FEWEST possible number of minutes from the instant one such double reading appears to the instant the next appears?
   A. 11   B. 30   C. 49   D. 60   E. 61

20. Each jar shown at the right contains 6 marbles. What is the FEWEST number of marbles that must be transferred to make the ratio: marbles in X:marbles in Y:marbles in Z = 3:2:1?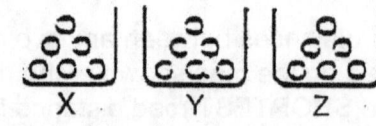
   A. 6   B. 5   C. 4   D. 3   E. 2

Questions 21-25.

DIRECTIONS: Questions 21 through 25 consist of two quantities, one in Column A and one in Column B. You are to compare the two quantities and in the space at the right write:
   A. if the quantity in Column A is greater;
   B. if the quantity in Column B is greater;
   C. if the two quantities are equal;
   D. if the relationship cannot be determined from the information given;
   An E response will not be scored.

21. Ann has 6 more marbles than Nancy, Nancy has 3 more marbles than Joe, and Joe has 4 more marbles than Pete.
Column A	Column B
The least number of marbles that must change hands if each is to have an equal number of marbles.	8

22.
Column A	Column B
Area of a circle with radius 1	Area of a square with side 1

23. $2x + 3 = y$
Column A	Column B
$20x + 20$	$10y$

24. 25% of x = 60
Column A	Column B
50% of x	120

25. $x < y < z$
Column A	Column B
xy	yz

KEY (CORRECT ANSWERS)

1. D
2. B
3. E
4. B
5. B

6. B
7. E
8. B
9. C
10. B

11. C
12. E
13. E
14. B
15. A

16. A
17. E
18. A
19. C
20. D

21. C
22. A
23. B
24. C
25. D

SOLUTIONS TO PROBLEMS

1. (D). The number in the fifth box is 8 + 5 = 13. The number in the sixth box is 13 + 8 = 21. Thus, the number in the seventh (shaded) box is 21 + 13 = 34.

2. (B). Point P is just a bit less than 2 boxes to the right of the dotted line. Thus, when the strip is folded along the dotted line, it will coincide with a point that is just a bit less than 2 boxes to the left of the dotted line, which is point B.

3. (E). $x = 180 - 40 = 140$. The angle designated as e is vertical, and therefore equal to 140. So. $x = e$.

4. (C). The number 0 is the center of itself because $0 = (1/2)(0)$.

5. (B). The expression *cdddc* is a word because the fourth letter is *d*, which is also the fourth letter of the English alphabet.

6. (B). In the given sentence, the letter *t* appears only once (in the word "cats"). Thus, $N(J) = 1$.

7. (E). Let J represent the original amount of money that Jane had and let B represent the original amount of money that Bill had. After Jane gave Bill $4, Jane had $J - 4$ dollars and Bill had $B + 4$ dollars. Since Jane still has $12 more than Bill, $J - 4 = 12 + B + 4$. Then $J = B + 12 + 4 + 4 = B + 20$. So, Jane originally had $20 more than Bill.

8. (B). The sum on the first row can be represented as $X + Y + 16$. The sum of the numbers on the diagonal from upper left to lower right is 32. This means that $X + Y + 16 = 32$, which simplifies to $X + Y = 16$. The sum of the numbers on the diagonal from upper right to lower left can be represented by $4Y$. Then $4Y = 32$, which leads to $Y = 8$. Finally, since $X + Y = 16$ and $Y = 8$, we find that $X = 8$.

9. (C). The lowest possible score would be if School C came in third place in both Events I and III. The score for School C would be $1 + 3 + 1 = 5$ points.

10. (B). The next mileage for which four of the five digits are the same is 62,666. Thus, the number of miles traveled is $62,666 - 62,222 = 444$.

11. (C). Since the next-to-last person left the room after 20 minutes, there must have been only 1 person left in the room. Let x represent the original number of people in the room. After 5 minutes, there were x/2 people in the room. After 10 minutes, there were x/4 people in the room. After 15 minutes, there were x/8 people in the room. After 20 minutes, there were x/16 people in the room. there would be (2)(2) = 4 people in the room at the 15-minute point, (4)(4) =

12. (E). The product of 9 and the triangle symbol must yield a number between 70 and 79, because $(9)(5) + 7 = 52$. The only digit that fits this requirement is 8. We check that $(582)(9) = 5238$.

13. (E). Look at the tens column. Let x represent the value of the box symbol. Then $x + 3 + x + 5 + x$, which simplifies to $3x + 8$, must be less than or equal to 15. This means that $3x < 7$, which means that $x < 7/3$. The only integer of the five choices that works is 2. As a check, note that $24 + 32 + 23 + 52 + 21 = 152$.

7 (#3)

14. (B). The shortest route involves the distances 6, 8, 9, and 5. The sum is 28.

15. (C). For this pattern, two black dots are followed by three unshaded boxes. Thus, the missing symbols are two unshaded boxes.

16. (A). Use K for knit and P for purl. The pattern appears as follows: KKKPPKKKPP.... This represents a sequence that repeats in blocks of five. We divide each of 77, 78, 79, and 80 by 5 and look at the remainders, which are 2, 3, 4, and 5. In the repeating block of KKKPP, the 2nd, 3rd, 4th, and 5th letters are K, K, P, P, which correspond to 2 knits and 2 purls.

17. (E). Dividing 253 by 24 yields 10.5416666..... days. Since (0.54166666...)(24) = 13, the amount of elapsed time is 10 days and 13 hours. Ten days from 4:00 PM on Saturday brings us to 4:00PM on Tuesday. Adding another 13 hours brings us to 5:00 AM on Wednesday.

18. (A). The current time is 1:35, which would represent the mirror image of the figure shown. Then adding 15 minutes to 1:35 would bring the time to 1:50.

19. (E). If the current time were 12:12, the next double reading would be 1:01. The difference in minutes between 12:12 and 1:01 is 49, which is the fewest number of minutes. For any other time with a double (such as 5:05), the next double reading would be in 61 minutes.

20. (D). There are a total of 18 marbles in the three jars. In order for the ratio X: Y: Z to be equal to 3 : 2 : 1, we would need 9 marbles in X, 6 marbles in Y and 3 marbles in Z. The least number of marbles that require a transfer would be 3 from Z to X.

21. (C). Using numerical values, assume that Ann has 15 marbles, Nancy has 9 marbles, Joe has 6 marbles, and Pete has 2 marbles. The total of 32 marbles must be split so that each person winds up with 8 marbles. Remove 7 marbles from Ann's pile and give 2 marbles to Joe and 5 marbles to Pete. Then Ann would have 8 marbles, Nancy still has 9 marbles, Joe would have 8 marbles, and Pete would have 7 marbles. Finally, remove 1 marble from Nancy's pile and give that marble to Pete. A total of 8 marbles have changed hands, where each person winds up with the same (8) number of marbles.

22. (A). The area of the circle is $\pi (1^2) = \pi$. The area of the square is $1^2 = 1$. We know that $\pi > 1$.

23. (B) $10y = 10(2x + 3) = 20x + 30$. This value is greater than $20x + 20$.

24. (C). If 25% of x = 60, then $x = 60/.25 = 240$. This means that 50% of x = 50% of 240 = 120. Then columns A and B match.

25. (D). Let $x = -7$, $y = -5$, and $z = -2$, so that $x < y < z$. Then $xy = 35$ and $yz = 10$, which leads to $xy > yz$. Now suppose that $x = 2$, $y = 5$, and $z = 7$. Then $xy = 10$ and $yz = 35$, which leads to $xy < yz$. The conclusion is indeterminate because it depends on the sign of y.

EXAMINATION SECTION
TEST 1

DIRECTIONS: Each question or incomplete statement is followed by several suggested answers or completions. Select the one that BEST answers the question or completes the statement. *PRINT THE LETTER OF THE CORRECT ANSWER IN THE SPACE AT THE RIGHT.*

1. Three dogs weigh 6, 10, and 12 kilograms, respectively. The weight of the lightest dog is how much less than the average (arithmetic mean) weight of the three dogs?
   A. 6 kg   B. 4 kg   C. $3^2/_3$ kg   D. $3^1/_3$ kg   E. $2^2/_3$ kg

   1.____

2. What is the average of $1/_5$ and $1/_7$?
   A. $1/_{12}$ B. $1/_6$ C. $6/_{35}$ D. $12/_{35}$ E. $36/_{35}$

   2.____

3. If the average (arithmetic mean) of -5 and x is -5, then x =
   A. 10   B. 5   C. 0   D. -5   E. -10

   3.____

4. A class took a math test that resulted in the following scores: 40, 50, 65, 65, 70, 85, 85, 85, 95.
   By how many points did the mode differ from the median?
   A. 0   B. 5   C. 10   D. 15   E. 20

   4.____

5. A teacher gave a test to 30 students and the average score was x. Scores on the test ranged from 0 to 90, inclusive.
   If the average score for the first 10 papers graded was 60, what is the difference between the greatest and least possible values of x?
   A. 20   B. 30   C. 40   D. 50   E. 60

   5.____

Questions 6-10.

DIRECTIONS: Questions 6 through 10 consist of two quantities, one in Column A and one in Column B. You are to compare the two quantities and in the space at the right write:
   A. if the quantity in Column A is greater;
   B. if the quantity in Column B is greater;
   C. if the two quantities are equal;
   D. if the relationship cannot be determined from the information given;
   An E response will not be scored.

6. On a certain test, the average score for the juniors was 87 and the average score for the sophomores was 81.

Column A	Column B
The average score for the total group	84

   6.____

7. $x + y = 10$

   Column A | Column B
   The average (arithmetic mean) of x and y | 5

8. $y = x + 1$

   Column A | Column B
   The average (arithmetic mean) of 7, 9, and x | The average (arithmetic mean) of 2, 13, and 7

9. In a school with 6 classrooms, there are more than 1 and less than 20 students in 1 classroom and exactly 20 students in each of the other 5 classrooms.

   Column A | Column B
   Average (arithmetic mean) of students per classroom | 20

10. The average (arithmetic mean) of 18, 30, x and y equals 12.
    $x > 0$

    Column A | Column B
    y | 0

11. The following scores were reported: 7, 9, 7, 4, 8, 3, 4, 7, 5
    Which of the following is(are) TRUE?
    I. The mean of the scores is not equal to any of the individual scores.
    II. The median of the scores is equal to the mode, and both are greater than the mean.
    III. If a score of 6 is added to the existing scores, none of the mean, median, or mode will change.
    The CORRECT answer is:
    A. II only B. I, II C. I, III
    D. II, III E. I, II, III

12. If for all numbers n, $\#n = n(n+1)(n+2)$, then $\frac{\#8}{\#4} =$

    A. #1 B. #2 C. #3 D. #4 E. #6

Questions 13-14.

DIRECTIONS: Questions 13 and 14 consist of two quantities, one in Column A and one in Column B. You are to compare the two quantities and in the space at the right write:
  A. if the quantity in Column A is greater;
  B. if the quantity in Column B is greater;
  C. if the two quantities are equal;
  D. if the relationship cannot be determined from the information given;
  An E response will not be scored.

These questions refer to the following definition of x, where x is any real number:

$$\boxed{x} = (x-1)^4 + (x-1)^2 + 1$$

13. Column A   Column B   13.____
    $\boxed{1}$ 1

14. Column A   Column B   14.____
    $\boxed{10}$ $\boxed{-10}$

Questions 15-16.

DIRECTIONS: Questions 15 and 16 refer to the following definition:

A	B
C	D

A block sum is a figure, like the one above, that has the following properties:
1. A, B, C, and D are digits from 1 to 9, inclusive.
2. A + B = 10C + D

For example,

5	8
1	3

is a block sum because 1, 3, 5, and 8 satisfy property 1 and 5 + 8 = 13 satisfies property 2.

15. If the figure at the right is a block sum, what is the value of A + B?

A	B
1	2

    A. 12
    B. 3
    C. 2
    D. 1
    E. It cannot be determined from the information given

    15.____

16. If the figure at the right is a block sum, what digit does D represent?

9	7
C	D

    A. 1
    B. 3
    C. 6
    D. 1
    E. It cannot be determined from the information given

    16.____

17. SALES OF FIVE PRODUCTS OF COMPANY X

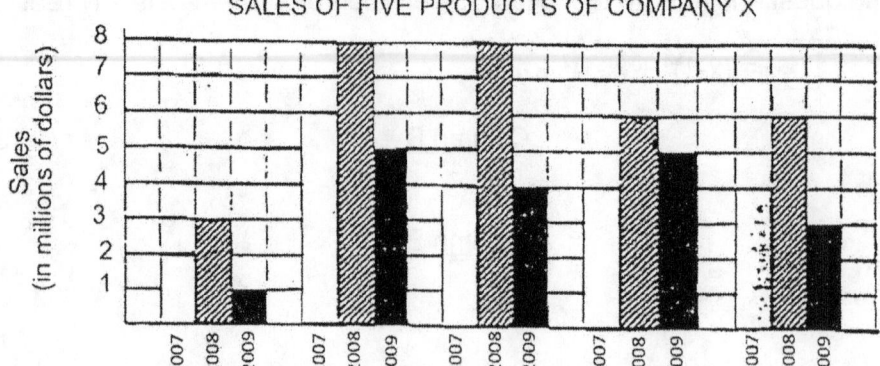

For which of the five products (A, B, C, D, and E) shown in the above graph was the percent increase in sales from 2007 to 2008 the same as the percent decrease from 2008 to 2009?

A. A   B. B   C. C   D. D   E. E

Questions 18-19.

DIRECTIONS: Questions 18 and 19 are to be answered on the basis of the following graph.

VOLUMES OF SALES FOR A 10-MONTH PERIOD FOR TWO SALESPEOPLE

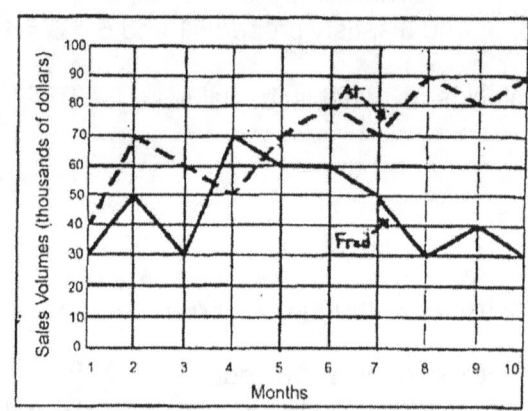

18. Consider Al's sales record from month 4 to month 5. What was the percent increase?

A. 25%   B. $33\frac{1}{3}$%   C. 40%   D. $133\frac{1}{3}$%   E. 175%

19. How much greater (in thousands of dollars) were the sales for Fred's best month than Al's worst month?

A. 10   B. 20   C. 30   D. 40   E. 70

20. If $a \neq 0$, then, $\dfrac{(-2a)^2}{-2a^3}$

A. -4   B. -1   C. 1   D. 3   E. 4

21. If $6 + x + y = 20$ and if $x + y = k$, then $20 - k$ is equal to
    A. 14
    B. 9
    C. 6
    D. $3^2/_3$
    E. none of the above

    21.____

22. If $x + y = k$ and $x = y = 1/k$, then when $k \neq 0$, $x^2 - y^2 =$
    A. $1/k$
    B. k
    C. k^2
    D. 2
    E. 1

    22.____

23. If $x^2 = 1$, then x^3 is equal to
    A. -3
    B. -1 only
    C. 1 only
    D. 3
    E. -1 or 1

    23.____

24. If $x = 2a$ and $y = \dfrac{1}{4a+2}$, what is y in terms of x?

    A. $\dfrac{1}{2x+2}$
    B. $\dfrac{1}{2x+4}$
    C. $\dfrac{2}{x+4}$
    D. $\dfrac{1}{8x+2}$
    E. $\dfrac{1}{8x+4}$

    24.____

25. On a certain typing assignment, Bob types 2 times as many pages per hour as Sam, and he makes 3 times as many errors per page as Sam. If Sam averages 1 error every 15 minutes, how many errors does Bob average in an hour?
    A. 2
    B. 3
    C. 6
    D. 12
    E. 24

    25.____

26. At a sale, the original price of an item was discounted by 20 percent, and the discounted price was reduced by an additional 5 percent for paying cash. If the original price was x dollars, which of the following represents the amount paid in dollars for a cash purchase of this item at the sale?
    A. 0.75x
    B. 0.76x
    C. 0.79x
    D. 0.80x
    E. 0.85x

    26.____

Questions 27-33.

DIRECTIONS: Questions 27 through 33 consist of two quantities, one in Column A and one in Column B. You are to compare the two quantities and in the space at the right write:
    A. if the quantity in Column A is greater;
    B. if the quantity in Column B is greater;
    C. if the two quantities are equal;
    D. if the relationship cannot be determined from the information given;
    An E response will not be scored.

27. 1 skedallion = 4.6 skippers
    2 phantoms = 9.3 skippers
    Column A   Column B
    Value of one skedallion   Value of one phantom

    27.____

28. $x > 1$
    Column A   Column B

    $\dfrac{x+x+x}{x \cdot 2}$ $\dfrac{3}{x^2}$

    28.____

29. $x \neq \pm 2$

    Column A: $\dfrac{x^2+4x+4}{x+2}$

    Column B: $\dfrac{x^2-4}{x-2}$

30. $x^2 + 8x + 15 = 0$

    Column A: x^2+8x

    Column B: 15

31. $x + 27 = 10$
    $2x - 27 = 5$

    Column A: x

    Column B: y

32. $2x + 2 < 1$

    Column A: x

    Column B: 0

33. $xy = 6$
    $x^2 + y^2 = 13$

    Column A: $(x+y)^2$

    Column B: 18

34. $(45)^2 + 2(45)(55) + (55)^2 =$
    A. 5,050 B. 9,100 C. 9,900 D. 10,000 E. 14,950

35. From which of the following statements must it follow that $x > y$?
    A. $x = 27$ B. $2x = y$ C. $x + 2 = y$
    D. $x - 2 = y$ E. None of the above

36. Ms. Smith is S years sold and is 3 years older than Ms. Lopez. In terms of S, how many years old was Ms. Lopez 2 years ago?
    A. $S - 5$ B. $S - 3$ C. $S - 2$ D. $S - 1$ E. $S + 1$

37. If k is a positive integer such that k/3 is an even integer and k/2 is an odd integer, which of the following statements must be TRUE?
    I. k is even
    II. $(k/2)^2$ is even
    III. $k/2 - k/3$ is odd
    The CORRECT answer is:
    A. I only   B. II only   C. III only   D. I, II   E. I, III

38. If a car travels x kilometers in t hours and 20 minutes, what is its AVERAGE speed in kilometers per hour?

    A. $\dfrac{x}{t+20}$ B. $\dfrac{t+20}{x}$ C. $x(t+\frac{1}{3})$ D. $\dfrac{t+\frac{1}{3}}{x}$ E. $\dfrac{x}{t+\frac{1}{3}}$

39. A 20-centimeter wire is cut into exactly three pieces. If the first piece is 3 centimeters shorter than the second piece and the third piece is 4 centimeters shorter than the second piece, what is the length, in centimeters, of the SHORTEST piece?

    A. 1   B. 3   C. 4   D. 5

40. Carol has twice as many books as Beverly has. After Carol gives Beverly 5 books, she still has 10 more books than Beverly has. How many books did Carol have originally?

    A. 15   B. 20   C. 30   D. 40

KEY (CORRECT ANSWERS)

1. D	11. B	21. C	31. A
2. C	12. A	22. E	32. B
3. D	13. C	23. E	33. A
4. D	14. B	24. A	34. D
5. E	15. A	25. E	35. D
6. D	16. C	26. B	36. A
7. C	17. E	27. B	37. E
8. C	18. C	28. A	38. E
9. B	19. C	29. C	39. D
10. B	20. E	30. B	40. D

TEST 2

DIRECTIONS: Each question or incomplete statement is followed by several suggested answers or completions. Select the one that BEST answers the question or completes the statement. *PRINT THE LETTER OF THE CORRECT ANSWER IN THE SPACE AT THE RIGHT.*

1. In the figure shown at the right, if AB is parallel to DE, then x =
   A. 105
   B. 90
   C. 80
   D. 75
   E. 65

   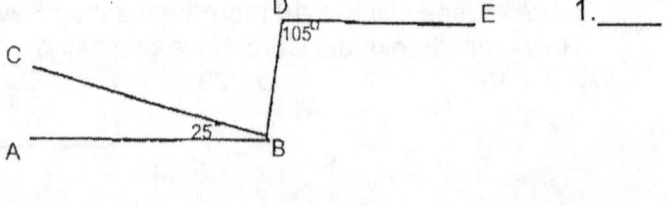

   1._____

2. In the figure shown at the right, $l \parallel m$. Which of the following pairs of angles must be equal?
   A. 1 and 3
   B. 2 and 3
   C. 3 and 5
   D. 4 and 6
   E. 5 and 7

   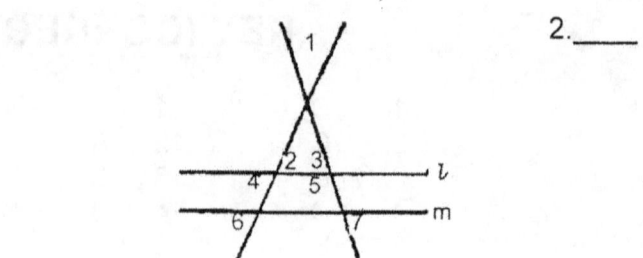

   2._____

3. In the figure shown at the right, ACD is a line segment. What is the value of x?
   A. 30
   B. 33
   C. 36
   D. 40
   E. 45

   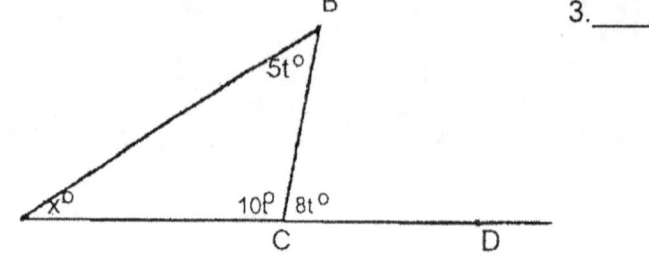

   3._____

4. If l_1, l_2, and l_3 intersect as shown at the right, then x =
   A. 30
   B. 50
   C. 60
   D. 90
   E. 100

   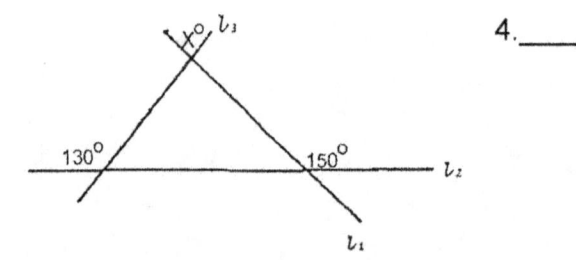

   4._____

66

Questions 5-8.

DIRECTIONS: Questions 5 through 8 consist of two quantities, one in Column A and one in Column B. You are to compare the two quantities and in the space at the right write:
- A. if the quantity in Column A is greater;
- B. if the quantity in Column B is greater;
- C. if the two quantities are equal;
- D. if the relationship cannot be determined from the information given;

An E response will not be scored.

5.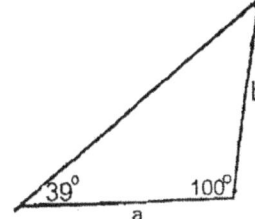

Column A	Column B
a	b

6.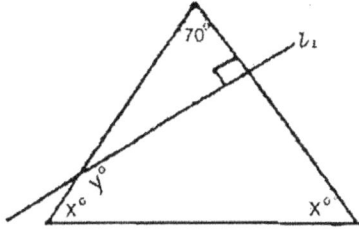

Column A	Column B
2x	y

7.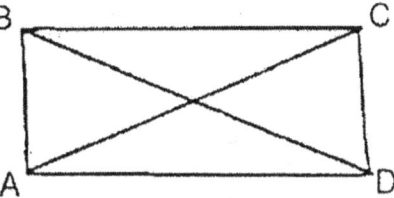

Note: Figure not drawn to scale.
In parallelogram ABCD, ∠ABC ≠ ∠BAD

Column A	Column B
Length of AC	Length of BD

8.

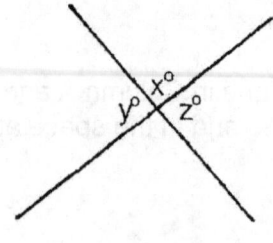

x + y + z = 4x

Column A	Column B
³/₂x	y

9. In the figure shown at the right, line r intersects line s at p.
If another line m is drawn through p with angles formed as indicated in the figure, then what is the value of y in terms of x?
   A. 60
   B. x
   C. 2x
   D. 180 – x
   E. 180 – 2x

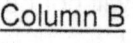

9.____

10. In the figure shown at the right, the 4 shaded areas are squares.
The area of the unshaded region of the rectangle is
   A. $\ell w - 4x^2$
   B. $(\ell-2x)(w-2x)$
   C. $(\ell-x)(w-x)$
   D. $\ell x + wx$
   E. $(\ell-4x)(w-4x)$

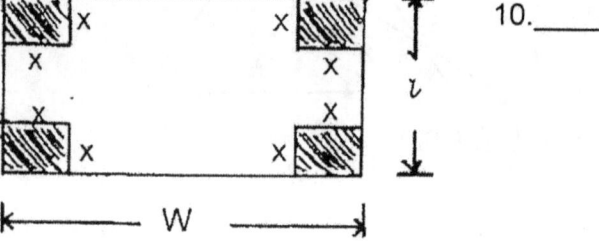

10.____

11. In the figure shown at the right, if one circle has radius r and the other has diameter r, what is the area of the shaded region?
   A. π/2
   B. 3πr/4
   C. πr/2
   D. πr²/2
   E. 3πr²/4

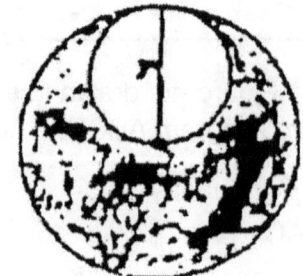

11.____

12. The figure shown at the right is a square. What is its area?
    A. 9
    B. 4
    C. 1
    D. ¼
    E. It cannot be determined from the information given

12.____

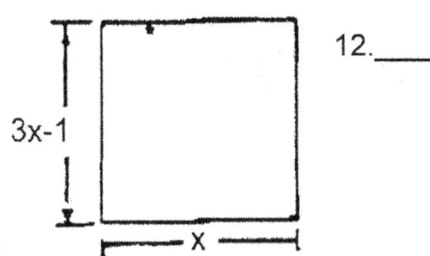

13. In the figure shown at the right, the two axes divide the enclosed region into four regions that have the same size and shape. Of the following, which is CLOSEST to the area of the entire enclosed region?
    A. 7
    B. 10
    C. 19
    D. 22
    E. 29

13.____

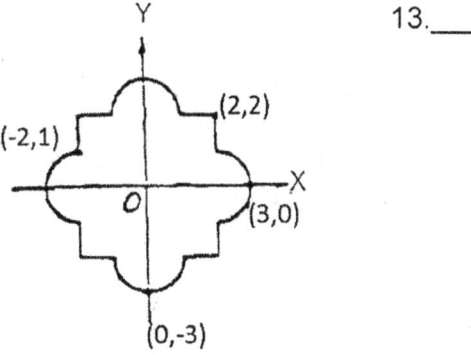

14. If the perimeter of square A is double that of square B, then the area of A is how many times the area of B?
    A. ½   B. 1   C. 2   D. 3   E. 4

14.____

Questions 15-16.

DIRECTIONS: Questions 15 and 16 consist of two quantities, one in Column A and one in Column B. You are to compare the two quantities and in the space at the right write:
  A. if the quantity in Column A is greater;
  B. if the quantity in Column B is greater;
  C. if the two quantities are equal;
  D. if the relationship cannot be determined from the information given;
  An E response will not be scored.

15.

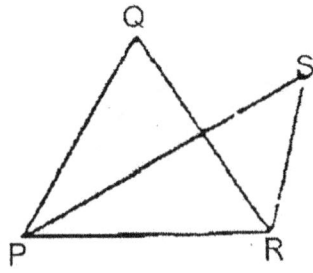

15.____

Perimeter of △PQR = Perimeter of △PSR

Column A
PQ + QR

Column B
PS + SR

16.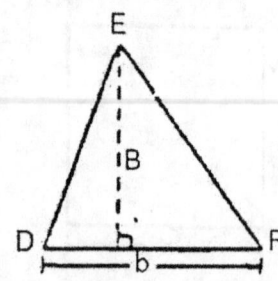

Note: Figures now drawn to scale

Column A	Column B
Area of △DEF	Area of △GHJ

17. What is the circumference of the circle shown at the right?
    A. 5π
    B. 10π
    C. $25/2\pi$
    D. 20π
    E. 25π

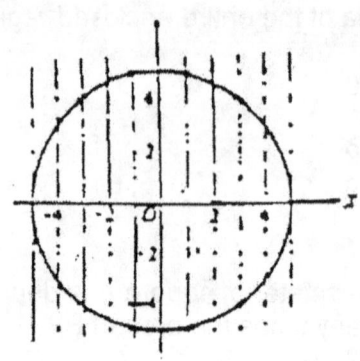

18. What is the diameter of a circle with circumference 1?
    A. π B. 1 C. ½ D. $1/\pi$ E. $-\pi + 1$

19. A circular track 400 meters in diameter is shown in the figure at the right. A runner starts at P, directly south of the center of the track, and runs counter-clockwise. At the end of exactly how many meters of travel will the runner be at the point where he is traveling directly north?
    A. 25π B. 100π C. 400π D. 800π E. $1,000\pi$

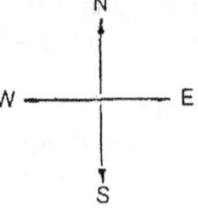 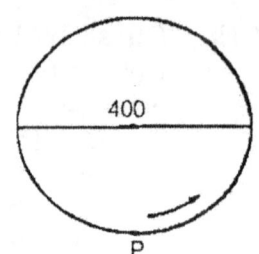

20. In the figure shown at the right, inscribed ABC is equilateral. If the radius of the circle is r, then the length of arc AXB is
    A. $2\pi r/3$
    B. $4\pi r/3$
    C. $3\pi r/2$
    D. $\pi r^2/3$
    E. $2\pi r^2/3$

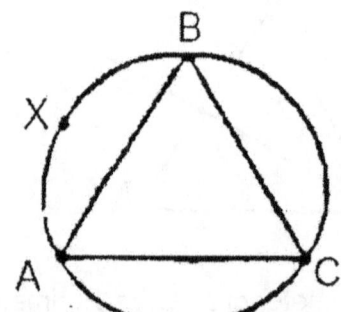

Questions 21-24.

DIRECTIONS: Questions 21 through 24 consist of two quantities, one in Column A and one in Column B. You are to compare the two quantities and in the space at the right write:
- A. if the quantity in Column A is greater;
- B. if the quantity in Column B is greater;
- C. if the two quantities are equal;
- D. if the relationship cannot be determined from the information given;

An E response will not be scored.

21.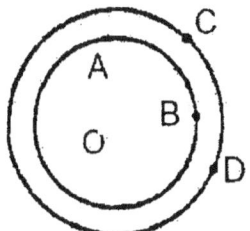

    Note: Figure not drawn to scale.
    Minor arcs AB and CD have equal length, and each lies on a different circle with center O.

Column A	Column B
Degree measure of minor arc AB	Degree measure of minor arc CD

22.
Column A	Column B
The length of the hypotenuse of a right triangle with legs of lengths 8 and 6	The length of the hypotenuse of a right triangle with legs of lengths of 12 and 5

23.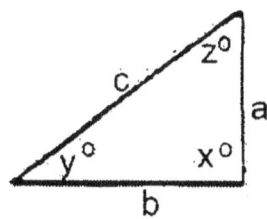

    Note: Figure not drawn to scale.
    $180 > x > y + z$

Column A	Column B
c^2	$a^2 + b^2$

21.____

22.____

23.____

24.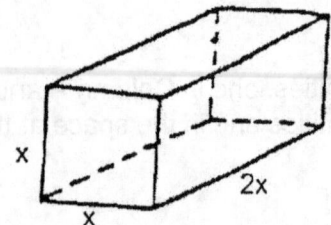

Column A	Column B
Total surface area of the rectangle solid shown	$10x^2$

25. A 25-foot ladder is placed against a vertical wall of a building, with the bottom of the ladder standing on concrete 7 feet from the base of the building. If the top of the ladder slips down 4 feet, then the bottom of the ladder will slide out _____ feet.
    A. 4   B. 5   C. 6   D. 7   E. 8

26. In the figure shown at the right, if an edge of each small cube has length 2, what is the volume of the entire rectangle solid?
    A. 192
    B. 144
    C. 72
    D. 52
    E. 48

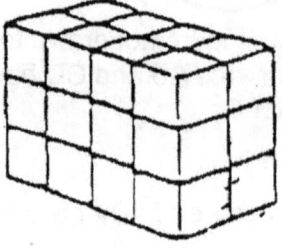

27. What is the volume of a cube with surface area $54x^2$?
    A. $9x^2$ B. $27x^3$ C. $81x^2$ D. $81x^3$ E. $729x^3$

28.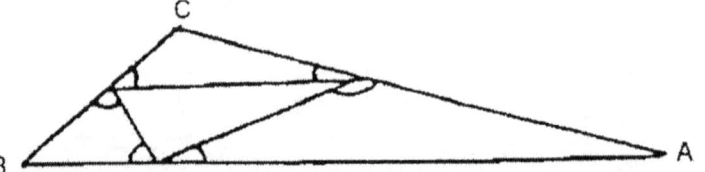

In the figure above, if ABC is a triangle, what is the sum of the degree measures of the marked angles?
    A. 90   B. 180   C. 270   D. 360

29. What is the sum of the degree measures of all the exterior angles indicated by arrows in the figure shown at the right?
    A. 360
    B. 920
    C. 1440
    D. 2880

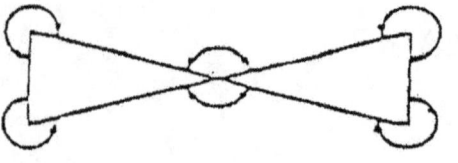

30. In the figure shown at the right, what is the average (arithmetic mean) degree measure of the 8 marked angles?
    A. 75
    B. 90
    C. 135
    D. 240

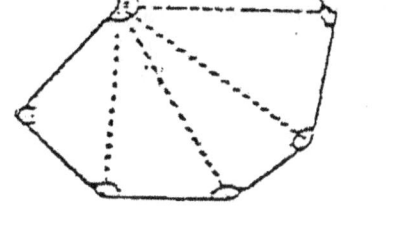

31. If $\frac{x+y}{x} = \frac{3}{2}$ then $\frac{y}{x} =$
    A. 1/5
    B. 1/4
    C. 1/3
    D. 1/2

32. Last year, Sue attended half the number of movies that Jim did and Pam attended 1/3 the number of movies that Jim did.
    If Pam attended 6 movies, how many movies did Sue attend?
    A. 3
    B. 9
    C. 13
    D. 15

33. $1 - \frac{1}{2} - \frac{1}{4} - \frac{1}{8} - \frac{1}{16} =$
    A. 1/16
    B. 1/13
    C. 1/10
    D. 1/8

34. In the figure shown at the right, what is the value of x?
    A. 22.5
    B. 23.5
    C. 30.5
    D. 32.5

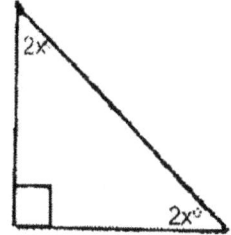

35. If 42(66+x) = 4200, then x =
    A. 25
    B. 30
    C. 34
    D. 45

36. In the figure shown at the right, if points P and Q have coordinates as shown, what is the combined area of the two shaded rectangles?
    A. 28
    B. 36
    C. 54
    D. 75

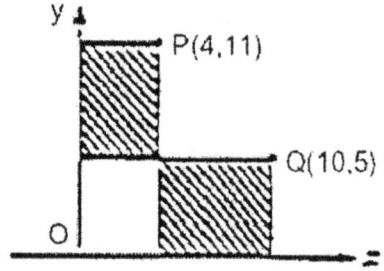

37. It took Chris 200 seconds to solve a puzzle.
    If it took Kim 160 seconds to solve the same puzzle, by what fraction of a minute was Chris' time longer than Kim's?
    A. 2/3
    B. 3/4
    C. 5/6
    D. 11/12

38. One out of 5 residents of Central Village were born in that village. If its population is 12,000, what is the TOTAL number of residents who were NOT born in Central Village?

   A. 2,400   B. 3,800   C. 5,400   D. 9,600

38.____

39. In the figure shown at the right, what is the value of x + y + z?

   A. 1,200
   B. 3,600
   C. 4,800
   D. 5,400

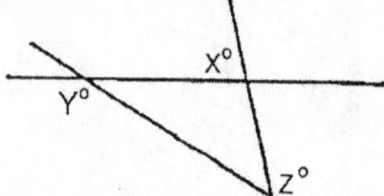

39.____

40. PP
    +QQ
    ‾‾‾
    RR

   If P, Q, and R are digits in the correctly worked addition problem above and P = 2Q, what is one possible value of R?

   A. 2   B. 4   C. 6   D. 8

40.____

KEY (CORRECT ANSWERS)

1.	C	11.	E	21.	A	31.	D
2.	D	12.	D	22.	B	32.	B
3.	A	13.	D	23.	A	33.	A
4.	E	14.	E	24.	C	34.	A
5.	A	15.	C	25.	E	35.	C
6.	B	16.	C	26.	A	36.	C
7.	D	17.	B	27.	B	37.	A
8.	C	18.	D	28.	D	38.	D
9.	E	19.	B	29.	C	39.	B
10.	A	20.	A	30.	C	40.	C

EXAMINATION SECTION
TEST 1

DIRECTIONS: Each question or incomplete statement is followed by several suggested answers or completions. Select the one that BEST answers the question or completes the statement. *PRINT THE LETTER OF THE CORRECT ANSWER IN THE SPACE AT THE RIGHT.*

1. In triangle PQR, $\angle Q = 80°$, $\angle P = 40°$, and PR = 10 in. What is the length of $\overline{PQ}$?

    A. 6.5 B. 7.6 C. 8.8 D. 9.7 E. 10.4

2. In the figure on the right, ABCD is a trapezoid inscribed in the circle with center at point O. $\overline{AB} // \overline{CD}$. If $\overline{AB}$ and $\overline{CD}$ are 4 units apart, AB = 4.5 units, OA = 5 units, and the shaded area = 58 square units, what is the length of $\overline{CD}$?

    A. 7.6
    B. 7.0
    C. 6.4
    D. 5.8
    E. 5.2

3. A license plate contains 3 letters followed by 3 digits. If repetition is allowed among the letters and NO repetition is permitted among the digits, how many different license plates are possible, assuming that the letter 0 and the digit 0 are NOT allowed?

    A. 6,955,200   B. 7,862,400   C. 7,875,000
    D. 8,858,300   E. 9,936,600

4. On Monday, an investor bought stock. By Tuesday, the stock had increased in value by 6%. By Thursday, the stock had decreased in value by 5% from Tuesday's value. If the stock was worth $422.94 on Thursday, what was its value on Monday?

    A. $425.90 B. $420.00 C. $418.75 D. $395.54 E. $377.36

5. A boy delivers papers for the New York Times, and he keeps 15% of all the money he collects. During one particular week, he kept $180.
How much money did he turn in to the Times?

    A. $1020 B. $1110 C. $1200 D. $1290 E. $1380

6. A rhombus and a square happen to have the same area. If the diagonals of the rhombus are 10 and 12, what is the perimeter of the square?

    A. 56.6 B. 50.2 C. 43.8 D. 37.4 E. 31.0

7. An auto bought in 2015 was worth $7000. If the value of this auto decreased by the same percent each year, and was worth $1750 in 2018, what was the constant percent decrease?

    A. 37% B. 45% C. 55% D. 63% E. 71%

8. The sum of an infinite geometric series is 200 and the common ratio is .15. What is the first term?

   A. 185   B. 170   C. 135   D. 80   E. 30

9. The volume of a sphere is 463 cubic inches. What is the length of the radius?

   A. 36.8   B. 28.8   C. 20.8   D. 12.8   E. 4.8

10. 1 tennis racket and 4 balls cost $27.30, whereas 3 tennis rackets and 8 balls cost $80.10. What does a tennis racket cost?

    A. $25.10   B. $25.30   C. $25.50   D. $25.70   E. $25.90

11. Y varies inversely as the cube root of W, when W = 8 and Y = 10. What is the approximate value of Y when W = 40?

    A. 8.05   B. 6.95   C. 5.85   D. 4.75   E. 3.65

12. In the figure on the right, $\overline{GI}$ is parallel to $\overline{HJ}$. If FI = 10, IJ = 12, and GI = 5, what is the length of $\overline{HJ}$?

    A. 6
    B. 7 2/3
    C. 9 1/3
    D. 11
    E. 12 2/3

13. A wheel which has a diameter of 9.6 inches makes 6 revolutions per second. How many feet does this wheel travel in 1 minute?

    A. 905   B. 2478   C. 6124   D. 10,858   E. 34,560

14. If $(2x - 3)^{3/4} = 6.2$, what is the value of x to the nearest tenth?

    A. 1.8   B. 3.7   C. 5.6   D. 7.2   E. 8.8

15. What is the sum of the first 65 terms of the following arithmetic sequence: -10, -4, 2, 8, ...?

    A. 12,350   B. 12,155   C. 12,025   D. 11,830   E. 11,700

16. A description of any point (x,y) in Quadrant 4 of the coordinate plane would be (x,y), where _____ and _____.

    A. x>0; y = 0   B. x<0; y<0   C. x = 0; y>0
    D. x<0; y>0   E. x>0; y<0

17. Bob has a collection of nickels and quarters with a total value of $3.65. If there are 5 more quarters than nickels, how many nickels are there?

    A. 13   B. 12   C. 10   D. 9   E. 8

18. What is the area of a triangle whose sides are 3, 5, 6?

    A. $\sqrt{45}$ B. $\sqrt{56}$ C. $\sqrt{68}$ D. $\sqrt{80}$ E. $\sqrt{90}$

19. Which one of the following represents a graph with the same x-intercept as the graph of 3x + y = 10?

    A. x + 3y = 10
    B. 3x - y = -10
    C. 6x - y = 20
    D. 3x + y = -20
    E. 6x + y = 18

    19._____

20. Using the formula h = 150t - 16t², what is the value of t when h = 256.5?

    A. 1.75   B. 2.25   C. 2.75   D. 3.25   E. 3.75

    20._____

21. In △ABC, a = 12, b = 5, and ∠C=100°. What is the length of side c?

    A. 13.8   B. 14.3   C. 14.8   D. 15.3   E. 15.8

    21._____

22. Which one of the following represents the correct solution to x² + x - 12 > 0?

    A. x<3 or x>-4
    B. x>-3 or x<4
    C. x<-3 or x>4
    D. x>3 or x<-4
    E. -3<x<4

    22._____

23. $400 is invested in a bank at an annual rate of 6% compounded monthly. What is the amount after 1.5 years? (to the nearest dollar)

    A. $403   B. $417   C. $438   D. $466   E. $501

    23._____

24. A sector of a circle has an area of 60 square units, and the central angle is 72°. What is the length of the radius?

    A. 9.8   B. 9.5   C. 9.2   D. 8.9   E. 8.6

    24._____

25. If water weighs 62.5 pounds per cubic foot, what is the weight in pounds of water contained in a cylinder with a radius of 4 feet and a height of 5 feet?

    A. 1148   B. 2354   C. 3672   D. 4760   E. 5236

    25._____

KEY (CORRECT ANSWERS)

1.	C	11.	C
2.	D	12.	D
3.	C	13.	A
4.	B	14.	D
5.	A	15.	D
6.	E	16.	E
7.	A	17.	E
8.	B	18.	B
9.	E	19.	C
10.	C	20.	B

21.	A
22.	D
23.	C
24.	A
25.	E

SOLUTIONS TO PROBLEMS

1. $\angle R = 180° - 80° - 40° = 60°$. Then, $\dfrac{PQ}{\sin 60°} = \dfrac{PR}{\sin 80°}$ So, PQ/.866 = 10/.985. PQ 8.8

2. $25\pi - (\dfrac{1}{2})(4)(4.5+CD) = 58$. Solving, CD ≈ 5.8

3. The number of possibilities = (25)(25)(25)(9)(8)(7) = 7,875,000

4. Letting x = value on Monday, (1.06x)(.95) = $422.94 Solving, x = $420.00

5. Let x = amount he collected. Then, .15x = $180, so x = $1200 Finally, $1200 - $180 = $1020

6. Area of rhombus = (1/2)(10)(12) = 60. Then, each side of the square = $\sqrt{60}$ ≈ 7.746. Finally, perimeter ≈ (7.746)(4) ≈ 31.0

7. Let x = rate of decay (in decimal form). Then, $1750 = 7000(1-x)^3$, $.25 = (1-x)^3$, .63 = 1-x, so x = .37 = 37%

8. Let x = first term. $200 = \dfrac{x}{1-.15}$. Solving, x = 170

9. $463 = \dfrac{4}{3}\pi R^3$, so $R^3 ≈ 110.533$, and R ≈ 4.8

10. Let x = cost of a tennis racket and y = cost of a ball. Then, x + 4y = $27.30 and 3x + 8y = $80.10. So, x = $25.50 and y = $0.45.

11. $\dfrac{10}{Y} = \dfrac{\sqrt[3]{40}}{\sqrt[2]{8}} ≈ \dfrac{3.42}{2}$. Solving, Y ≈ 5.85

12. $\dfrac{FI}{FJ} = \dfrac{GI}{HJ}$, So $\dfrac{10}{22} = \dfrac{5}{HJ}$. Solving, HJ = 11

13. 1 revolution = (9.6)(π) ≈ 30.16 inches. Then, 6 revolutions ≈ 180.96 inches, which translates to (180.96)(60) = 10,857.6 inches per minute. Finally, 10,857.6 ÷ 12 ≈ 905 feet

14. $[(2x-3)^{\frac{3}{4}}]^{\frac{4}{3}} = (6.2)^{\frac{4}{3}}$, so 2x-3 ≈ 11.39. Then, x ≈ 7.2

15. The sum = 65/2[(2)(-10)+(65-1)(6)] = 11,830

16. In Quadrant 4, x must be positive and y must be negative.

17. Let x = number of nickels. Then, $.05x + .25(x+5) = 3.65$. Solving, $x = 8$

18. Area = $\sqrt{s(s-a)(s-b)(s-c)}$, where s = 1/2 the perimeter; a, b, c = sides. So, area = $\sqrt{7(7-3)(7-5)(7-6)} = \sqrt{56}$

19. The x-intercept of both $3x+y = 10$ and $6x-y = 20$ is $(10/3, 0)$

20. $256.5 = 150t - 16t^2$, so $16t^2 - 150t + 256.5 = 0$
    Then, $t = [150 \pm \sqrt{150^2 - (4)(16)(256.5)}]/(2)(16) = 7.125$ and 2.25

21. $c = \sqrt{5^2 + 12^2 - (2)(5)(12)\cos 100°} \approx \sqrt{189.838} \approx 13.8$

22. Rewrite as $(x+4)(x-3) > 0$. Then, if both factors are positive, $x>3$. However, if both factors are negative, $x<-4$.

23. Amount = $400(1 + .06/12)^{18}$ = $438

24. Area of circle = $(60)(360/72) = 300$. Then, $300 = (\pi)(R^2)$, so $R \approx 9.8$

25. Weight = (62.5) (volume) = $(62.5)(1/3 \pi)(4^2)(5) \approx 5236$

TEST 2

DIRECTIONS: Each question or incomplete statement is followed by several suggested answers or completions. Select the one that BEST answers the question or completes the statement. *PRINT THE LETTER OF THE CORRECT ANSWER IN THE SPACE AT THE RIGHT.*

1. Mary buys a one-year subscription to Reader's Digest. She has elected to pay the monthly rate of $1.30. Had she chosen to pay each week, she would have saved 6 2/3% over the one-year period.
   What would have been her weekly payment?

   A. .26   B. .28   C. .30   D. .32   E. .34

   1._____

2. The volume of a pyramid with a square base is 100 cubic inches. If the height = 10 inches, what is the length, in inches, of the base?

   A. 4.5   B. 4.7   C. 5.1   D. 5.3   E. 5.5

   2._____

3. If cos x = P, which one of the following expressions represents cos 2x?

   A. 2P-1
   B. 2P
   C. $2P^2-1$
   D. $2P^2+1$
   E. $2P^2+P+1$

   3._____

4. The numeral 1111 in base 3 would appear as what numeral in base 6?

   A. 2222   B. 1616   C. 555   D. 318   E. 104

   4._____

5. Let f(x) = 3x, g(x) = x^2-3, and h(x) = $\sqrt{x+1}$. What is the value of f(g(3)) - g(h(15))?

   A. 5   B. 7   C. 9   D. 11   E. 13

   5._____

6. If x^2 = 9 and y^2 = 25, what is the lowest possible value of x-y?

   A. -10   B. -8   C. -6   D. -4   E. -2

   6._____

7. What is the remainder when 931^{400} is divided by 5?

   A. 4   B. 3   C. 2   D. 1   E. 0

   7._____

8. 8, _____, _____, _____, 42, _____, _____, x If the above is an arithmetic sequence, what is the value of x?

   A. 59 1/2   B. 61 1/2   C. 63 1/2   D. 65 1/2   E. 67 1/2

   8._____

9. An ordinary die is tossed twice. What is the probability of getting two different even numbers?

   A. 1/12   B. 1/9   C. 1/6   D. 1/3   E. 1/2

   9._____

10. If 6 people working at the same rate can complete a project in 5 days, what fractional part of that job can 2 people do in 4 days?

    A. 1/4   B. 4/15   C. 1/3   D. 3/5   E. 8/11

    10._____

11. John needs 2/3 hour to mow a lawn. If John and Susan can mow a lawn in 1/4 hour while working together, what fraction of an hour would Susan need to mow the lawn working alone?

    A. 1/6   B. 2/5   C. 5/12   D. 1/2   E. 11/12

12. A person who is 68 inches tall casts a shadow which is 80 inches. What is the angle of elevation from the end of the shadow to the top of the person?

    A. 26°   B. 32°   C. 40°   D. 52°   E. 58°

13. If $4\sec^2 x - 9 = 0$, what is the value of x if 270° < x < 360°?

    A. 312°   B. 318°   C. 326°   D. 332°   E. 340°

14. A triangle has the following coordinates for its vertices A, B, C: A = (0,0), B = (1,2), C = (4,1). What is the perimeter?

    A. 7.9   B. 8.3   C. 8.7   D. 9.1   E. 9.5

15. The symbol * is defined as follows: n* = (n-1)(n)(n+1) for any integer n. What is the value of 8* 4*?

    A. 6.0   B. 6.8   C. 7.6   D. 8.4   E. 9.2

16. The fuel gauge on an auto shows 1/5 full. After 11 gallons of gas are added, the gauge shows 3/4 full. What is the number of additional gallons required in order for the fuel gauge to show that the gas tank is completely full?

    A. 5   B. 6   C. 7   D. 8   E. 9

17. If x>y, which one of the following is always true?

    A. x-y>1   B. $xy>y^2$ C. $x^2>y^2$ D. x+1>y   E. x+y>y

18. In this diagram, GJ = FJ and ∠H = 90°. If GH = 24 and JH = 6, what is the value of FG?

    A. 35
    B. 37
    C. 39
    D. 41
    E. 43

19. In a room of 25 people, 14 are smokers and 10 drink beer. Some are both beer drinkers and smokers. If 4 people are neither smokers nor drinkers, how many people are both smokers and drinkers?

    A. 6   B. 5   C. 4   D. 3   E. 2

20. Let x be an integer so that 2x+9 has a value greater than 10 and less than 30. For how many values of x will 2x+9 be divisible by 5?

    A. 4   B. 3   C. 2   D. 1   E. 0

21. Given T = {2, 3, 4, 5}, how many different subsets contain an odd number of elements?

A. 2 B. 3 C. 5 D. 6 E. 8

22. What is the sum of the series $\frac{1}{2}+\frac{1}{6}+\frac{1}{18}+\frac{1}{54}+...?$

    A. 3/4 B. 19/24 C. 4/5 D. 5/6 E. 16/25

23. N gallons of paint are needed to paint a house. Each gallon will paint 10 square yards. If the total area to be painted is done by 5 people, each working at the same speed, how many square feet will each person paint?

    A. 2N B. 5N C. 10N D. 18N E. 27N

24. Let f(x) = {x + 5, if x > 0
              {x - 5, if x < 0
    What is the range of this function?

    A. {y:-5 < y ≤ 5}
    B. {y:y ≥ .5 or y < - 5}
    C. {y:-5 ≤ y<5}
    D. {y:y > 5 or y ≤ - 5}
    E. {y:y = 5 or y = -5}

25. In this diagram, MN = NK and ∠KNP = 72°. What is the measurement of, ∠KML ?

    A. 144°
    B. 135°
    C. 126°
    D. 117°
    E. 108°

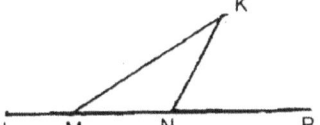

KEY (CORRECT ANSWERS)

1. B
2. E
3. C
4. E
5. A
6. B
7. D
8. E
9. C
10. B

11. B
12. C
13. A
14. E
15. D
16. A
17. D
18. C
19. D
20. B

21. E
22. A
23. D
24. B
25. A

SOLUTIONS TO PROBLEMS

1. ($1.30)(12) = $15.60. A discount of 6 2/3% means a new annual price of (15.60)(.93 1/3) = $14.56. Finally, $14.56 ÷ 52 = .28

2. Volume = (1/3) (Area of base) (height). Let x = side of base. Then, 100 = (1/3x^2)(10). So, x^2 = 30, and x = $\sqrt{30}$ ≈ 5.5

3. For any x, cos 2x = 2$\cos^2$x - 1 = 2P^2-1

4. 1111 in base 3 means (1)(3^3)+(1)(3^2)+(1)(3)+l = 40 in base 10. The numberal 104 in base 6 means (1)(6^2)+(0)(6)+4 = 40 in base 10 also.

5. f(g(3)) = f(6) = 18 and g(h(15)) = g(4) = 13 Finally, f(6)-g(4) = 5

6. x = 3 or -3 and y = 5 or -5. The possible values of x-y are: 3-5 = -2, 3-(-5) = 8, -3-5 = -8, -3-(-5) = 2, so the least of these values is -8

7. 931^{400} must end in 1. Any number ending in 1, when divided by 5, will leave a remainder of 1.

8. (42-8) ÷ 4 = 8 1/2. Then, x = 42+(3)(8 1/2) = 67 1/2

9. There are 36 possibilities when tossing one die twice. The 6 ways of getting the desired results are 24, 26, 42, 46, 62, 64. Then, 6/36 = 1/6

10. (2)(4)/(6)(5) reduces to 4/15

11. Let x = Susan's time working alone. Then, $\frac{1}{4} / \frac{2}{3} + \frac{1}{4} / x = 1$
    Simplifying, 3/8 + 1/4x = 1. Solving, x = 2/5

12. Let x = required angle. Then, tan x = 68/80, so x ≈ 40°

13. By factoring, (2sec x - 3)(2sec x + 3) = 0. Then, x = Arcsec3/2 and x = Arcsec(- 3/2). Since 270°< x < 360°, solve only x = Arcsec3/2 ≈ 312°

14. $AB = \sqrt{(1-0)^2 + (2-0)^2} = \sqrt{5}$; $AC = \sqrt{(4-0)^2 + (1-0)^2} = \sqrt{17}$
    $BC = \sqrt{(4-1)^2 + (1-2)^2} = \sqrt{10}$ Then, $\sqrt{5} + \sqrt{17} + \sqrt{10} \approx 9.5$

15. 8* = (7)(8)(9) = 504, 4* = (3)(4)(5) = 60. Then, 504/60 = 8.4

16. 3/4 - 1/5 = 11/20 Let x = capacity of the tank. Then, 11 = (11/20)(x), so x = 20. Finally, the gauge shows 3/4 full; thus, only (1/4)(20) = 5 additional gallons are needed.

17. Since x + 1 > x and it is given that x > y, x + 1 > y. Each of the other choices can be shown to be false by choosing x = -3 and y = -4 (for example).

18. $GJ = \sqrt{24^2+6^2} = \sqrt{612} = FJ$. $FH = 6+\sqrt{612} \approx 30.7$

    Now, $FG = \sqrt{GH^2+FH^2} \approx \sqrt{576+942.5} \approx 39$

19. Let x = number of those who drink and smoke, 14-x = number who only smoke, 10-x = number who only drink. Since 4 people neither smoke nor drink, x+(14-x) + (10-x) = 21. Solving, x = 3

20. If 2x+9>10, x>1/2 and if 2x+9<30, x<10 1/2. Thus, x ε {1,2,3,...,10}. The values of 2x+9 are 11, 13, 15, 17, ..., 29. Among these numbers there are exactly 3 which are divisible by 5, namely 15, 20, 25.

21. There are 4 subsets with exactly one element, namely {2}, {3}, {4}, {5}. There are also 4 subsets with exactly three elements, namely {2, 3, 4}, {2, 3, 5}, {2, 4, 5}, {3, 4, 5}. Thus, there are a total of 8 subsets.

22. For this infinite geometric series, sum = $\dfrac{1}{2} \div (1 - \dfrac{\frac{1}{6}}{\frac{1}{2}}) = \dfrac{3}{4}$

23. N gallons will paint 10N square yards = 90N square feet. Each person will paint 90N ÷ 5 = 18N square feet.

24. If x ≥ 0, y ≥ 5 and if x<0, y<-5. Thus, the range is {y:y ≥ 5 or y<-5>.

25. ∠KNP = 72° = ∠KMN + ∠NKM. Since MN = NK, ∠KMN = ∠NKM = 1/2(72°) = 36°. Finally, ∠KML = 180° - 36° = 144°

TEST 3

DIRECTIONS: Each question or incomplete statement is followed by several suggested answers or completions. Select the one that BEST answers the question or completes the statement. *PRINT THE LETTER OF THE CORRECT ANSWER IN THE SPACE AT THE RIGHT.*

1. Five children are to be assigned to 5 different seats. If Roy and Judy must be assigned to the first 2 seats, but not necessarily in that order, how many different seating arrangements are possible?

   A. 3   B. 6   C. 12   D. 24   E. 120

   1.____

2. The numeral 234 in base 6 would appear as what numeral in base 8?

   A. 102   B. 112   C. 124   D. 136   E. 144

   2.____

3. How many numbers between 20 and 50 are both odd and divisible by 3?

   A. 8   B. 7   C. 6   D. 5   E. 4

   3.____

4. In this diagram, $\overline{QT}$ is parallel to $\overline{RS}$. QT = 12, RS = 18, and TS = 5. What is the value of PT?

   A. 11
   B. 10
   C. 9
   D. 8
   E. 7

   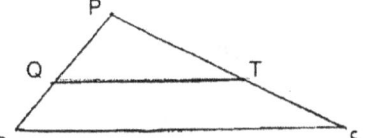

   4.____

5. This year's enrollment at Central High School is *only* 80% of last year's enrollment. If there was a decrease of 90 students from last year to this year, how many students are enrolled this year?

   A. 240   B. 360   C. 450   D. 560   E. 720

   5.____

6. If $x^2 = 5 \pmod 7$ and $0 < x < 10$ with x an integer, how many solutions are there?

   A. 0   B. 1   C. 2   D. 3   E. 4

   6.____

7. If x>w and x(w-x) = 0, which one of the following must be true?

   A. w = 0   B. x = 0   C. w > 0   D. x < 0   E. w-x = 0

   7.____

8. The symbol $\ominus$ is defined as follows: $x \ominus y = x^2 - y$. What is the value of $4 \ominus 3 \ominus 2$?

   A. 9   B. 23   C. 57   D. 145   E. 167

   8.____

9. The number 506 is which term of the arithmetic sequence -12, -5, 2, 9, ...?

   A. 71st   B. 73rd   C. 75th   D. 77th   E. 79th

   9.____

10. Let $g(x) = \{x^3+4,$ if $x \geq 0$
    $\leftarrow \{x^2+3,$ if $x<0$
    What is the range of this function?

    10.____

87

A. {y:y>3} B. {y:y ≥ 0}
C. {All real numbers} D. {y:y>4}
E. {y:3<y<4}

11. An ordinary coin is flipped 4 times. What is the probability of exactly 3 tails, but not in succession?

   A. 1/16 B. 1/8 C. 3/16 D. 1/4 E. 3/8

12. For a particular rectangular solid, the length, width, and height are given by 2x, x, and 3x, respectively. If the difference between the volume and total surface area is 32, what is the area of a face consisting of the width and height?

   A. 16 B. 24 C. 32 D. 48 E. 96

13. In this figure, O is the center of the circle. If ∠M= 20° and = $\widehat{SR}$ 30°, what is the measurement of ∠MON ?

   A. 95°
   B. 100°
   C. 105°
   D. 110°
   E. 115°

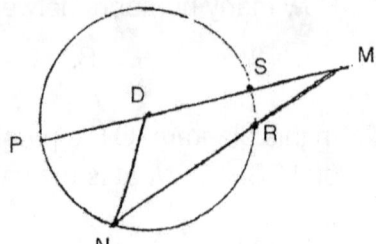

14. In a certain right triangle ABC, ∠C = 90°. If tan ∠A = 2/x, which of the following is the correct representation for sin ∠B ?

   A. $\dfrac{2}{\sqrt{x+2}}$ B. $\dfrac{x+2}{\sqrt{x^2+4}}$ C. $\dfrac{2}{\sqrt{x^2+4}}$ D. $\dfrac{x}{\sqrt{x+2}}$ E. $\dfrac{x}{\sqrt{x^2+4}}$

15. If the length and width of rectangle A are 20% and 30% less, respectively, than the length and width of rectangle B, the area of rectangle A would be _____ percent less than the area of rectangle B.

   A. 32 B. 38 C. 44 D. 50 E. 56

16. In a certain school, each student gets a grade of A, B, C, or D. If 1/6 of the students got A's, 1/4 got B's, 2/5 got C's, and 66 students got D's, how many students received B's?

   A. 40 B. 65 C. 90 D. 115 E. 140

17. Suppose x ranges in value between .001 to .01, y ranges in value from .0001 to .1, and z ranges in value from .1 to 10. What is the maximum value of x ÷ (yz)?

   A. 10,000 B. 1000 C. 100 D. 10 E. 1

18. In a class of 25 students, 1/5 of all the students scored at least 91 out of 100 on the final exam. What was the maximum average for all 25 students on this exam?

   A. 83 B. 86 C. 89 D. 92 E. 95

19. How many different arrangements of the letters in the word ACCEPT are possible? 19.____

   A. 360   B. 480   C. 540   D. 600   E. 720

20. What are the solutions to the equation $\tan^2 x - 5\tan x - 6 = 0$, where $0° \leq x \leq 180°$? 20.____

   A. 72°, 117°   B. 45°, 81°   C. 99°, 135°
   D. 63°, 72°   E. 81°, 135°

21. If $\cos x = .3$, what is the value of $\cos 2x$ if $0° \leq x \leq 90°$? 21.____

   A. -.56   B. -.60   C. -.75   D. -.82   E. -.91

22. If a chemist has 120 pints of a 20% iodine solution, how many pints of water would have to be added to produce a 15% iodine solution? 22.____

   A. 30   B. 35   C. 40   D. 45   E. 50

23. If X = {4, 5, 6, 7, 8} and Y = {1, 3, 5, 7, 9}, what is the set represented by $(X \cup Y) - (X \cap Y)$? 23.____

   A. {1, 3, 4, 6, 8, 9}   B. {1, 3, 5, 6, 7, 8, 9}
   C. {1, 5, 7, 9}   D. {1, 4, 6, 8}
   E. {1, 3, 4, 5, 6, 7, 8, 9}

24. What is the sum of all the odd integers from 101 to 199 inclusive? 24.____

   A. 5800   B. 6400   C. 6800   D. 7200   E. 7500

25. Jason is x years old and is 7 years older than Cindy. How old was Cindy 4 years ago? 25.____

   A. x-15   B. x-11   C. x-4   D. x-3   E. x+3

KEY (CORRECT ANSWERS)

1. C
2. D
3. D
4. B
5. B

6. A
7. B
8. E
9. C
10. A

11. B
12. D
13. D
14. E
15. C

16. C
17. B
18. D
19. A
20. E

21. D
22. C
23. A
24. E
25. B

SOLUTIONS TO PROBLEMS

1. If Roy is given the 1st seat and Judy is assigned the 2nd seat, there are 3! = 6 ways of arranging the other three children.
   By reversing the seating for Roy and Judy, there are another 3! = 6 seating arrangements. 3! + 3! = 12

2. In base 6, 234 means $(2)(6^2)+(3)(6)+4 = 94$ in base 10.
   In base 8, 136 means $(1)(8^2)+(3)(8)+6 = 94$ in base 10 also.

3. The 5 numbers are 21, 27, 33, 39, 45.

4. Let PT = x, PT/PS = QT/RS, so $\frac{x}{x+5}=\frac{12}{18}=\frac{2}{3}$. Solving, x = 10

5. Let x = last year's enrollment, .80x = this year's enrollment. Then, x - .80x = 90, so x = 450. Thus, .80x = 360

6. If $x^2 \equiv 5 \pmod 7$, then x^2-5 must be divisible by 7.
   If 0<x<10, the nine values of x^2-5 are: -4, -1, 4, 11, 20, 31, 44, 59, 76. None of these numbers is divisible by 7.

7. Since x>w, w-x<0. Now, if x(w-x) = 0, x = 0 necessarily.

8. $4 \ominus 3 = 4^2 - 3 = 13$. Then, $13 \ominus 2 = 13^2 - 2 = 167$

9. Let n = numbered term. Then, 506 = -12+(n-1)(7). Solving, n = 75

10. If $x \geq 0$, g(x) = y ≥ 4 and if x<0, g(x) = y>3. (Note: x^2>0 for any x<0). Thus, the range is {y:y>3}.

11. The only correct sequences are THTT and TTHT. (H = heads, T = tails) Since there are 16 sequences, the probability = 2/16=1/8

12. Volume = $(2x)(x)(3x) = 6x^3$, surface area = $(2)(2x)(x)+2(2x)(3x) + (2)(x)(3x) = 22x^2$. Then, $6x^3 - 22x^2 = 32$. This simplifies to $3x^3 - 11x^2 - 16 = 0$. Then, $(x - 4)(3x^2 + x + 4) = 0$. A rational root is x = 4 = width. The height = 3x = 12. Finally, (4)(12) = 48

13. $\angle M = 1/2 (\widehat{PN}-\widehat{SR})$, so $20° = 1/2(\widehat{PN} -30°)$. Then, $\widehat{PN} = 70°$.
    If $\widehat{PN} = 70°$, $\angle PON = 70°$ also. Finally, $\angle MON = 180°-70° = 110°$

14. $AB = \sqrt{x^2+4}$. Tan $\angle A = \frac{BC}{AC} = \frac{2}{x}$, so sin $\angle B = \frac{AC}{AB} = \frac{x}{\sqrt{x^2+4}}$

15. Let x,y = length and width of rectangle B. Then, .8x, .7y = length and width of rectangle Area of rectangle B = xy, whereas area of rectangle A = .56xy. This means that the area of rectangle A = 1 - .56 = .44 = 44% less than the area of rectangle B.

16. $1 - \frac{1}{6} - \frac{1}{4} - \frac{2}{5} = \frac{11}{60}$. so, $66 \div \frac{11}{60} = 360$ students in the school. Then, (1/4)(360) = 90 got B's.

17. To maximize x ÷ (yz), choose the largest x, the smallest y, and the smallest z. Then, .01 ÷ [(.0001) (.1)] = 1000

18. If (1/5) (25) = 5 students scored 100 and the other 20 students scored 90, the class average would have been [(5)(100)+(20)(90)] ÷ 25 = 92

19. The number of different arrangements $\frac{6!}{2!} = \frac{720}{2} = 360$ = Note: n! = (n)(n-1)(n-2)(...)(1)

20. Rewrite the equation as (tan x-6)(tan x+1) = 0 Then, x = arctan 6 ≈ 81° and x = arctan - 1 = 135°

21. Cos 2x = cos²x - sin²x. If cos x = .3, cos²x = .09 and sin²x = 1 - cos²x = .91. Finally, .91 - .09 = .82, and since 2x is in the 2nd quadrant, cos 2x = -.82

22. Let x = pints of water added. The amount of iodine in the resulting solution remains (120)(.20) = 24 pints. Then, 24/(120+x) = .15. Solving, x = 40

23. (X ∪ T)-(X ∩ Y) = {1, 3, 4, 5, 6, 7, 8, 9} - {5, 7} = {1, 3, 4, 6, 8, 9}

24. There are 50 odd numbers between 101 and 199, inclusive. Sum = 50/2(101+199) = 7500

25. Cindy's current age is x-7. Then, 4 years ago, her age was x - 7 - 4 = x - 11

TEST 4

DIRECTIONS: Each question or incomplete statement is followed by several suggested answers or completions. Select the one that BEST answers the question or completes the statement. *PRINT THE LETTER OF THE CORRECT ANSWER IN THE SPACE AT THE RIGHT.*

1. In this figure, = 50°, $\overline{PS}$ bisects bisects ∠PQR, $\overline{SQ}$ bisects ∠PQR, and PQ = QR. What is the measurement of the larger ∠PSQ ?

    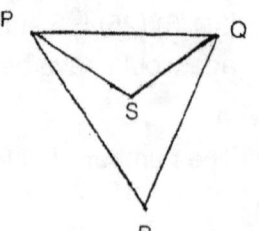

    A. 215°
    B. 225°
    C. 235°
    D. 245°
    E. 255°

2. Points A, B, C, D are collinear, but are not necessarily positioned in that order. A is midway between B and D. BD = 18, BC = 23, and DC = 5.
   What is the length of $\overline{AC}$?

    A. 13 B. 14 C. 15 D. 16 E. 17

3. How many even numbers between 1 and 1000 are divisible by both 9 and 15?

    A. 9 B. 10 C. 11 D. 12 E. 13

4. A 70-inch wire is cut into 5 pieces. After the first piece is cut, each succeeding piece is 3 inches longer than the preceding piece.
   What is the length of the longest piece?

    A. 16" B. 18" C. 20" D. 22" E. 24"

5. A jar contains 3 white beans, 2 black beans, and 4 red beans. A person takes two beans out of the jar, one at a time with no replacement.
   What is the probability of getting two white beans?

    A. 2/9 B. 1/9 C. 1/10 D. 1/12 E. 2/25

6. Let ⊕ be defined as follows: x ⊕ y = the number of prime numbers between x and y, NOT including x or y. Which one of the following has the same value as 9 ⊕ 20?

    A. 14 ⊕ 23 B. 22 ⊕ 33 C. 25 ⊕ 36 D. 29 ⊕ 42 E. 30 ⊕ 45

7. ℓ_1, ℓ_2, ℓ_3 intersect as shown. What is the measurement of the angle denoted by x?

   A. 39°
   B. 37°
   C. 35°
   D. 33°
   E. 31°

8. Let the function h(x) be defined as follows:
   h(x) = { 5x + 1, if x>1
           {-2x + 3, if x<1
   What is the range of h(x)?

   A. {y:y>3}   B. {y:y>1}   C. {y:y>6}
   D. {y:y<1}   E. {y:y<3}

9. If the length of a rectangle is decreased by 10% and the width is decreased by 20%, by what percent is the area decreased?

   A. 30%   B. 28%   C. 26%   D. 24%   E. 22%

10. Bill begins working on a project at 1:00 PM. At 3:00 PM, he is joined by Beverly, and together they complete the project by 6:00 PM. If Beverly had done the entire project by herself, she would have required 6 hours.
    If Bill had no help on this project, at what time would he have finished it?

    A. 11:00 PM   B. 10:30 PM   C. 10:00 PM
    D. 9:30 PM   E. 9:00 PM

11. If (5w-2)(1/w) = 0, what value(s) is(are) correct for w?

    A. 2/5,0   B. 5/2,0   C. 5/2   D. 0   E. 2/5

12. For this triangle, XY = 20, YZ = 15, and ∠Y = 130°.
    What is the approximate area of △XYZ?

    A. 85
    B. 100
    C. 115
    D. 125
    E. 150

13. On a certain typing assignment, Pamela types 3 times as many pages as Beth, but she makes 50% more errors per page than Beth does.
    If Beth averages 1 error every 10 minutes, how many errors does Pamela average in one hour?

    A. 18   B. 21   C. 24   D. 27   E. 30

14. How many different subsets of {1, 2, 3, 4} do NOT contain the element 3? Do NOT count the empty set.

A. 4   B. 5   C. 6   D. 7   E. 8

15. There are 20 people at a party. A tray used to make ice cubes is 9 inches long, 6 inches wide, and 5 inches high. Assume these measurements refer to the space to be filled with ice cubes 2 inches on each edge, and that the tray is used only once to make ice cubes. If each person at the party needs 2 ice cubes for drinks, what percent of these people will not get any ice cubes?

    A. 40%   B. 35%   C. 25%   D. 20%   E. 15%

16. A 60-ounce container of salt water contains 25% salt. How many ounces of this solution must be removed and replaced with the same number of ounces of salt so that the solution contains 30% salt?

    A. 3   B. 3 1/2   C. 4   D. 4 1/2   E. 5

17. A sample consists of four 2's, five 3's, six 6's, and three 7's. What is the positive difference between the mean and median of this sample?

    A. .03   B. .06   C. .09   D. .12   E. .15

18. If $f(x) = 2x-10$ and $g(x) = 10-x^2$, what is the positive difference between $f(g(-1))$ and $g(f(-1))$?

    A. 110   B. 126   C. 142   D. 158   E. 174

19. How would the number 205 appear if it were written in base 5?

    A. 41   B. 130   C. 210   D. 1241   E. 1310

20. Given a rectangle with a length of 18 and a width of 6, and the largest possible circle inscribed in this rectangle, what is the area inside this rectangle but outside the inscribed circle?

    A. 80   B. 83   C. 86   D. 89   E. 92

21. There are x gallons of paint available to paint a room. After y gallons have been used, what percent of the paint has not been used?

    A. 100(x-y)/x   B. 100y/x   C. y/[100(x-y)]
    D. x/[100(y-x)]   E. 100x/y

22. What is the period of the function $Y = 3 \cos 2x/5$?

    A. $\dfrac{2\pi}{5}$ B. $\dfrac{6\pi}{5}$ C. 2π D. 3π E. 5π

23. If $z-w \equiv 5 \pmod 8$, which of the following is a possible value for $3z-3w$?

    A. 75   B. 63   C. 52   D. 40   E. 33

24. What is the sum of the 6 exterior angles indicated by arrows in this figure?

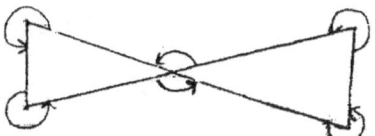

   A. $1080°$
   B. $1260°$
   C. $1440°$
   D. $1620°$
   E. $1800°$

25. If $x \triangle y$ is defined as $\dfrac{1}{x^2 - y^2}$, an undefined expression is

   A. $2 \triangle 1$ B. $3 \triangle -3$ C. $0 \triangle 1$ D. $4 \triangle 0$ E. $-1 \triangle -2$

KEY (CORRECT ANSWERS)

1. D
2. B
3. C
4. C
5. D

6. E
7. E
8. B
9. B
10. A

11. E
12. C
13. D
14. D
15. A

16. C
17. B
18. C
19. E
20. A

21. A
22. E
23. B
24. C
25. B

SOLUTIONS TO PROBLEMS

1. $\angle RPQ = \angle R = 50°$, because $PQ = QR$. $\angle RPS = (1/2)(50°) = 25°$
   $\angle PQR = 180° - 50° - 50° = 80°$, so $\angle SQR = (1/2)(80°) = 40°$
   Finally, larger $\angle PSQ = 360° - 25° - 50° - 40° = 245°$

2. Since $BC = BD + DC$, D must lie between B and C. Also, since A is midway between B and D and $BD<BC$, the points appear as B, A, D, C from left to right. Now, $AD = (1/2)(BD) = 9$ and since $DC = 5$, $AC = AD + DC = 14$

3. The lowest even number divisible by 9 and 15 is 90. Since $1000 \div 90 = 11\ 1/9$, there are 11 multiples of 90 which are less than 1000, namely: 90, 180, 270, 360, 450, 540, 630, 720, 810, 900, and 990.

4. Let x = shortest piece. The other 4 pieces are $x + 3$, $x + 6$, $x + 9$, $x + 12$. Then, $x + (x + 3) + (x + 6)+(x + 9)+(x + 12) = 70"$ Solving, $x = 8"$. The longest piece $= x + 12 = 20"$

5. The probability for the first bean to be white is $3/9 = 1/3$.
   For the second draw, only 8 beans are left, of which 2 are white. Here the probability is $2/8 = 1/4$ The combined probability is $1/3 \cdot 1/4 = 1/12$

6. $9 \oplus 20 = 4$, since the primes 11, 13, 17, 19 lie between 9 and 20. $30 \oplus 45 = 4$ also, since the primes 31, 37, 41, 43 lie between 30 and 45

7. $\angle PQR = 180° - 137° = 43°$, $\angle QPR = 180° - 74° = 106°$ $\angle PRQ = x = 180° - \angle PQR - \angle QPR = 31°$

8. If $x>1$, $h(x)>(5)(1)+1 = 6$. If $x<1$, $h(x)>(-2)(1)+3 = 1$ Combining these statements, the range is $\{y:y>1\}$.

9. Let x, y represent the original length and width of the rectangle. Then, $.90x$ and $.80y$ represent the reduced length and width. The reduced area $= .72xy$, which represents a 28% decrease from the area of the original rectangle.

10. Let x = time Bill would need working alone. The actual hours he works both alone and with Beverly is 5, while the actual hours Beverly works (with Bill) is 3. Since Beverly would have needed 6 hours working alone, $5/x + 3/6 = 1$. Solving, $x = 10$ hours. Finally, 1:00 PM + 10 hours = 11:00 PM

11. Since it is impossible for $1/w$ to be 0, $5w-2 = 0$. Solving, $w = 2/5$

12. 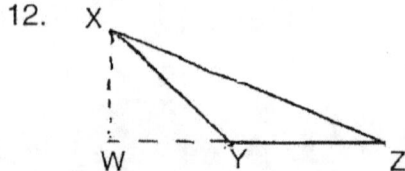 Extend YZ to W so that $\overline{XW}$ is the height of $\triangle XYZ$. $\angle XYW = 180° - 130° = 50°$. $XW = XY \sin 50° = 15.32$ Finally, area $= (1/2)(15)(15.32) \approx 115$

13. The number of errors that Pamela would average in 10 minutes $= (1)(3)(1.5) = 4.5$. The factor of 3 is used because Pamela is typing 3 times as fast as Beth. The factor of 1.5 represents a 50% increase per page in the error rate. Finally, since 1 hour = (10 minutes)(6), Pamela averages $(4.5)(6) = 27$ errors in one hour.

14. The 7 subsets are: {1}, {2}, {4}, {1, 2}, {1, 4}, {2, 4}, and {1, 2, 4}.

15. The number of ice cubes that will fit into the tray = (9/2) (6/2) (5/2), with each factor rounded DOWN to the nearest integer. This means (4)(3)(2) = 24 cubes will fit into the tray. This will serve 24 ÷ 2 = 12 people, since each person needs 2 ice cubes. Then, 8 people will not get any ice cubes, and 8 ÷ 20 = 40%.

16. Let x = number of ounces removed from the original solution. The amount of salt initially = (.25)(60) = 15 ounces. When x ounces are removed, the amount of salt removed is .25x ounces.
    Now, x ounces of salt are added back. At this point, 15 - .25x + x = 15 + .75x = the amount of salt in the final solution, which will still hold 60 ounces total. Thus, 15 + .75x = (.30)(60) = 18. Solving, x = 4

17. The median of 18 numbers is the average of the 9th and 10th numbers = (3+6)/2 = 4.5. The mean of this sample is [(4)(2)+(5)(3)+(6)(6)+(3)(7)] ÷ 18 ≈ 4.44
    Then, 4.5 - 4.44 = .06

18. $f(g(x)) = f(10-x^2) = 2(10-x^2) - 10 = 10 - 2x^2$, so $f(g(-1)) = 8$. $g(f(x)) = g(2x-10) = 10-(2x-10)^2$ $= -4x^2 + 40x - 90$, so $g(f(-1)) = -134$. Finally, $8-(-134) = 142$

19. $205 = (1)(5^3)+(3)(5^2)+(1)(5^1)+(0)(5^0)$, so the number 205 appears as 1310 in base 5.

20. The area of the rectangle = (18) (6) = 108. The largest inscribed circle has a diameter of 6. Its area = $(\pi) (radius)^2 = (\pi)(3)^2 \approx 28$. The area inside the rectangle but outside the circle ≈ 108 - 28 = 80

21. After y gallons have been used, x-y gallons of paint are left. Then, (x-y)/x represents the fraction of paint left. To convert to a percent, multiply (x-y)/x by 100 to get 100(x-y)/x

22. Given Y = Acos Bx; A, B constants; the period is given by 2π/B. Thus, 2π/2/5 = 5π

23. z-w = 5, 13, 21, 29, ..., so 3z - 3w = 15, 39, 63, 87, ... The only value on the 3z-3w list which is given is 63

24. The sum of all 6 exterior angles plus the 6 interior angles of the two triangles is (5)(360°) = 1800°, since this is equivalent to the sum of all the angles surrounding 5 points. Now, the sum of the 6 interior angles = 2(180°) = 360°, since they represent the angles in two triangles. Finally, the 6 exterior angles add up to 1800° - 360° = 1440°

25. $\frac{1}{x^2-y^2} = \frac{1}{(x-y)(x+y)}$. This expression is undefined if x-y = 0 or x+y = 0. In selection B, x = 3, y = -3, so $3\Delta-3 = \frac{1}{(3-(-3))(3+(-3))} = \frac{1}{(6)(0)}$ = undefined

TEST 5

DIRECTIONS: Each question or incomplete statement is followed by several suggested answers or completions. Select the one that BEST answers the question or completes the statement. *PRINT THE LETTER OF THE CORRECT ANSWER IN THE SPACE AT THE RIGHT.*

1. Which one of the following numbers contains the most distinct prime factors?
   A. 500   B. 720   C. 840   D. 960   E. 1000

2. John is 5 years younger than Molly. In 9 years, John's age will be 4/5 of Molly's age. How old is John now?
   A. 9   B. 11   C. 13   D. 16   E. 19

3. In this diagram, 0 is the center of the circle; G, J, H, and K are points on the circle. $\overline{GH}$ is a diameter; $\angle GJK = (2)(\angle KJH)$. If arc GK is 8 inches, how many inches is $\overline{OG}$?

   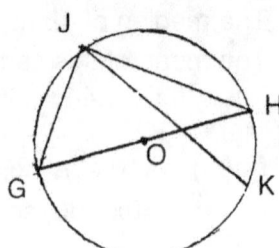

   A. $\dfrac{4}{\pi}$

   B. $\dfrac{6}{\pi}$

   C. $\dfrac{8}{\pi}$

   D. $\dfrac{10}{\pi}$

   E. $\dfrac{12}{\pi}$

4. How many positive odd integers less than 70 are divisible by 3?
   A. 10   B. 11   C. 12   D. 13   E. 14

5. Janice can type 25 memos in 1 hour. Working together, Janice and Ellen can type 38 memos in 48 minutes. How many minutes would Ellen require to type 27 memos?
   A. 72   B. 66   C. 54   D. 48   E. 42

6. In right triangle ABC, if sec $\angle A$ = 2.5, then tan $\angle A \approx$
   A. .4   B. .9   C. 1.6   D. 2.3   E. 3.5

7. If $(x+y)^2 = 60$ and $x^2+y^2 = 36$, what is the value of $(x-y)^2$?
   A. 6   B. 12   C. 30   D. 48   E. 54

8. The year 2333 contains 3 consecutive digits which are the same. How many years after 2333 is the next year that also contains 3 consecutive digits which are the same?
   A. 100   B. 105   C. 111   D. 120   E. 133

9. The area of the shaded region is 10π and = 80°. What is the length of arc AC?

   A. 5.6
   B. 7.8
   C. 9.4
   D. 11.5
   E. 13.2

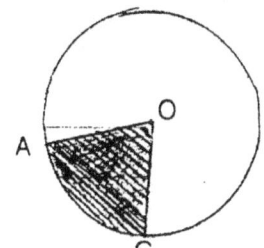

9.____

10. If $f(x) = x^2+1$ and $g(x) = 4x-2$, what is the value of $f^{-1}(g^{-1}(5))$?

   A. $\frac{\sqrt{3}}{2}$ B. 1   C. $\frac{\sqrt{5}}{2}$ D. $\frac{\sqrt{7}}{2}$ E. 2

10.____

11. If exactly two of the three integers x, y, z are odd, which one of the following must also be odd?

   A. x+y+z   B. x+yz   C. x^2+yz   D. 5xyz   E. xyz+3

11.____

12. Let ⊕ be defined as follows: ⊕ x = x^2-1 if x<0 and x^2+1 if x ≥ 0. What is the value of ⊕ 3 ÷ ⊕ - 2?

   A. 9/2   B. 10/3   C. 8/5   D. 3/2   E. 5/4

12.____

13. A club had $50 in its treasury and held a raffle to raise money. Each raffle ticket was sold for $2.50, and $100 was given away in prizes.
    If the treasury showed a final balance of $400, how many raffle tickets were sold?

   A. 150   B. 160   C. 170   D. 180   E. 190

13.____

14. Al, Betty, and Cindy are assigned to 3 chairs which are situated in a straight line. What is the probability that Al will be seated next to Betty?

   A. 1/6   B. 1/3   C. 1/2   D. 2/3   E. 3/4

14.____

15. Two cars leave a specific location at the same time, with car A traveling east and car B traveling west. After 3 1/2 hours, the cars are 315 miles apart.
    If car A averaged 6 miles per hour faster than car B, how many miles had car B traveled after 2 1/2 hours?

   A. 90   B. 95   C. 105   D. 110   E. 120

15.____

16. If ∠Q = 75°, ∠R = 55°, PQ = 8°, what is the approximate value of PR?

   A. 9.4
   B. 10.2
   C. 11.3
   D. 12.5
   E. 13.8

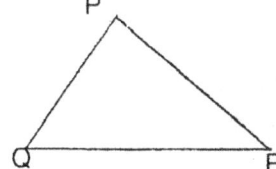

16.____

17. In this figure, O is the center of the circle, MT = TN = 5, and KT = 2. What is the length of $\overline{ON}$?

    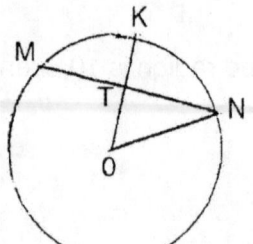

    A. 6.75
    B. 7.25
    C. 7.75
    D. 8.25
    E. 8.75

18. In this figure, O is the center of the circle, $\angle B = 25°$, $\widehat{DE} = 40°$, and $\widehat{AD} = 110°$. What is the measurement of $\angle C$?

    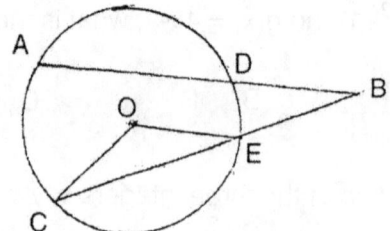

    A. 20°
    B. 22°
    C. 25°
    D. 28°
    E. 30°

19. A basketball team has won 70% of the 20 games it has played this year. What is the MAXIMUM number of losses allowed in the remaining 40 games this year so that the team's winning percent for the entire year is at least 60%?

    A. 14   B. 16   C. 18   D. 20   E. 22

20. For how many integer values of x will 4x+7 be an integer greater than 20 and less than 80?

    A. 12   B. 13   C. 14   D. 15   E. 16

21. Tickets for a play cost $7 each for adults and $3 each for children. If 300 tickets were purchased for a total of $1360, how many adults' tickets were purchased?

    A. 80   B. 115   C. 150   D. 185   E. 220

22. Let P = {5, 10, 15, 20} and Q = {10, 15, 20, 25}. Suppose x represents any number in set P and y represents any number in set Q.
    How many different values of x ÷ y are possible?

    A. 12   B. 13   C. 14   D. 15   E. 16

23. In a certain marching band, exactly 2/7 of the musicians play the trumpet. Also, 1/3 of the trumpet players can play the trombone.
    If more than 5 musicians can play both these instruments, what is the MINIMUM number of musicians in this marching band?

    A. 53   B. 49   C. 35   D. 21   E. 15

24. The mean of x, y, and z is 18, whereas the mean of 2x, y, and 2z is 28. What is the mean of x and z? 24._____

    A. 5   B. 8   C. 10   D. 12   E. 15

25. In which one of the following samples is the mode equal to the median? 25._____

    A. 6, 6, 6, 7, 7, 8   B. 5, 6, 6, 7, 8, 8, 8   C. 4, 5, 6, 6, 7, 7, 7
    D. 5, 6, 7, 8, 8, 9   E. 6, 6, 7, 7, 7, 8

KEY (CORRECT ANSWERS)

1. C
2. B
3. E
4. C
5. A

6. D
7. B
8. C
9. C
10. A

11. E
12. B
13. D
14. D
15. C

16. A
17. B
18. E
19. C
20. D

21. B
22. B
23. A
24. E
25. E

SOLUTIONS TO PROBLEMS

1. $500 = 2^2 \cdot 5^3$, $720 = 2^4 \cdot 3^2 \cdot 5$, $840 = 2^3 \cdot 3 \cdot 5 \cdot 7$, $960 = 2^6 \cdot 3 \cdot 5$, $1000 = 2^3 \cdot 5^3$. Thus, 840 contains four distinct prime factors.

2. Let x = John's age now and x+5 = Molly's age now. Then, x+9 = 4/5(x+14). Solving, x = 11.

3. $\angle GJH = 90°$, since it is an inscribed angle with $\overset{\frown}{GH}$ as the intercepted arc. If x = $\angle KJN$, $2x = \angle GJK$. So, $3x = 90°$, $x = 30°$, $2x = 60°$. Then, $\overset{\frown}{GK} = (2)(60°) = 120° = 8$ inches. The circumference = $360° = 24$ inches. Finally, $\overline{OG}$ = radius = $\dfrac{24}{2\pi} = \dfrac{12}{\pi}$ inches.

4. The 12 numbers which meet the stated requirements are: 3, 9, 15, 21, 27, 33, 39, 45, 51, 57, 63, 69.

5. Janice can type (25/60)(48) = 20 memos in 48 minutes. Then, Ellen types 38 - 20 = 18 memos in 48 minutes. Finally, Ellen needs (48/18)(27) = 72 minutes to type 27 memos.

6. Let AC = 2 and AB = 5, so sec $\angle A$ = 5/2 = 2.5. Then, BC = $\sqrt{5^2 - 2^2} \approx 4.58$. Now, $\tan \angle A = \dfrac{BC}{AC} \approx \dfrac{4.58}{2} \approx 2.3$

7. $(x+y)^2 = x^2+2xy+y^2 = 60$ and $x^2+y^2 = 36$, so $2xy = 24$. Then, $(x-y)^2 = x^2-2xy+y^2 = x^2+y^2-2xy = 36 - 24 = 12$

8. 111 years after the year 2333 is the year 2444.

9. The area of the circle = $(10\pi)(360/80) = 45\pi$. Then, the radius = $\sqrt{45} \approx 6.71$. Now, $80° \approx 1.4$ radians, so arc AC = $(6.71)(1.4) \approx 9.4$

10. $g^{-1}(x) = \dfrac{x+2}{4}$, $f^{-1}(x) = \sqrt{x-1}$, so $f^{-1}(g^{-1}(x)) = \sqrt{\dfrac{x+2}{4} - 1} = \sqrt{(x-2)/4}$. Then, $f^{-1}(g^{-1}(5)) = \sqrt{3/4} = \sqrt{3}/2$

11. xyz must be even if exactly two of these numbers are odd, so xyz+3 = even + odd = odd number. The other 4 choices would be even if x is even.

12. $\oplus 3 = 3^2+1 = 10$, $\oplus -2 = (-2)^2 - 1 - 3$. So, $\oplus 3 \div \oplus -2 = 10/3$

13. Let x = number of raffle tickets sold. Then, 50 + 2.50x - 100 = 400. Simplifying, 2.50x = 450. Thus, x = 180

14. Using initials, there are six possible arrangements: ABC, CAB, BAC, CBA, ACB, BCA. In the first four arrangements, Al is next to Betty. So, the probability is 4/6 = 2/3

15. Let x, x + 6 = speeds in miles per hour for car B, A, respectively. Then, $3\frac{1}{2}x + 3\frac{1}{2}(x+6) = 315$, so x = 42. The distance car B traveled in 2 1/2 hours = (42)(2 1/2) = 105 miles

16. Let PR = x. $\dfrac{8}{\sin 55°} = \dfrac{x}{\sin 75°}$, so x = (8sin 75°) ÷ sin 55° ≈ 9.4

17. Since MT = TN, $\overline{KO} \perp \overline{NM}$. In right triangle TON, let ON = x, OT = x-2 (OT = OK-KT). Then, $(x-2)^2 + 5^2 = x^2$. Simplifying, $x^2-4x+4+25 = x^2$. Solving, x = 7.25

18. $\angle B = 1/2 (\overset{\frown}{AC}-\overset{\frown}{DE})$; so $25° = 1/2(\overset{\frown}{AC} -40°)$, and this means $\overset{\frown}{AC} = 90°$. $\overset{\frown}{CE} = 360° - \overset{\frown}{AC} - \overset{\frown}{AD} - \overset{\frown}{DE} = 120°$. $\angle O = \overset{\frown}{CE} = 120°$ and since OC = OE, $\angle C = (180°-120°)/2 = 30°$

19. The team has already won (.70)(20) = 14 games. There are a total of 60 games for the year, and for a winning percent of 60%, the team must win (.60)(60) = 36 games. Thus, the team must win 36 - 14 = 22 of the remaining 40 games. Finally, the maximum number of losses allowed in the remaining games = 40 - 22 = 18

20. If 4x+7>20, x>3.25 and if 4x+7<80, x<18.25. The allowable integer values of x are 4,5,6,...,18. This represents 15 numbers.

21. Let x = number of adults' tickets, 300-x = number of children's tickets. Then, 7x+3(300-x) = 1360. Solving, x = 115

22. The 13 different values would be: 1/5, 1/4, 1/3, 2/5, 1/2, 3/5, 2/3, 3/4, 4/5, 1, 1 1/3, 1 1/2, 2.

23. Let x = minimum number of band members. Then, we get 2/7 · 1/3 x > 5. So, 2/21-x > 5 and x > 52.5. Thus, x = 53

24. (x + y + z)/3 =18, so x + y + z = 54. Likewise, (2x + y + 2z)/3 = 28, so 2x + y + 2z = 84. By subtraction, x + z = 30, so (x + z)/2 = mean of x and z = 15

25. For the sample 6, 6, 7, 7, 7, 8, the mode = median = 7
    In choice A, mode = 6 and median = 6.5
    In choice B, mode = 8 and median = 7
    In choice C, mode = 7 and median = 6
    In choice D, mode = 8 and median = 7.5

EXAMINATION SECTION
TEST 1

DIRECTIONS: Each question or incomplete statement is followed by several suggested answers or completions. Select the one that BEST answers the question or completes the statement. *PRINT THE LETTER OF THE CORRECT ANSWER IN THE SPACE AT THE RIGHT.*

1. What is the range of the function $g(x) = \sqrt{3-6x} - 10$?

   A. $\{y|y \geq \frac{1}{2}\}$ B. $\{y|y \geq -10\}$
   C. {All real numbers}   D. $\{y|y \geq 2\}$
   E. $\{y|y \geq 3\}$

2. A sphere and a right circular cone have the same volume. If the cone has a base area of 36π and a height of 8, what is the radius of the sphere?

   A. 9.0   B. 7.8   C. 6.6   D. 5.4   E. 4.2

3. If the product of five integers is positive, then what is the maximum number of integers which could be negative?

   A. 1   B. 2   C. 3   D. 4   E. 5

4. The probability of event A occurring is .24, the probability of event B occurring is .33, and the probability of at least one of the events A or B occurring is .48. What is the probability that both events A and B occur?

   A. .09   B. .17   C. .25   D. .39   E. .57

5. Z varies jointly as X and the square of Y. By what percent will Z change if X is decreased by 10% and Y is increased by 8%?

   A. 2.0% decrease   B. 2.0% increase
   C. 5.0% increase   D. 8.5% increase
   E. 12.5% increase

6. The operation * is defined as follows: $x*y = \frac{x+y}{x-y}$.

   What is the value of 3*4*5?

   A. $-\frac{7}{5}$ B. -1   C. $\frac{1}{6}$ D. $\frac{5}{7}$ E. 6

7. What are the solution(s) to the equation $\tan^2 x + 5\tan x + 4 = 0$, given $0° \leq x \leq 360°$?

   A. 135° and 315°   B. 104°, 135°, 284°, 315°
   C. 104°   D. 135°, 284°, 315°
   E. 104°, 135°, 284°

8. Which one of the following functions has a period of 3?
   Y =

   A. $2\sin 3x$
   B. $3\sin 3\pi x$
   C. $\sin\dfrac{3\pi x}{2}$
   D. $4\sin\dfrac{2\pi x}{e}$
   E. $\dfrac{2}{3}\sin\pi x$

9. Which one of the following situations for triangle ABC is NOT possible?
   ∠A = _____, BC = _____, AC = _____

   A. 30°; 6; 12
   B. 40°; 7; 10
   C. 50°; 8; 9
   D. 60°; 9; 11
   E. 70°; 10; 8

10. What is the maximum value of the function $f(x) = -3x^2 + 2x + 5$?

    A. 5 1/2   B. 5 1/3   C. 5   D. 4 2/3   E. 4 1/2

11. For which values of K will the equation $Kx^2 + 9x + 3 = 0$ have 2 complex roots?

    A. K > 6 3/4
    B. K > 9
    C. K < 3
    D. K < 0
    E. K > 1/3

12. Water fills up a right triangular prism at the rate of 15 cubic inches per second. The triangular base has an area of 25 cubic inches and it requires 2 minutes to fill this prism to 3/4 capacity.
    What is the height of this prism, in inches?

    A. 16   B. 32   C. 48   D. 80   E. 96

13. In a certain company, 3/4 of the workers have college degrees, and 3/4 of the workers with college degrees are married.
    What fraction of the workers in this company have college degrees, but are not married?

    A. 1/16   B. 3/16   C. 5/16   D. 7/16   E. 9/16

14. An ellipse is given by the equation $\dfrac{(x-1)^2}{25} + \dfrac{(y-1)^2}{9} = 1$.
    Which one of the following represents the location of one focus?

    A. (5, -1)   B. (5, 0)   C. (5, 1)   D. (5, 3)   E. (5, 4)

15. From a deck of 52 cards, what is the probability of drawing a spade on the first draw and a club on the second draw, given that the cards are drawn without replacement?

    A. 169/2704   B. 13/204   C. 1/4   D. 13/51   E. 1/2

16. From a group of 16 girls and 12 boys, a committee of 3 girls and 2 boys is to be selected. How many different committees are possible?

    A. 98,280   B. 68,520   C. 36,960   D. 14,404   E. 1152

17. PQRS is a parallelogram in which RS = 18, PSR = 110°, and the perimeter = 42. To the nearest integer, what is the area?   17._____

   A. 63
   B. 60
   C. 57
   D. 54
   E. 51

18. How many positive integers less than 1000 contain at LEAST one 6 as a digit?   18._____
   A. 190   B. 215   C. 238   D. 253   E. 271

19. If $5^x = 10$, what is the value of x^5?   19._____
   A. 6.0   B. 4.8   C. 3.5   D. 1.2   E. 0.1

20. For which one of the following functions is the domain equal to the range?   20._____
   A. $f(x) = (5x+1)/(2x-1)$ B. $g(x) = (4x+3)/(4x-3)$
   C. $h(x) = (2x+1)/(3x-2)$ D. $m(x) = (3x+2)/(2x-5)$
   E. $n(x) = (6x+5)/(3x-5)$

21. If $(x^3+1)/(x+1) = 3$, what is the value of x^2-x?   21._____
   A. 2   B. 3   C. 4   D. 5   E. 6

22. If $2\sin x = 3\cos x$, $0° \le x \le 360°$, what is the measurement of x?   22._____
   A. 74°   B. 68°   C. 62°   D. 56°   E. 50°

23. If $f(x) = x+3$ and $g(x) = 3x-1$, what is the value of $f^{-1}(g^{-1}(1))$?   23._____
   A. 17/3   B. 11/3   C. 1/3   D. -2/3   E. -7/3

24. Which one of the following equations represents a circle with center at (3,-4)?   24._____
   A. $x^2 + y^2 + 6x - 8y + 21 = 0$
   B. $x^2 + y^2 - 6x + 8y + 24 = 0$
   C. $2x^2 + y - 12x + 18 = 0$
   D. $6x + y^2 - 8y + 20 = 0$
   E. $5x^2 + 3y^2 = 15$

25. What is the value of $\sum_{n=1}^{\infty} \frac{3}{4}(\frac{2}{3})^{n-1}$?   25._____
   A. 1/2   B. 3/4   C. 9/4   D. 9/2   E.

KEY (CORRECT ANSWERS)

1.	B		11.	A
2.	E		12.	E
3.	D		13.	B
4.	A		14.	A
5.	C		15.	B
6.	C		16.	C
7.	B		17.	E
8.	D		18.	E
9.	D		19.	A
10.	B		20.	C

21.	A
22.	D
23.	E
24.	B
25.	C

SOLUTIONS TO PROBLEMS

1. The smallest possible value of $\sqrt{3-6x}$ is 0, when $x = \frac{1}{2}$. Thus, the smallest g(x) or y value = 0 - 10 = -10

2. The volume of the cone = $(\frac{1}{3})(36\pi)(8) = 96\pi$. Then, $96\pi = \frac{4}{3}R^3$, and $R^3 = 72$. Finally, $R = \sqrt[3]{72} \approx 4.2$

3. If an even number of integers are negative, their product is positive. Given 5 integers, 4 is the maximum value of even integers which are each negative.

4. Let P(A), P(B), P(A or B), P(A and B) represent the various probabilities of each event. P(A or B) = P(A) + P(B) - P(A and B). Thus, .48 = .24 + .33 - P(A and B). Solving, P(A and B) = .09

5. $Z = KXY^2$ originally. The changed Z value, where K is a constant, is $(K)(.90X)(1.08Y)^2 = 1.04976KXY^2$. This represents an increase of approximately 5.0%.

6. $3*4 = \frac{3+4}{3-4} = -7$. Then, $-7*5 = \frac{-7+5}{7-5} = \frac{-2}{-12} = \frac{1}{6}$

7. Rewrite equation as (tan x +1)(tan x + 4) = 0. Then for tan x + 1 = 0, x = 135° and 315°. For tan x + 4 = 0, x = 104° and 284°.

8. If Y = A sin Bx, A and B are constants, the period is given by $\frac{2\pi}{B}$. Since $\frac{2\pi}{B} = 3$, $B = \frac{2\pi}{3}$

9. For △ABC to be impossible, BC must be less than AC sin ∠A, and 9 < (11)(sin 60°) ≈ 9.5

10. Rewrite equation as $f(x) -3(x-\frac{1}{3})^2 + 5\frac{1}{3}$. The vertex is located at $(\frac{1}{3}, 5\frac{1}{3})$. so, $5\frac{1}{3}$ is the maximum f(x) value.

11. In order to have 2 complex roots, $9^2 - (4)(k)(3) < 0$. This means 81 - 12k < 0. Solving, k > 6 3/4

12. It requires $(120)(\frac{4}{3}) = 160$ seconds to fill up the prism.

    Then, volume = (160)(15) = 2400 cubic inches. Finally, height = 2400 ÷ 25 = 96 inches.

13. $\frac{3}{4}$ of the workers have college degrees and $(\frac{3}{4})(\frac{3}{4})=\frac{9}{16}$ have college degrees and are married. Then, $\frac{3}{4}-\frac{9}{16}=\frac{3}{16}$ of the workers have college degrees but are not married.

14. The center of the ellipse is (1,-1). The distance from the center to a focus = $\sqrt{25-9}=4$. Since the major axis lies on the line Y = -1, one focus must be stationed at (5,-1). Incidentally, the other focus is located at (-3,-1).

15. The probability of drawing a spade then a club, without replacement
$(\frac{13}{52})(\frac{13}{51})=(\frac{1}{4})(\frac{13}{51})=\frac{13}{204}$

16. The number of committees = $(_{16}C_3)(_{12}C_2) = (\frac{16 \cdot 15 \cdot 14}{3!})(\frac{12 \cdot 11}{2!}) = (560)(66) = 36,960$

17. The width = $\frac{1}{2}$ (42) - 18 = 3. Area = (18)(3)(sin 110°) ≈ 51

18. From 1 - 100, there are 19 integers with at least one 6.
This situation is repeated in the groups 101 - 200, 201 - 300, 301 - 400, 401 - 500, 701 - 800, 801 - 900, and 901 - 1000. From 501 - 600, there are 20 such integers; and from 601 to 700, there are 99 such integers. The grand total becomes (8)(19) + 20 + 99 = 271

19. If $5^x = 10$, then x = $\text{Log}_{10} 10 \div \text{Log}_{10} 5$ ≈ 1.4307.
Then, 1.4307^5 ≈ 6.0

20. h(x) = (2x+1)/(3x-2). The domain and range are all numbers except 2/3.

21. Algebraically, $(x^3+1)/(x+1) = x^2 - x + 1$. Now, $x^2 - x + 1 = 3$, so, $x^2-x = 2$.

22. Rewrite as sin x/cos x = $\frac{3}{2}$. Since tan x = sin x/cos x, 3 x = arctan $\frac{3}{2}$ ≈ 56°

23. $g^{-1}(x) = (x+1)/3$ and $f^{-1}(x) = x-3$. Then, $f^{-1}(g^{-1}(x)) = f^{-1}(x+1)/3) = (x+1)/3-3 = (x-8)/3$.
Finally, $f^{-1}(g^{-1}(1)) = (1-8)/3 = -\frac{7}{3}$

24. Rewrite as $(x^2-6x+9) + (y^2+8y+16) -1=0$, which becomes $(x-3)^2 + (y+4)^2 = 1$. This is a circle centered at (3,-4) with a radius of 1.

25. This is a geometric series: $\frac{3}{4}+(\frac{3}{4})(\frac{2}{3})+(\frac{3}{4})(\frac{2}{3})^2+\ldots$

The sum $\frac{3}{4}/(1-\frac{2}{3})=\frac{3}{4}/\frac{1}{3}=\frac{9}{4}$

TEST 2

DIRECTIONS: Each question or incomplete statement is followed by several suggested answers or completions. Select the one that BEST answers the question or completes the statement. *PRINT THE LETTER OF THE CORRECT ANSWER IN THE SPACE AT THE RIGHT.*

1. $1, \frac{2}{3}, \frac{2}{9}, \frac{8}{27}, \ldots$ In this sequence, each number (after the first number) is two-thirds of the positive difference of the preceding two numbers. What would be the sixth number in this sequence?

   A. 10/243   B. 4/81   C. 32/243   D. 40/243   E. 32/81

2. The equation of line l_1 is $x = 6$. The slopes of lines l_2 and l_3 are $\frac{1}{2}$ and 1/5, respectively. If point P lies halfway between A and B, what is the y-coordinate of P?

   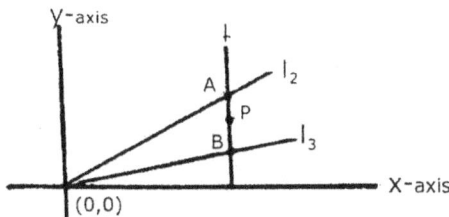

   A. 7/20
   B. 13/10
   C. 31/20
   D. 9/5
   E. 21/10

3. Suppose x is a positive factor of 18, and y is a positive factor of 30. If $x \neq 18$ and $y \neq 30$, what is the maximum value of $y \div (x+1)$?

   A. 25/3   B. 15/2   C. 5/2   D. 15/9   E. 30/19

4. A machine is designed to make 3 round holes, then 4 square holes. If this pattern is always repeated, what would be the shapes of the 66th, 67th, 68th, and 69th holes?

   A. 2 round, 2 square   B. 1 square, 3 round
   C. 1 round, 3 square   D. 3 square, 1 round
   E. 3 round, 1 square

5. As a customer in a certain bank, a person's identification number must contain four digits, with repetition allowed. The first digit must be a 0, 1, or 2; the last digit must be odd. How many different identification numbers can be assigned by this bank?

   A. 960   B. 1080   C. 1215   D. 1500   E. 1920

6. If $8^{x+1} = 16^{2x-3}$, what is the value of y in the equation $9^x = 3^{2y-1}$?

   A. 7/2   B. 10/3   C. 25/9   D. 19/8   E. 21/16

7. A function has zeros at 5i, -5i, and 3. If this function is represented as $y = f(x)$, what is the value of $f(-1)$?

   A. -75   B. -85   C. -100   D. -104   E. -112

8. An auto bought in 1985 was worth $7000, but in 1988 was only worth $1750. If this auto depreciated by the same percent each year, what would be its approximate value in 1990?

   A. $575   B. $695   C. $745   D. $825   E. $955

9. In △ PQR, LP = 80°, Q = 40°, and PR = 10. What is the approximate length of $\overline{PQ}$?

   A. 13.5   B. 12.3   C. 11.4   D. 9.6   E. 8.8

10. If cos 2x - cos x = 0 and 0° ≤ x < 360°, how many values of x will satisfy this equation?

    A. 1   B. 2   C. 3   D. 4   E. 5

11. In this diagram, ∠K = 90°, JM = $\sqrt{33}$, JK = 5, and $\overline{KM}$ is 3 times as long as $\overline{KL}$. What is the length of $\overline{LM}$?

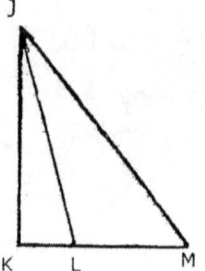

A. $\frac{1}{2}\sqrt{2}$

B. $\frac{2}{3}\sqrt{2}$

C. $\frac{4}{3}\sqrt{2}$

D. $\frac{3}{2}\sqrt{2}$

E. $\frac{5}{2}\sqrt{2}$

12. Line l_1 is described by the equation x+4y = 5. If line l_2 is perpendicular to l_1 and contains the point (1,2), what is the x-intercept of l_2?

    A. 9/2   B. 7/4   C. 3/2   D. 3/4   E. 1/2

13. A large spherical object is to be painted. The radius of this object is 5 feet and it can be determined that 1 container of paint will cover a surface area of 30 square feet.
    If a painter uses the contents of 1 container in 20 minutes, how many hours (approximately) will be required to paint this entire spherical object?

    A. 2.7   B. 3.5   C. 4.6   D. 5.8   E. 6.7

14. A pyramid with a square base has the same volume as half a rectangular solid. The height of the two solids are equal. If the length and width of the rectangular solid are 12 and 9, respectively, what is the approximate length of each side of the base of the pyramid?

    A. 8.3   B. 9.4   C. 10.5   D. 11.6   E. 12.7

15. Suppose g(x) is a function of x given by: $g(x) = \sqrt{3-6x} - 10$. Let T = the domain and V = the range of g(x). Which of the following sets describes $T \cap V$?

    A. $\{t: -10 \leq t \leq 2\}$
    B. $t: t \geq 2$ or $t \leq -10$
    C. $\{t: -10 \leq t \leq \frac{1}{2}\}$
    D. $\{t: t \geq \frac{1}{2}$ or $t \leq -10\}$
    E. {All real numbers}

16. For which one of the following equations would the graph show an amplitude of $\frac{3}{2}$ and a period of $\frac{2}{3}$?

    A. $\frac{2}{3} \cos \frac{2x}{3}$
    B. $-\frac{2}{3} \cos \frac{4\pi x}{3}$
    C. $\frac{3}{4} \cos \frac{2\pi x}{3}$
    D. $-\frac{3}{2} \cos 3\pi x$
    E. $\frac{2}{3} \cos 2px$

17. What is the value of the following summation expression: $\sum_{i=5}^{22}(2i^2+12)$?

    A. 7422   B. 7530   C. 7638   D. 7746   E. 7854

18. What is the value of the following summation expression: $\sum_{n=1}^{\infty}\frac{3}{4}(\frac{2}{3})^{n-1}$?

    A. $\frac{9}{4}$ B. $\frac{3}{2}$ C. $\frac{5}{4}$ D. $\frac{1}{2}$ E. $\frac{1}{4}$

19. What is the length of the circumference of the circle whose equation is $x^2 + y^2 + 10y = 144$?

    A. 12π B. 13π C. 20π D. 24π E. 26π

20. In a Normal Distribution of data, the mean is 30 and the standard deviation is 4. If the number 24 is one of the data and has a frequency of 10, which one of the following data values would have a frequency lower than 10?

    A. 37   B. 34   C. 31   D. 28   E. 25

21. Heights among people are nearly normally distributed with a mean of 67 inches and a standard deviation of 2.5 inches. If 500 people are randomly selected, approximately how many of them would be expected to be shorter than 64 inches?

    A. 49   B. 58   C. 66   D. 77   E. 85

22. Using the formula Area = $\frac{2}{3}$ bh for a parabola bounded by a line segment perpendicular to its axis of symmetry, where b = length of this segment and h = distance from this segment to the vertex, what is the approximate area bounded by the parabola whose equation is y = -1/3x^2 + 2x + 1 and the line y = -1?

    A. 25.8   B. 30.1   C. 34.4   D. 38.6   E. 42.9

23. Which one of the following absolute value inequalities has *only* the solution x = -2?

    A. |3x+6| < 0   B. |3x+6| < -2   C. |3x+6| ≤ 0
    D. |3x+6| ≥ 0   E. |3x+6| > -2

24. In paying back a loan on a monthly basis, suppose Jeff's balance after the third payment is $875.40. If the annual rate is 15.6% compounded monthly and his constant monthly payment is $120.00, what amount of his fourth payment will be credited toward reducing the loan's principal?

    A. $98.22   B. $100.82   C. $103.42   D. $106.02   E. $108.62

25. On a standardized test, Mary answered 74 of the 80 questions, and left the other 6 questions blank. Each correct answer was worth 2 pounds and for each wrong answer, she lost 1/2 point. Mary's final score was 133. On this same test, David answered correctly the same number of questions as Mary but had no wrong answers. What was David's final score?

    A. 142   B. 140   C. 138   D. 136   E. 134

KEY (CORRECT ANSWERS)

1.	D	11.	C
2.	E	12.	E
3.	B	13.	B
4.	C	14.	E
5.	D	15.	C
6.	A	16.	D
7.	D	17.	D
8.	B	18.	A
9.	A	19.	E
10.	C	20.	A

21.	B
22.	A
23.	C
24.	E
25.	D

SOLUTIONS TO PROBLEMS

1. The fifth number $=\frac{2}{3}(\frac{8}{27}\cdot\frac{2}{9})=\frac{4}{81}$. Then, the sixth number $=\frac{2}{3}(\frac{8}{27}\cdot\frac{4}{81})=\frac{40}{243}$

2. To find the y-coordinate of point A, $\frac{y-0}{6-0}=\frac{1}{2}$, so y = 3

   To find the y-coordinate of point B, $\frac{y-0}{6-0}=\frac{1}{5}$, so y $\frac{6}{5}$

   Finally, the y-coordinate of point P = $(3+\frac{6}{5})/2=\frac{21}{10}$

3. x can be 1, 2, 3, 6, or 9; y can be 1, 2, 3, 5, 6, 10, or 15. In order to maximize y ÷ (x+1), choose the largest y and the smallest x. Then, 15 ÷ (1+1) = 15/2 is the maximum value.

4. After 63 holes, the pattern would repeat, since 63 is divisible by 7. So, the 66th through 69th holes would represent the equivalent of the 3rd through 6th holes in this pattern, which is: round, square, square, square.

5. There are 3 choices for the first digit, 10 choices for each of the second and third digits, and 5 choices (1, 3, 5, 7, 9) for the fourth digit. The total number of I.D. numbers = (3)(10)(10)(5) = 1500

6. $8^{x+1} = 16^{2x-3}$ can be written as $(2^3)^{x+1} = (2^4)^{2x-3}$, which becomes $2^{3x+3} = 2^{8x-12}$. So, 3x + 3 = 8x - 12, and x = 3.
   Now, $9^3 = 3^{2y-1}$ can be written as $(3^2)^3 = 3^6 = 3^{2y-1}$.
   Then, 6 = 2y - 1 and so y = $\frac{7}{2}$

7. y = f(x) = (x-5i)(x+5i)(x-3) = $x^3 - 3x^2 + 25x - 75$. Then, f(-1) = $(-1)^3 - 3(-1)^2 + 25(-1) - 75$ = -104

8. Let x = rate of depreciation. Then, 1750 = 7000$(1-x)^3$. Then, X ≈ .37, 1- X ≈ .63. The value of the auto in 1990 = 1750(.63)2 ≈ $695

9. ∠R = 180° - 80° - 40° = 60°. Then, $\frac{PQ}{\sin\angle R}=\frac{PR}{\sin\angle Q}$, so we get
   PQ/sin 60° = 10/sin 40°. Solving, PQ = 13.5

10. Cos 2x can be written as $2\cos^2 x - 1$, so $2\cos^2 x - \cos x - 1 = 0$ Rewrite as (cos x-1)(2cos x+1) = 0. Then, for cos x = 1, x = 0°; for cos x = $-\frac{1}{2}$, x = 120° and 240°

11. $KM = \sqrt{(\sqrt{33})^2 - 5^2} = \sqrt{8} = 2\sqrt{2}$ Let KL = x, so $2\sqrt{2} = 3x$ and $x = \frac{2}{3}\sqrt{2}$. Now,

    $LM = 2\sqrt{2} - \frac{2}{3}\sqrt{2} = \frac{4}{3}\sqrt{2}$

12. Since the slope of l_1 is $-\frac{1}{4}$ and l_2 is perpendicular to l_1, the slope of l_2 is 4. The equation for l_2 becomes y = 4x+B, where B = y-intercept. By substitution, 2 = 4(1) + B, so B = -2. Now, y = 4x-2 is the equation for l_2 and its x-intercept is found by substituting 0 for y. Thus, 0 = 4x-2, so $x = \frac{1}{2}$

13. The surface area of a sphere is $4\pi r^2$, where r = radius. This sphere has a surface area of $(4\pi)(5^2) = 100\pi$ square feet.

    This will require $100\pi \div 30 = \frac{10\pi}{3}$ containers of paint.

    The number of minutes needed = $(\frac{10\pi}{3})(20) \approx 209, \approx 3.5$ hours.

14. The volume of a pyramid = $\frac{1}{3}$ Bh, where B = area of base, h = height. For a rectangular solid, volume = Lwh, which represent length, width, and height. Since heights are equal and the pyramid's volume = half the rectangular solid's volume, $\frac{1}{3}B = \frac{1}{2}$ Lw. So, B = $(\frac{3}{2})$ (L)(W) = $(\frac{3}{2})$ (12)(9) = 162. Each side of the base $=\sqrt{162} \approx 12.7$

15. The domain is given by x such that $\sqrt{3-6x} \geq 0$; this means x ≤ 1/2. Since the lowest value of $\sqrt{3-6x}$ is 0, the minimum value of g(x) is -10. $T \cap V = \{t: -10 \leq t \leq 1/2\}$

16. For y = A cos Bx, the amplitude = |A| and the period = $|\frac{2\pi}{B}|$

    In selection D, amplitude = 3/2 and period = $2\pi/3\pi$ = 2/3

17. $\sum_{i=5} 22(2i^2 + 12) = \sum_{i=1} 22(2i^2+12) - \sum_{i=1}^{4}(2i^2+12)$ = 2[(22)(23)(45)/6] + (12)(22) - {2[(4)(5)(6) + (12)(4)]} = 7746

18. $\sum_{n=1}^{\infty} \frac{3}{4}(\frac{2}{3})^{n-1} = \frac{3}{4} + (\frac{3}{4})(\frac{2}{3}) + (\frac{3}{4})(\frac{2}{3})^2 + ... \frac{3/4}{1-2/3}$ = 9/4

19. Rewrite the equation as $(x-0)^2 + (y+5)^2 = 169$. This describes a circle centered at $(0,-5)$ with a radius of $\sqrt{169} = 13$.
The circumference $= (2\pi)(13) = 26\pi$

20. In a Normal Distribution, the further away from the mean which a particular data lies, the lower its frequency. 37 lies further from 30 than the distance from 24 to 30.

21. Convert 64 to a z-score (standard score) by the calculation $(64-67)/2.5 = -1.2$. Using a table of Normal Distribution values, Prob$(z<1.2) \approx .1151$. Finally, $(.1151)(500) \approx 58$

22. Rewrite $y = -1/3x^2 + 2x + 1$ as $y = -1/3(x-3)^2 + 4$, so the vertex is $(3,4)$. To locate the two points where the line $y = -1$ intersects the parabola, solve $-1 = -1/3x^2 + 2x + 1$. This can be simplified to $x^2 - 6x - 6 = 0$, from which $x \approx 6.87$ and $x \approx -.87$. The length of the line segment ≈ 7.74 and the height to the vertex $= 5$. Area $\approx (2/3)(7.74)(5) = 25.8$

23. Since $|3x+6|$ must be at least 0, $|3x+6| \leq 0$ can be simplified to $|3x+6| = 0$. Then, $3x + 6 = 0$, so $x = -2$

24. The amount of his fourth payment which is credited to paying the interest $= (875.40)(.156/12) \approx \$11.38$. Then, the amount credited toward reducing the principal $= \$120.00 - \$11.38 = \$108.62$

25. Let x = number of correct answers on Mary's test. Let y = number of wrong answers. Then, $x + y = 74$ and $2x - 1/2y = 133$. Solving, $x = 68$, $y = 6$. Thus, David must have answered 68 questions correctly, with no wrong answers. His final score was $(68)(2) = 136$

TEST 3

DIRECTIONS: Each question or incomplete statement is followed by several suggested answers or completions. Select the one that BEST answers the question or completes the statement. *PRINT THE LETTER OF THE CORRECT ANSWER IN THE SPACE AT THE RIGHT.*

1. In a right circular cone, water is being poured in at the rate of 80 cubic inches every minute. If the slant height is 25 in. and the vertical height is 20 in., how many mimites would be needed to fill two-thirds of this cone?

    A. 31   B. 35   C. 39   D. 43   E. 47

    1.____

2. Let the operation @ be defined as follows: x @ y = the sum of all odd numbers between (but NOT including) x and y.
   What is the value of (50 @ 650) - (54 @ 649)?

    A. 104   B. 429   C. 753   D. 1077   E. 1400

    2.____

3. At the Airtight Security Company, all employees must wear badges. Each badge has an identification number which consists of two letters, followed by two digits. (There are 10 digits, 0 through 9). The first letter must be one of the five vowels, followed by a non-vowel. The first digit must be odd, followed by any different digit. How many different badge numbers are possible?

    A. 2625   B. 4725   C. 5250   D. 5850   E. 6500

    3.____

4. If $|x-3| \leq 1/2$ and $|y-2| \leq 3$, what is the maximum value of $|x-y|$?

    A. 81/2   B. 71/2   C. 51/2   D. 41/2   E. 21/2

    4.____

5. The 20th term of a geometric sequence is 1/2 and the 14th tern is 8. To the nearest hundredth, what is the value of the common ratio?

    A. .63   B. .67   C. .71   D. .75   E. .79

    5.____

6. What is the minimum cardinality of a set for which the total number of proper subsets is more than 1,000,000?

    A. 24   B. 22   C. 20   D. 18   E. 16

    6.____

7. Let n(x) mean the number of elements in set x. Suppose sets x, y, z have the following properties: $n(x \cup y \cup z) = 70$, $n(x \cap y \cap z) = 3$, $n(x \cap z) = 18$, $n(y \wedge z) = 11$, $n(x) = 30$, $n(y) = 44$, and $n(z) = 28$.
   What is the value of $n(x \cap y)$?

    A. 5   B. 6   C. 7   D. 8   E. 9

    7.____

8. For a 50-digit number, it is known that the sum of the first 47 digits (from left to right) is 77. If the entire number is divisible by 20, which one of the following could represent the last 3 digits?

    A. 040   B. 160   C. 190   D. 220   E. 380

    8.____

119

9. A closed rectangular tank measures 2' by 3' by 4'. It is filled with water to two-thirds of its capacity. As the tank is placed flat on its sides, the water depth changes. What is the maximum possible difference in water depths?

   A. 1/3'   B. 2/3'   C. 1'   D. 1 1/3'   E. 2'

10. A number n has x distinct prime factors. If n is a positive odd integer, how many distinct prime factors are there for 2n?

    A. x   B. x+1   C. x+2   D. 2x   E. 2x+1

11. If $i = \sqrt{-1}$, what is the reciprocal of $5+3i$?

    A. $\dfrac{5-3i}{34}$ B. $\dfrac{5-3i}{16}$ C. $\dfrac{5-3i}{4}$ D. $\dfrac{5-3i}{10}$ E. $\dfrac{5-3i}{2}$

12. Points (1, 5) and (-1, 9) lie on a parabola. If the minimum value of y is found when x = 2, what is the minimum y value?

    A. 1 1/2   B. 2 1/2   C. 3 1/2   D. 4 1/2   E. 5 1/2

13. Which one of the following represents one of the foci for the ellipse whose equation is given by $16x^2 + 25y^2 = 16$?

    A. (-5/3, 0)   B. (-3/4, 0)   C. (-3/5, 0)   D. (5/4, 0)   E. (4/3, 0)

14. Which one of the following represents the equation of a circle for which a diameter has endpoints at (-6, 3) and (2, 5)?

    A. $(x+4)^2 + (y-8)^2 = 64$
    B. $(x+3)^2 + (y-7)^2 = 40$
    C. $(x+3)^2 + (y-6)^2 = 35$
    D. $(x+2)^2 + (y-5)^2 = 21$
    E. $(x+2)^2 + (y-4)^2 = 17$

15. A sample consists of three 6's, two 7's, and three of an unknown number. If the sample mean is 10, what is the value of the unknown number?

    A. 17   B. 16   C. 15   D. 14   E. 13

16. What is the approximate distance between the centers of the circles given by $x^2 + y^2 - 12x + 10y + 20 = 0$ and $8x^2 + 8y^2 + 16x + 2y - 1 = 0$?

    A. 5.3   B. 6.1   C. 6.9   D. 7.7   E. 8.5

17. If sec x = y, which one of the following must be true?

    A. $x = \arctan(y^2-1)^{1/2}$
    B. $y = \text{arcsec } x$
    C. $x = \arcsin(y^2+1)$
    D. $y = \arccos(1-x)$
    E. $x = \text{arccot}(y-1)^{3/2}$

18. A coin is tossed 80 times. If the probability of getting tails on any single toss is .75, what is the probability of getting exactly 65 tails?

    A. .14   B. .11   C. .08   D. .05   E. .02

19. In a certain obtuse triangle, the sides are 7, 7, and x. Which of the following accurately describes all the possible values of x?

   A. $7 < x < 7\sqrt{2}$
   B. $7 \leq x \leq 7\sqrt{2}$
   C. $7 < x < 14$
   D. $7\sqrt{2} < x < 14$
   E. $7\sqrt{2} \leq x \leq 14$

20. $\begin{array}{r} AB \\ +CD \\ \hline AAA \end{array}$ In this addition problem, A, B, C each represent a non-zero digit. What is the value of A + B + C + D? (A, B, C, D are all different.)

   A. 15   B. 18   C. 21   D. 24   E. 27

21. An inlet pipe can fill a pool in 15 minutes and an outlet pipe can empty this pool in 40 minutes. Suppose the inlet pipe is used alone for 10 minutes, after which time both the inlet and outlet pipes are used until the pool is full.
For how many minutes will the outlet pipe have been used?

   A. 8   B. 9   C. 10   D. 11   E. 12

22. If $f(x) = 4e^x - 1$ and $g(x) = \log_{10}x$, what is the value of $f(g(2))$?

   A. 5.7   B. 4.4   C. 3.6   D. 2.3   E. 1.5

23. James takes 1/2 hour to get to work if he travels on the highway. If he travels on local roads, the trip is 3 miles shorter but requires 4/5 hour. His average speed on the highway is 24 miles per hour faster than his average speed on the local roads. What is his average speed, in mph, on the highway?

   A. 46   B. 48   C. 50   D. 52   E. 54

24. At a party, there are 5 husband-wife couples. If each wife gives a gift to everyone except her own husband, how many gifts are given?

   A. 20   B. 30   C. 35   D. 40   E. 50

25. What is the limiting value of $(3+x+2x^2)/(6+4x+3x^2)$ as x approaches infinity?

   A. 7/10   B. 2/3   C. 1/2   D. 3/7   E. 1/4

KEY (CORRECT ANSWERS)

1. C
2. C
3. B
4. D
5. A

6. C
7. B
8. E
9. D
10. B

11. A
12. D
13. C
14. E
15. B

16. E
17. A
18. D
19. D
20. C

21. A
22. B
23. E
24. D
25. B

SOLUTIONS TO PROBLEMS

1. Volume = $\frac{1}{3}\pi R^2 H$, where R = radius, H = vertical height. The radius = $\sqrt{25^2-20^2} = 15$ = 15 in., so the volume = $(\frac{1}{3}\pi)(225)(20) \approx$ 4712.4 cu.in. Then, two-thirds volume $\approx$ 3141.6 cu.in. Finally, 3141.6 ÷ 80 $\approx$ 39 minutes

2. 50 @ 650 = 51 + 53 + 55 + ... + 649 and 54 @ 649 = 55 + 57 + 59 + ... + 647. Upon subtraction, the result is 51 + 53 + 649 = 753

3. The number of different badge numbers = (5)(21)(5)(9) = 4725

4. If $|x-3| \leq 1/2$, $2\,1/2 \leq x \leq 3\,1/2$. If $|y-2| \leq 3$, $-1 \leq y \leq 5$. The maximum value of $|x-y| = |3\,1/2-(-1)| = 4\,1/2$

5. In a geometric sequence, the nth term = ar^{n-1}, where a = first term and r = common ratio. Then, $ar^{19} = 1/2$ and $ar^{13} = 8$. Dividing the first equation by the second equation, $r^6 = 1/6$. So, $r = (1/16)^{1/6} \approx .63$

6. Given a set with n elements (cardinality of n), the total number of proper subsets = 2^n-1. If $2^n-1 > 1,000,000$,
n > Log 1,000,001 < Log 2 $\approx$ 19.93. Thus, the smallest allowable value of n is 20

7. $n(x \cup y \cup z) = n(x) + n(y) + n(z) - n(x \cap y) - n(x \cap z) - n(y \cap z) + n(x \cap y \cap z)$. So, 70 = 30 + 44 + 28 - n(x∩z) -18-11+3. Solving, n(x∩y)=6

8. In order to divide by 20, the number must end in 0 and the sum of the digits must be a number divisible by 4. If the last 3 digits are 380, the sum of all 50 digits will be 88

9. The volume of water in the tank = (2/3)(2x3x4) = 16 cu.ft.
If the 4 ft. and 2 ft. sides are flat, the water level = 2 ft.
If the 4 ft. and 3 ft. sides are flat, the water level = 1 1/3 ft.
If the 2 ft. and 3 ft. sides are flat, the water level = 2 2/3 ft.
The maximum difference in water depths = 2 2/3- 1 1/3= 1 1/3 ft.

10. The number 2n has the same prime factors as the odd number n, with the addition of the factor 2. Thus, 2n has only one more factor than n.

11. The reciprocal of 5+3i is $\frac{1}{5+3i} = \frac{1}{5+3i} \cdot \frac{5-3i}{5-3i} = \frac{5-3i}{25-9i^2} = \frac{5-3i}{34}$

12. The equation of this parabola is $y = A(x-2)^2 + B$, where A, B are constants. Since (1,5) and (-1,9) lie on this parabola, $5 = A(1-2)^2 + B$ and $9 = (-1-2)^2 + B$. Then, A = 1/2, B = 4 1/2, so $y = 1/2(x-2)^2 + 4\,1/2$. When x = 2, y = 4 1/2

13. Rewriting the equation as $\frac{x^2}{1}+\frac{y^2}{16/25}=1$, the ellipse is centered at (0,0), the major axis $=2(\sqrt{1})=2$, and the length of the minor axis $=2(\sqrt{16/25})=\frac{8}{5}$. Then, a = half the length of the 4 major axis = 1 and b = half the length of the minor axis $=\frac{4}{5}$. So, c = distance from center to either focus $=\sqrt{a^2-b^2}=\frac{3}{5}$. Thus, one focus is located at $(-\frac{3}{5},0)$. The other focus is found at $(\frac{3}{5},0)$.

14. The center of this circle is the midpoint of the line segment joining (-6,3) and (2,5) = (-2,4). The length of the diameter $= \sqrt{(-6-2)^2+(3-5)^2}=\sqrt{68}=2\sqrt{17}$. So, the radius' length $=\sqrt{17}$. The equation is $(x+2)^2 + (y-4)^2 = 17$

15. Let x = sample mean. Then, $\frac{(3)(6)+(2)(7)+3x}{8}=10$. Solving, x = 16

16. Rewrite $x^2 + y^2 - 12x + 10y + 20 = 0$ as $(x-6)^2 + (y+5)^2 = 41$ and rewrite $8x^2 + 8y^2 + 16x + 2y - 1 = 0$ as $(x+1)^2+(y+\frac{1}{8})^2=\frac{73}{65}$
The centers of these circles are (6,-5) and (-1,-1/8), 0 respectively. The distance between these centers = $\sqrt{[6-(-1)]^2+[-5-(-1/8)]^2} \approx \sqrt{72.8} \approx 8.5$

17. $\tan^2 x + 1 = \sec^2 x$, so $\tan^2 x = y^2-1$. Then, $\tan x = (y^2-1)^{\frac{1}{2}}$, and $x = \arctan(y^2-1)^{\frac{1}{2}}$,

18. The probability is given by $({}_{80}C_{65})(.75)^{65}(.25)^{15}$, where ${}_{80}C_{65}$ means the number of combinations of 80 items taken 65 at a time. Since ${}_{80}C_{65} \approx 6.636 \times 10$, $({}_{80}C_{65})(.75)^{65}(.25)^{15} \approx .05$

19. The obtuse angle must lie between the two sides which are 7. The 3rd side must be less than the sum of the other two sides, so x < 14. Also, since the obtuse angle lies opposite side $x^2 > 7^2+7^2$, so $x > \sqrt{98} = 7\sqrt{2}$. Thus, $7/2 < x < 14$

20. Since the sum of two 2-digit numbers is a 3-digit number, A = 1. Now in the ten's column, 1 + C = 1, and since C ≠ 0, C = 9. In the units column, B + D = 11 (B+D ≠ 1, since this would force B = 0 or D = 0). Thus, A+B+C+D=21

21. Let x = number of minutes the outlet pipe is used, x + 10 = number of minutes the inlet pipe is used. Then, (10+x)/15 -x/40 = 1. Solving, x = 8

22. $f(y(x)) = f(\log_{10}x) = 4e^{\log 10x} - 1$. Now, $f(g(2)) = 4e^{\log 102} 1 \approx 4e^{.301} - 1 \approx 4.4$

23. Let x = highway speed, x-24 = local road's speed. Then, $\frac{1}{2}x = \frac{4}{5}(x-24)+3$, since the trip on local roads is 3 miles o shorter than the trip on the highway. Solving, x = 54 miles per hour.

24. Each wife gives a gift to 8 other people (everyone except her husband). Since there are 5 wives, (8)(5) = 40 gifts are exchanged.

25. If f(x)/g(x) represent two functions of x with the identical highest exponent, the limiting value as x approaches infinity is the ratio of the respective coefficients of the highest exponent of x. Thus, the limit = 2/3

TEST 4

DIRECTIONS: Each question or incomplete statement is followed by several suggested answers or completions. Select the one that BEST answers the question or completes the statement. *PRINT THE LETTER OF THE CORRECT ANSWER IN THE SPACE AT THE RIGHT.*

1. George just bought 3 replacement cutters for his electric shaver. As he was unpacking the new cutters, he accidentally mixed them with the 3 old cutters.
   If all 6 cutters look identical, what is the probability that he will insert at least 2 replacement cutters when he randomly selects any 3 cutters?

   A. $\dfrac{1}{10}$ B. $\dfrac{1}{5}$ C. $\dfrac{1}{3}$ D. $\dfrac{2}{5}$ E. $\dfrac{2}{3}$

2. Suppose Sharon deposits $800 at the end of each of the months January, February, March, and April into a bank which pays annual interest at 6% compounded monthly. What is the accumulated value of these deposits at the end of April?

   A. $3392   B. $3336   C. $3280   D. $3224   E. $3200

3. A particular dance routine calls for 2 steps forward, 3 steps backward, and 1 complete turn. If each of the movements counts as one beat, which of the following is the correct sequence for the 40th, 41st, 42nd, and 43rd beats if the given sequence is always repeated?

   A. 1 backward, 1 turn, 2 forward
   B. 2 backward, 1 turn, 1 forward
   C. 2 forward, 2 backward
   D. 1 forward, 3 backward
   E. 1 turn, 2 forward, 1 backward

4. A function has zeros at 3i, -3i, and -2. Which of the following is the location of the y-intercept?

   A. (0, -2)   B. (0, 4)   C. (0, 8)   D. (0, 14)   E. (0, 18)

5. Suppose (m)(n)(p) = 60, and m<n<p. If m, n, p are positive integers and m>1, what is the smallest possible value of mp?

   A. 6   B. 9   C. 12   D. 15   E. 20

6. If 8Ln(-x) = 1/2, what is the value of e^x? (approximately)

   A. .345   B. .254   C. .172   D. .125   E. .063

7. The height of an object is given by $h = -16t^2 + 160t + 100$, where h = height in feet (above ground level) and t = time in seconds. What is the maximum height, in feet, which this object will reach?

   A. 350   B. 425   C. 500   D. 575   E. 650

8. A closed cylinder has a surface area of 308 square inches. If the height is three times as large as the radius, how long, in inches, is the radius?

   A. 5.6   B. 4.9   C. 4.2   D. 3.5   E. 2.8

9. A sphere with a radius of 4 feet is being filled with liquid at the rate of 5 cubic feet per minute. How many minutes are required to fill this sphere to 80% capacity?

A. 43   B. 47   C. 50   D. 54   E. 57

10. What is the value of $\lim_{x \to \infty} (2x+5x^2)/(5+3x^2)$?

A. $\frac{2}{5}$ B. $\frac{7}{8}$ C. $\frac{5}{3}$ D. $\frac{9}{5}$ E. $\frac{11}{4}$

11. What is the approximate area of a circle whose equation is given by $x^2+y^2-6x+12y+9 = 0$?

A. 89   B. 97   C. 105   D. 113   E. 121

12. A parabola contains the points (1,3) and (7,3). The maximum y value is found when x = 4. If the y-intercept is (0,.9), what is the maximum y value?

A. 5.2   B. 5.7   C. 6.2   D. 6.7   E. 7.2

13. In the diagram shown at the right, $\angle Q = 15$, PR = 40, and O is the center of the circle. If RT = 10 inches, what is the approximate length, in inches, of PS?

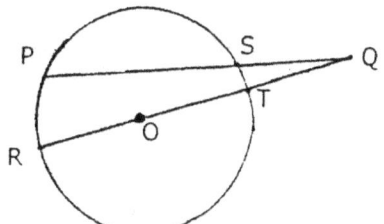

A. 17.3
B. 15.8
C. 14.3
D. 12.8
E. 11.3

14. If $x=\dfrac{w}{y^2}$ and $y=\dfrac{w^2}{y}$, which of the following is equivalent to $\dfrac{w}{y}$?

A. $\sqrt[3]{xt}$ B. $\sqrt{xt}$ C. x^3/t^3 D. x^2t^2 E. x^3t^3

15. An annuity of $15,000 per year is to be paid out at the end of the years 1997, 1998, and 1999. If money is worth 12% per year compounded annually, what is the value of this annuity at the end of 1996?

A. $24,817   B. $28,587   C. $32,367   D. $36,027   E. $40,157

16. A large tank holds 60 liters of a solution which is 30% acid. How many liters should be drained and replaced with pure acid to raise the solution to 40% acid?

A. 8.57   B. 9.47   C. 10.37   D. 11.27   E. 12.17

17. 3 apples, 2 oranges, and 5 pears cost $2.90; 2 apples, 5 oranges, and 4 pears cost $3.39; 5 apples, 3 oranges, and 2 pears cost $3.07. What is the cost of 4 apples, 1 orange, and 3 pears?

A. $2.33   B. $2.56   C. $2.79   D. $3.02   E. $3.25

18. There are 3 jars of marbles, each with 8 marbles. If the ratio of marbles is changed to 4:3:1, how many marbles must be taken from the jar which will eventually have the fewest marbles?

   A. 6   B. 5   C. 4   D. 3   E. 2

19. In the diagram shown at the right, KLMIIP is a regular pentagon, L, M, Q are collinear, and P, N, R are collinear. What is the value of $\angle Q + \angle R$?

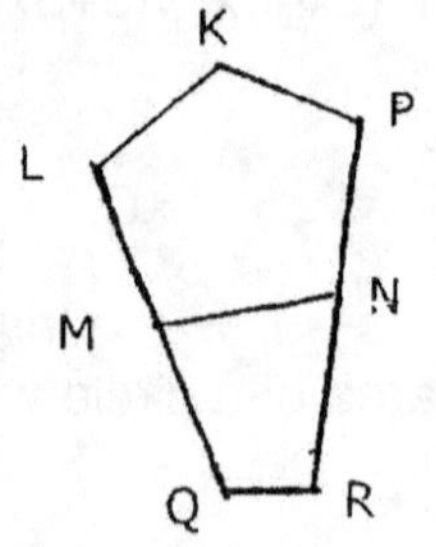

   A. 180°
   B. 192°
   C. 204°
   D. 216°
   E. 228°

20. A sample of numbers has a mean of 20 and a standard deviation of 3. One particular number in this sample has a standard score of 2. What is its actual raw score?

   A. 6   B. 16   C. 26   D. 36   E. 46

21. If $3\cos^2 x + 4\cos x - 4 = 0$, what are all the allowable values of x if $0° \le x \le 360°$?

   A. 228°
   B. 48°, 132°
   C. 228°, 312°
   D. 132°
   E. 48°, 312°

22. The foci of an ellipse are located at (-7,0) and (7,0). The length of the major axis is 50. What is the ratio of the major axis to the minor axis?

   A. $\dfrac{25}{7}$ B. $\dfrac{25}{24}$ C. $\dfrac{24}{25}$ D. $\dfrac{7}{24}$ E. $\dfrac{7}{25}$

23. Janet bought a total of 30 items, consisting of pens and pencils. If the cost of each pen was $.45 and she bought x pens, which of the following expressions represents the cost of each pencil if the total cost of all 30 items is C?

   A. (C-.45x)/(30-x)
   B. (30C-.45x)/(.45-x)
   C. (C-.45)/(x-30)
   D. (30C-.45x)/(30-x)
   E. (30C-x)/(x-.45)

24. Let $f(x) = 3e^{-x}$ and $h(x) = \operatorname{Ln} 2x$. What is the exact value of $[f(x)][h^{-1}(x)]$?

   A. $\dfrac{2}{5}$ B. $\dfrac{2}{3}$ C. $\dfrac{3}{4}$ D. $\dfrac{5}{4}$ E. $\dfrac{3}{2}$

25. How many different permutations are possible when using all the letters in the word INTENTIONAL?

   A. 39,916,800
   B. 15,735,400
   C. 3,628,800
   D. 1,663,200
   E. 940,600

KEY (CORRECT ANSWERS)

1. B
2. D
3. B
4. E
5. C

6. A
7. C
8. D
9. A
10. C

11. D
12. B
13. E
14. A
15. D

16. A
17. A
18. B
19. D
20. C

21. E
22. B
23. A
24. E
25. D

SOLUTIONS TO PROBLEMS

1. The total number of combinations of 3 items from 6 is $(6)(5)(4)/3! = 20$. The number of combinations of exactly 2 correct (new) cutters is $_3C_2 = (3)(2)/2! = 3$ and the number of combinations of all 3 correct cutters is 1. Thus, the required probability = $(3+1)/20 = 1/5$

2. Each month, the interest is $.06/12 = .005$. The accumulated value of all 4 deposits = $\$800(1.005)^3 + \$800(1.005)^2 + \$800(1.005)^1 + \$800 \approx \$3224$

3. After 6 beats, the sequence repeats. Since $40 \div 6$ leaves a remainder of 4, the 40th beat corresponds to the 4th beat. The correct sequence would correspond to the 4th, 5th, 6th, and 1st beats, which are 2 backward, 1 turn, 1 forward.

4. Let $y = f(x) = (x-3i)(x+3i)(x-2) = x^3 + 2x^2 + 9x + 18$. When $x = 0$, $y = 18$

5. Since m must be at least 2, there are only 3 possible combinations for m, n, p, respectively, namely: 2, 3, 10; 2, 5, 6; and 3, 4, 5. The second combination shows the least value of $mp = 12$.

6. $8\text{Ln}(-x) = 1/2$ is equivalent to $\text{Ln}(-x) = \dfrac{1}{16}$. This becomes $-x = e^{\frac{1}{16}}$, so $x \approx -1.0645$. Finally, $e^{1.0645} \approx .345$.

7. Rewrite $h = -16t^2 + 160t + 100$ as $h = -16(t-5)^2 + 500$. When $t = 5$, this object's height = 500 feet, which is the maximum height.

8. The surface area = $2\pi R^2 + 2\pi RH$, where R = radius, H = height. Since $H = 3R$, we have $308 = 2\pi R^2 + 6\pi R^2 = 8\pi R^2$. Then, $R = \sqrt{38.5/\pi} \approx 3.5$

9. The volume $= \dfrac{4}{3}\pi R^3 = (\dfrac{4}{3\pi})(64) \approx 268$ cubic feet. Then, $(.80)(268) = 214.4$. Finally, $214.4 \div 5 \approx 43$ minutes.

10. $\underset{x \to \infty}{\text{Limit}}[f(x)/g(x)]$ = ratio of coefficients of highest exponents of $f(x)$, $g(x)$ if those exponents are equal. Therefore, the limit = $\dfrac{5}{3}$

11. Rewrite the equation as $(x-3)^2 + (y+6)^2 = 36$. The radius must be $\sqrt{36} = 6$, so the area = $(\pi)(6^2) \approx 113$

12. $y = A(x-h)^2 + k$ is the general equation, where (h,k) is the vertex. Since $(1, 3)$ lies on the parabola, $3 = A(1-h)2 + k$, and since the maximum y value occurs when $x = 4$, $3 = A(1-4)^2 + k$ or $3 = 9A + k$. The point $(7, 3)$ would also lead to $3 = 9A + k$. Since $(0, .9)$ lies on this curve, $.9 = A(0-4)^2 + k$ or $.9 = 16A + k$. Then, by subtraction, $2.1 = -7A$, so $A = -.3$. By substitution, $k = 5.7$, and so $(4, 5.7)$ is the highest point on the parabola.

13. $\angle Q = \frac{1}{2}(PR-ST)$, so $15° = \frac{1}{2}(40°-ST)$. This means $ST = 10°$, so $PS = 180° - 40° - 10° = 130°$. The circumference $= (\pi)(10) \approx 31.4$ inches. Finally, the length of PS =
$PS = 31.4(\frac{130°}{360°}) \approx 11.3$

14. $xt = \frac{w}{y^2} \cdot \frac{w^2}{y} = \frac{w^3}{y^3} = (\frac{w}{y})^3$. Then, $\sqrt[3]{xt} = \frac{w}{y}$

15. The annuity's value at the end of 1996 = $15,000(1.12)^{-1} + $15,000(1.12)^{-2} + $15,000(1.12)^{-3} \approx $36,027

16. Let x = amount of the original solution drained. Then, $[.30(60-x)+x] \div 60 = .40$. Solving, $x \approx 8.57$ liters

17. Let x = cost of 1 apple, y = cost of 1 orange, z = cost of 1 pear. Then, $3x + 2y + 5z = 2.90, $2x + 5y + 4z = 3.39, $5x + 3y + 2z = 3.07. This leads to $x = .30$, $y = .35$, $z = .26$. Then, $4(.30) + 1(.35) + 3(.26) = 2.33

18. $24 \div (4+3+1) = 3$, so the number of marbles in the jars will be 12, 9, 3, respectively. The last jar will have lost 5 marbles.

19. Any exterior angle of KLMNP would have a measurement of $360° \div 5 = 72°$. Since $\angle NMQ = \angle MNR = 72°$, and the sum of all four angles in MQRN must be $360°$, $\angle Q + \angle R = 360° - 72° - 72° = 216°$

20. Let x = raw score. Then, $(x-20) \div 3 = 2$. Solving, $x = 26$

21. Rewrite the equation as $(3\cos x - 2)(\cos x + 2) = 0$. $\cos x + 2 = 0$ has no solution, but for $3\cos x - 2 = 0$, $x = \arccos \frac{2}{3} \approx 48°, 312°$

22. The length of the minor axis $= 2\sqrt{25^2 - 7^2} = 48$. Then, $\frac{50}{48} = \frac{25}{24}$

23. Let Q = cost of 1 pencil. Then, $.45x + (30-x)(Q) = C$. Solving, $Q = (C-.45x)/(30-x)$

24. Given $y = Ln2x$, to find $y^{-1}(x)$, rewrite as $x = Ln2y$ and solve for y. Then, $y = e^{x-Ln2} = e^x/2$. So, $h^{-1}(x) = e^x/2$ and $[f(x)][h^{-3}(x)] = (3e^{-x})(e^x/2) = \frac{3}{2}$

25. Since there are 11 letters, including 3 N's, 2 T's and 2 I's, the number of different permutations is given by $11!/(3! \cdot 2! \cdot 2!) = 39,916,800/24 = 1,663,200$

TEST 5

DIRECTIONS: Each question or incomplete statement is followed by several suggested answers or completions. Select the one that BEST answers the question or completes the statement. *PRINT THE LETTER OF THE CORRECT ANSWER IN THE SPACE AT THE RIGHT.*

1. A function Y = g(x) has zeros at 1, 4i and -4i. What is the value of g(2)?

   A. -12   B. -4   C. 4   D. 12   E. 20

2. A cylinder with a radius of 6 inches is being filled with water at the rate of 20 cubic inches per minute. If it takes 8.5 minutes to fill this cylinder to 50% capacity, what is the measurement of the height, in inches?

   A. 7   B. 9   C. 11   D. 13   E. 15

3. Mike deposits a fixed amount at the end of each month into a bank account which pays annual interest at 9% compounded monthly. If he deposits this amount at the end of each month January through June, and the present value of these deposits is approximately $1519.85, what is the amount of each month's deposit?

   A. $320   B. $305   C. $290   D. $275   E. $260

4. For any group of data, $p(x) = \left(\dfrac{L_x + \frac{1}{2}Ex}{N}\right)(100)$ is a formula which can be used to find the percentile for a given value x. P(x) is the percentile, Lx is the number of data less than x, EX is the number of data equal to x, and N is the total number of data.

   Given the sample 3, 3, 3, 2, 9, 5, 4, 4, what is the percentile for the number 4, to the nearest integer?

   A. 44   B. 50   C. 63   D. 75   E. 88

5. Bill traveled a total of 100 miles, part of which was city driving and the rest was highway driving. The total trip took 3 hours and his average rate for city driving was 20 miles per hour.
   If he traveled x miles in the city, which of the following represents his average driving rate on the highway?

   A. (100x)(x)/60
   B. x(60-x)/(100-x)
   C. (60)(20-x)/(100-x)
   D. (20)(100-x)/(60-x)
   E. (x)(100-x)/(3x-20)

6. If $\tan^2 x - 4\tan x - 5 = 0$ and $180° < x < 270°$, what is the approximate value of cos x - sin x?

   A. 1.38   B. 1.18   C. .98   D. .78   E. .58

7. A 90-digit positive integer has the 4 right-most digits missing. If the sum of the other 86 digits is 602 and the entire number is divisible by 9, which of the following could represent the last four digits, in order from left to right?

   A. 2341   B. 3253   C. 4515   D. 5192   E. 6743

8. If $\log_{10}x + \log_{10}Y = \log_{10}50$, and $x^2 + y^2 = 70$, what is the approximate value of $(x+y)^3$? 8._____

   A. 5081   B. 2217   C. 942   D. 170   E. 13

9. What is the approximate distance from the point (3,2) to the line represented by $2x + 5y - 10 = 0$? 9._____

   A. .75   B. .84   C. .93   D. 1.02   E. 1.11

10. If $w^3 - w^2 = n$ and w is a positive integer, which one of the following could be a value of n? 10._____

    A. 270   B. 180   C. 90   D. 50   E. 20

11. For the parabola $(y-1)^2 = 20x$, what is the equation of the directrix? 11._____
    x =

    A. -20   B. -5   C. -1   D. 1   E. 5

12. Given the equation $kx^2 - 9y^2 = 144$, if one asymptote is represented as $y=\frac{4}{3}x$, what is the distance between the foci of this hyperbola? 12._____

    A. 4   B. 8   C. 10   D. 16   E. 20

13. What is the sum of the first 10 terms of the series $1+\frac{3}{4}+\frac{9}{16}+\frac{27}{48}+....?$ 13._____

    A. 3.77   B. 3.85   C. 3.98   D. 4.12   E. 4.25

14. In the diagram shown at the right, O is the center of the circle, $\overline{PR}$ and $\overline{QS}$ are chords, $\angle PTS=95°$, $\widehat{PVS} = 160°$, and the circumference = 36π inches. What is the length, in inches, of $\widehat{QR}$? 14._____

    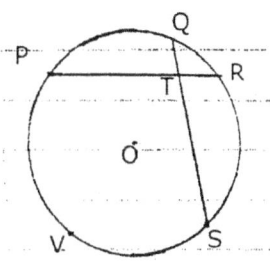

    A. 6π B. 5π C. 4π D. 3π E. 2π

15. How many different permutations are possible when using all the letters of the word APPROPRIATED? 15._____

    A. 15,751,000   B. 17,456,600   C. 19,958,400
    D. 21,654,200   E. 23,352,800

16. Two different mixtures of gasohol are available, one with 5% alcohol and the other containing 12% alcohol. How many gallons of the 12% mixture must be added to 60 gallons of the 5% mixture to produce a mixture containing 9% alcohol? 16._____

    A. 72   B. 80   C. 88   D. 96   E. 104

17. Bob and Linda are painting the lateral surface of an object in the shape of a right circular cone. Bob can paint an area of 10 square feet each minute. The radius of the cone is 14 feet and the height is 20 feet.
If Bob and Linda working together can paint the entire lateral area in 70 minutes, approximately how many square feet per minute can Linda paint alone?

    A. 9.5   B. 12.4   C. 15.3   D. 18.2   E. 21.1

18. In this diagram, square MNPQ has a length of 8 on each side, arc MRP is an arc of the circle with center at Q, arc MTP is an arc of the circle with center at N. What is the area of the shaded region?

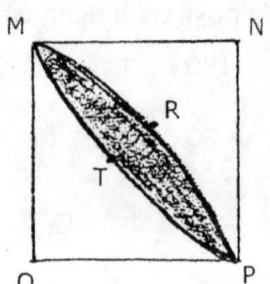

    A. $32\pi - 64$
    B. $16\pi - 32$
    C. $64 - 16\pi$
    D. $32 - 8\pi$
    E. $16 - 4\pi$

19. What is the length of the longest diagonal of a regular hexagon with a perimeter of 72?

    A. 12   B. 16   C. 20   D. 24   E. 28

20. What is the value of $\lim_{x \to \infty} (3+4x+6x^2)/(8x^2+3x+2)$?

    A. $\frac{3}{8}$ B. $\frac{3}{4}$ C. $\frac{3}{2}$ D. $\frac{4}{3}$ E. $\frac{8}{3}$

21. Let A, B, C represent 3 sets such that $A \cup B = A$ and $C \cup B = C$. which one of the following statements MUST be true?

    A. A is a subset of C
    B. $C = A \cup B$
    C. A equals C
    D. $A \cap B \cap C$ = empty set
    E. B is a subset of A and C

22. A sample of numbers has a mean of 30. One particular raw score is 66, and its standard score is 4.8. What is the value of the sample standard deviation?

    A. 7.5   B. 8.2   C. 8.9   D. 9.6   E. 10.3

23. Y varies jointly as W and Z^2. By approximately what percent will Y decrease if W is decreased by 10% and Z is decreased by 20%?

    A. 54   B. 48   C. 42   D. 36   E. 30

24. Which of the following represents the complete set of values of x satisfying (4x-1)(x+4) < 0?   24._____

    A. $-4 < x < \dfrac{1}{4}$ B. $-4 < x < -\dfrac{1}{4}$ C. $-\dfrac{1}{4} < x < 4$

    D. $-\dfrac{1}{4} < x < \dfrac{1}{4}$ E. $-\dfrac{1}{4} < x < 4$

25. Define Δ as follows: $x \Delta y = (x+2)/(y-2)$. What would be the value of $3 \Delta 4 \Delta 5$?   25._____

    A. $\dfrac{8}{15}$ B. $\dfrac{7}{10}$ C. $\dfrac{5}{6}$ D. $\dfrac{4}{3}$ E. $\dfrac{3}{2}$

KEY (CORRECT ANSWERS)

1. E   11. B
2. B   12. C
3. E   13. A
4. C   14. D
5. D   15. C

6. D   16. B
7. A   17. C
8. B   18. A
9. E   19. D
10. B 20. B

21. E
22. A
23. C
24. A
25. E

SOLUTIONS TO PROBLEMS

1. Since the zeros are 1, 4i, and -4i, g(x) can be written as $(x-1)(x-4i)(x+4i) = x^3 - x^2 + 16x - 16$. Thus, $g(2) = 2^3 - 2^2 + 16(2) - 16 = 20$

2. Volume $= \frac{1}{3}\pi R^2 H$. $(20)(8.5) = 170$ cubic inches = 50% of the volume, so $V = (170)(2) = 340$ cubic inches. Then, $340 = (\frac{1}{3}\pi)(6^2)(H)$ Solving, $H \approx 9$

3. Let D = the amount of each month's deposit. Then, $\$1519.85 = (D)[1-(1+.0075)^{-6}]/.0075$. This reduces to $\$1519.85 = (D)(5.8456)$. Solving, $D \approx \$260$. Note that .0075 is the monthly interest on 9% annual interest.

4. $P(4) = [4+1/2 \cdot 2] \div 8][100] = 62.5 \approx 63$

5. Let R = highway rate. Then, $\frac{x}{20} + \frac{100-x}{R} = 3$.
   This simplifies to $(100-x)/R = (60-x)/20$. Solving, $R = (20)(100-x)/(60-x)$.

6. Rewrite the equation as $(\tan x - 5)(\tan x + 1) = 0$, which leads to $x \approx 78.7°, 135°, 258.7°$, and $315°$. Since we have $180° < x < 270°$, use $x = 258.7°$. Now, $\cos 258.7° - \sin 258.7° \approx .78$

7. If the last four digits were 2341, the sum of all 90 digits would be 612. Since 612 is divisible by 9, the entire number must also be divisible by 9.

8. Since $\log_{10} x + \log_{10} y = \log_{10} xy = \log_{10} 50$, $xy = 50$ and $2xy = 100$. Now, $x^2 + 2xy + y^2 = (x^2+y^2) + 2xy = (x+y)^2 = 170$ Finally, $(x+y)^3 = [(x+y)^2]^{\frac{3}{2}} = (170)^{\frac{3}{2}} \approx 2217$

9. The distance from any point (x_1, y_1) to a line $Ax + By + C = D$ is given by $|A \cdot x_1 + B \cdot y_1 + C|/\sqrt{A^2+B^2}$. In this example, $|2 \cdot 3 + 5 \cdot 2 - 10|/\sqrt{2^2+5^2} = 6/\sqrt{29} \approx 1.11$

10. If $w = 6$, $6^3 - 6^2 = 180 = n$. If $w^3 - w^2 = n$ for any of the other four n values, w would not be an integer.

11. Given any parabola which can be written as $(y-h)^2 = 4cx$, the vertex is located at $(0,h)$ and the equation of the directrix is $x = -c$. In this example, $c = 5$, so $x = -5$ is the directrix equation

12. Rewrite the given equation as $\frac{x^2}{144/k} - \frac{y^2}{16} = 1$; since $y = \frac{4}{3}x$ an asymptote, $b = 4$, $a = 3$, $144/k = 3^2 = 9$, so $k = 16$. Then, $c^2 = a^2 + b^2 = 25$, so $c = 5$. The two foci are found at $(5,0)$ and $(-5,0)$, so the distance between them is 10.

13. The sum of a geometric series is given by $\frac{a-ar^n}{1-r}$, where a = first term, r = common ratio, and n = number of terms. Thus, we have $\frac{1-(1)(.75)^{10}}{1-.75} \approx 3.77$

14. $\angle PST = \frac{1}{2}(PVS+QR)$, so $95° = \frac{1}{2}(160°+QR)$. Then, we get QR = 30°. Let x = length of QR. Then, $\frac{x}{36\pi} = \frac{30}{360}$ Solving, $x = 3\pi$

15. Since there are 12 letters, including 2 A's, 3 P's, and 2 R's, the number of permutations = 12!/(2!3!.2!) = 19,958,400

16. Let x = number of gallons of the 12% mixture required. Then, (60)(.05) + (x)(.12) = (x+60)(.09). Solving, x = 80

17. The lateral area = $(\pi)(R)(S)$, where R = radius = 14 ft. and S = lateral height
    $= \sqrt{R^2+H^2} = \sqrt{14^2+20^2} \approx 24.4$ ft.
    So, lateral area = $(\pi)(14)(24.4) \approx 1073$ sq.ft. Let x = Linda's rate per minute. Then, $1073 \div (10+x) = 70$ Solving, $x \approx 5.3$

18. Connect M to N. Each of triangles MNP and MQP has an area of (1/2)(8)(8) = 32. The region enclosed by Q and arc MRP is a quarter circle with an area of $\frac{1}{4}\pi(8^2) = 16\pi$ region enclosed by N and arc MTP. Let x = shaded area. Then, $16\pi + 16\pi - x =$ area of square $= 64$. Solving, $x = 32\pi - 64$

19. Each side of ABCDEF = 72/6 = 12. △AGF is a 30°-60°-90° triangle, and so is △EHD. Thus, since $\angle AFG = \angle HED = 30°$, $AG = HD = \frac{1}{2}$ any side of ABCDEF = 6. GH = FE = 12. Finally, AD = 6 + 12 + 6 = 24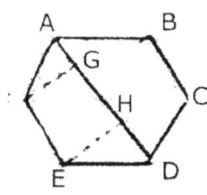

20. If f(x), g(x) are functions of the same degree, $\lim_{x \to \infty}[f(x)/g(x)] =$ ratio of leading (highest) coefficients $= \frac{6}{8} = \frac{3}{4}$

21. If $A \cup B = A$, B must be a subset of A. Likewise, if $C \cup B = C$, B is a subset of C.

22. Let y = standard deviation. Then, 4.8 = (66-30)/y Solving, y = 7.5

23. $Y = KWZ^2$, where K is a constant. The new $Y = (K)(.90W)(.80Z)2 = .576KWZ^2$. The percent decrease = $(1-.576) \cdot 100 \approx 42$

24. If 4x-1 < 0 and x+4 > 0, then x < 1/4 and x > -4, so $-4 < x < \frac{1}{4}$. Note: If 4x-1 > 0 and x+4 < 0, this would imply that $x > \frac{1}{4}$ and x < -4, which is not possible.

25. $3 \triangle 4 = (3+2)/(4-2) = \frac{5}{2}$. Then, $\frac{5}{2} \triangle 5 = (\frac{5}{2}+2)/(5-2) = \frac{9}{2} \div 3 = \frac{3}{2}$

MATHEMATICS

EXAMINATION SECTION
TEST 1

DIRECTIONS: Each question or incomplete statement is followed by several suggested answers or completions. Select the one that *BEST* answers the question or completes the statement. *PRINT THE LETTER OF THE CORRECT ANSWER IN THE SPACE AT THE RIGHT.*

1. If r + q = s and r + q + s = w, what does w equal in terms of r and q? 1.____

   A. 2r + q   B. 2q + r   C. 2r + 2q
   D. r + q + s   E. 2s + 2r + q

2. In a circle a chord is cut off so that it equals the radius. How many degrees are there in the central angle formed by two radii and this chord? 2.____

   A. 50   B. 52   C. 54   D. 57   E. 60

3. Find the shaded area formed by 4 overlapping squares, each having a 3" side and a 1" overlap. 3.____

   A. 36
   B. 32
   C. 30
   D. 24
   E. 22

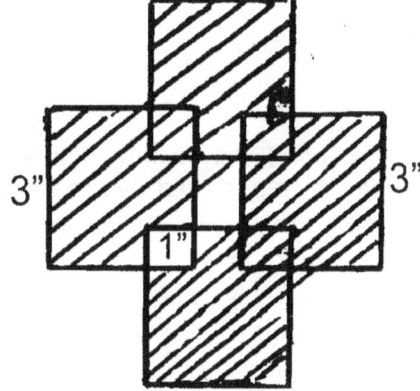

4. $(x+y)^2 - x^2 - y^2 = (?)$ 4.____

   A. 2xy   B. xy   C. 0   D. $2x^2 + 2y^2$ E. y^2

5. If x - 2 = x - 2, what does x equal numerically? 5.____

   A. Only 0   B. Any number   C. 7
   D. 2   E. 5

6. What approximate percent of 72 is 43? 6.____

   A. 56   B. 57   C. 58   D. 60   E. 61

7. What is the area of the shaded triangle? 7.____

   A. 9 1/2
   B. 10
   C. 10 1/2
   D. 11
   E. 12

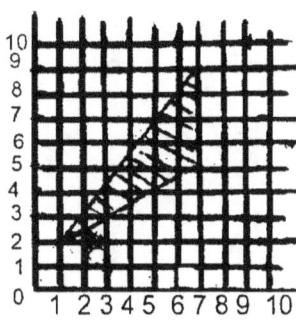

8. In a marine base 12% of the men are from California and 4% of these marines are from Anaheim. What percent of the men are from Anaheim?

    A. 48   B. 4.8   C. .48   D. .048   E. .0048

9. A book shelf is 4 feet long. How many books will fit on the shelf if each book is 3 1/3 inches thick?

    A. 11   B. 12   C. 13   D. 14   E. 15

10. The areas of the complete circles are x, y, and z. The areas of the portions of the circles are r, s, t, u and w. What is the area of x + y - z?

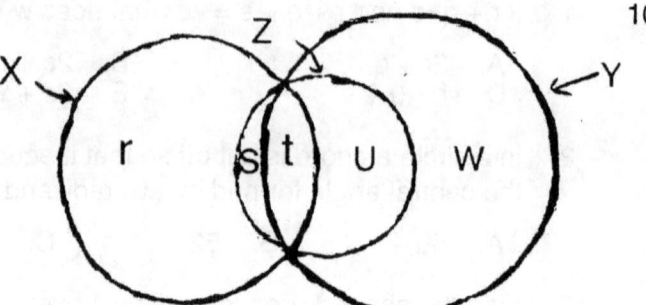

    A. r + t + w
    B. r + 2t + w
    C. s + t + u
    D. r + s + w
    E. s + u + w

Questions 11-15.

DIRECTIONS: Each of the questions below is followed by two statements, labeled (1) and (2), in which certain data are given. In these questions you do not actually have to compute an answer, but rather you have to decide whether the data given in the statement are *sufficient* for answering the question. Using the data given in the statements *plus* your knowledge of mathematics and everyday facts, you are to print in the space at the right the letter

    A. if statement (1) *ALONE* is sufficient but statement (2) alone is not sufficient to answer the question asked;
    B. if statement (2) *ALONE* is sufficient but statement (1) alone is not sufficient to answer the question asked;
    C. if *BOTH* statements (1) and (2) *TOGETHER* are sufficient to answer the question asked, but *NEITHER* statement *ALONE* is sufficient;
    D. if *EACH* statement is sufficient by itself to answer the question asked;
    E. if statements (1) and (2) *TOGETHER* are *NOT* sufficient to answer the question asked and additional data specific to the problem are needed.

11. The distance to John's house is 40 miles from his college. John went to school Friday but then returned home. *How long* did the entire trip take?

    (1) If John went 40 miles per hour faster it would have taken him half the time.
    (2) He traveled at a uniform rate, both going and coming, of 40 miles per hour.

12. $4x - 8y = 4$. $y = ?$

    (1) $x - 2y = 0$
    (2) $x = 5$

13. There are 75 people in the town that attend either meeting x or meeting y or both. How many attend each meeting?

    (1) 30 people attend meeting x *only*
    (2) 45 people attend meeting y

14. In triangle RST, how many degrees is angle R if

    (1) RS/ST = 1 (2) RS/TR = 1
    angle R = 60 degrees

15. In triangle RST, angle S is 90 degrees and SR = ST. Find the area of triangle RST.

    (1) SR = 5
    (2) RT = $5\sqrt{2}$

KEY (CORRECT ANSWERS)

1. C 6. D
2. E 7. E
3. B 8. C
4. A 9. D
5. B 10. A

11. D
12. B
13. E
14. C
15. D

SOLUTIONS TO PROBLEMS

1. Since $r + q = s$ and $r + q + s = w$, we get $r + q + r + q = w$. Simplified, $w = 2r + 2q$

2. In a circle with center O, if chord equals the radius, that $\triangle$ AOB is equilateral. Then, the central angle = 60°.

3. By adding up the areas of the 4 large squares, each little square has been added twice. The shaded area will be $(4)(3^2) - 4(1^2) = 32$ sq.in.

4. $(x + y)^2 - x^2 - y^2 = x^2 + 2xy + y^2 - x^2 - y^2 = 2xy$

5. Since $x - 2 = x - 2$ is an identity, x can equal any number.

6. $43/72 = .597 \approx 60\%$

7. Area = $(1/2)(base)(height) = (1/2)(4)(6) = 12$

8. The percent of men from Anaheim is $(.04)(.12) = .0048 = .48\%$

9. 4 ft. = 48 in. Then, $48 \div 3\frac{1}{3} = 14.4$. So, 14 books will fit on the shelf.

10. $x + y - z = (r+s+t) + (t+u+w) - (s+t+u) = r + t + w$

11. Let x = rate. Statement 1 alone is sufficient, since we could solve $40/(x + 40) = 1/2(40/x)$, yielding $x = 40$.
Thus, time = 1 hour. Statement 2 alone is also sufficient since letting x = time we get $x = 40/40 = 1$ hour.

12. Statement 1 alone will not be sufficient to solve for y, since substituting $x = 2y$ into the given equation yields $4(2y) - 8y = 4$ which has no solution. Statement 2 alone would be sufficient.
If $x = 5$, $(4)(5) - 8y = 4$, so $y = 2$.

13. Statement 1 alone would not be sufficient because we don't know how many people attended meeting y only and how many attended both x and y. Statement 2 alone is not sufficient because we don't know how many of the 45 attended both x and y, versus how many attended only y. Finally, the two statements together are still insufficient.

14. Each of statements 1 and 2 separately is not sufficient to find $\angle R$, but together they imply that RS = ST = TR. So, $\angle R = 60°$.

15. Statement 1 alone is sufficient because ST = SR = 5. Then, the area of the triangle is $(1/2)(5)(5) = 12.5$. Statement 2 alone is also sufficient because given RT = $5\sqrt{2}$ and SR = ST, we let SR = x. Then, $x^2 + x^2 = (5\sqrt{2})^2$. Solving, $x = 5$. Area of triangle = $(1/2)(5)(5) = 12.5$.

TEST 2

DIRECTIONS: Each question or incomplete statement is followed by several suggested answers or completions. Select the one that BEST answers the question or completes the statement. PRINT THE LETTER OF THE CORRECT ANSWER IN THE SPACE AT THE RIGHT.

1. A man runs 220 yards in 20.7 seconds. The first 90 yards he runs in 11.8 seconds. In approximately *how many* seconds does he run the first 100 yards if he runs the last 130 yards at a uniform rate?

    A. 12.0　　B. 12.2　　C. 12.5　　D. 12.7　　E. 13.0

2. The symbol $\begin{vmatrix} a & b \\ c & d \end{vmatrix}$ is called the *determinant* of the quantities a, b, c, d. The value of the determinant is (ad-bc). Find the value of the determinant $\begin{vmatrix} 2 & 3 \\ 3 & 1 \end{vmatrix}$

    A. 3　　B. -7　　C. 5　　D. 7　　E. -5

3. In the figure, angle B is obtuse, AP = 8, BP = 5, and Q is any point on AB. Which of the following expresses possible values of the length of PQ?

    A. 8 > PQ > 5
    B. 8 > 5 > PQ
    C. 5 > PQ > 8
    D. PQ > 8 > 5
    E. None of these

4. If a man buys several articles for n cents per dozen and sells them for n/9 cents per article, *what* is his profit, in cents, on each article?

    A. n/36　　B. n/12　　C. 3n/4　　D. 4n/3　　E. n/18

5. Five billion dozen eggs are used in the United States each year. If every twelfth egg is made into powder, *how many* billion eggs per year are powdered?

    A. 2　　B. 2 1/2　　C. 3　　D. 4　　E. 5

6. The symbols ° and * designate two different mathematical operations. If a° (b*c) = a°b*a°c, then the operation ° is said to be *distributive* with respect to the operation *. If ° represents the operation of multiplication (x), then * may represent which of the following operations:

    I. +　　II. -　　III. ÷

    The CORRECT answer is:

    A. I only　　　　　　B. II only　　　　　　C. I and II only
    D. I, II, and III　　　E. None of these

7. If the *additive inverse* of a number a is termed (-a) in the real number system, find the additive inverse of -7/2

    A. 2/2　　B. 2/7　　C. -7　　D. -2　　E. 7/2

143

8. If x = ay, where y does not equal zero, express a in terms of x and y.

    A. - y/x   B. x/y   C. xy   D. x+y   E. x-y

9. Which of the following has *no* finite value that can be determined?

    A. 0/3   B. 3 x 0   C. 0 - 3
    D. 3/0   E. None of these

10. The coordinates of P_1 are (1,4). What are the coordinates of P_2?

    A. (2,3)
    B. (1,2)
    C. (5,2)
    D. (2,2)
    E. (5,3)

Questions 11-15.

DIRECTIONS: Each of the data sufficiency problems below consists of a question and two statements, labeled (1) and (2), in which certain data are given. You have to decide whether the data given in the statements are *sufficient* for answering the question. Using the data given in the statements *plus* your knowledge of mathematics and everyday facts, you are to print in the space at the right the letter

A. if statement (1) *ALONE* is sufficient, but statement (2) alone is not sufficient to answer the question asked;
B. if statement (2) *ALONE* is sufficient, but statement (1) alone is not sufficient to answer the question asked;
C. if *BOTH* statements (1) and (2) *TOGETHER* are sufficient to answer the question asked, but *NEITHER* statement *ALONE* is sufficient;
D. if *EACH* statement *ALONE* is sufficient to answer the question asked;
E. if statements (1) and (2) *TOGETHER* are *NOT* sufficient to answer the question asked, and additional data specific to the problem are needed.

11. Given triangle ABC. How many degrees in angle A?

    (1) AB = AC
    (2) Angle B = 40 degrees

12. There are 24 pencils in a box. How many have both erasers and dull points?

    (1) 21 have erasers
    (2) 3 have dull points

13. Given equilateral triangle ABC and hexagon DEFGHI formed as in the figure. What is the ratio of the area of the hexagon to the area of triangle ABC?

    (1) Triangles ADE, BFG and CHI are all equilateral
    (2) AD = CH = BF

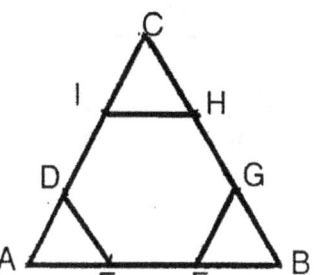

14. A and B go on a 300-mile trip by car. They take turns driving, each driving for eight hours. Find the average rate of each.

    (1) A drove 48 miles more than B
    (2) A averaged 6 miles an hour faster than B

15. A table is 30 inches long and 9 inches wide. It is covered by three overlapping napkins each 9 inches wide. *How long* is each of the napkins?

    (1) All three napkins are of equal length
    (2) If the table were 1 1/2 times as long as it is now, the napkins would just cover the table without overlapping.

KEY (CORRECT ANSWERS)

1. C	6. C
2. B	7. E
3. A	8. B
4. A	9. D
5. E	10. D

11. C
12. E
13. E
14. D
15. C

SOLUTIONS TO PROBLEMS

1. $(220 - 90) \div (20.7 - 11.8) \approx 14.6$ yds. per second for the last 130 yards. The time needed to run the 10 yards from the 90-yard marker to the 100-yard marker $10 \div 14.6 \approx .7$ sec. = Since he ran the first 90 yards in 11.8 seconds, his time, in seconds, for the first 100 yards $= 11.8 + .7 = 12.5$.

2. $\begin{vmatrix} 2 & 3 \\ 3 & 1 \end{vmatrix} = (2)(1) - (3)(3) = -7$

3. In $\triangle PQB$, $\overline{PQ}$ must be the longest side since $\angle B$ is obtuse. Then, $PQ > 5$. In $\triangle APQ$ $\angle Q$ is obtuse, so $AP = 8$ must be the longest side. This implies $PQ < 8$. Finally, $8 > PQ > 5$.

4. n cents per dozen articles means n/12 cents per article. His profit in cents on each article $= n/9 - n/12 = n/36$.

5. Five billion dozen ÷ 1 dozen = 5 billion.

6. Only statements I and II are correct since $a \cdot (b+c) = a \cdot b + a \cdot c$ and $a \cdot (b-c) = a \cdot b - a \cdot c$.

7. The additive inverse of $-7/2 = -(-7/2) = +7/2$

8. If $x = ay$, dividing by y yields $a = x/y$

9. 3/0 has no finite value since division by zero has no meaning.

10. Since P_2 lies 1 unit to the right and 2 units below P_1, the coordinates of P_2 are (2,2).

11. If $AB = AC$, then $\angle B = \angle C$, but we cannot determine the measurement of $\angle A$. If $\angle B$ is known to be $40°$, $\angle A + \angle C$ must equal $180°$, but we could not determine $\angle A$. These two statements together would be sufficient to determine $\angle A$. Since $\angle B = 40°$, $\angle C = 40°$. Then, $\angle A = 180° - 40° - 40° = 100°$.

12. The two statements together are insufficient. For example, we might have 21 pencils with erasers and no dull points along with 3 pencils with dull points but no erasers. Another possibility is 20 pencils with erasers and no dull points, 3 pencils with dull points and no erasers, 1 pencil with both an eraser and a dull point, and 1 pencil with no eraser and no dull point.

13. Statement 1 alone is not sufficient to determine the sides of the hexagon. Statement 2 alone is not sufficient since we do not know if $\triangle ADE$, $\triangle BFG$, $\triangle CIH$ are equilateral. So the sides of the hexagon are still unknown. Together, statements 1 and 2 are still not sufficient. (The required information would be: $\triangle ADE$, $\triangle BFG$, $\triangle CHI$ are equilateral and $AD = DI = IC$.)

14. Statement 1 alone is sufficient. Let x = distance driven by B and x + 48 = distance driven by A. Then, x + x + 48 = 300, so x = 126, x + 48 = 174. The average rates of A and B are 174/8 = 21.75 and 126/8 = 15.75. Using statement 2 alone, let x = average rate for B and x + 6 = average rate for A. Then, (x+6)(8) + 8x = 300. Thus, x = 15.75, x + 6 = 21.75.

15. Each statement alone is not sufficient, but taken together let x = each napkin's length.
Then, 3x = (30)(1 1/2) = 45.
Thus, x = 15.

TEST 3

DIRECTIONS: Each question or incomplete statement is followed by several suggested answers or completions. Select the one that *BEST* answers the question or completes the statement. *PRINT THE LETTER OF THE CORRECT ANSWER IN THE SPACE AT THE RIGHT.*

Questions 1-10.

DIRECTIONS: In each of the problems below, do *not solve the problem,* but simply indicate one of the following choices:
   A. if not enough information is given to solve the problem;
   B. if just enough information is given to solve the problem;
   C. if statement (1) is needed to solve the problem, but not statement (2);
   D. if statement (2) is needed to solve the problem, but not statement (1);
   E. if neither statement (1) nor (2) is needed to solve the problem.

1. The bases of an isosceles trapezoid are 6 and 10.
   Find the area of the trapezoid.

   (1) The diagonals of the trapezoid are 9.
   (2) The lower base angles are acute.

2. How far is A from C?

   (1) A is 10 miles from B.
   (2) B is 15 miles from C.

3. A cylindrical glass 6 inches high is full of water. How many lbs. of water does the glass contain?

   (1) A cubic foot of water weighs 62.5 pounds.
   (2) The diameter of the glass is 4 inches.

4. Find the height of the flagpole.

   (1) The shadow of a yardstick is 4 ft. long.
   (2) At the same time and place the shadow of a flagpole is 36 ft.

5. A man has 18 coins consisting of nickles and dimes.
   HOW many of each are there?

   (1) The total value is $1.20.
   (2) There are twice as many nickles as dimes.

6. Find each number.

   (1) Three numbers are in the ratio 5:7:9.
   (2) The middle number is equal to half the sum of the first and third numbers.

7. How many pounds of each does he use?

   (1) A dealer mixes coffee worth $1.80 a pound with coffee worth $2.10 a pound.
   (2) The mixture sells for $1.98 a pound.

8. The area of a square is 36 square inches. Find the side of the square. 8.____

   (1) A rectangle is formed equal in area to the square.
   (2) The length of the rectangle is 3 inches more than a side of the square.

9. Find the number of dollars invested at each rate. 9.____

   (1) A man invests a certain amount of money, part at 6% and the rest at 8%.
   (2) The total annual income from the two investments is $290.

10. Find each integer. 10.____

    (1) The sum of three consecutive integers is 33.
    (2) The largest of the three integers is 2 more than the smallest.

KEY (CORRECT ANSWERS)

1. C   6. A
2. A   7. A
3. B   8. E
4. B   9. A
5. D   10. C

SOLUTIONS TO PROBLEMS

1. 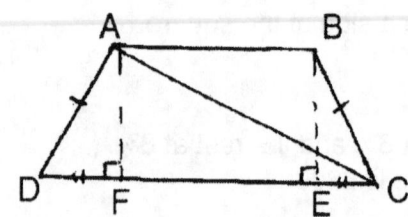 Let AB = 6, DC = 10. Using statement 1, in right triangle AFC, FC = 6 + 2 = 8, AC = 9, so The area of the trapezoid $\frac{1}{2}(\sqrt{17})(6 + 10)$ or $8\sqrt{17}$. This means statement 2 will not be needed.

2. There is insufficient information to find the distance from A to C. (Note that AC = 25 ONLY if points A, B, C are collinear.)

3. Using both statements together, the volume of the glass is Since a cubic foot of water weighs 62.5 pounds, the weight of water in the glass = $(62.5)(\frac{2}{3}\pi)$ = $41\frac{2}{3}\pi$ pounds.

4. Using both statements together, let x = height of the flagpole. Then, x/36 = 3/4. Thus, x = 27 ft.

5. Statement 1 is not needed. With statement 2 alone, let x = number of dimes, 2x = number of nickels. Then, x + 2x = 18, so x = 6. There are 6 dimes and 12 nickels.

6. Let the three numbers be represented as 5x, 7x, 9x. Since 7x = 1/2(5x + 9x) anyway, statement 2 is not needed. We now conclude that there is insufficient information to find each number.

7. There is insufficient information to find the number of pounds of each type of coffee. The only conclusion we can reach is that UNEQUAL number of pounds of each type is used since $1.98 \neq (1.80 + 2.10) / 2$.

8. From the given information, each side of the square Neither of statements 1 nor 2 is needed.

9. Let x = amount invested at 6%, y = amount invested at 8%. Then, .06x + .08y = 290, if we use both statements. This is still insufficient to find x or y.

10. From statement 1, x, x + 1, x + 2 could represent the integers. Then, x + x + 1 + x + 2 = 33. Solving, the numbers are 10, 11, and 12. This means statement 2 will not be needed.

TEST 4

DIRECTIONS: Each question or incomplete statement is followed by several suggested answers or completions. Select the one that BEST answers the question or completes the statement. PRINT THE LETTER OF THE CORRECT ANSWER IN THE SPACE AT THE RIGHT.

Questions 1-5.

DIRECTIONS: Each of the data sufficiency problems below consists of a question and two statements, labeled (1) and (2), in which certain data are given. You have to decide whether the data given in the statements are *sufficient* for answering the question. Using the data given in the statements *plus* your knowledge of mathematics and everyday facts (such as the number of days in June or the meaning of *counterclockwise*), you are to print in the space at the right of the letter:

A. if statement (1) ALONE is sufficient, but statement (2) alone is not sufficient to answer the question asked;
B. if statement (2) ALONE is sufficient, but statement (1) alone is not sufficient to answer the question asked;
C. if BOTH statements (1) and (2) TOGETHER are sufficient to answer the question asked, but NEITHER statement ALONE is sufficient;
D. if EACH statement ALONE is sufficient to answer the question asked;
E. if statements (1) and (2) TOGETHER are NOT sufficient to answer the question asked, and additional data specific to the problem are needed.

1. Which side of △ RST is the longest?

   (1) < S = 54 degrees, < T = 36 degrees
   (2) < R is a right angle

2. Is the sum of the three integers, x, y, and z, odd?

   (1) xyz = 105
   (2) The sum and the difference of any two of the numbers are each even, and y is odd.

3. What is the two-digit number Q?

   (1) The sum of its digits is 13 and the product of its digits is 36.
   (2) If it were multiplied by 2, the result would still be a two-digit number. .

4. If x and y are integers, is x+y odd?

   (1) xy = 6
   (2) x-y is odd.

5. x + y + z = (?)

   (1) x + y = 3
   (2) x + z = 5

6. Two variables in a scientific experiment are such that their product is always 1. If, for a certain time, one variable is greater than zero, less than 1, and decreasing, then which of the following describes the second variable?

    A. Greater than 1 and increasing
    B. Greater than 1 and decreasing
    C. Not changing
    D. Less than 1 and increasing
    E. Less than 1 and decreasing

7. If x, y, z, and w are all real numbers and none of them is zero, which of the following expressions can equal zero?

    I. $x+y+z+w$
    II. $x^2 + y^2 + z^2 + w^2$
    III. $x^3 + y^3 + z^3 + w^3$
    IV. $x^4 + y^4 + z^4 + w^4$

    The CORRECT answer is:

    A. I only   B. III only   C. II and IV only
    D. I and III only   E. I, II, III, and IV

8. If $x(x-y) = 0$ and if y does not equal zero, which of the following is true?

    A. $x = 0$ B. Either $x = 0$ or $x = y$ C. $x = y$
    D. $x^2 = y$ E. Both $x = 0$ and $x - y = 0$

9. If n is an integer and if the following are arranged in order, which integer is in the middle?

    A. n+3   B. n-9   C. n-4
    D. n+6   E. n-1

10. If ϕ is an operation on the positive numbers, for which of the following definitions of is $x \phi y = y \phi x$?

    A. $x \phi y = x/y$
    B. $x \phi y = x - y$
    C. $x \phi y = x(x + y)$
    D. $x \phi y = \dfrac{yx}{y+x}$
    E. $x \phi y = x^2 + xy^2 + y^4$

11. In the figure to the right, a card is covering part of the left number which is known to be in the hundred thousands. Which of the following is the only number that could possibly be the above product?

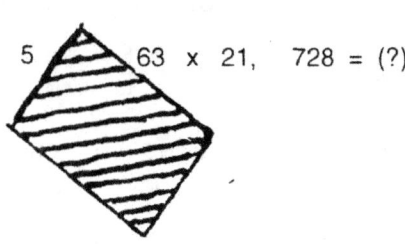
5   63 x 21, 728 = (?)

    A. 1, 107, 130, 464
    B. 1, 107, 130, 466
    C. 11, 076, 130, 444
    D. 11, 076, 130, 464
    E. 11, 076, 130, 466

12. If $x^2 + 2xy + y^2 = k$, where x and y are positive integers and x is odd and y is even, which of the following statements is true?

    A. k is odd and a perfect square
    B. k is even and a perfect square
    C. k is odd and not a perfect square
    D. k is even and not a perfect square
    E. None of these

13. If the average of 13 consecutive whole numbers is odd, then the product of the first and last of these numbers must necessarily be

    A. odd   B. even
    C. a multiple of 7   D. a multiple of 13
    E. a multiple of the average of the 13 numbers

14. How many of the numbers between 100 and 300 begin or end with 2?

    A. 20   B. 40   C. 180   D. 100   E. 110

15. A prime number is a number that can be divided only by itself and one. Which of the following is NOT a prime number?

    A. 101   B. 93   C. 53   D. 47   E. 17

16. If $2x + 2 > 8$, x must be

    A. < 8   B. < 5   C. > 3   D. > 4   E. > 6

17. Which one of the following must be excluded so that the remaining four are consistent?

    A. a > b   B. a > d   C. b > c   D. c > a   E. d > c

18. The sides of a triangle are 9, 12, and x. What are all the values of x for which the triangle will be acute?

    A. x < 21
    B. x > 3
    C. 3 < x < 21
    D. x < 15
    E. $3\sqrt{7} < x > 15$

19. The fraction a/b (a and b positive) will have a value greater than 2 if

    A. 2a = 2b   B. a > b   C. a > 2
    D. a > 2b   E. 2b > a

20. If Tom knows that x is an integer > 3 but < 8 and Charley knows that x is an integer > 6 but < 11, then Tom and Charley can *correctly* conclude that

    A. x can be exactly determined
    B. x may be either of 2 values
    C. x may be any of 3 values
    D. x may be any of 4 values
    E. there is no value of x satisfying these conditions

KEY (CORRECT ANSWERS)

1. D
2. D
3. C
4. D
5. E

6. A
7. D
8. B
9. E
10. D

11. D
12. A
13. A
14. E
15. B

16. C
17. D
18. E
19. D
20. A

SOLUTIONS TO PROBLEMS

1. From statement 1, $\angle S = 54°$, $\angle T = 36°$, so $\angle R = 90°$. Then the hypotenuse $\overline{ST}$ of this right triangle must be the longest. From statement 2, $\overline{ST}$ must be the hypotenuse, and so must be the longest side. Each of statements 1 and 2 is sufficient to find the longest side of $\triangle RST$.

2. From statement 1, if $xyz = 105$, then all three numbers must be odd. This implies $x + y + z$ is odd. From statement 2, y is odd and since $|x-y|$, $|x-z|$, $|z-y|$ must each be even, we know that x and z must also be odd. Thus, $x + y + z$ must be odd. Each of statements 1 and 2 is sufficient.

3. Let $10x + y$ represent Q. From statement 1 alone, $x + y = 13$ and $xy = 36$. Solving this system of equations, $x = 9$ and $y = 4$ or $x = 4$ and $y = 9$. Q = 49 or 94. Now using statement 2, we have $2(10x + y) < 100$. With both statements 1 and 2, Q must be 49 since 2(94) exceeds 100.

4. From statement 1, if $xy = 6$, one of x,y is odd and the other is even. So, $x + y$ must be odd. From statement 2, $x - y$ is odd would mean that one of x, y is odd and the other is even. Again, $x + y$ must be odd. Each of statements 1 and 2 is sufficient.

5. Using both statements together, we could determine only that $z - y = 2$. This would still be insufficient to determine the value of $x + y + z$.

6. If $0 < x < 1$, $xy=1$, and x is decreasing, then y must be increasing and $y > 1$. For example, if $x = .5$ and $y = 2$, when x decreases to .25, $y = 4$.

7. $x + y + z + w$ could be zero. (For example, $x = 1$, $y = -1$, $z = 2$, $w = 2$.) Those same values would also make $x^3 + y^3 + z^3 + w^3 = 0$. But $x^2 + y^2 + z^2 + w^2 > 0$ and $x^4 + y^4 + z^4 + w^4 > 0$. Only statements I and III could be zero.

8. Given $x(x-y) = 0$ and $y \neq 0$, then $x = 0$ or $x-y = 0$.
This means $x = 0$ or $x = y$.

9. The 5 selections arranged in ascending order are: n-9, n-4, n-1, n+3, n+6. Thus, n-1 is the middle integer.

10. If $x \phi y = \dfrac{xy}{x+y}$, then $y \phi x = \dfrac{yx}{y+x}$, which is equivalent to $\dfrac{xy}{x+y}$. Thus, $x \phi y = y \phi x$.

11. Since $500{,}000 \times 21{,}728 > 11{,}000{,}000{,}000$, only choices C, D, E are possible. Since the last digits of each factor are 3 and 8, respectively, the product must end in 4. We now eliminate choice E. Consider the first line of the multiplication. $8 \times 3 = 4$ with a carry of 2 and $8 \times 6 + 2 = 0$ digit in the ten's column. Another contribution to the ten's column will be the result of multiplying 3 (from the unknown number) by 2 (from 21,728) to get a 6 digit. The answer must now have a digit of $0 + 6 = 6$ in the ten's column. Only choice D is possible. Note: $11{,}076{,}130{,}464 \div 21{,}728 = 509{,}763$.

12. $x^2 + 2xy + y^2 = (x+y)^2 = k$. Since x is odd and y is even, $x + y$ is odd and so is $(x+y)^2$ an odd number. This means that k is odd and a perfect square.

13. The average of 13 consecutive whole numbers must be the 7th number. If this 7th number is odd, then both the first and last numbers must also be odd. Consequently, their product must be odd.

14. There are 10 numbers between 100 and 200 (non-inclusive) which end with a 2, namely 102, 112, 122,..., 182, 192. Between 200 and 300 (inclusive), there are 100 numbers beginning with a 2 (and some ending with a 2 as well), namely, 200, 201, 202,..., 298, 299. The total of numbers satisfying the given requirements = 100 + 10 = 110.

15. 93 is not a prime number since it has factors other than 1 and 93, namely 3 and 31.

16. If $2x + 2 > 8$, then $2x > 6$, so $x > 3$.

17. By excluding choice D, there is consistency among the others, so that a > b or d and b or d > c.

18. If x is the largest side, then $x^2 = 9^2 + 12^2$ will result in a right triangle. Solving, $x = 15$. This would mean if $x \geq 15$, this will not be an acute triangle. (If $x \geq 15$, this will be an obtuse triangle.) Now suppose x is the smallest side. The largest angle will lie opposite the side which is 12. We know that $12^2 = 9^2 + x^2 - (2)(9)(x) \cdot \cos$ (angle opposite 12). To maintain an acute triangle, cos (any angle) must be positive. To insure this, $12^2 - 9^2 - x^2$ must be negative. This leads to $x^2 > 144 - 81 = 63$, so $x > \sqrt{63} = 3\sqrt{7}$. Finally, the restrictions on x are $3\sqrt{7} < x > 15$.

19. If $a/b > 2$, then $a > 2b$. (Both a, b > 0.)

20. If x fulfills both $3 < x < 8$ and $6 < x < 11$, then $x = 7$ (if x must be an integer).

BASIC FUNDAMENTALS OF MATHEMATICS

PRINCIPLES AND APPLICATIONS

CONCISE TEXT

WITH PROBLEMS AND ANSWERS

* ARITHMETIC
* ALGEBRA
* LOGARITHMS
* GEOMETRY
* TRIGONMETRY

BASIC FUNDAMENTALS OF MATHEMATICS

		Paragraphs	Page
Chapter 1.	INTRODUCTION	1, 2	2
2.	PERCENTAGE	3–12	3
3.	RATIO AND PROPORTION		
Section I.	Ratio	13–15	5
II.	Proportion	16–21	7
Chapter 4.	POWERS AND ROOTS	22–25	9
5.	ALGEBRA		
Section I.	Introduction	26–31	
II.	Positive and negative numbers	32–42	
III.	Fundamental operations	43–50	
IV.	Factoring	51–61	
V.	Algebraic fractions	62–69	
VI.	Exponents and radicals	70–76	
VII.	Imaginary and complex numbers	77–79	
VIII.	Equations	80–86	
IX.	Quadratic equations	87–94	
Chapter 6.	GRAPHS		
Section I.	Basic characteristics of graphs	95–99	29
II.	Graphing equations	100–103	32
Chapter 7.	POWERS OF TEN	104–111	34
8.	LOGARITHMS	112–127	38
9.	PLANE GEOMETRY	128–142	43
10.	TRIGONOMETRY		
Section I.	Basic trigonometric theory	143–153	
II.	Natural trigonometric functions	154–164	
III.	Trigonometric laws	165–173	
Chapter 11.	RADIANS	174–176	59
12.	VECTORS	177–181	61
	ANSWERS TO PROBLEMS		62

BASIC FUNDAMENTALS OF MATHEMATICS

CHAPTER 1
INTRODUCTION

1. PURPOSE AND SCOPE

   a. Purpose. This section provides the basic mathematics required by students and candidates in all fields, including beginning and advanced students.

   b. Scope. This section covers those principles and applications of arithmetic, algebra, logarithms, geometry, and trigonometry that are required for practical understanding.

2. MATHEMATICS AND TESTING

   Skill in the use of mathematics, particularly arithmetic, algebra, and trigonometry, is essential in all fields of testing, including mental and general ability, school, college entrance, aptitude, achievement, civil service, professional, and advanced or graduate examinations.

CHAPTER 2
PERCENTAGE

3. General

a. Definition. Percentage is the process of computation in which the basis of comparison is a *hundred*. The term *percent*—from *per*, *by*, and *centum*, *hundred*—means *by* or *on the hundred*. Thus, 2 percent of a quantity means two parts of every hundred parts of the quantity.

b. Symbol. The symbol of percentage is %. Percent may also be indicated by a fraction or a decimal. Thus, $5\% = \frac{5}{100} = .05$. Figure 1 shows the relationship between fractions, decimals, and percentage.

c. Base, Rate, and Percentage.
(1) The *base* is the number on which the percentage is computed.
(2) The *rate* is the amount (in hundredths) of the base to be estimated.
(3) The *percentage* is a part or proportion of a whole expressed as so many per hundred. Percentage is the portion of the base determined by the rate.

4. Conversion of Decimal to Percent

To change a decimal to percent, move the decimal point two places to the right and add the percent symbol.

Example: Change .375 to percent.
  Move decimal point two places to right: 37.5
  Add percent symbol: 37.5%

5. Conversion of Fraction to Percent

To convert a fraction to percent, divide the numerator by the denominator and convert to a decimal. Then, convert the decimal to percent (par. 4).

Example: Change fraction $\frac{5}{8}$ to percent.
  Divide numerator by denominator: $5 \div 8 = .625$
  Convert decimal to percent: 6.25 = 62.5%
  Thus, $\frac{5}{8} = 62.5\%$.

6. Conversion of Percent to Decimal

To change a percent to a decimal, omit the percent symbol and move the decimal point two places to the left.

Example 1: Change 15% to a decimal.
  Omit percent symbol: 15% becomes 15
  Move decimal point two places to the left: 15 becomes .15
  Thus, 15% = .15.

Example 2: Change 110% to a decimal.
  Omit percent symbol: 110% becomes 110
  Move the decimal point two places to the left: 110 becomes 1.10.
  Thus, 110% = 1.10.

7. Conversion of Percent to Fraction

To change a percent to a fraction, first change the percent to a decimal (par. 6) and then to a fraction. Reduce the fraction to its lowest terms.

Example 1: Change 25% to a fraction.
  Change to a decimal: 25% = .25
  Change to a fraction: $.25 = \frac{25}{100}$
  Reduce fraction to lowest terms: $\frac{25}{100} = \frac{1}{4}$
  Thus, $25\% = \frac{1}{4}$.

Example 2: Change 37.5% to a fraction.
  Change to a decimal: 37.5% = .375
  Change to a fraction: $.375 = \frac{375}{1000}$
  Reduce fraction to lowest terms: $\frac{375}{1000} = \frac{3}{8}$
  Thus, $37.5\% = \frac{3}{8}$.

8. Finding Percentage

a. General. To find the percent of a number, write the percent as a decimal and multiply the number by this decimal. In this case, the *base* and *rate* are given. The problem is to find the percentage.

Example 1: Find 5% of 140 (140 is the base, 5% is the rate, and the product is the percentage).
  5% of 140 = .05 × 140 = 7

Example 2: Find 5.2% of 140.
  5.2% of 140 = .052 × 140 = 7.28

Example 3: Find 150% of 36.
  150% of 36 = 1.50 × 36 = 54

Example 4: Find $\frac{1}{2}$% of 840.
  $\frac{1}{2}\% = .5\%$
  .5% of 840 = .005 × 840 = 4.20
  Thus, $\frac{1}{2}$% of 840 = 4.20.

b. Application of Percentage. In communications-electronics, typical applications of percentage computation are used in determining tolerance values of resistors or in determining the efficiencies of motors and generators.

9. Finding Rate

To find the percent one number is of another, write the problem as a fraction, change the fraction to a decimal, and write the decimal as a percent. In this case, the *percentage* and *base* are given. The problem is to find the *rate*.

Example 1: 3 is what percent of 8? (3 is the percentage, 8 is the base, and the quotient is the rate.)
  $\frac{3}{8} = .375$

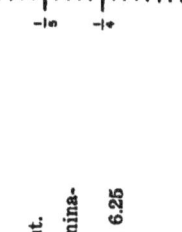

Figure 1. Relationship between fractions, decimals, and percentage.

$.375 = 37.5\% = 37\frac{1}{2}\%$

Therefore, 3 is $37\frac{1}{2}\%$ of 8.

Example 2: What percent of 542 is 234?

$\frac{234}{542} = .4317+$ (round off)

$.432 = 43.2\%$

Therefore, 234 is 43.2% of 542.

Example 3: 125 is what percent of 50?

$\frac{125}{50} = 2.50$

$2.50 = 250\%$

Therefore, 125 is 250% of 50.

10. Finding Base Numbers

To find a number when a percent of the number is known, first find 1% of the number, and then find 100% of the number. In this case, the *percentage* of the number and the *rate* are given. The problem is to find the *base*.

Example 1: 42 is 12% of what number?

12% (base number) = 42

1% (base number) = $\frac{42}{12} = 3.50$

100% (base number) = $100 \times 3.50 = 350$

Therefore, the base number is 350.

Example 2: 45 is 150% of what number?

150% (base number) = 45

1% (base number) = $\frac{45}{150} = .3$

100% (base number) = $100 \times .3 = 30$

Therefore, the base number is 30.

11. Expressing Accuracy of Measurements in Percent

a. *Relative error* is the accuracy of a measurement expressed in percent of the total measurement. In determining the relative error, it is first necessary to establish the *limit of error*.

b. The *limit of error* is the difference between the *true value* and the *measured value*. Assume that the reading on a scale, to the nearest tenth of an inch, is 2.2 inches. If the true value is 2.15 inches, the limit of error is the difference between 2.15 and 2.20, or .05 inch.

c. *Relative error* is computed by solving the ratio $\frac{\text{LIMIT OF ERROR}}{\text{MEASURED VALUE}}$, and expressing the result as a percent. In the scale reading above, the relative error $= \frac{.05}{2.2} = 2.27\%$, or 2.3%.

12. Review Problems—Percentage

a. Show each of the following in three forms—as a fraction or mixed number, as a decimal, and as a percent:

(1) $\frac{3}{5}$
(2) 50%
(3) .375
(4) $\frac{1}{4}$
(5) $62\frac{1}{2}\%$
(6) .6
(7) $\frac{3}{10}$
(8) 70%
(9) 2.25
(10) $1\frac{7}{8}$
(11) .08
(12) $\frac{3}{50}$
(13) .18
(14) $1\frac{1}{4}\%$
(15) .025
(16) .05
(17) $8\frac{1}{3}\%$
(18) $37\frac{1}{2}\%$
(19) 105%
(20) 4%

b. Evaluate the following:

(1) 250% of 60
(2) 125% of 40
(3) 200% of 2
(4) 225% of 400

c. What percent of a number is—

(1) 1.5 times the number?
(2) $2\frac{3}{4}$ times the number?
(3) $\frac{3}{2}$ times the number?
(4) $5\frac{1}{2}$ times the number?

d. Find the following:

(1) $\frac{2}{5}\%$ of 410
(2) $\frac{3}{5}\%$ of 416,000
(3) $\frac{2}{5}$ of 85
(4) 5.2% of 85

e. Solve the following problems:

(1) Find the relative error for a limit of error of .05 inch in measuring 24.2 inches.
(2) Find the relative error for a limit of error of 2 inches in measuring 200 yards.

f. Find the number when—

(1) 12% of the number is 52
(2) 15% of the number is 375
(3) 32% of the number is 166.4
(4) 8% of the number is 16
(5) 84% of the number is 168

CHAPTER 3
RATIO AND PROPORTION

Section I. RATIO

13. Understanding Ratio

It is often desirable, for the purpose of comparison, to express one quantity in terms of another quantity of the same kind. One way to express this relationship is by means of a *ratio*. For example, if one resistor has a resistance of 800 ohms and another has a resistance of 100 ohms, the first resistor has 8 times as much resistance as the second. In other words, the ratio between the resistors is 8 to 1.

14. Expressing Ratio

Ratio can be expressed in four different ways. For example, the ratio of 12 to 3 can be expressed as follows: 12 to 3, 12:3, 12 ÷ 3, or $\frac{12}{3}$. The numbers 12 and 3, which are the terms of the ratio, are called the *antecedent* and the *consequent*, respectively. The antecedent is the dividend or the numerator; the consequent is the divisor or denominator.

15. Obtaining Value of Ratio

Both terms of any ratio may be multiplied and divided by the same number without changing the value of the expression. In the ratio $\frac{12}{3}$, for example, the 12 is divided by 3, giving the value of 4. This means that the ratio 12:3 is equal to the ratio 4:1.

Example 1: What is the ratio of 6:2?
$$\frac{6}{2} = 3, \text{ or } 3:1$$

Example 2: What is the ratio of 7:3?
$$\frac{7}{3} = 2\frac{1}{3} \text{ or } 2\frac{1}{3}:1$$

Example 3: Find the ratio of the areas (par. 26) of two squares the sides of which are 6 and 8 inches, respectively. The areas of similar figures are in the same ratios as the squares of their like dimensions.
$$8:6^2 = 64:36$$
$$\frac{64}{36} = 1\frac{28}{36} = 1\frac{7}{9} \text{ or } 1\frac{7}{9}:1$$

Thus, the second square (8 inches on a side) is $1\frac{7}{9}$ times as large as the first square (6 inches on a side).

Section II. PROPORTIONS

16. Understanding Proportion

A proportion is a statement of equality between two ratios. If the value of one ratio is equal to the value of another ratio, they are said to be in proportion. For example, the ratio 3:6 is equal to the ratio 4:8. Therefore, this can be written 3:6 :: 4:8 or 3:6 = 4:8. In any proportion, the first and last terms are called the *extremes*; the second and third terms are called the *means* (fig. 2).

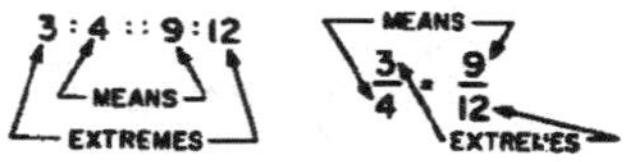

Figure 2. Terms of proportion.

17. Rules of Proportion

There are three rules of proportion that are used in determining an unknown quantity.

They also can be used to prove that the proportion is true.

a. In any proportion, *the product of the means equals the product of the extremes.*

Example 1: 3:4 :: 9:12.
3 × 12 = 36 (product of extremes)
4 × 9 = 36 (product of means)

Example 2: $\frac{3}{4} = \frac{9}{12}$.

Note. When the proportion is expressed in fractional form, the numerator of one fraction is multiplied by the denominator of the other fraction. This process is called *cross-multiplication*.

3 × 12 = 36 (product of extremes)
4 × 9 = 36 (product of means)

b. In any proportion, *the product of the means divided by either extreme gives the other extreme.*

Example: 6:8 :: 18:24.
8 × 18 = 144 (product of means)
144 ÷ 6 = 24 (one extreme)
144 ÷ 24 = 6 (other extreme)

c. In any proportion, *the product of the extremes divided by either mean gives the other mean.*

Example: 5:7 :: 15:21
5 × 21 = 105 (product of extremes)
105 ÷ 7 = 15 (one mean)
105 ÷ 15 = 7 (other mean)

18. Solving for Unknown Term

As demonstrated in paragraph 49, the unknown term of a proportion can be determined if the other three terms are known.

Example 1: In the proportion $\frac{5}{10} = \frac{10}{y}$, solve for y (the unknown quantity). Find the product of the means:
10 × 10 = 100
Find the product of the extremes: 5 × y = 5y

The products of the means and extremes are equal: 5y = 100
Divide both sides by 5:
$$\frac{5y}{5} = \frac{100}{5}$$
$$y = 20$$
Therefore, $\frac{5}{10} = \frac{10}{20}$.

Example 2: In the proportion 6:12 :: 24:y, solve for y.
Write the proportion in fractional form:
$$\frac{6}{12} = \frac{24}{y}$$
Cross-multiply.
6y = 288
Divide both sides by 6.
$$\frac{6y}{6} = \frac{288}{6}$$
$$y = 48$$
Therefore, 6:12 :: 24:48.

Example 3: In the proportion $\frac{z}{20} = \frac{5}{10}$, solve for z.
Cross-multiply.
10z = 100
Divide both sides by 10.
$$\frac{10z}{10} = \frac{100}{10}$$
$$z = 10$$
Therefore, $\frac{10}{20} = \frac{5}{10}$.

19. Stating Ratios for Problems in Proportion

When setting up a proportion problem, be sure to state the ratios correctly. Analyze each problem carefully to determine whether the unknown quantity will be greater or lesser than the known term of the ratio in which it occurs. Arrange the terms of the ratio as shown below, and solve for the unknown quantity as explained in paragraph 18.

$$\frac{LESSER}{GREATER} = \frac{LESSER}{GREATER}, \text{ or } LESSER : GREATER :: LESSER : GREATER$$

Example: The weight of 15 feet of iron pipe is 8 pounds. What is the weight of 255 feet of the same pipe? Let the unknown quantity be represented by the letter y. Since ratios must express a relation between quantities of the same kind, one ratio must be between feet and feet and the other between pounds and pounds.

Study the problems; 255 feet of pipe will weigh more than 15 feet of pipe. Arrange the first ratio in the order LESSER to GREATER—15 feet:

255 feet, or $\frac{15}{255}$.

Arrange the second ratio in the same order—LESSER to GREATER—8 pounds: y pounds, or $\frac{8}{y}$.

Write the proportion and solve.

15:255 = 8:y, or

$$\frac{15}{255} = \frac{8}{y}$$

$15y = 255 \times 8$

$15y = 2040$

$y = \frac{2040}{15}$

$y = 136$ pounds

20. Inverse Proportion

a. The ratio 2:3 is the inverse of the ratio 3:2. In proportion, when a second ratio is equal to the inverse of the first ratio, the elements are said to be *inversely proportional.*

b. Two numbers are inversely proportional when one increases as the other decreases. In this case, their product is always the same. In problems dealing with pulleys, the speeds of different size pulleys connected by belts are inversely proportional to their diameters. A smaller pulley rotates faster than a larger pulley.

Example 1: A pulley 30 inches in diameter is turning at a speed of 300 revolutions per minute. If this pulley is belted to a pulley 15 inches in diameter (fig. 3), determine the speed at which the smaller pulley is turning.

Let the speed of the smaller pulley be represented by y. Study the problem; the first ratio will be between inches and the second will be between revolutions per minute (rpm). Also note that the second pulley is smaller than the first and must make more revolutions than the first. Therefore, the answer will be a number larger than 300.

Arrange the ratios in the order LESSER to GREATER.

First ratio:

15:30, or $\frac{15}{30}$

Second ratio:

300:y, or $\frac{300}{y}$

The proportion:

15:30 = 300:y, or $\frac{15}{30} = \frac{300}{y}$

Solve the proportion:

$$\frac{15}{30} = \frac{300}{y}$$

$15y = 300 \times 30$

$15y = 9000$

$y = \frac{9000}{15}$

$y = 600$ rpm

Example 2: A 24-inch pulley is fixed to a drive shaft that is turning at the rate of 400 rpm. This pulley is belted to a 6-inch pulley. Determine the speed of the smaller pulley in revolutions per minute. Driving pulley (400 rpm, 24 inches in diameter). Driven pulley (y rpm, 6 inches in diameter).

$$\frac{6}{24} = \frac{400}{y}$$

$6y = 400 \times 24 = 9,600$

$y = 1,600$ rpm

21. Problems Using Proportion

a. A steel plate ½ inch thick, 12 inches wide, and 9 feet long weighs 183.6 pounds. What is the weight of a piece of steel plate of the same thickness and width if it is 16 feet 6 inches long?

b. If three men complete a certain job in 8 days, how many days would it take seven men to complete the same job, considering that they will work at the same speed?

c. If 3 resistors cost 25 cents, find the cost of 60 resistors at the same rate?

d. If the upkeep on 62 trucks for a year is $3,100, what would be the upkeep on 28 such trucks for 1 year at the same rate?

e. At a given temperature, the resistance of a wire increases with its length. If the resistance of a wire per 1,000 feet at 68°F is .248 ohm, what is the resistance of 1,500 feet; of 1,200 feet; of 1,850 feet; of 3,600 feet?

f. If 21-gage wire weighs 2.452 pounds per 1,000 feet, what is the weight of 1,150 feet; 1,540 feet; 1,680 feet; 349 yards?

g. The speeds of gears running together are inversely proportional to the number of teeth in the gears. A driving gear with 48 teeth meshes with a driven gear with 16 teeth. If the driving gear turns at the rate of 100 rpm, how many rpm are made by the driven gear?

h. A 36-tooth gear running at a speed of 280 rpm drives another gear with 64 teeth. What is the speed of the other gear?

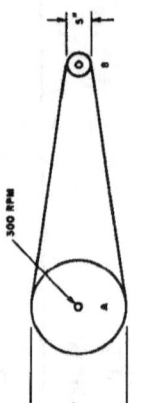

Figure 3. Pulleys and inverse ratio.

CHAPTER 4
POWERS AND ROOTS

22. Powers

There are many times in mathematics when a number must be multiplied by itself a number of times, such as $4 \times 4 \times 4 \times 4 \times 4$. This is written as 4^5 and is described as 4 raised to the fifth power. A number multiplied by itself once is said to be raised to the second power (squared). Thus, 5×5 is written 5^2. The number 2, written to the right and above the number 5, is the *exponent*; the number 5 is the *base*. The base number is a *factor* of a number written in exponential form because the product is evenly divisible by the base.

23. Roots

The root of a number is that number which, when multiplied by itself a given number of times, will equal the given number. The square root of 25 is 5, since 5×5 or 5^2 equals 25. The third root (cube root) of 216 is 6, since $6 \times 6 \times 6$ or 6^3 equals 216. The fourth root of 81 is 3, since $3 \times 3 \times 3 \times 3$ or 3^4 equals 81. Extraction of a root is generally indicated by placing, in front of the number, a *radical sign* ($\sqrt{}$). A small figure is placed in the angle at the front of the sign to indicate the root to be taken. If the small figure is omitted, it is understood that the operation required is square root.

Thus,

$\sqrt{25} = 5$
$\sqrt[3]{216} = 6$
$\sqrt[4]{81} = 3$

24. Finding Square Root of a Number

a. Finding Square Root by Mental Calculation. In some instances, the square root can be determined mentally from a knowledge of common multiplication. For example, $\sqrt{25}$ is 5, since 5×5 or $5^2 = 25$. Similarly, $\sqrt{144}$ is 12, since 12×12 or $12^2 = 144$.

b. Finding Square Root by Arithmetical Process. In most cases, the square root of a number must be determined by a mathematical process. If the number is a perfect square, the square root will be an integral number; if the number is not a perfect square, the square root will be a continued decimal.

Example 1: Evaluate $\sqrt{3398.89}$.

Step 1. Starting at the decimal point, mark off the digits in pairs in both directions.

$\sqrt{33\ 98.89}$

Step 2. Place the decimal point for the answer directly above the decimal point that appears under the radical sign.

Step 3. Determine by inspection the largest number that can be squared without exceeding the first pair of digits—33. The answer is 5, since the square of any number larger than 5 will be greater than 33. Place the 5 above the first pair of digits.

$\sqrt{33\ 98.89}$
 5

Step 4. Square 5 to obtain 25, and place it under 33. Subtract 25 from 33 and obtain 8. Bring down the next pair of digits—98.

$\sqrt{33\ 98.89}$
 5
 25
 898

Step 5. Double the answer, 5, to obtain a trial divisor of 10. Divide the trial divisor into all but the last digit of the modified remainder. It will go into 89 eight times. Place the 8 above the second pair of digits, and also place the 8 to the right of the trial divisor. Thus, the true divisor is 108. Multiply 108 by 8 and obtain 864. Subtract 864 from 898 to obtain 34. Bring down the next pair of digits—89.

$\sqrt{33\ 98.89}$
 5 8
 25
 898
$2 \times 5 = 10$ [8]   864
[8] $\times 108 =$ 3489

Note. With each new successive digit in the answer:
 1. Place the digit in the answer above the pair of digits involved.
 2. Place the same digit to the right of the trial divisor to obtain the true divisor.
 3. Multiply the digit by the true divisor. (Do not use the square boxes in actual problems.)

Step 6. Double the answer, 58, to obtain a trial divisor of 116. Divide the trial divisor into all but the last digit of the remainder. It will go into 348 three times. Place the 3 above the third pair of digits, and also place the 3 to the right of the trial divisor. Thus, the true divisor is 1163. Multiply 1163 by 3 to obtain 3489. Subtract 3489 from 3489. There is no remainder. Therefore 3398.89 is a perfect square and its square root is 58.3.

$\sqrt{33\ 98.89}$
 5 8. 3
 25
 898
 864
$2 \times 58 = 116$ [3]   3489
[3] $\times 1163 =$ 3489

Step 7. Check the answer by squaring $58.3 — 58.3^2 = 3398.89$. The complete calculation is shown below:

$\sqrt{33\ 98.89}$
 5 8. 3
 25
 898
$2 \times 5 = 10$ [8]   864
[8] $\times 108 =$ 3489
$2 \times 58 = 116$ [3]   3489
[3] $\times 1163 =$

Example 2: Evaluate $\sqrt{786.808}$.

Step 1. Starting at the decimal point, mark off the digits in pairs in both directions.

$\sqrt{07\ 86.80\ 80}$

Note. The extreme left-hand group may have only one digit. However, there must be an even number of digits to the right of the decimal point. If necessary, add a zero.

Step 2. Place the decimal point for the answer directly above the decimal point that appears under the radical sign.

Step 3. Determine the largest number that can be squared without exceeding the first digit—7. The answer is 2, since the square of any whole number larger than 2 will be greater than 7. Place the 2 above the 7.

$\sqrt{07\ 86.80\ 80}$
 2

Step 4. Square 2 to obtain 4 and place it under 7. Subtract 4 from 7 to obtain 3. Bring down the next pair of digits—86.

$\sqrt{07\ 86.80\ 80}$
 2
 4
 386

Step 5. Double the answer, 2, to obtain a trial divisor of 4. Divide the trial divisor into all but the last digit of the modified remainder. It will go into 38 nine times. Place the 9 above the second pair of digits, and also place the 9 to the right of the trial divisor. The true divisor is 49. Multiply 49 by 9 to obtain 441. However,

441 cannot be subtracted from 386, so the next lower digit must be tried. Substitute 8 for 9 in both the answer and the divisor and multiply 48 by 8 to obtain 384. Subtract 384 from 386 to obtain a remainder of 2. Bring down the next pair of digits—80.

```
         2 9.
    √07 86.80 80
       4
       ‾‾‾
       386
2 × 2 = 4  [9]
[9] × 49 =   441
```

```
         2 8.
    √07 86.80 80
       4
       ‾‾‾
       386
       384
       ‾‾‾
         280
2 × 2 = 4  [8]
[8] × 48 =   384
```

Step 6. Double the answer, 28, to obtain a trial divisor of 56. Divide the trial divisor into all but the last digit of the remainder. Since it is not possible to divide 56 into 28, place a zero above the third pair of digits and bring down the next pair of digits—80.

```
         2 8. 0
    √07 86.80 80
       4
       ‾‾‾
       386
       384
       ‾‾‾
         28080
2 × 28 = 56  280
```

Step 7. Multiply 280 by 2 to obtain a trial divisor of 560. Divide the trial divisor into all but the last digit of the remainder. It will go 5 times. Place the 5 above the fourth pair of digits, and also place the 5 to the right of the trial divisor. Thus, the true divisor is 5605. Multiply 5605 by 5 to obtain 28025. Subtract 28025 from 28080. There is a remainder of 55. Thus, the square root of 786.808 is 28.05, with a remainder of 55. A more exact answer can be obtained by adding pairs of zeros and continuing the square root process.

```
              2 8. 0 5
         √07 86.80 80
            4
            ‾‾‾
            386
            384
            ‾‾‾
              28080
2 × 280 = 560 [5]   28025
[5] × 5605 =          ‾‾‾‾‾
                         55
```

Check the answer by squaring 28.05 and adding the remainder ($28.05^2 + .0055$). Place the extreme right digit of the remainder under the extreme right digit of the squared number. The complete calculation is shown below:

```
              2 8. 0 5
         √07 86.80 80
            4
            ‾‾‾
            386
            384
            ‾‾‾
              28080
2 × 2 = 4 [8]
[8] × 48 =
2 × 28 = 56
2 × 280 = 560 [5]   26025
[5] × 5605 =          ‾‾‾‾‾
                         55
```

25. Review Problems—Square Root

a. Solve the following:

(1) $\sqrt{441}$
(2) $\sqrt{10089}$
(3) $\sqrt{2500}$
(4) $\sqrt{8.40}$
(5) $\sqrt{2510.01}$
(6) $\sqrt{4901.4001}$
(7) $\sqrt{7482.25}$
(8) $\sqrt{5759.2921}$

b. Solve the following to nearest thousandth.

(1) $\sqrt{5}$
(2) $\sqrt{7}$
(3) $\sqrt{11}$
(4) $\sqrt{13}$
(5) $\sqrt{15}$
(6) $\sqrt{17}$

c. The current (in amperes) flowing through a resistor can be determined by taking the square root of the quotient obtained by dividing the value of power supplied to the resistor (in watts) by the value of the resistance (in ohms). Thus, if a resistance of 300 ohms is absorbing 60 watts of power, it is drawing a current of $\sqrt{\dfrac{60}{300}}$ amperes. This equals about .447 ampere. In the same manner, find the value of current for each of the following values of power and resistance:

	Power (watts)	Resistance (ohms)	Current (amperes)
(1)	25	1,000	?
(2)	50	7,000	?
(3)	40	500	?
(4)	75	60	?

CHAPTER 5
ALGEBRA

Section I. INTRODUCTION

26. General

a. Algebra is an extension of arithmetic. All of the four basic operations of arithmetic—addition, subtraction, multiplication and division—apply also to algebra. Arithmetic deals only with particular numbers; algebra may also employ letters or symbols to represent numbers.

b. Algebra is often referred to as the shorthand language of mathematicians. The simplest example of the algebraic language is the formula, in which letters are used to represent words or numbers. For example, the area (A) of a rectangle can be determined by multiplying the length (l) by the width (w). Algebraically, this is stated as $A = lw$.

27. Algebraic Expressions and Terms

a. An *algebraic expression* is the representation of any quantity in algebraic signs and symbols; for example, $2x - 7$. A *numerical algebraic expression* consists entirely of numerials and signs, such as $8 - (6 \times 2)$. A *literal algebraic expression* contains only letters and symbols, such as $ax - ay$.

b. Each algebraic expression contains two or more terms, separated by one of the signs of operation $(+, -, \div, \times)$. The expression $3x - 4xy - 2y$, for example, contains three terms: $3x$, $4xy$, and $2y$. If the terms have the same letters and exponents, such as $3a^2x$, $9a^2x$, and $12a^2x$, they are called *similar terms*. Terms that do not contain the same letters and exponents, such as $3ab^2$, $3a^2b$, and $3x^2y$, are *dissimilar terms*.

c. If an algebraic expression contains one term, such as $3abc$ or $5a^4x^2$, it is called a *monomial*; if it contains two terms, such as $x - y$, it is called a *binomial*; and if it contains three terms, such as $5x^2 - 3xy - 2y^3$, it is called a *trinomial*. A more general rule of algebraic expressions states that any expression containing more than one term is called a *polynomial*.

28. Signs of Operation

In algebra, the conventional signs of operation $(+, -, \times$ and $\div)$ retain the same meaning as in arithmetic. In algebra, however, certain other signs may be used.

a. *Multiplication* may be indicated as follows:

Arithmetic	Algebra
$a \times b$	ab
$a \times b$	$a \cdot b$
$a \times b$	$(a)(b)$

b. *Division* may be indicated as follows:

Arithmetic	Algebra
$x \div y$	$\dfrac{x}{y}$
$(a+b) \div (a-b)$	$\dfrac{a+b}{a-b}$

c. The arithmetical signs for both *addition* and *subtraction* are retained in algebra.

Arithmetic	Algebra
$4 + 5$	$4 + 5$
$a - b$	$a - b$

29. Coefficients

Any factor of a product is known as a coefficient of the remaining factors. In the term $2x$, 2 is the numerical coefficient of x, f is the coefficient of $2x$, and x is the coefficient of $2f$. However, it is common practice to speak of the numerical part of the term as the coefficient. If a term contains no numerical coefficient, the number 1 is understood. Thus, abc is $1 \, abc$, and xyz is $1 \, xyz$.

30. Subscripts

In expression such as $R_1 + R_2 + R_3$, the small numbers or letters written to the right and below the literal terms are called subscripts. Subscripts are used to designate different values of a variable quantity. They are read: R sub 1, R sub 2, etc.

31. The Radical Sign

The radical sign $(\sqrt{\;})$ has the same meaning in algebra as in arithmetic (ch. 5). Thus, the expression $z = 2\sqrt{R^2 + x^2}$ states that z is equal to 2 times the square root of $R^2 + x^2$.

Section II. POSITIVE AND NEGATIVE NUMBERS

32. Signed Numbers

Only positive numbers are used in arithmetical operations, but both *positive* and *negative* numbers may appear in algebraic expressions. The plus sign $(+)$ is used to indicate a positive number and the minus sign $(-)$ to indicate a negative number. If the sign is omitted, the number is understood to be positive. Positive and negative numbers are called *signed numbers*.

33. Need for Negative Numbers

The need for negative numbers may be seen from the succession of subtraction below:

$$\begin{array}{cccccccc}
6 & 6 & 6 & 6 & 6 & 6 & 6 & 6 \\
-0 & -1 & -2 & -3 & -4 & -5 & -6 & -7 & -8 & -9 \\
\hline
6 & 5 & 4 & 3 & 2 & 1 & 0 & -1 & -2 & -3
\end{array}$$

When the subtrahend is greater than the minuend, the difference becomes less than zero and the negative sign is placed before the difference. Thus, a negative number may be defined as a number less than zero.

34. Application of Positive and Negative Numbers

In technical work, many scales are calibrated above and below (or to the right and left of) a center point designated 0 (zero). For example, the degrees of temperature indicated on a thermometer scale are measurements of distance taken on a scale in opposite directions from some point chosen to represent a reference or zero point. Temperature is always so many degrees above or below zero. In mathematics, it is convenient to indicate that a temperature is so many degrees above or below zero by prefixing the reading with a positive or negative sign. Thus, 45° above zero is +45° and 15° below zero is −15°. Similarly, in electronic and electrical measuring instruments, scales are often calibrated to read positive numbers on one side of a zero and negative numbers on the other.

35. Graphical Representation of Positive and Negative Numbers

a. *Principle.* Positive and negative numbers may be represented graphically as shown in figure 4. The zero is the reference point. This graph can be used to illustrate both addition and subtraction.

b. *Addition.* To add numbers graphically, start at the zero reference point and mark off the first number, going to the right if the number is positive, or to the left if the number is

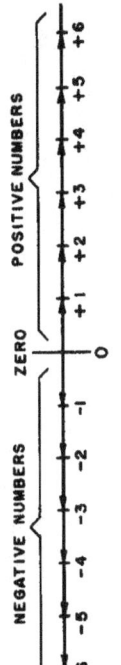

Figure 4. Graphical representation of positive and negative numbers.

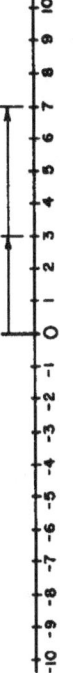

Figure 5. Graphical representation of addition of positive numbers.

negative. From this new point, mark off the second number, again going to the right if the number is positive, or to the left if it is negative. The number of units between zero and the final point is the sum of the two numbers. This procedure can be continued for more than two numbers. Figure 5 shows graphical addition of positive numbers; figures 6 and 7 show graphical addition of negative numbers; and figure 8 shows the addition of a combination of a positive and a negative number. Figures 6 and 7 show that the order in which the negative numbers are taken does not affect the answer.

c. Subtraction. To subtract numbers graphically, change the sign of the subtrahend (number to be subtracted) and proceed as for addition. Figure 9 shows the subtraction of $+3$ from $+5$ to obtain the difference of $+2$.

36. Absolute Value of a Number

The numerical value of a number, without regard to its sign, is called the *absolute value*

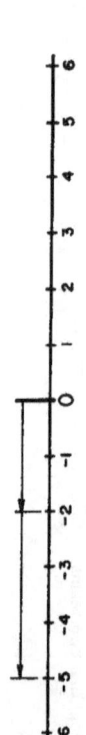

Figure 6. Graphical representation of addition of negative numbers (-3 and -2).

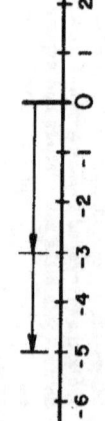

Figure 7. Graphical representation of addition of negative numbers (-1 and -5).

of the number. Thus, the absolute value of -3 or $+3$ is 3. This is written $|3|$.

37. Addition of Positive and Negative Numbers

a. Positive Numbers. To add two or more positive numbers, find the sum of their absolute values and prefix the sum with a plus sign. When there is no possibility of misunderstanding, the plus sign is usually omitted.

Example: Add $+4$, $+5$, and $+6$
$+4 + (+5) + (+6) = +15$ or 15

b. Negative Numbers. To add two or more negative numbers, find the sum of their absolute values and prefix the sum with a minus sign.

Example: Add -4, -5, and -6
$-4 + (-5) + (-6) = -15$

c. Positive and Negative Numbers. To add a positive and a negative number, find the difference between their absolute values and prefix the sum with the sign of the number that has the greater absolute value. This is called *algebraic addition*. When three or more positive and negative numbers are to be added, first find the sum of all positive numbers, and then the sum of all negative numbers. Add these sums algebraically as above.

Example 1: Add $+6$ and -9.
$+6 + (-9) = -3$

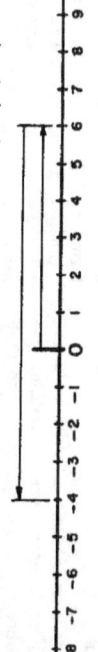

Figure 8. Graphical representation of addition of positive and negative numbers.

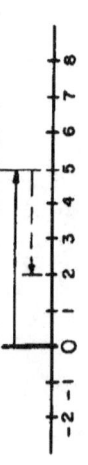

Figure 9. Graphical representation of subtraction of positive numbers.

Example 2: Add $+5$, -8, $+12$, and -6.
$+5 + (+12) = +17$
$-8 + (-6) = -14$
$(+17) + (-14) = +3$

38. Subtraction of Positive and Negative Numbers

To subtract positive and negative numbers, change the sign of the subtrahend and proceed as in addition (par. 37).

a. Positive Numbers.

Example 1: Subtract $+2$ from $+5$.
$+5 - (+2) = +5 - 2 = +3$ or 3

Example 2: Subtract $+5a^2$ from $+6a^2$.
$+6a^2 - (+5a^2) = +6a^2 - 5a^2$
$= +1a^2 = a^2$

b. Negative Numbers.

Example 1: Subtract -3 from -5.
$-5 - (-3) = -5 + 3 = -2$

Example 2: Subtract $-4a$ from $-2a$.
$-2a - (-4a) = -2a + 4a = +2a$ or $2a$

c. Positive and Negative Numbers.

Example 1: Subtract -2 from $+5$.
$+5 - (-2) = +5 + 2 = +7$ or 7.

Example 2: Subtract $-3x^2$ from $+5x^2$.
$+5x^2 - (-3x^2) = +5x^2 + 3x^2$
$= +8x^2$ or $8x^2$

39. Multiplication of Positive and Negative Numbers

a. Numbers Having Like Signs. If the two numbers to be multiplied have the same signs, the product is positive.

Example 1: Multiply $+5$ by $+3$.
$(+5)(+3) = +15$ or 15

Example 2: Multiply -5 by -3.
$(-5)(-3) = +15$ or 15

b. Numbers Having Unlike Signs. If the two numbers to be multiplied have unlike signs, the product is negative.

Example 1: Multiply -5 by $+3$.
$(-5)(+3) = -15$

Example 2: Multiply $+5$ by -3.
$(+5)(-3) = -15$

c. Several Positive and Negative Numbers. To multiply several positive and negative numbers, multiply the numbers in groups of two in the order in which they appear.

Example 1:
Multiply $(-5)(+3)(+7)(-2)(-4)$.
$(-5)(+3)$ $(+7)(-2)$ (-4)
$= (-15)$ (-14) (-4)
$=$ $(+210)$ (-4)
$=$ -840

Example 2:
Multiply $(+7)(+2)(-5)(-3)(-1)(-4)$.
$= (+7)(+2)$ $(-5)(-3)$ $(-1)(-4)$
$= (+14)$ $(+15)$ $(+4)$
$= (+210)$ $(+4)$
$=$ 840

40. Division of Positive and Negative Numbers

a. Numbers Having Like Signs. The quotient of two numbers that have the same signs is positive.

Example 1: Divide -15 by -5.
$-15 \div -5 = +3$ or 3

Example 2: Divide $+24$ by $+6$.
$+24 \div +6 = +4$ or 4

b. Numbers Having Unlike Signs. The quotient of two numbers that have opposite signs is negative.

Example 1: Divide 35 by -7.
$+35 \div -7 = -5$

Example 2: Divide $-8,998$ by 28.
$-8988 \div 28 = -321$

41. Order of Signs

When only addition and subtraction signs appear in a series of terms, addition and subtraction procedures may be performed in any order. However, when multiplication and division signs appear in the same series with addition and subtraction signs, the multiplication and division must be performed first, and then the addition and subtraction.

Example 1: Evaluate $15 + 5 - 3 + 4 - 8$.

Step 1. Add the $+$ terms:
$15 + 5 + 4 = 24$

Step 2. Add the $-$ terms:
$(-3) + (-8) = -11$

Step 3. Add the $+$ terms and the $-$ terms algebraically:
$24 - 11 = 13$.

Example 2: Evaluate $9 \times 4 + 6 - 3 + 5 \times 2$.

Step 1. Perform the multiplication first:
$(9 \times 4) + 6 - 3 + (5 \times 2) =$
$(36) + 6 - 3 + (10)$

Step 2. Add the $+$ terms:
$36 + 6 + 10 = 52$

Step 3. Add the $-$ terms:
$52 - 3 = 49$

Example 3: Evaluate $81 \div 9 - 3 + 6 - 15 + 4 \times 5$.

Step 1. Perform the division:
$(81 \div 9) - 3 + 6 - 15 + (4 \times 5) = (9) - 3 + 6 - 15 + (4 \times 5)$

Step 2. Perform the multiplication:
$9 - 3 + 6 - 15 + (4 \times 5) = 9 - 3 + 6 - 15 + (20)$

Step 3. Add the $+$ terms:
$9 + 6 + 20 = 35$

Step 4. Add the $-$ terms:
$(-3) + (-15) = -18$

Step 5. Add the $+$ terms and the $-$ terms algebraically:
$35 - 18 = 17$.

42. Review Problems—Positive and Negative Numbers

a. Add the following:
 (1) 23 and -6
 (2) 21 and 37
 (3) -54 and 33
 (4) $-43°$ and $-96°$
 (5) 682 volts and -934 volts

b. Subtract the following:
 (1) -104 amperes from 147 amperes
 (2) -37 volts from -45 volts
 (3) $.64cy$ from $.0025cy$
 (4) $21.36ax^2$ from $-10.63ax^2$
 (5) $-.986x^2y$ from $.824x^2y$

c. Find the product of the following:
 (1) -6.4 and 2.8
 (2) $3, -6,$ and 4
 (3) $-\frac{2}{3}, \frac{6}{7},$ and $-\frac{2}{5}$
 (4) $3.01, -.02,$ and -1.26
 (5) $-.0025, 150, -.10,$ and $.075$
 (6) $-2, 5, 3, -1,$ and 4

d. Divide:
 (1) 36 by 4
 (2) $-\frac{5}{7}$ by $\frac{3}{4}$
 (3) -5.6 by $-.008$
 (4) -750 by -3
 (5) $\frac{1}{3}$ ampere by $\frac{1}{2}$ ampere
 (6) -3750 by 150

e. Evaluate the following:
 (1) $2 + 3 - 9$
 (2) $3 + 4 + 2 \times 5 - 3$
 (3) $2 - 3 \times 9$
 (4) $3 \times 4 + 2 \times 5 - 3$
 (5) $5 + 8 \times 7 - 2 \times 11 + 7$
 (6) $28 \div 14 - 8 + 16 + 3 \times 2$
 (7) $46 - 18 + 3 \times 4 - 8 + 12$
 (8) $5 - 3 + 6 \times 4 + 40$
 (9) $8 - 16 + 4 \times 3 - 10 \times 5$
 (10) $15 \div 5 - 3 + 2 \times 10 - 2$

Section III. FUNDAMENTAL OPERATIONS

43. Addition and Subtraction of Algebraic Expressions

a. *General.* Only similar algebraic terms—those that are exactly alike in all respects other than numerical coefficients—may be added or subtracted. For example, the sum of $3x^2y$ and $5x^2y$ is $8x^2y$. Dissimilar terms cannot be added or subtracted directly, but the processes of addition or subtraction can be indicated by the use of plus or minus signs. For example, the sum of $4x^2y$ and $2xy^2$ is $4x^2y + 2xy^2$.

b. *Procedure.* To add or subtract algebraic expressions, arrange the terms so that like terms are in the same vertical column, and preferably in descending order of powers. Add or subtract the terms according to the rules of signed numbers (pars. 37 and 38).

Example 1: Add $x^3 - 3x^2 + 1, x^3 + x - 3,$ and $x^2 + x + 1$.

$$\begin{array}{r} x^3 - 3x^2 + 1 \\ x^3 + x - 3 \\ x^2 + 2x + 1 \\ \hline 2x^3 - 2x^2 + 2x - 1 \end{array}$$

Example 2: Subtract $x^4 + 3x^3 + x - 1$ from $x^4 + x^3 - x + 2$.

$$\begin{array}{r} x^4 + x^3 - x + 2 \\ -(x^4 + 3x^3 - x + 1) \end{array}$$

Remove parentheses and change signs.

$$\begin{array}{r} x^4 + x^3 - x + 2 \\ -x^4 - 3x^3 - 2x + 3 \\ \hline x^4 - 3x^3 - 2x + 3 \end{array}$$

44. Multiplication and Division of Monomials

a. *Multiplication.* In multiplying monomials, multiply the numerical coefficients and write this result as the coefficient of the product. After the coefficient, write each literal factor with an exponent equal to the sum of all the exponents of that letter in the original factors.

For example, $3a^n \cdot 2a^m = 6a^{n+m}$.

Example 1: Multiply x^3 by x^3.
$x^3 \cdot x^3 = x^{3+3} = x^6$

Example 2: Multiply $x, x^3,$ and x^{10}.
$x^1 \cdot x^3 \cdot x^{10} = x^{1+3+10} = x^{14}$

Example 3: Multiply x^3y^4 by $3xy^3$.
Step 1. Multiply the coefficients:
$1 \cdot 3 = 3$

Step 2. Multiply the two factors having the base x:
$x^3 \cdot x = x^{3+1} = x^4$

Step 3. Multiply the two factors having the base y:
$y^4 \cdot y^3 = y^{4+3} = y^7$

Step 4. The product is:
$x^3y^4 \cdot 3xy^3 = 3x^4y^7$

Example 4: Multiply x^2y^4z and wx^3yz^5.
$x^2y^4z \cdot wx^3yz^5 = wx^{2+3}y^{4+1}z^{1+5}$
$x^{2+3} = x^5$
$y^{4+1} = y^5$
$z^{1+5} = z^6$
Therefore, $x^2y^4z \cdot wx^3yz^5 = wx^5y^5z^6$.

b. *Division.* In dividing a monomial by a monomial, divide the numerical coefficient of the dividend by the coefficient of the divisor and write the result as the coefficient of the quotient. After the coefficient, write each literal factor with an exponent equal to its exponent in the dividend minus its exponent in the divisor. Thus, to divide $6a^n$ by $3a^m$ (n greater than m), $\frac{6a^n}{3a^m} = 2a^{n-m}$.

Example 1: Divide x^3 by x^2.
$\frac{x^3}{x^2} = x^{3-2} = x^1 = x$

Example 2: Divide $5x^4yz^3$ by $6x^2z^2$.
$\frac{5x^4yz^3}{6x^2z^2} = \frac{5}{6} x^{4-2} z^{3-2}$
$= \frac{5}{6} x^2yz$ or $\frac{5x^2yz}{6}$

c. *Removal of Parentheses and Brackets.*

(1) In multiplying a quantity in parentheses by a given factor, multiply each term inside the parentheses by that factor and drop the parentheses. If the factor is a negative quantity, the sign of every term inside the parentheses is changed. For example, $-5(a - b + c) = -5a + 5b - 5c$.

(2) When an algebraic expression, such as $5x - 4[x - 2(x - 3)]$, has more than one grouping symbol (parentheses and brackets), remove the inside grouping symbol first and then successively remove the outer grouping symbols.

Example 1: Simplify $5x - 4[x - 2(x - 3)]$.
$$5x - 4[x - 2(x - 3)] = 5x - 4[x - 2x + 6]$$
$$= 5x - 4x + 8x - 24$$
$$= 9x - 24$$
$$= 3(3x - 8)$$

Example 2: Simplify $4a - \{6a - 2b + 2[2a - b + 42] - (c + 2b)\}$.
$$4a - \{6a - 2b + 2[2a - b + 42] - (c + 2b)\}$$
$$= 4a - \{6a - 2b + 4a - 2b + 84 - c - 2b\}$$
$$= 4a - 6a + 2b - 4a + 2b + 84 + c + 2b$$
$$= -6a + 6b + c - 84$$

Example 3: Simplify $-(-1[-(x - y - z) + 29] - 39 + 2y - z)$.
$$-(-1[-(x - y - z) + 29] - 39 + 2y - z)$$
$$= -(-1[-x + y + z + 29] - 39 + 2y - z)$$
$$= -(+x - y - z - 29 - 39 + 2y - z)$$
$$= -x + y + z + 29 + 39 - 2y + z$$
$$= -x - y + 2z + 68$$

45. Raising Algebraic Functions to Powers

To raise an algebraic function to a power, multiply the exponents. Thus, $(a^n)^m = a^{nm}$.

Example 1: Simplify $(5^2)^4$.
$$(5^2)^4 = 5^{2 \cdot 4} = 5^{12}$$

Example 2: Simplify $(2ab)^3$.
$$(2ab)^3 = 2ab \cdot 2ab \cdot 2ab = 8a^3b^3$$
or $2^{1 \cdot 3} a^{1 \cdot 3} b^{1 \cdot 3} = 8a^3b^3$

Example 3: Simplify $(ax^2)^3$.
$$(ax^2)^3 = a^{1 \cdot 3} x^{2 \cdot 3} = a^3 x^6$$

Example 4: Simplify $[(x^5)^3]^5$.
$$[(x^5)^3]^5 = [x^{5 \cdot 3}]^5 = [x^{15}]^5 = x^{1 \cdot 15 \cdot 5} = x^{60}$$

Example 5: Simplify $\left(\dfrac{2}{x^2}\right)^5$.
$$\left(\dfrac{2}{x^2}\right)^5 = \dfrac{2^{1 \cdot 5}}{x^{2 \cdot 5}} = \dfrac{2^5}{x^{10}} = \dfrac{32}{x^{10}}$$

46. Negative Exponents

The rule for dividing monomials (par. 44b) also holds when the exponents of the denominator is greater than the exponent of the numerator. For example, $a^1 \div a^5 = a^{1-5} = a^{-4}$; however, a quantity such as a^{-3} may be written as $\dfrac{1}{a^3}$.

Example: Multiply x^2, x^{-1}, and $\dfrac{1}{x^3}$.

Step 1. Write down the factors of the multiplication:
$$x^2 \cdot x^{-1} \cdot \dfrac{1}{x^3}$$

Step 2. Place all factors in the numerator:
$$x^2 \cdot x^{-1} \cdot x^{-3}$$

Step 3. Multiply the factors (add their exponents):
$$x^{2-1-3} = x^{-2}$$

47. Zero Exponents

The zero power of any quantity is equal to 1. For example $x^2 \cdot x^{-2} = x^0$ when the exponents are added. However, x^{-2} can also be written $\dfrac{1}{x^2}$; in this case, $x^2 \cdot x^{-2} = \dfrac{x^2}{x^2} = 1$.

Therefore, $x^0 = 1$. Any number (except zero) raised to the zero power is equal to 1.

Example: Solve $\dfrac{x^2 y^3}{z} \cdot \dfrac{z^4}{xy} \div \dfrac{x^3 y^2}{z^3}$.

$$\dfrac{x^2 y^3}{z} \cdot \dfrac{z^4}{xy} \div \dfrac{x^3 y^2}{z^3} = \dfrac{x^2 y^3 z^4}{xyz} \div \dfrac{x^3 y^2}{z^3} = \dfrac{x^2 y^3 z^4}{xyz} \cdot \dfrac{z^3}{x^3 y^2} = \dfrac{x^2 y^3 z^7}{x^4 y^3 z} = x^{2-4} y^{3-3} z^{7-1}$$
$$= x^{-2} y^0 z^6 = x^{-2} \cdot 1 \cdot z^6 = \dfrac{z^6}{x^2}$$

48. Multiplication of Polynomials

a. By a Monomial. To multiply a polynomial by a monomial, multiply each term in the polynomial separately by the monomial and add the products. Observe the rules for the multiplication of signed numbers (par. 39) and exponents (par. 44a).

Example 1: Multiply $3a + 2ab + 5c$ by $2b$.
$$\begin{array}{r} 3a + 2ab + 5c \\ 2b \\ \hline 6ab + 4ab^2 + 10bc \end{array}$$

Example 2: Multiply $ad - ae + af$ by $3a^2$.
$$\begin{array}{r} ad - ae + af \\ 3a^2 \\ \hline 3a^3d - 3a^3e + 3a^3f \end{array}$$

Example 3: Multiply $3x^2y^2 - 2xy^3 + 5x^4y$ by $4x^3y$.
$$\begin{array}{r} 3x^2y^2 - 2xy^3 + 5x^4y \\ 4x^3y \\ \hline 12x^5y^3 - 8x^4y^4 + 20x^7y^2 \end{array}$$

b. By a Polynomial. To multiply a polynomial by another polynomial, multiply each term of one polynomial by each term of the other and add the products.

Example 1: Multiply $(a + b)$ by $(a + b)$.
$$\begin{array}{r} a + b \\ a + b \\ \hline a^2 + ab \\ ab + b^2 \\ \hline a^2 + 2ab + b^2 \end{array}$$

Example 2: Multiply $2x + 3y$ by $2x + 3z$.
$$\begin{array}{r} 2x + 3y \\ 2x + 3z \\ \hline 4x^2 + 6xy \\ + 6xz + 9yz \\ \hline 4x^2 + 6xy + 6xz + 9yz \end{array}$$

Example 3: Multiply $5x^3 - 6xy + 3y^2$ by $x + y$.
$$\begin{array}{r} 5x^3 - 6xy + 3y^2 \\ x + y \\ \hline 5x^4 - 6x^2y + 3xy^2 \\ + 5x^3y - 6xy^2 + 3y^3 \\ \hline 5x^4 - x^2y - 3xy^2 + 3y^3 \end{array}$$

49. Division of Polynomials

a. By a Monomial. To divide a polynomial by a monomial, divide each term of the polynomial by the monomial.

Example 1: Divide $3a^2 + 4ab + 5ac$ by a.
$$\dfrac{3a^2 + 4ab + 5ac}{a} = 3a + 4b + 5c$$

Example 2: Divide $7x^2 + 14xy - 21ax^2$ by $7x$.
$$\dfrac{7x^2 + 14xy - 21ax^2}{7x} = x + 2y - 3ax$$

Example 3: Divide $4r(s + t) - r^4(s + t)^2 + qr^2(s + t)^3$ by $r^2(s + t)$.
$$\dfrac{4r(s + t) - r^4(s + t)^2 + qr^2(s + t)^3}{r^2(s + t)}$$
$$= \dfrac{4r(s + t)}{r^2(s + t)} - \dfrac{r^4(s + t)^2}{r^2(s + t)} + \dfrac{qr^2(s + t)^3}{r^2(s + t)}$$
$$= \dfrac{4}{r} - r^2(s + t) + q(s + t)^2$$

b. By a Polynomial. To divide a polynomial by a polynomial, just arrange the dividend and the divisor according to descending powers of one variable, starting with the highest powers at the left. Then proceed as shown in the examples below. If there is a remainder, write it as the numerator of a fraction the denominator of which is the divisor.

Example 1: Divide $ab + ac + db + dc$ by $a + d$.

Step 1. Divide the first term of the divisor, a, into the first term of the dividend, ab. The quantity a is contained in the first term, ab, b times. Write b as the first term of the quotient.

$$a + d \overline{)ab + ac + db + dc}$$

$$\; b$$

Step 2. Multiply both terms of the divisor by b:

$$a + d \overline{)ab + ac + db + dc}$$
$$ab + db$$

Step 3. Subtract the result from the original dividend:

$$a + d \overline{)ab + ac + db + dc}$$
$$\underline{ab + db}$$
$$ac + dc$$

Step 4. Divide the first term of the divisor into the first term of the

remainder. It is contained in the first term, ac, c times. Write c as the second term of the quotient.

$$a + d \overline{)ab + ac + db + dc}$$
$$ b + c$$

Step 5. Multiply both terms of the divisor by c and subtract. There is no remainder:

$$a + d \overline{)ab + ac + db + dc}$$
$$\underline{ab + db}$$
$$ac + dc$$
$$\underline{ac + dc}$$

Step 6. Therefore,
$$\frac{ab + ac + db + dc}{a + d} = b + c.$$

Example 2: Divide $x^2 + 2xy + y^2$ by $x + y$.

$$x + y \overline{)x^2 + 2xy + y^2}$$
$$ x + y$$
$$\underline{x^2 + xy}$$
$$xy + y^2$$
$$\underline{xy + y^2}$$

Therefore,
$$\frac{x^2 + 2xy + y^2}{x + y} = x + y.$$

Example 3: Divide $6a^2 - ab - 27ac - 15b^2 + 7bc + 30c^2$ by $3a - 5b - 6c$.

$$3a - 5b - 6c \overline{)6a^2 - ab - 27ac - 15b^2 + 7bc + 30c^2}$$
$$ 2a + 3b - 5c$$
$$\underline{6a^2 - 10ab - 12ac}$$
$$ 9ab - 15ac - 15b^2 + 7bc + 30c^2$$
$$\underline{9ab - 15b^2 - 18bc}$$
$$ -15ac + 25bc + 30c^2$$
$$ \underline{-15ac + 25bc + 30c^2}$$

50. Review Problems—Fundamental Operations

a. Add the following algebraic expressions:

(1) $2a^4 + 3a^2b^3 + 5b^4$, $a^4 - 5a^2b^3 - 2b^4$, and $3a^4 - 2a^2b^3 + b^4$.

(2) $3E - 2RI - 15ZI$, $6RI + 2AZI$, and $-2E - RI + 11ZI$.

(3) $10w - 4x + 3y + 6z$, $2x - 5w + y$, $3z - 2x - y$, and $6y - 4w - z + 5x$.

b. Subtract the following algebraic expressions:

(1) $-7ax - 2by + cz$ from $12ax + 15by - 8cz$.

(2) $10w - 3y - 4z + 6x$ from $3x + 5y - 2z - 15w$.

(3) $8a^2 + 10ab - 4b^2$ from $12a^2 - 24ab + 2b^2$.

c. Simplify:

(1) $7a^0$
(2) $(5x + 9)^0$
(3) $(3x^2 + 7x + 1)^0$

d. Perform the indicated operations:

(1) $l^a \cdot l^4$
(2) $y^{a+1} \cdot y^b$
(3) $y^{a+1} \cdot y^{b-1}$
(4) $\dfrac{r^{10}}{r^4}$
(5) $(R^3)^m$
(6) $\dfrac{r^{a+5}}{r^4}$

e. Express with positive exponents:

(1) $4x^{-4}$
(2) $r^{-1} x^{-1}$
(3) $(6a)^{-2v}$
(4) $l^{-3} R^{-1}$
(5) $2^{-3} a^2 b^{-3}$
(6) $\dfrac{3EI^{-1} R^{-1}}{4}$

f. Perform the indicated operations:

(1) $(5ab)(2a^2 - 3ab + 7b^2)$
(2) $4a(a^2 + 3a + 1)$
(3) $(i^2 + 3i + 9)(i - 3)$
(4) $(2x^2 + 3xy - y^2)(x^2 + xy + y^2)$
(5) $(3x^2 - 2xy - 5y^2)(3x^2 + 2xy - 5y^2)$
(6) $[(x - 1)a - (x - 1)c] \div [(x - 1)ac]$
(7) $(3rL - rR^2) \div rR$
(8) $(5a^3b - 10a^5b^2 + 15a^6b^4) \div 5a^3b$
(9) $(1 + 2z^4 + 4z^3 + 7z) \div (3 + z^2 - z)$
(10) $(100b^3 - 13b^2 - 3b) \div (3 + 25b)$

Section IV. FACTORING

51. Understanding Factoring

Factoring is the breaking up of an expression into the *factors* or *individual parts* of which it is composed. In other words, to factor an algebraic expression means to find two or more expressions which, when multiplied together, will result in the original expression. For example, since $3 \cdot 5 = 15$, 3 and 5 are the factors of 15; since $4 \cdot a \cdot b = 4ab$, 4, a, and b, are the factors of $4ab$; since $a(x + y) = ax + ay$, a and $(x + y)$ are the factors of $ax + ay$.

52. Factors of Positive Integers

It is often difficult to determine at a glance the factors of which a number is composed. There are many different combinations of numbers that would result in an answer of 36; for example, the desired factors for 36 in a certain problem might $36 \cdot 1$, $18 \cdot 2$, $12 \cdot 3$, $9 \cdot 4$, $6 \cdot 6$, $2 \cdot 2 \cdot 9$, $4 \cdot 3 \cdot 3$, $2 \cdot 3 \cdot 6$, and so on.

53. Factors of a Monomial

Because the factors of a monomial are evident, usually a monomial is not separated into its prime factors. The factors of a^3b^2c are $a \cdot a \cdot a \cdot b \cdot b \cdot c$, and the factors of $15a^2b$ are $3 \cdot 5 \cdot a \cdot a \cdot b$.

54. Square Root of a Monomial

The square root of an algebraic expression is one of its two equal factors. Thus, the square root of 49 is 7, the square root of 81 is 9, the square root of a^2 is a, and the square root of x^2y^2 is xy. As discussed in paragraph 31, the radical sign is used to indicate the square root of a number. Actually, every number has two square roots, one positive and one negative. If no sign precedes the radical, the positive or *principal root* is understood. For example, $\sqrt{9} = +3$. If a negative sign *precedes the radical*, however, the negative root is intended. Thus, $-\sqrt{9} = -3$. When dealing with literal terms, the values of the various factors often are unknown. Therefore, *when extracting the square root of a monomial, extract the square root of the numerical coefficient, divide the exponents of the literal terms by 2, and prefix the square root with the plus or minus* ($\pm$) *sign*, which denotes that either the positive or negative root may be the correct one.

Example 1: $\sqrt{x^{16}y^4} = \pm x^8y^2$.
Example 2: $\sqrt{49a^4b^2} = \pm 7a^2b$.

55. Cube Root of a Monomial

The cube root of a monomial is one of its three equal factors. The index 3 in the angle of the radical sign ($\sqrt[3]{}$) indicates cube root (par. 31). To *extract the cube root of a monomial, extract the cube root of the numerical coefficient, divide the exponents of the literal terms by 3, and prefix the cube with the same sign as that of the monomial.*

Example 1: $\sqrt[3]{a^3y^3} = a^2y$.
Example 2: $\sqrt[3]{27x^{12}y^6z^3} = 3x^4y^2z$.
Example 3: $\sqrt[3]{-64x^3y^3} = -4x^2y$.

56. Factors of a Polynomial

a. Common Monomial Factor. In an algebraic expression, the type of factor which can be recognized most easily is the monomial factor (single letter or number) which is common to each term in the expression. For instance, in the expression $xa + xb + xc$, the x is a factor common to each of the terms. Thus, the expression $xa + xb + xc$ can be written $x(a + b + c)$. This relationship is shown pictorially in figure 10. Since the area of a rectangle is equal to its base multiplied by its altitude (par. 136b), the area of the uppermost rectangle in figure 10 is x times a, or xa. The areas of the center and lower rectangles are xb and xc, respectively. The area of the large rectangle formed by the three small rectangles is equal to its base x times its altitude $(a + b + c)$, or $x(a + b + c)$. Since the area of the large

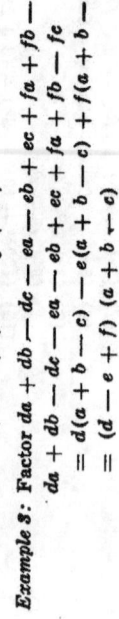

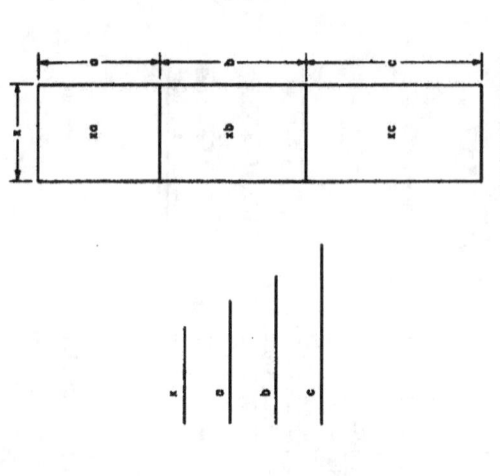

Figure 10. Common monomial factors.

rectangle is equal to the sum of the areas of the three smaller rectangles, then $x(a + b + c)$ is equal to $xa + xb + xc$. This shows that the factor x can be removed from $xa + xb + xc$ and the expression written $x(a + b) + xc$. Accuracy of factoring can be checked by multiplying the two factors together—the product should be the original expression. Thus, $x(a + b + c) = xa + xb + xc$. *To factor a polynomial, the terms of which have a common monomial factor, determine the largest factor common to all of the terms, divide the polynomial by this factor, and write the quotient in parentheses preceded by the monomial factor.* The first factor contains all that is common to all of the terms; it may consist of more than one literal number and may be to a power higher than the first.

Example 1: Factor $x^3 - 7x^2 + 4x$.
$x^3 - 7x^2 + 4x = x(x^2 - 7x + 4)$

Example 2: Factor $abx + aby - abz$.
$abx + aby - abz = ab(x + y - z)$

Example 3: Factor $2ax^5 - 4bx^3 + 6cx^2 = 2x^2(a - 2^2 + 3^c)$

b. Binomial Factors. Sometimes binomial factors are not immediately apparent, and an algebraic term may appear to have no common factors. For example, the expression $am + bm + an + bn$ may seem to have no factors in common. However, the first pair, $am + bm$, has a common factor, m, and the second pair, $an + bn$, has a common factor, n. Factoring out the common factors, the expression becomes $m(a + b) + n(a + b)$. Since there are two terms containing a common factor $(a + b)$, this factor can be removed to make the expression $(a + b) (m + n)$. Thus, the factors are $(a + b)$ and $(m + n)$. This relationship is shown pictorially in figure 11. Starting with

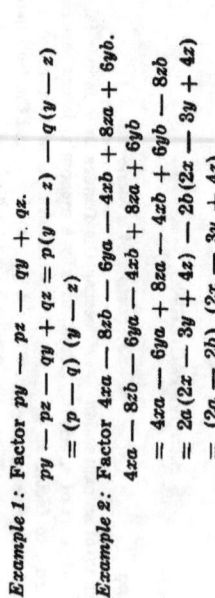

the upper left-hand rectangle and going clockwise, the areas of the four rectangles are am, am, bm, and bn. The area of the large rectangle formed by the four smaller rectangles is its base $(m + n)$ times its altitude $(a + b)$, or $(m + n) (a + b)$. Since the area of the large rectangle is equal to the sum of the areas of the four smaller rectangles, then $(m + n) (a + b)$ is equal to $am + am + bm + bn$. This shows that the expression $am + bm + an + bn$ can be factored into $(m + n)$ and $(a + b)$. To check the factoring, multiply $(a + b)$ by $(m + n)$; the product is $am + an + bm + bn$. Since the addition of terms can be expressed in any order, the factoring is correct.

Example 1: Factor $py - pz - qy + qz$.
$py - pz - qy + qz = p(y - z) - q(y - z)$
$= (p - q) (y - z)$

Example 2: Factor $4xa - 8xb - 6ya - 4zb + 8za + 6yb$.
$4xa - 8xb - 6ya - 4zb + 8za + 6yb$
$= 4xa - 6ya + 8za - 4xb - 4zb + 6yb - 8zb$
$= 2a(2x - 3y + 4z) - 2b(2x - 3y + 4z)$
$= (2a - 2b) (2x - 3y + 4z)$
$= 2(a - b) (2x - 3y + 4z)$

Example 3: Factor $da + db - dc - ea - eb + ec + fa + fb - fc$.
$da + db - dc - ea - eb + ec + fa + fb - fc$
$= d(a + b - c) - e(a + b - c) + f(a + b - c)$
$= (d - e + f) (a + b - c)$

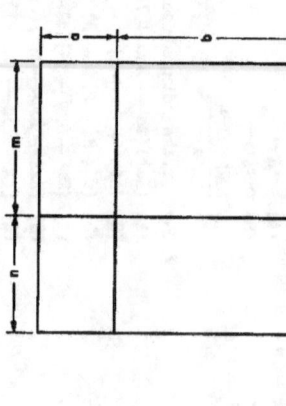

Figure 11. Binomial factors.

57. Factors of the Square of a Binomial

a. Square of Sum of Two Numbers. The square of the sum of two numbers is a special product that should be readily recognized to aid in factoring algebraic expressions. *The square of the sum of two numbers equals the square of the first, plus twice the product of the first and second, plus the square of the second.* Conversely, the factors of $a^2 + 2ab + b^2$ are $(a + b)(a + b)$ or $(a + b)^2$. This relationship is shown in figure 12. The areas of the four rectangles, as shown on the figure, are a^2, ab, ab, and b^2. The area of the large rectangle formed by the four smaller rectangles is equal to its base $(a + b)$ times its altitude $(a + b)$, or $(a + b)^2$. Since the area of the large rectangle is equal to the sum of the areas of the four smaller rectangles, then $(a + b)^2$ is equal to $a^2 + ab + ab + b^2$, or $a^2 + 2ab + b^2$. This shows that the expression $a^2 + 2ab + b^2$ can be factored into $(a + b)(a + b)$, or $(a + b)^2$. Figure 13 shows a similar relationship in which nine small rectangles form one large rectangle.

In this case, the area of the large rectangle is $(a + 2b)^2$ and the sum of the areas of the nine smaller rectangles is $a^2 + 4ab + 4b^2$; consequently, $(a + 2b)$ and $(a + 2b)$ are factors of $a^2 + 4ab + 4b^2$. Thus, the factors of the square of one number, plus twice the product of the first and second number, plus the square of the second number are the square of the sum of the two numbers.

Example: Factor $4b^2 + 16db + 16d^2$.

$$4b^2 + 16db + 16d^2 = (2b + 4d)(2b + 4d)$$
$$= (2b + 4d)^2$$
$$= [2(b + 2d)]^2$$
$$= 2^2(b + 2d)^2$$

To prove the factoring:

$$(2b + 4d)^2 = (2b)^2 + 2(2b)(4d) + (4d)^2$$
$$= 4b^2 + 16db + 16d^2$$

Note that 4 (that is, 2^2) may be removed before factoring the rest of the expression—this often simplifies computation.

$$4(b^2 + 4bd + 4d^2) = 4(b + 2d)^2$$

b. Square of Difference of Two Numbers. The square of the difference of two numbers equals the square of the first, minus twice the product of the first and second, plus the square of the second. For example, $(a - b)^2 = a^2 - 2ab + b^2$. The factors of $a^2 - 2ab + b^2$ are $(a - b)(a - b)$ or $(a - b)^2$. This relationship is shown pictorially in figure 14. The area of the large rectangle formed by the four small rectangles is a^2. The areas of the four smaller rectangles are shown on the illustration. The area of the upper left-hand rectangle is $(a - b)^2$. It is also equal to the area of the large rectangle minus the areas of the other three rectangles, or $a^2 - b(a - b) - b(a - b) - b^2$. This can be further simplified as follows:

$$a^2 - b(a - b) - b(a - b) - b^2$$
$$a^2 - 2b(a - b) - b^2$$
$$a^2 - 2ab + 2b^2 - b^2$$
$$a^2 - 2ab + b^2$$

Therefore, $(a - b)^2 = a^2 - 2ab + b^2$, and $(a - b)$ and $(a - b)$ are factors of $a^2 - 2ab + b^2$. Thus, the factors of the square of one number, minus twice the product of the first and the second, plus the square of the second are the square of the difference of the two numbers.

Example:

Factor $9b^2 - 12bd + 4d^2$.

$$9b^2 - 12bd + 4d^2 = (3b - 2d)(3b - 2d)$$
$$= (3b - 2d)^2$$

To prove the factoring:

$$(3b - 2d)^2 = (3b)^2 - 2(3b)(2d) + (2d)^2$$
$$= 9b^2 - 12bd + 4d^2$$

58. Factors of Difference of Two Squares

The product of the sum and difference of two numbers is equal to the difference of their squares. Thus, $(a + b)(a - b) = a^2 - b^2$. To factor the difference of two squares, extract the square roots, then write the sum of the roots as one factor and the difference of the roots as the other factor. Thus, the factors of $a^2 - b^2$ are $(a + b)(a - b)$.

Example:

Factor $4x^2 - 9y^2$.

$$4x^2 - 9y^2 = (2x + 3y)(2x - 3y)$$

To prove the factoring:

$$(2x + 3y)(2x - 3y)$$
$$= (2x)^2 + (2x)(3y) - (2x)(3y) - (3y)^2$$
$$= 4x^2 - 9y^2$$

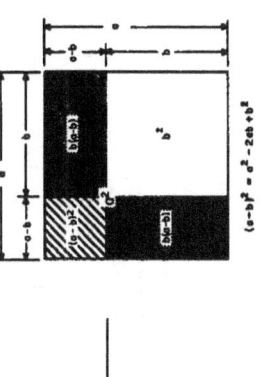

Figure 14. Square of difference of two numbers.

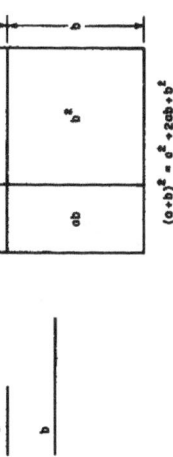

Figure 12. Square of sum of two numbers.

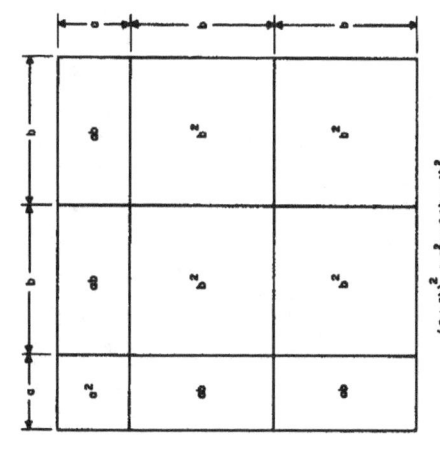

Figure 13. Factors of square of positive binomial.

59. Factors of Trinomials

a. Trinomials Such as $x^2 + x(a + b) + ab$. The factors of a trinomial consisting of the square of the common term, the product of the common term and the algebraic sum of the unlike terms, and the product of the unlike terms are two binomials that have one term in common and the other term unlike. Thus, the factors of $x^2 + x(a + b) + ab$ are $(x + a)(x + b)$ where x is the common term, and a and b are the unlike terms. As proof, the product of $(x + a)(x + b)$ is $x^2 + xa + xb + ab$. By factoring the two terms which have a common factor, x, the original trinomial $x^2 + x(a + b) + ab$ is obtained.

Example: Factor $9r^2 + 6r(s + t) + 4st$.

To prove the factoring:

$9r^2 + 6r(s + t) + 4st = (3r + 2s)(3r + 2t)$

$(3r + 2s)(3r + 2t) = (3r)^2 + (3r)(2s) + (3r)(2t) + (2s)(2t)$
$= 9r^2 + 6rs + 6rt + 4st$
$= 9r^2 + 6r(s + t) + 4st$

b. Trinomials Such as $x^2 + 6x + 8$. To factor a trinomial of the form $x^2 + 6x + 8$, $x^2 - 6x + 8$, $x^2 + 6x - 8$, or $x^2 - 6x - 8$, much of the work is done by trial and error. The problem is to find two factors of the final term which, when added together, will give the coefficient of the middle term. Taking the first of the trinomials above, the factors of 8 are $8 \cdot 1$ and $4 \cdot 2$. Since $4 + 2 = 6$ and $8 + 1 = 9$, the factors that will be used are 4 and 2. With regards to signs, *if the sign of the two factors are alike and will be the same as the sign of the middle term*. Thus, the factors of $x^2 + 6x + 8$ are $(x + 4)$ and $(x + 2)$, and the factors of $x^2 - 6x + 8$ are $(x - 4)$ and $(x - 2)$. *If the sign of the final term is negative, however, the signs containing the two terms of each binomial factor are unlike; the larger factor will take the sign of the middle term.* For example, the factors of $x^2 + 2x - 8$ are $(x + 4)$ and $(x - 2)$, and the factors of $x^2 - 2x - 8$ are $(x - 4)$ and $(x + 2)$.

Example 1: Factor $y^2 + 12y + 32$.
$y^2 + 12y + 32 = (y + 8)(y + 4)$

Example 2: Factor $z^2 - 11z + 30$.
$z^2 - 11z + 30 = (z - 6)(z - 5)$

Example 3: Factor $r^2 + 4r - 12$.
$r^2 + 4r - 12 = (r + 6)(r - 2)$

Example 4: Factor $s^2 - 8 - 20$.
$s^2 - 8 - 20 = (s - 5)(s + 4)$

c. Trinomials Such as $6a^2 - 11a - 10$. The procedure used to factor trinomials of this type is an extension of the procedure described in b above and as shown in the example below.

Example: Factor $6a^2 - 11a - 10$.

Step 1. Find two numbers that, when multiplied together, form the left-hand term, $6a^2$.
$(6a)(a) = 6a^2$
$(2a)(3a) = 6a^2$

Step 2. Find two numbers that, when multiplied together, form the right-hand term, -10.
$(10)(-1) = -10$
$(5)(-2) = -10$
$(-10)(1) = -10$
$(-5)(2) = -10$

Step 3. By trial and error, set up two binomial expressions containing factors from step 1 in the left-hand term and factors from step 2 in the right-hand term. The proper selection of factors should give the middle term of the trinomial when the binomials are multiplied.
$(2a + 5)(3a - 2)$ (first trial)
$6a^2 + 15a - 4a - 10 = 6a^2 + 11a - 10$ (multiplying out)

The middle term obtained does not match the middle term of the given trinomial. The numerical value is correct, but the sign is wrong. Make a second trial with the signs in the binomials changed.
$(2a - 5)(3a + 2)$
$6a^2 - 15a + 4a - 10 = 6a^2 - 11a - 10$

Step 4. Since the second trial results in the correct trinomial, the factors of $6a^2 - 11a - 10$ are $(2a - 5)$ and $(3a + 2)$.

Note. The method of trial and error used above may not work in every case. Other arrangements of factors and signs must be tried until the correct results are obtained.

60. Factors of Two Cubes

a. Sum of Two Cubes. The factors of the sum of two cubes, such as $x^3 + y^3$, are $(x + y)$ and $(x^2 - xy + y^2)$. In this case, the binomial is an expression of the sum of the primes minus the product of the primes. This is seen readily by dividing $x^3 + y^3$ by $x + y$.

Thus,

$$x + y \overline{\smash{\big)}\, \begin{array}{r} x^2 - xy + y^2 \\ x^3 \end{array}}$$

$$\begin{array}{r} x^3 + x^2y \\ - x^2y \\ - x^2y - xy^2 \\ + xy^2 + y^3 \\ + xy^2 + y^3 \end{array}$$

Example 1: Factor $z^3 + 8$.
$z^3 + 8 = (z + 2)(z^2 - 2z + 4)$

To prove the factoring:

$$z + 2 \overline{\smash{\big)}\, \begin{array}{r} z^2 - 2z + 4 \\ z^3 \end{array}}$$

$$\begin{array}{r} z^3 + 2z^2 \\ - 2z^2 \\ - 2z^2 - 4z \\ 4z + 8 \\ 4z + 8 \end{array}$$

b. Difference of Two Cubes. The factors of the difference of two cubes, such as $x^3 - y^3$, are $(x - y)(x^2 + xy + y^2)$. These factors are an expression of the difference of the primes times the sum of the squares plus the product of the primes. As in the sum of two cubes, factoring can be proved by dividing the product by the binomial factor.

Example 1: Factor $a^3 - b^3$.

$a^3 - b^3 = (a - b)(a^2 + ab + b^2)$

To prove the factoring:

$$a - b \overline{\smash{\big)}\, \begin{array}{r} a^2 + ab + b^2 \\ a^3 \end{array}}$$

$$\begin{array}{r} a^3 - a^2b \\ a^2b \\ a^2b - ab^2 \\ ab^2 - b^3 \\ ab^2 - b^3 \end{array}$$

Example 2: Factor $z^3 - 27$.
$z^3 - 27 = (z - 3)(z^2 + 3z + 9)$

To prove the factoring:

$$z - 3 \overline{\smash{\big)}\, \begin{array}{r} z^2 + 3z + 9 \\ z^3 \end{array}}$$

$$\begin{array}{r} z^3 - 3z^2 \\ 3z^2 \\ 3z^2 - 9z \\ 9z - 27 \\ 9z - 27 \end{array}$$

Example 2:

Factor $r^3 + 125x^3$.
$r^3 + 125x^3 = (r + 5x)(r^2 - 5rx + 25x^2)$

To prove the factoring:

$$r + 5x \overline{\smash{\big)}\, \begin{array}{r} r^2 - 5rx + 25x^2 \\ r^3 \end{array}}$$

$$\begin{array}{r} r^3 + 5r^2x \\ - 5r^2x \\ - 5r^2x - 25rx^2 \\ 25rx^2 + 125x^3 \\ 25rx^2 + 125x^3 \end{array}$$

Example 3: Factor $64s^3 - 216t^3$.
$64s^3 - 216t^3 = (4s - 6t)(16s^2 + 24st + 36t^2)$

To prove the factoring:

$$\begin{array}{r} 16s^2 + 36t^2 \\ 4s - 6t \overline{)64s^3 + 216t^3} \\ \underline{64s^3 - 96s^2t} \\ 96s^2t \\ \underline{96s^2t - 144st^2} \\ 144st^2 - 216t^3 \\ \underline{144st^2 - 216t^3} \end{array}$$

61. Review Problems—Factoring

a. Factor:

(1) $25 + 5 - 30$
(2) $8 + 4 - 32$
(3) $9 - 18 + 21$
(4) $7r - 21r + 35r$
(5) $10x + 8y + 6z$

b. Find the values of the indicated powers:

(1) $(7xy^3)^2$
(2) $(-2w^5)^2$
(3) $(8a^2b^4)^2$
(4) $(9a^3x)^3$
(5) $(-3bz^4)^3$

c. Find the value of each of the following:

(1) $\sqrt{5^2}$
(2) $\sqrt{4^3}$
(3) $\sqrt{a^2b^6}$
(4) $\sqrt{36y^2z^4}$

(5) $\sqrt{100a^2b^{10}}$
(6) $\sqrt{16a^2 \cdot 5^2}$
(7) $\sqrt[3]{-27}$
(8) $\sqrt[3]{-x^9}$
(9) $\sqrt[3]{(-8)^2}$
(10) $\sqrt[3]{125x^{12}y^{15}z^6}$

d. Factor:

(1) $3x + 6$
(2) $5a^2 + 15a$
(3) $10x^3 - 14x^2 - 2x$
(4) $6axy + 9bzx - 12cz$
(5) $m^3 + m^2 - 5mx$
(6) $3a^5 - 6a^4b - 3a^3b^2$
(7) $7ry^3 - 14ry^3 + 21ry^3$
(8) $12x^2am + 14xa^2m + 16xam^2$
(9) $rr_1^2 + rr_2^2$
(10) $\frac{1}{4}c^3d - \frac{1}{8}c^2d^2 + \frac{1}{16}cd^3$

Section V. ALGEBRAIC FRACTIONS

62. General

Algebraic fractions play an important part in equations for electrical and electronic circuits. These fractions can be added, subtracted, multiplied, and divided in the same manner as arithmetical fractions.

63. Changing Signs of Fractions

a. The sign preceding a fraction is the sign of the fraction. It refers to the fraction as a whole and not to either the numerator or the denominator. In addition, the numerator and denominator each has a sign. For example, in the fraction $-\frac{3a}{5b}$, the sign of the fraction is minus, the sign of the numerator is plus, and the sign of the denominator is plus. Any two of the three signs can be changed without changing the value of the fraction.

Thus, $-\frac{3a}{5b} = \frac{-3a}{5b} = \frac{3a}{-5b}$.

Therefore, the sign of the fraction is not changed if the signs of both the numerator and the denominator are changed. Also, the sign of the fraction must be changed if the sign of either the numerator or denominator, but not both, is changed.

b. If the numerator or denominator is a polynomial, the sign of each term should be changed, not just the first sign. For example,

$$\frac{a-b}{c-d} = +\frac{-(a-b)}{c-d} = \frac{-a+b}{c-d} = \frac{b-a}{c-d}.$$

c. If the numerator or denominator is in factored form, change only the sign of one of the factors, not both. Thus,

$$\frac{(x-y)(x-2y)}{x+y} = \frac{(x+y)(x-2y)}{x+y} = \frac{(y-x)(x-2y)}{x+y}.$$

64. Changing Form of Algebraic Fractions

In algebra, as in arithmetic, any fraction can be changed to an equivalent fraction by multiplying or dividing both the numerator and denominator by the same term or number except zero. This will not change the value of the fraction. For example, to change the fraction $\frac{3}{5}$ to a fraction with 10 as its denominator, multiply both the numerator and the denominator by 2. Thus,

$$\frac{3}{5} = \frac{3 \cdot 2}{5 \cdot 2} = \frac{6}{10}.$$

Similarly, to change the fraction $\frac{x}{y}$ to a fraction with yz as its denominator, the denominator is changed to yz by multiplying by z; the numerator also is multiplied by z to become xz. Thus,

$$\frac{x}{y} = \frac{x \cdot z}{y \cdot z} = \frac{xz}{yz}.$$

Example 1: Change $\frac{4}{a-3}$ to a fraction with $a^2 - 9$ as its denominator.

$$\frac{4}{a-3} = \frac{4 \cdot (a+3)}{(a-3)(a+3)} = \frac{4(a+3)}{a^2-9}$$

Example 2: Change $\frac{4r-3}{6r}$ to a fraction with $18r^4s$ as its denominator.

$$\frac{4r-3}{6r} = \frac{(4r-3) \cdot 3rs}{6r \cdot 3rs} = \frac{3rrs(4r-3)}{18r^2s}$$

65. Reducing Fractions to Lowest Terms

As in arithmetic, when the numerator and denominator of a fraction have no common factor other than 1, the fraction is said to be in its lowest terms. The fraction $\frac{3}{8}, \frac{a}{b}$, and $\frac{p+q}{p-q}$, therefore, are in their lowest terms since the numerator and denominator of each fraction have no other factor except 1. The fractions $\frac{6}{12}$ and $\frac{3a}{9a^2}$ are not in their lowest terms. The fraction $\frac{6}{12}$ can be reduced to its lowest term by dividing both the numerator and denominator by 6. Similarly, the fraction $\frac{5y}{15y^2}$ can be reduced to $\frac{1}{3y}$ by dividing the numerator and denominator by $5y$. Thus, to reduce a fraction to its lowest terms, factor the numerator and denominator into prime factors and cancel the factors common to both (since they are equal to $\frac{1}{1}$).

Example 1: Reduce $\frac{6y}{8y^2}$ to lowest terms.

$$\frac{6y}{8y^2} = \frac{2y(3)}{2y(4y)} = \frac{3}{4y}$$

Example 2: Reduce $\frac{xab^2}{xcb}$ to lowest terms.

$$\frac{xab^2}{xcb} = \frac{xb(ab)}{xb(c)} = \frac{ab}{c}$$

Example 3: Reduce $\dfrac{a^2 - b^2}{4a + 4b}$ to lowest terms.

$$\dfrac{a^2 - b^2}{4a + 4b} = \dfrac{(a+b)(a-b)}{4(a+b)} = \dfrac{a-b}{4}$$

Example 4: Reduce $\dfrac{2a^2 + 4ab + 2b^2}{2a + 2b}$ to lowest terms.

$$\dfrac{2a^2 + 4ab + 2b^2}{2a + 2b} = \dfrac{2(a+b)(a+b)}{2(a+b)} = \dfrac{a+b}{1} = a+b$$

66. Finding Lowest Common Denominator

The lowest common denominator (LCD) of two or more fractions is the smallest term or number that is divisible by each of the denominators. Inspect to find this term or number, divide the LCD by the denominator of each fraction, and multiply both the numerator and denominator by the quotient. For example, when changing the fractions $\tfrac{2}{3}$ and $\tfrac{4}{5}$ to fractions which have an LCD, inspection shows that 15 is the smallest number which is divisible by both 3 and 5. Thus, the fractions $\tfrac{2}{3}$ and $\tfrac{3}{5}$ become $\tfrac{10}{15}$ and $\tfrac{9}{15}$. Similarly, the LCD of $\dfrac{4xy}{3a^2}$ and $\dfrac{6z}{4ab}$ is $12a^2b$ because this is the smallest term that is divisible by both $3a^2$ and $4ab$. Thus, the fraction $\dfrac{4xy}{3a^2}$ and $\dfrac{6z}{4ab}$ become $\dfrac{16xyb}{12a^2b}$ and $\dfrac{18za}{12a^2b}$, respectively. When fractions have factors with exponents in the denominators, the highest power of each distinct factor is used to form the LCD. For example, consider the problem of finding the LCD of fractions having the following denominators: x^3y^2z, $x^2y^4z^3$, y^4z^2, x^2y^4. The LCD is $x^3y^4z^3$ because x^3, y^4, and z^3 are the highest powers of x, y, and z in any one denominator.

Example: Change $\dfrac{3a}{a^2 - b^2}$ and $\dfrac{4b}{a^2 - ab - 2b^2}$ to equivalent fractions having an LCD.

Step 1. Factor each denominator into its prime factors:

$$\dfrac{3a}{a^2 - b^2} = \dfrac{3a}{(a+b)(a-b)}$$

$$\dfrac{4b}{a^2 - ab - 2b^2} = \dfrac{4b}{(a+b)(a-2b)}$$

Step 2. The lowest common multiple of the denominators is the LCD:

$$(a+b)(a-b)(a-2b)$$

Step 3. Divide the LCD by the denominators:

$$(a+b)(a-b)(a-2b) \div (a+b)(a-b) = a - 2b$$
$$(a+b)(a-b)(a-2b) \div (a+b)(a-2b) = a - b$$

Step 4. Change $\dfrac{3a}{(a+b)(a-b)}$ into a fraction having $(a+b)(a-b)(a-2b)$ as its denominator:

$$\dfrac{3a}{(a+b)(a-b)} = \dfrac{3a(a-2b)}{(a+b)(a-b)(a-2b)}$$

Step 5. Change $\dfrac{4b}{(a+b)(a-2b)}$ into a fraction having $(a+b)(a-b)(a-2b)$ as its denominator.

$$\dfrac{4b}{(a+b)(a-2b)} = \dfrac{4b(a-b)}{(a+b)(a-b)(a-2b)}$$

Step 6. Therefore, $\dfrac{3a}{a^2 - b^2} = \dfrac{3a(a-2b)}{(a+b)(a-b)(a-2b)}$

and $\dfrac{4b}{a^2 - ab - b^2} = \dfrac{4b(a-b)}{(a+b)(a-b)(a-2b)}$

67. Addition and Subtraction of Algebraic Fractions

a. Addition. The addition of algebraic fractions is similar to the corresponding operation in arithmetic. To add two or more fractions having a common denominator, add the numerators and place the result over the common denominator. If the fractions have different denominators, convert them to fractions with an LCD. The sum of the fractions is equal to the algebraic sum of the numerators divided by the LCD. Simplify the numerator and reduce the result to its lowest terms. If possible, factor or combine for further simplification.

Example: Find the sum of $\dfrac{2x}{x+y}$ and $\dfrac{2y}{x-y}$.

The LCD is $(x+y)(x-y)$. Therefore,

$$\dfrac{2x}{x+y} + \dfrac{2y}{x-y} = \dfrac{2x(x-y)}{(x+y)(x-y)} + \dfrac{2y(x+y)}{(x+y)(x-y)}$$

$$= \dfrac{2x(x-y) + 2y(x+y)}{(x+y)(x-y)}$$

$$= \dfrac{2x^2 - 2xy + 2xy + 2y^2}{(x+y)(x-y)}$$

$$= \dfrac{2x^2 + 2y^2}{(x+y)(x-y)}$$

$$= \dfrac{2(x^2 + y^2)}{x^2 - y^2}$$

b. Subtraction. To subtract two fractions having a common denominator, subtract the numerator of the subtrahend from the numerator of the minuend and place the result over the common denominator. If the denominators are different, find the LCD and subtract, as shown below.

Example: Subtract $\dfrac{8}{x^2 + 6x - 16}$ from $\dfrac{9}{x^2 + 7x - 18}$.

The LCD is $(x-2)(x+8)(x+9)$. Therefore,

$$\dfrac{9}{x^2 + 7x - 18} - \dfrac{8}{x^2 + 6x - 16}$$

$$= \dfrac{9(x+8)}{(x-2)(x+8)(x+9)} - \dfrac{8(x+9)}{(x-2)(x+8)(x+9)}$$

$$= \dfrac{9(x+8) - 8(x+9)}{(x-2)(x+8)(x+9)}$$

$$= \dfrac{9x + 72 - 8x - 72}{(x-2)(x+8)(x+9)}$$

$$= \dfrac{x}{(x-2)(x+8)(x+9)}$$

68. Multiplication and Division of Algebraic Fractions

a. Multiplication. The process of multiplication of algebraic fractions is the same as in arithmetic. The product of two or more fractions is the product of the numerators divided by the product of the denominators. The operation may be simplified by dividing common factors in the numerator and denominator by the same factor.

Example 1: Multiply $\frac{6a^2b}{7x}$ by $\frac{21x^2y}{24a^2b}$.

The first numerator and the second denominator are divisible by $6a^2b$; the first denominator and the second numerator are divisible by $7x$. Therefore:

$$\frac{\overset{1}{\cancel{6a^2b}}}{\cancel{7x}} \cdot \frac{\overset{3xy}{\cancel{21x^2y}}}{\underset{4}{\cancel{24a^2b}}} = \frac{3xy}{4}$$

Example 2: Multiply $\frac{a^2+2ab+b^2}{a-b}$ by $\frac{a^2-2ab+b^2}{a+b}$.

$$\frac{a^2+2ab+b^2}{a-b} \cdot \frac{a^2-2ab+b^2}{a+b} = \frac{(a+b)(a+b)}{a-b} \cdot \frac{(a-b)(a-b)}{a+b}$$

$$= \frac{\cancel{(a+b)}(a+b)\cancel{(a-b)}(a-b)}{\cancel{(a-b)}\cancel{(a+b)}}$$

$$= (a+b)(a-b)$$

$$= a^2 - b^2$$

b. Division. To divide algebraic fractions, multiply the dividend by the reciprocal of the divisor. Thus, to divide by x, multiply by the reciprocal of x, that is $\frac{1}{x}$. In other words, invert the divisor and proceed as in multiplication.

Example 1: Divide $\frac{2a+2b}{a-3}$ by $\frac{a^2-b^2}{2a-6}$.

$$\frac{2a+2b}{a-3} \div \frac{a^2-b^2}{2a-6} = \frac{2a+2b}{a-3} \cdot \frac{2a-6}{a^2-b^2}$$

$$= \frac{2(a+b)}{a-3} \cdot \frac{2(a-3)}{(a+b)(a-b)}$$

$$= \frac{2 \cdot 2}{a-b}$$

$$= \frac{4}{a-b}$$

Example 2: Divide $\frac{z^2-z-6}{z^2-25}$ by $\frac{z^2+z-12}{z^2-z-20}$.

$$\frac{z^2-z-6}{z^2-25} \div \frac{z^2+z-12}{z^2-z-20} = \frac{z^2-z-6}{z^2-25} \cdot \frac{z^2-z-20}{z^2+z-12}$$

$$= \frac{(z-3)(z+2)}{(z-5)(z+5)} \cdot \frac{(z-5)(z+4)}{(z-3)(z+4)}$$

$$= \frac{z+2}{z+5}$$

69. Review Problems—Algebraic Fractions

a. Changing Signs of Fractions. Solve for the unknown.

(1) $\frac{4x+3}{6} - \frac{x-9}{4} = 5$

(2) $\frac{z-2}{4} - \frac{1}{2}$

(3) $\frac{r+4}{3} - \frac{r-2}{5} = 2$

(4) $\frac{4x-3}{6x} - \frac{4x+5}{3x} = 2$

(5) $\frac{7t+2}{3} = 3$

(6) $\frac{x-4}{3} + \frac{2x-5}{6} = 3$

(7) $\frac{2r+3}{5} - \frac{3r+2}{4} = 2$

(8) $\frac{7x-4}{3} + \frac{x-5}{5} = \frac{1}{5}$

b. Equivalent Fractions. Supply missing terms.

(1) $\frac{4}{8} = \frac{?}{16}$

(2) $\frac{1}{c} = \frac{?}{cx}$

(3) $\frac{3}{r-s} = \frac{?}{r^2-s^2}$

(4) $\frac{a-8}{1} = \frac{?}{3}$

(5) $\frac{l-6}{l-3} = \frac{?}{(l-3)(l-9)}$

(6) Change $\frac{4E^2}{R}$ into an equivalent fraction of which the denominator is $2I^2 R$.

(7) Change $\frac{1}{3rfc}$ into an equivalent fraction of which the denominator is $6\pi f^2 c$.

c. Lowest Common Denominator. Reduce to equivalent fractions having an LCD.

(1) $\frac{1}{R}, \frac{1}{R^2}, \frac{1}{r}$

(2) $\frac{1}{a+1}, \frac{x}{a-1}$

(3) $\frac{b}{2x}, \frac{c}{3x}$

(4) $\frac{y}{2}, \frac{y}{2y+6}$

(5) $\frac{2}{c}, \frac{3}{c+1}$

(6) $\frac{i}{e-5}, \frac{i}{2e-10}$

(7) $\frac{y}{c^2-d^2}, \frac{z}{c-d}$

d. Addition and Subtraction of Fractions. Perform the indicated operations.

(1) $\frac{1}{a} + \frac{4}{a} + \frac{7}{a}$

(2) $\frac{s}{t} + \frac{s+4}{2t} + \frac{s+3}{4t}$

(3) $\frac{3a}{4x^2y} + \frac{5b}{6xy^3}$

(4) $\frac{z^2-1}{2} + \frac{z^2-4}{4}$

(5) $\frac{3c-2d}{4cd^2} + \frac{2c-3d}{3c^2d}$

(6) $\frac{(r+1)(r-3)}{r^2+2r-15} + \frac{(r-2)(r+5)}{r^2+2r-15}$

(7) $3y - \frac{1}{4}$

(8) $\frac{a+b}{a-b} - \frac{a-b}{a+b}$

(9) $\frac{32}{25q^2} - \frac{16}{5q}$

(10) $\frac{3t-2t}{4tv^2} - \frac{2t-3t}{3t^2v}$

e. Multiplication and Division of Fractions. Perform the indicated operations.

(1) $\frac{9y^2}{16} \cdot \frac{2}{3}$

(2) $\frac{a^5}{b^4} \cdot \frac{a^6}{b^5}$

(3) $\frac{3x^2}{49y^2z} \cdot \frac{7yz^2}{9xm}$

(4) $\left(\frac{1}{r} - \frac{1}{s}\right)\left(r - \frac{r^2}{s}\right)$

(5) $\frac{2z^4-5xy-3y^2}{z^2-9y^2} \cdot \frac{3x+9y}{10x^2+5xy}$

(6) $\frac{a^2+2ab+b^2}{a^2-b^2} \cdot \frac{a+b}{a^2-2ab+b^2}$

(7) $3z \div \frac{1}{5}$

(8) $\frac{5ba^3}{6cd} \div 5b$

(9) $\frac{12s^4t}{20uv} \div \frac{3st}{4u^2v}$

(10) $\left(e+2-\frac{3}{e}\right) \div \left(e+1-\frac{2}{e}\right)$

Section VI. EXPONENTS AND RADICALS

70. General

Chapter 4 presents exponents and roots consisting only of whole numbers. However, to use exponents and radicals to solve many equations and formulas, a knowledge of additional operations is required.

71. Fractional Exponents

a. General. A fractional exponent is merely another way of expressing the root of a number. For example, the cube root of x usually is written $\sqrt[3]{x}$; however, it also can be written $x^{\frac{1}{3}}$. Similarly, $\sqrt{2}$ also can be written $2^{\frac{1}{2}}$.

b. Application. Fractional exponents have a practical value in simplifying algebraic problems. They follow the same rules as exponents that consist of integers, and can be added, subtracted, multiplied, or divided in the same way; thus

$$a^{\frac{1}{2}} \cdot a^{\frac{1}{2}} = a^{\frac{1}{2}+\frac{1}{2}} = a^1 = a, \text{ and } a^{\frac{1}{3}} \cdot a^{\frac{1}{3}} \cdot a^{\frac{1}{3}} = a^{\frac{1}{3}+\frac{1}{3}+\frac{1}{3}} = a^1 = a.$$

In other words, $a^{\frac{1}{2}}$ is one of two equal factors of a, and $a^{\frac{1}{3}}$ is one of three equal factors of a or the square cube root of a; therefore, $a^{\frac{1}{2}} = \sqrt{a}$ and $a^{\frac{1}{3}} = \sqrt[3]{a}$.

c. Changing from Radical Form to Exponential Form. To change a radical expression to exponential form, remove the radical sign and annex a fractional exponent to the radicand (number under the radical sign). The numerator of the fractional exponent is the power of the radicand, and the denominator is the index of the root.

Example 1: Change $\sqrt{a^3}$ to exponential form and simplify.

$$\sqrt{a^3} = (a^3)^{\frac{1}{2}}$$

Multiplying exponents and simplifying:

$$(a^3)^{\frac{1}{2}} = a^{3 \cdot \frac{1}{2}} = a^{\frac{3}{2}} = \sqrt{a}$$

Therefore, $\sqrt{a^3} = \sqrt{a}$.

Example 2: Change $\sqrt[3]{8a^2b^3}$ to exponential form and simplify.

$$\sqrt[3]{8a^2b^3} = \sqrt[3]{2^3a^2b^3} = (2^3a^2b^3)^{\frac{1}{3}} = 2^{3 \cdot \frac{1}{3}} a^{2 \cdot \frac{1}{3}} b^{3 \cdot \frac{1}{3}}$$
$$= 2^1 a^{\frac{2}{3}} b^{\frac{3}{3}} = 2^1 a^{\frac{2}{3}} b^1 = 2b \sqrt[3]{a^2}$$

d. Changing from Exponential Form to Radical Form. To change an expression with a fraction exponent to a radical form, make the base of the fractional exponent the radicand, the numerator of the exponent the power of the radicand, and the denominator of the exponent the index of the root.

Example 1: Change $4^{\frac{1}{2}}$ to radical form.

$$4^{\frac{1}{2}} = \sqrt{4}$$

Example 2: Change $3^{\frac{2}{3}}$ to radical form.

$$3^{\frac{2}{3}} = \sqrt[3]{3^2} = \sqrt[3]{9}$$

Example 3: Change $(5a^2b)^{\frac{2}{3}}$ to radical form.

$$(5a^2b)^{\frac{2}{3}} = \sqrt[3]{(5a^2b)^2}$$
$$= \sqrt[3]{25a^4b^2}$$

72. Simplification of Radicals

a. Removing a Factor from the Radicand. The form in which a radical expression is written may be changed without altering its numerical value. Sometimes there is a question as to what actually is the simplest form for an expression. For instance, consider the simplification of an expression such as $\sqrt{1250}$: $\sqrt{1250} = \sqrt{2.5^4} = 5^2\sqrt{2} = 25\sqrt{2}$. The expression $25\sqrt{2}$ usually is accepted as being simpler than $\sqrt{1250}$. As a general rule, the fewer the factors under the radical sign, the simpler the expression. Thus, a radicand may be separated into two factors, one of which is the greater power whose root can be taken. The root of this factor may then be written as the coefficient of a radical of which the other factor is the radicand.

Example 1: Simplify $\sqrt{50}$.

$$\sqrt{50} = \sqrt{25 \cdot 2}$$
$$= \sqrt{25} \cdot \sqrt{2}$$
$$= 5\sqrt{2}$$

Example 2: Simplify $\sqrt[4]{32a^7b^5}$.

$$\sqrt[4]{32a^7b^5} = (2^5a^7b^5)^{\frac{1}{4}}$$
$$= 2^{\frac{5}{4}}a^{\frac{7}{4}}b^{\frac{5}{4}}$$
$$= 2^{1\frac{1}{4}}a^{1\frac{3}{4}}b^{1\frac{1}{4}}$$
$$= 2a \sqrt[4]{2a^3b^5}$$

b. Rationalizing Denominator. Rationalizing a denominator containing a radical means to eliminate the radical in the denominator. For example, to rationalize the expression $\frac{1}{\sqrt[3]{2}}$, first change the denominator into an expression having a fractional exponent; thus, $\frac{1}{\sqrt[3]{2}} = \frac{1}{2^{\frac{1}{3}}}$; then multiply the denominator by a number that will make its exponent equal to 1. This operation eliminates the radical sign below the line. In this case, $2^{\frac{2}{3}}$ is such a factor; thus $2^{\frac{1}{3}} \cdot 2^{\frac{2}{3}} = 2^1 = 2$. Such multiplication can be performed without changing the value of the fraction if the numerator also is multiplied by the same number; thus $\frac{1}{2^{\frac{1}{3}}} \cdot \frac{2^{\frac{2}{3}}}{2^{\frac{2}{3}}} = \frac{2^{\frac{2}{3}}}{2^{\frac{1}{3}+\frac{2}{3}}} = \frac{2^{\frac{2}{3}}}{2}$. Finally, changing the numerator into radical form, $\frac{\sqrt[3]{2^2}}{2} = \frac{\sqrt[3]{4}}{2}$. Therefore, to rationalize a denominator, multiply both the numerator and the denominator by a number that will make the exponent in the denominator equal to 1; then simplify the radicand in the numerator. The examples below illustrate the method of rationalizing a few different types of denominators.

Example 1: Rationalize $\frac{1}{3^{\frac{2}{3}}}$.

$$\frac{1}{3^{\frac{2}{3}}} = \frac{1}{3^{\frac{2}{3}}} \cdot \frac{3^{\frac{1}{3}}}{3^{\frac{1}{3}}} = \frac{3^{\frac{1}{3}}}{3} = \frac{\sqrt[3]{3}}{3}$$

Example 2: Rationalize $\frac{1}{\sqrt{8}}$.

First simplify $\sqrt{8}$.

$$\sqrt{8} = \sqrt{4 \cdot 2} = \sqrt{4} \cdot 2^{\frac{1}{2}} = 2 \cdot 2^{\frac{1}{2}}$$
$$\frac{1}{\sqrt{8}} = \frac{1}{2 \cdot 2^{\frac{1}{2}}} = \frac{2^{\frac{1}{2}}}{2 \cdot 2^{\frac{1}{2}} \cdot 2^{\frac{1}{2}}} = \frac{\sqrt{2}}{4}$$

Example 3: Rationalize $\frac{1}{\sqrt{7}}$.

Here the square root in the denominator is being multiplied by itself, making the number a perfect square.

$$\frac{1}{\sqrt{7}} = \frac{1}{\sqrt{7}} \cdot \frac{\sqrt{7}}{\sqrt{7}} = \frac{\sqrt{7}}{\sqrt{7}\sqrt{7}} = \frac{\sqrt{7}}{7}$$

c. Practical Application. The processes of the simplification of radicals and rationalization of denominators are useful when computing decimals. It is necessary to know, however, that $\sqrt{2} = 1.414$, $\sqrt{3} = 1.732$, etc. For example, consider the problem of evaluating $\frac{1}{\sqrt{2}}$. One way of evaluating this problem is to divide 1 by 1.414. This evaluation is a long-division problem of some length, however. A much more simple way is to rationalize—thus $\frac{1}{\sqrt{2}} = \frac{\sqrt{2}}{2}$, and dividing 1.414 by 2 gives the result, 0.707.

73. Addition and Subtraction of Radicals

As discussed in paragraph 27b, terms that are alike in all respects, except for their coefficients, are called *similar terms*. Similarly, radicals that have the same index and the same radicand and differ only in their coefficients are called *similar radicals*. For example, $-5\sqrt{3}$, $2\sqrt{3}$, and $\sqrt{3}$ are similar radicals. Similar radicals may be added or subtracted in the same way that similar terms are added and subtracted. However, if the radicands are not alike and cannot be reduced to a common radicand, they are dissimilar and addition and subtraction can only be indicated; thus to add or subtract radicals, reduce them to their simplest form, then combine similar radicals, and indicate the addition or subtraction of dissimilar radicals.

Example 1: Perform the indicated operations.

$4\sqrt{6} - 5\sqrt{6} - \sqrt{6} + 10\sqrt{6} = 8\sqrt{6}$

Example 2: Add.

$\sqrt{48a} + \sqrt{\frac{a}{3}} + \sqrt{3a} = 4\sqrt{3a} + \frac{1}{3}\sqrt{3a} + \sqrt{3a}$
$= \frac{16}{3}\sqrt{3a}$

Example 3: Perform the indicated operations.

$\sqrt[9]{16r^2} - r\sqrt[3]{4r} + \sqrt[9]{64r^3} = \sqrt[9]{(4r)^2} - r\sqrt[3]{4r} + \sqrt[9]{(4r)^3}$
$= (4r)^{\frac{2}{9}} - 4(4r)^{\frac{1}{3}} + (4r)^{\frac{3}{9}}$
$= \sqrt[3]{4r} - r\sqrt[3]{4r} + \sqrt[3]{4r}$
$= \sqrt[3]{4r}(2-r)$

Example 4: Perform the indicated operations.

$2\sqrt{6} + \sqrt[9]{\frac{2}{3}} - \sqrt{36} + \sqrt[9]{\frac{2}{3}} = 2\sqrt{6} + \sqrt{\frac{2}{3}} - \sqrt{6}$
$= 2\sqrt{6} + \sqrt[9]{\frac{2}{3}} - \sqrt{6}$
$= 2\sqrt{6} + 3\sqrt{6} - \sqrt{6}$
$= 4\sqrt{6}$

74. Multiplication of Radicals

a. Radicals With Same Indexes. Radicals can be multiplied and combined under the same radical sign even though they differ in value, provided the index of the radicals are the same. To multiply a radical expression when radicals are of the same order, first multiply the coefficients, then multiply the radicands, and then simplify, if possible. For example, $2\sqrt{3} \cdot 3\sqrt{5} = 6\sqrt{15}$. If the radicand is a perfect square, simplify the result by extracting the square root. Remember that there are two square roots, one positive and one negative; thus, $6\sqrt{3} \cdot 4\sqrt{3} = 24\sqrt{9} = 24(\pm 3) = \pm 72$. When polynomial expressions, either or both of which involve radicals, are to be multiplied, proceed in the same manner as with literal polynominal expressions (par. 48). For example, $(\sqrt{3} + 2\sqrt{5}) \times (\sqrt{3} - 2\sqrt{5}) =$

$\sqrt{3} + 2\sqrt{5}$
$\sqrt{3} - 2\sqrt{5}$
$\overline{\sqrt{9} + 2\sqrt{15}}$
$\quad -2\sqrt{15} - 4\sqrt{25}$
$\overline{\sqrt{9} \quad\quad -4\sqrt{25}} = \pm 3 - 4(\pm 5)$
$= \pm 3 \pm 20$
$= 3 \pm 20 \text{ or } -3 \pm 20$
$= \pm 17 \text{ or } \pm 23$

Example 1: Multiply $2\sqrt[3]{3a}$, $5\sqrt[3]{4a}$, and $3\sqrt[3]{18a}$.

$2\sqrt[3]{3a} \cdot 5\sqrt[3]{4a} \cdot 3\sqrt[3]{18a} = 2 \cdot 5 \cdot 3 \cdot \sqrt[3]{3a} \cdot \sqrt[3]{4a} \cdot \sqrt[3]{18a}$
$= 30\sqrt[3]{216a^3}$
$= 30 \cdot 6a$
$= 180a$

Example 2: Multiply $\sqrt[4]{8t^3}$ and $\sqrt[4]{4t^2s}$.

$\sqrt[4]{8t^3} \cdot \sqrt[4]{4t^2s} = \sqrt[4]{32t^5s}$
$= \sqrt[4]{2^4 \cdot 2 \cdot t^4 \cdot t \cdot s}$
$= 2t\sqrt[4]{2ts}$

b. Radicals With Different Indexes. To multiply radicals when the indexes are different, first express them as radicals with a common index (or common fractional exponent) and proceed as in *a* above. The common index is the lowest common multiple of the indexes of the original radicals.

Example 1: Multiply $\sqrt{2} \cdot \sqrt[3]{4}$.

$\sqrt{2} \cdot \sqrt[3]{4} = \sqrt{2} \cdot \sqrt[3]{2^2}$
$= 2^{\frac{1}{2}} \cdot 2^{\frac{2}{3}}$
$= 2^{\frac{3}{6}} \cdot 2^{\frac{4}{6}}$
$= 2^{\frac{7}{6}}$
$= 2^{\frac{6}{6}} \cdot 2^{\frac{1}{6}}$
$= 2 \cdot 2^{\frac{1}{6}} \text{ or } 2\sqrt[6]{2}$

Example 2: Multiply $\sqrt[3]{4x} \cdot \sqrt[4]{8x^3}$.

$\sqrt[3]{4x} \cdot \sqrt[4]{8x^3} = \sqrt[12]{(4x)^4} \cdot \sqrt[12]{(8x^3)^3}$
$= \sqrt[12]{2^8 \cdot x^4} \cdot \sqrt[12]{2^9 \cdot x^9}$
$= \sqrt[12]{2^{17} \cdot x^{13}}$
$= \sqrt[12]{2^{12} \cdot 2^5 \cdot x^{12} \cdot x}$
$= 2x\sqrt[12]{2^5 \cdot x}$
$= 2x\sqrt[12]{32x}$

75. Division of Radicals

a. Monomial Radical Expressions. The division of radicals is essentially the opposite of multiplication. When radicals are of the same order, the division of two radicals may be expressed under one radical sign—for example, $\frac{\sqrt{4}}{\sqrt{2}} = \sqrt{\frac{4}{2}} = \sqrt{2}$. When radicals are of different orders, they must be expressed as radicals having the same index or be changed to fractional exponents.

Example 1: Divide $\sqrt{15}$ by $\sqrt{5}$.

$\frac{\sqrt{15}}{\sqrt{5}} = \sqrt{\frac{15}{5}} = \sqrt{3}$

Example 2: Divide $\sqrt[3]{x^2y}$ by $\sqrt[3]{y^7}$.

$\frac{\sqrt[3]{x^2y}}{\sqrt[3]{y^7}} = \sqrt[3]{\frac{x^2y}{y^7}} = \sqrt[3]{\frac{x^2}{y^6}} = \frac{x}{y^2}\sqrt[3]{x^2}$

Example 3: Divide $\sqrt{35}$ by $\sqrt{15}$.

$\frac{\sqrt{35}}{\sqrt{15}} = \sqrt{\frac{35}{15}}$
$= \sqrt{\frac{7}{3}}$
$= \frac{1}{3}\sqrt{21}$

Example 4: Divide $\sqrt{4ab} \sqrt[3]{2ab}$ by $\sqrt[6]{4a^5b^3}$.

$\frac{\sqrt{4ab}\sqrt[3]{2ab}}{\sqrt[6]{4a^5b^3}} = \frac{\sqrt[6]{(4ab)^3} \cdot \sqrt[6]{(2ab)^2}}{\sqrt[6]{4a^5b^3}}$
$= \sqrt[6]{\frac{64a^3b^3 \cdot 4a^2b^2}{4a^5b^3}}$
$= \sqrt[6]{64b^2}$
$= \sqrt[6]{2^6 b^2} \text{ or } (2^6b^2)^{\frac{1}{6}}$
$= 2\sqrt[3]{b}$

b. Binomial Expressions With Radical in Divisor. When the divisor is a binomial in which one or more of the terms contains a square root, division is performed by first rationalizing the divisor. Multiply the numerator and denominator of the fraction by the denominator with the sign between the terms changed; then simplify the denominator.

Example 1: Divide 3 by $4 + \sqrt{6}$.

$\frac{3}{4 + \sqrt{6}} = \frac{3}{4+\sqrt{6}} \cdot \frac{4-\sqrt{6}}{4-\sqrt{6}}$
$= \frac{3(4-\sqrt{6})}{16-6}$
$= \frac{3}{10}(4-\sqrt{6})$

Example 2: Divide $\sqrt{1+x} - \sqrt{1-x}$ by $\sqrt{1+x} + \sqrt{1-x}$.

$$\frac{\sqrt{1+x}-\sqrt{1-x}}{\sqrt{1+x}+\sqrt{1-x}} \cdot \frac{\sqrt{1+x}-\sqrt{1-x}}{\sqrt{1+x}-\sqrt{1-x}}$$

$$= \frac{(1+x) - 2\sqrt{1-x^2} + (1-x)}{(1+x) - (1-x)}$$

$$= \frac{2 - 2\sqrt{1-x^2}}{2x}$$

$$= \frac{1 - \sqrt{1-x^2}}{x}$$

76. Review Problems—Exponents and Radicals

a. Simplify.

(1) $2^{\frac{1}{2}}(2^{\frac{1}{4}})$
(2) $(8^{\frac{1}{3}})^2$
(3) $\sqrt{50}$
(4) $\sqrt[3]{\frac{1}{16}}$
(5) $\sqrt{18x - 9}$
(6) $\sqrt[3]{\frac{6x^{3a}}{y^a}}$
(7) $(x^{10}y^5)^{\frac{1}{5}}$
(8) $(d^8c^4)^{\frac{1}{4}}$
(9) $\left(\frac{64r^4}{g^3}\right)^{\frac{1}{2}}$
(10) $(a^2b^4)^{\frac{1}{4}}$

b. Express with radical signs.

(1) $4^{\frac{1}{2}}$
(2) $\frac{1}{a^2b^{\frac{1}{3}}}$
(3) $6^{\frac{2}{3}}$
(4) $(8f)^{\frac{1}{2}}$
(5) $5x^{-5}$
(6) $\frac{1}{a^{\frac{2}{3}}c^{1.5}}$
(7) $\frac{1}{6r^3}$
(8) $(8 a^2b^3)^{\frac{1}{3}}$
(9) $(2r_1 + 3r_2)^{\frac{1}{2}}$
(10) $3(x^4y^2)^{\frac{1}{2}}$

c. Express with fractional exponents.

(1) $\sqrt[4]{a^3}$
(2) $\sqrt[3]{6x}$
(3) $6x\sqrt[3]{a^2}$
(4) $\sqrt[5]{x^2}$
(5) $\sqrt{3a^3b^5}$
(6) $y^3\sqrt[4]{a^3}$
(7) $8\sqrt[3]{3c}$
(8) $9\sqrt{a^7}$
(9) $3b\sqrt[5]{cd^3}$
(10) $\sqrt[3]{(x-y)^3}$

d. Simplify by removing suitable factors from radicand.

(1) $\sqrt{12}$
(2) $\sqrt{63}$
(3) $\sqrt{63x^4}$
(4) $2\sqrt{72a^5b^4}$
(5) $\sqrt{605d^3}$
(6) $\sqrt{81^4k}$
(7) $3\sqrt{63pz^2}$
(8) $2d^{-2}\sqrt{108d^7d^8}$
(9) $5a\sqrt{81a^3b^5}$
(10) $16w^5x\sqrt{98w^{14-3}x^3y^2z}$

e. Rationalize denominators.

(1) $\frac{1}{\sqrt{50}}$
(2) $\frac{1}{\sqrt{4x}}$
(3) $\frac{2a}{\sqrt{3a}}$
(4) $\frac{1}{\sqrt[3]{x}}$
(5) $\frac{1}{\sqrt[4]{8ax^3}}$

(6) $\frac{1}{\sqrt[3]{8} - 2x}$
(7) $\frac{a+b}{\sqrt[3]{a^2}}$
(8) $\frac{a}{\sqrt[4]{a^2bc}}$
(9) $\frac{1}{\sqrt[3]{(s+1)^2}}$
(10) $\frac{i+3}{\sqrt[4]{(i+3)^2}}$

f. Simplify.

(1) $6\sqrt{4} - 3\sqrt{4} + 2\sqrt{4}$
(2) $6\sqrt{45} - 2\sqrt{20}$
(3) $x - \sqrt{\frac{3x^2}{4}}$
(4) $\frac{a}{2} + \sqrt{\frac{9a^2}{2}}$
(5) $\sqrt{rst} + rt\sqrt{\frac{s}{rt}}$
(6) $\sqrt{\frac{x+y}{x-y}} - \sqrt{\frac{x-y}{x+y}}$
(7) $\sqrt{5} + 3\sqrt{x} + 5\sqrt{x}$
(8) $7\sqrt{a} - 4\sqrt{5} - 2\sqrt{5}$
(9) $4\sqrt{x-y} + 3\sqrt{x+y} - 8\sqrt{x-y}$
(10) $3\sqrt{125a^3b^3} + b\sqrt{20a^3} - \sqrt{500a^3b^3}$

g. Find product and simplify.

(1) $3\sqrt{5} \cdot 4\sqrt{2}$
(2) $2\sqrt[3]{9} \cdot 3\sqrt[3]{3}$
(3) $4\sqrt[3]{a^2b^5} \cdot 2\sqrt{3z^2}$
(4) $\sqrt{4x^2} \cdot 2\sqrt{3x^2}$
(5) $\sqrt[3]{4x^2y^2} \cdot \sqrt[3]{4pq^4x^3} \cdot \sqrt[5]{4xy^4}$
(6) $2\sqrt[3]{2pq^4} \cdot \sqrt[3]{4pq^4x^3} \cdot 3\sqrt[3]{8pq^4x^3}$
(7) $(\sqrt{a} + \sqrt{b} + \sqrt{c})^2$
(8) $a\sqrt{x}(a\sqrt{ax} + x\sqrt{ax} + \sqrt{ax})$
(9) $\sqrt{9} - \sqrt{17} \cdot \sqrt{9} + \sqrt{17}$
(10) $\sqrt[3]{x^2y^4} \cdot \sqrt{256a^8}$

h. Divide and simplify.

(1) $\frac{\sqrt{12}}{\sqrt{3}}$
(2) $\frac{\sqrt[3]{625y}}{\sqrt[3]{5y}}$
(3) $\frac{\sqrt[3]{16x^2}}{\sqrt[3]{2x}}$
(4) $\frac{3zy}{\sqrt{zu}}$
(5) $\frac{\sqrt{6}-2}{2}$
(6) $\frac{\sqrt{30a}\sqrt[4]{24a^2}\sqrt[3]{72a}}{\sqrt[5]{5a}}$
(7) $\frac{\sqrt{2}+\sqrt{c}}{\sqrt{c}+2\sqrt{2}}$
(8) $\frac{4\sqrt{3}-3\sqrt{2}}{\sqrt{6}} \div \frac{\sqrt{10}}{4\sqrt{3}+3\sqrt{2}}$
(9) $\frac{\sqrt{e^2+f^2}+f}{\sqrt{e^2+f^2}-f}$
(10) $\frac{2b+\sqrt{1-4b^3}}{2b-\sqrt{1-4b^3}}$

Section VII. IMAGINARY AND COMPLEX NUMBERS

77. Imaginary Numbers

a. Indicated Square Root of Negative Numbers.

(1) In the study of roots to this point, only the roots of positive numbers have been considered. Sometimes a negative expression will appear under the radical. Such an expression originally was given the designation *imaginary number* to distinguish it from real numbers. In electricity and electronics, however, so-called imaginary numbers are used for real physical calculations—the reactance of a large capacitor or inductor must be calculated by using this type of number.

(2) In multiplication, when a real number is multiplied by itself the result is always positive. For example, $+5 \cdot +5 = 25$, and $-5 \cdot -5 = 25$. Therefore, any number raised to a power having an even exponent will be positive because like signs are being multiplied. However, this is not true for the interpretation of an expression such as $\sqrt{-9}$. Any negative number can be regarded as the product of a positive number of the same absolute value and -1, and the square root of a negative

number can be written as the square root of a positive number times $\sqrt{-1}$; thus, $\sqrt{-9} = \sqrt{9}\sqrt{-1} = 3\sqrt{-1}$, with $\sqrt{-1}$ being the imaginary number. Most mathematics texts represent the imaginary number $\sqrt{-1}$ by the letter i. However, the letter I or i means current in electrical formulas; therefore, the letter j, commonly called the *operator j*, is used in electronics.

Example 1: $\sqrt{-36} = \sqrt{(-1)36} = \sqrt{-1} \cdot \sqrt{36} = \sqrt{-1} \cdot 6 = j6$

Example 2: $\sqrt{-Z^2} = \sqrt{(-1)Z^2} = \sqrt{-1} \cdot \sqrt{Z^2} = \sqrt{-1} \cdot Z = jZ$

Example 3: $-\sqrt{-9a^2} = -\sqrt{(-1)9a^2} = -\sqrt{-1} \cdot \sqrt{9a^2} = -\sqrt{-1} \cdot 3a = -j3a$

b. Powers of Operator j. Imaginary numbers follow the fundamental laws of addition, subtraction, multiplication, and division. They also can be raised to a power; thus, $j^3 = j^2 \cdot j = -1(j) = -j$, and $j^4 = j^2 \cdot j^2 = -1(-1) = 1$. The values of the powers of j are obtained as follows:

$j^1 = j = \sqrt{-1}$
$j^2 = j \cdot j = \sqrt{-1} \cdot \sqrt{-1} = -1;$
$j^3 = j \cdot j \cdot j = \sqrt{-1} \cdot \sqrt{-1} \cdot \sqrt{-1} = -1\sqrt{-1} = -j;$ and
$j^4 = j \cdot j \cdot j \cdot j = \sqrt{-1} \cdot \sqrt{-1} \cdot \sqrt{-1} \cdot \sqrt{-1} = j^2 \cdot j^2 = -1 \cdot -1 = 1;$ but
$j^5 = j \cdot j \cdot j \cdot j \cdot j = \sqrt{-1} \cdot \sqrt{-1} \cdot \sqrt{-1} \cdot \sqrt{-1} \cdot \sqrt{-1} = j^4 \cdot j = j^1 = \sqrt{-1},$ and the whole cycle starts over again. Therefore, j^4 can be eliminated as many times as it is contained in an expression, reducing the quantity to j, j^2, or j^3 and getting its value from the following:

$j = j = \sqrt{-1}$
$j^2 = -1$
$j^3 = -j$
$j^4 = 1$

Example 1: Simplify j^{13}.
$j^{13} = j^{12} \cdot j = j \cdot \sqrt{-1} = \sqrt{-1}$

Example 2: Simplify j^{27}.
$j^{27} = j^{24} \cdot j^3 = j^3 = -j = -\sqrt{-1}$

c. Addition and Subtraction of Imaginary Numbers. These numbers may be added or subtracted in the same manner that any algebraic expression is added or subtracted (par. 44). First change the expression to the j form; then treat the j as any other letter in an algebraic expression.

Example 1: Add $\sqrt{-25}$, $\sqrt{-36}$, and $\sqrt{-9}$.
$\sqrt{-25} + \sqrt{-36} + \sqrt{-9} = j5 + j6 + j3 = j14$

Example 2: Add $6\sqrt{-2} + 5\sqrt{-8} + 8\sqrt{-18}$.
$6\sqrt{-2} + 5\sqrt{-8} + 8\sqrt{-18} = j^3\sqrt{2} + j^5\sqrt{8} + j^8\sqrt{18}$
$= j^3\sqrt{2} + j(5 \cdot 2)\sqrt{2} + j(8 \cdot 3)\sqrt{2}$
$= (j^6 + j^{10} + j^{24})\sqrt{2}$
$= j^{40}\sqrt{2}$

Example 3: Subtract $\sqrt{-64}$ from $\sqrt{-36}$.
$\sqrt{-36} - \sqrt{-64} = j^6 - j^8 = -j^2$

Example 4: Subtract $4\sqrt{-8}$ from $6\sqrt{-18}$.
$6\sqrt{-18} - 4\sqrt{-8} = j(6 \cdot 3)\sqrt{2} - j(4 \cdot 2)\sqrt{2}$
$= (j^{18} - j^8)\sqrt{2}$
$= j^{10}\sqrt{2}$

d. Multiplication of Simple Imaginary Numbers. When multiplying two imaginary numbers, remember that $j^2 = -1$, $j^3 = -j$, and $j^4 = 1$ (b above); then, proceed as with any problem in multiplication (par. 45).

Example 1: Multiply $\sqrt{-16}$ and $\sqrt{-4}$.
$\sqrt{-16} \cdot \sqrt{-4} = j^4 \cdot j^2 = j^2 8 = (-1)8 = -8$

Example 2: Multiply $\sqrt{-81}$, $\sqrt{-25}$, and $\sqrt{-49}$.
$\sqrt{-81} \cdot \sqrt{-25} \cdot \sqrt{-49} = j^9 \cdot j^5 \cdot j^7 = j^3 315 = (-j)315 = -j315$

e. Division of Single Imaginary Numbers. In the division of two simple imaginary numbers, when both the dividend and divisor contain operator j, divide both by j and proceed as with ordinary integers. If a j remains in the denominator, the denominator must be rationalized because the j represents a radical expression. To rationalize, multiply both the numerator and denominator by the imaginary number.

Example 1: Divide $\sqrt{-100}$ by $\sqrt{-16}$.
$$\frac{\sqrt{-100}}{\sqrt{-16}} = \frac{\overset{1}{\cancel{j}} \cdot 10}{\underset{1}{\cancel{j}} \cdot 4} = 2\tfrac{1}{2}$$

Example 2: Divide 12 by $\sqrt{-6}$.
$$\frac{12}{\sqrt{-6}} = \frac{12}{j\sqrt{6}} = \frac{12}{j\sqrt{6}} \cdot \frac{j\sqrt{6}}{j\sqrt{6}} = \frac{j12\sqrt{6}}{j^2 6} = \frac{j2\sqrt{6}}{-1} = -j2\sqrt{6}$$

Example 3: Divide $\sqrt{-3}$ by $\sqrt{-4}$.
$$\frac{\sqrt{-3}}{\sqrt{-4}} = \frac{\overset{1}{\cancel{j}}\sqrt{3}}{\underset{1}{\cancel{j}}2} = \frac{\sqrt{3}}{2} \text{ or } \frac{1}{2}\sqrt{3}$$

Example 4: Divide 6 by j.
$$\frac{6}{j} = \frac{6}{j} \cdot \frac{j}{j} = \frac{j6}{j^2} = \frac{j6}{-1} = -j6$$

78. Complex Numbers

a. Operations With Complex Numbers. A *complex number* is a real number united to an imaginary number by a plus or minus sign; thus, $10 - j5$, $x + jy$, and $R + jx$ are complex numbers. Complex numbers are of great importance in alternating-current electricity in which many problems would be difficult to solve without their use. A complex number expressed in the form $x + jy$ may be considered a binomial; thus, the addition, subtraction, multiplication, and division of complex numbers are reduced to the corresponding operations with binomials in which one term is real and the other imaginary.

b. Addition and Subtraction of Complex Numbers. To add or subtract complex numbers, first combine the real parts, then combine the imaginary parts, and write the results as a binomial with the appropriate sign separating the real and imaginary terms.

Example 1: Add $3 + j5$ and $5 - j$.
$(3 + j5) + (5 - j) = 3 + j5 + 5 - j$
$= 8 + j4$

Example 2: Add $6 + \sqrt{-25}$ and $8\sqrt{-16}$.
$$(6 + \sqrt{-25}) + (8\sqrt{-16}) = 6 + j5 + (8 \cdot j4)$$
$$= 6 + j5 + j32$$
$$= 6 + j37$$

Example 3: Add $8 + \sqrt{-12}$ and $9 + \sqrt{-75}$.
$$(8 + \sqrt{-12}) + (9 + \sqrt{-75}) = 8 + j2\sqrt{3} + 9 + j5\sqrt{3}$$
$$= 17 + j7\sqrt{3}$$

Example 4: Subtract $7 - j6$ from $3 - j2$.
$$(3 - j2) - (7 - j6) = 3 - j2 - 7 + j6$$
$$= -4 + j4$$

Example 5: Subtract $2 - 3\sqrt{-4}$ from $10 + \sqrt{-4}$.
$$(10 + \sqrt{-4}) - (2 - 3\sqrt{-4}) = (10 + j2) - (2 - j6)$$
$$= 10 + j2 - 2 + j6$$
$$= 8 + j8 \text{ or } 8(1 + j)$$

Example 6: Subtract $3 + 7\sqrt{-24}$ from $5 + 3\sqrt{-6}$.
$$(5 + 3\sqrt{-6}) - (3 + 7\sqrt{-24}) = 5 + j3\sqrt{6} - [3 + j(7 \cdot 2)\sqrt{6}]$$
$$= 5 + j3\sqrt{6} - 3 - j14\sqrt{6}$$
$$= 2 - j11\sqrt{6}$$

c. *Multiplication of Complex Numbers.* As in addition and subtraction, when complex numbers are multiplied they are treated as ordinary binomials. Remember, however, that $j^2 = -1$.

Example 1: Multiply $3 - j6$ by $4 + j2$.

$$\begin{array}{r} 3 - j6 \\ 4 + j2 \\ \hline 12 - j24 \\ +j6 - j^2 12 \\ \hline 12 - j18 - j^2 12 = j12 - j18 - (-1)(12) \\ = 12 - j18 + 12 \\ = 24 - j18 \end{array}$$

Example 2: Multiply $8 - \sqrt{-5}$ by $-2 + \sqrt{-6}$.

$$\begin{array}{r} 8 - j\sqrt{5} \\ -2 + j\sqrt{6} \\ \hline -16 + j2\sqrt{5} + j8\sqrt{6} - j^2\sqrt{30} = -16 + j2\sqrt{5} + j8\sqrt{6} - (-1)\sqrt{30} \\ = -16 + j2\sqrt{5} + j8\sqrt{6} + \sqrt{30} \\ = -16 + \sqrt{30} + j(2\sqrt{5} + 8\sqrt{6}) \end{array}$$

d. *Division of Complex Numbers.* When dividing complex numbers, the denominator of the expression in its fractional form must first be rationalized (par. 74). To obtain a real number as a divisor, multiply both the numerator and denominator by the complex number of the denominator with its sign changed (called the *conjugate* of the complex number). In carrying out the multiplication, the complex expression is eliminated. Since $j^2 = -1$, the sign of the coefficient of j^2 is changed; the complex number thus becomes a real number to combine with the other real number in the denominator.

Example 1: Divide $3 + j4$ by $1 + j$.
$$\frac{3 + j4}{1 + j} = \frac{3 + j4}{1 + j} \cdot \frac{1 - j}{1 - j}$$
$$= \frac{3 + j - j^2 4}{1 - j^2}$$
$$= \frac{3 + j - (1-1)4}{1 - (-1)}$$
$$= \frac{3 + j + 4}{2}$$
$$= \frac{7}{2} + j\frac{1}{2}$$

Example 2: Divide 6 by $3 + \sqrt{-2}$.
$$\frac{6}{3 + \sqrt{-2}} = \frac{6}{3 + j\sqrt{2}} \cdot \frac{3 - j\sqrt{2}}{3 - j\sqrt{2}}$$
$$= \frac{6(3 - j\sqrt{2})}{(3 + j\sqrt{2})(3 - j\sqrt{2})}$$
$$= \frac{18 - j6\sqrt{2}}{9 - j^2 2}$$
$$= \frac{18 - j6\sqrt{2}}{11}$$

79. Review Problems—Imaginary and Complex Numbers

a. Simplify the radical, using operator j.
  (1) $\sqrt{-75}$
  (2) $\sqrt{-23}$
  (3) $-\sqrt{-64ax^2}$
  (4) $-\sqrt{100x^4y^4}$
  (5) $\sqrt{-\frac{1}{9}}$
  (6) $\sqrt[3]{-128x^6y^5}$

b. Add.
  (1) $-47 + j17$ and $63 + j92$
  (2) $27 - j11$ and $14 - j11$
  (3) $123 - j114$ and $-62 - j137$
  (4) $44 + j17$ and $-j7$
  (5) $6 + j10$ and $j1$
  (6) $14 + j15$ and $-16 - j62$

c. Subtract.
  (1) $-69 + j432$ from $710 + j61$
  (2) $14 - j121$ from $73 - j7$
  (3) $84 - j62$ from $62 - j47$
  (4) $-74 - j20$ from $81 - j81$
  (5) $-87 - j7$ from $82 + j16$
  (6) $-9 + j$ from $-j7$

d. Multiply.
  (1) $4 + \sqrt{-81}$ by $2 + \sqrt{-49}$
  (2) $2 + 2\sqrt{-2}$ by $3 + 3\sqrt{-3}$
  (3) $2 - j3$ by $2 + j3$
  (4) $(2 - j3)^2$
  (5) $(j^4 + j^2 + j^3 + j^4)^3$
  (6) $4 - j7$ by $8 + j2$
  (7) $f + jg$ by $f + jg$
  (8) $I + jE$ by $I - jE$
  (9) $8 - j13$ by $11 - j12$
  (10) $5 + \sqrt{-16}$ by $7 - \sqrt{-81}$

e. Divide.
  (1) 1 by $3 + j2$
  (2) $6 + j$ by j
  (3) $2 + j3$ by $3 - j4$
  (4) $4 + \sqrt{-9}$ by $2 - \sqrt{-1}$
  (5) $x + jy$ by $x - jy$
  (6) 10 by $1 + j^2$
  (7) 3 by $1 - j$
  (8) $3 + \sqrt{-25}$ by $4 - \sqrt{-4}$
  (9) $6 - j2$ by $4 - j7$
  (10) $I + jE$ by $I - jE$

Section VIII. EQUATIONS

80. General

An *equation* is a statement of equality between two expressions. For example, $x + y = 12$, $3x + 5 = 20$, and $3 \cdot 9 = 27$ are equations; therefore, all expressions separated by the equality sign are equations, whether the expressions are algebraic or arithmetical. The expression to the left of the equality sign is called the *left-hand member* of the equation; the expression to the right of the equality sign is called the *right-hand member*. Finding the values of the unknown quantities of an algebraic equation is known as solving the equation, and the answer is called the *solution*. If only one unknown is involved, the solution is also called the *root*.

81. Solving Simple Equations

a. Adding Same Quantity to Both Members of Equation. Equal quantities may be added to both sides of an equation without changing the equality.

Example 1: Solve the equation $x - 4 = 7$ for x.

$$x - 4 = 7$$
$$x - 4 + 4 = 7 + 4$$
$$x = 11$$

Example 2: Solve the equation $x - 7 = 14$ for x.

$$x - 7 = 14$$
$$x - 7 + 7 = 14 + 7$$
$$x = 21$$

b. Subtracting Same Quantity From Both Members of Equation. Equal quantities may be subtracted from both sides of an equation.

Example 1: Solve the equation $x + 2 = 5$ for x.

$$x + 2 = 5$$
$$x + 2 - 2 = 5 - 2$$
$$x = 3$$

Example 2: Solve the equation $x + 5 = 12$ for x.

$$x + 5 = 12$$
$$x + 5 - 5 = 12 - 5$$
$$x = 7$$

c. Multiplying Both Members of Equation by Same Quantity. Both sides of an equation can be multiplied by the same quantity.

Example 1: Solve the equation $\frac{x}{3} = 5$ for x.

$$\frac{x}{3} = 5$$
$$\frac{x}{3} \cdot \frac{3}{1} = 5 \cdot 3$$
$$x = 15$$

Example 2: Solve the equation $\frac{z}{3} + \frac{z}{9} = 4$ for z.

Multiply both sides of the equation by 9.

$$\left(\frac{z}{3} \cdot \frac{9}{1}\right) + \left(\frac{z}{9} \cdot \frac{9}{1}\right) = 4 \cdot 9$$
$$3z + z = 36$$
$$4z = 36$$
$$z = 9$$

d. Dividing Both Members of Equation by Same Quantity. Both sides of an equation may be divided by the same quantity.

Example 1: Solve the equation $3x = 12$ for x.

$$3x = 12$$
$$\frac{3x}{3} = \frac{12}{3}$$
$$x = 4$$

Example 2: Solve the equation $PV = RT$ for T.

$$PV = RT$$
$$\frac{PV}{R} = \frac{RT}{R}$$
$$T = \frac{PV}{R}$$

82. Solving More Difficult Equations

a. Transposition. The process of adding to or subtracting from both members of an equation (par. 81a and b) can be shortened by shifting a term or terms from one side of the equation to the other and changing the signs. This operation is called transposition.

Example 1: Solve the equation $6x + 4 = x - 16$ for x.

$$6x + 4 = x - 16$$
$$6x - x = -16 - 4$$
$$5x = -20$$
$$x = -4$$

Example 2: Solve the equation $2a + 2 = 2a + 2$ for a.

$$5a - 7 = 2a + 2$$
$$5a - 2a = 2 + 7$$
$$3a = 9$$
$$a = 3$$

b. Equations With Fractions. In solving a fractional equation, first find the LCD and multiply both members of the equation, term by term; then perform the operations in paragraph 81 or *a* above.

Example 1: Solve the equation $\frac{x}{2} + \frac{x}{3} = 10$ for x.

$$\frac{x}{2} + \frac{x}{3} = 10$$
$$\frac{3x + 2x}{6} = 10$$
$$\frac{5x}{6} = \frac{10}{1}$$
$$5x = 60$$
$$x = 12$$

Example 2: Solve the equation $\frac{x-1}{2} + x$ for x.

$$\frac{x-1}{2} + x = 3 + x$$
$$\frac{x-1}{2} = \frac{3+x}{1}$$
$$1(x-1) = 2(3+x)$$
$$x - 1 = 6 + 2x$$
$$x - 2x = 6 + 1$$
$$-x = 7$$
$$x = -7$$

Example 3: Solve the equation $\frac{2}{x+4} = \frac{4}{x-3} = \frac{2}{x-2} +$ for x.

$$\frac{2}{x+4} = \frac{4}{x-3} = \frac{2}{x-2} + \frac{4}{x-3}$$

$$\frac{2(x+4) + 2(x-2)}{(x-2)(x+4)} = \frac{4}{x-3}$$

$$\frac{2x + 8 + 2x - 4}{(x-2)(x+4)} = \frac{4}{x-3}$$

$$\frac{4x + 4}{(x-2)(x+4)} = \frac{4}{x-3}$$

$$(4x+4)(x-3) = 4(x-2)(x+4)$$

$$4x^2 - 8x - 12 = 4(x^2 + 2x - 8)$$

$$4x^2 - 8x - 12 = 4x^2 + 8x - 32$$

$$4x^2 - 4x^2 - 8x - 8x = -32 + 12$$

$$-16x = -20$$

$$16x = 20$$

$$x = \frac{20}{16} = \frac{5}{4} = 1\frac{1}{4}$$

83. Written Equations

Many practical problems are stated in words and must be translated into symbols before the rules of algebra can be applied. There are no specific rules for the translation of a written problem into an equation of numbers, signs, and symbols. The following general suggestions may be helpful in developing equations:

a. From the worded statement of the problem, select the unknown quantity (or one of the unknown quantities) and represent it by a letter, such as x. Write the expression, stating exactly what x represents and the units in which it is measured.

b. If there is more than one unknown quantity in the problem, try to represent each unknown in terms of the first unknown.

Example 1: In simple problems, an equation may be written by an almost direct translation into algebraic symbols; thus,

Seven times a certain voltage diminished by 3
$$7 \times E - 3$$

gives the same result as the voltage increased by 75,
$$= E + 75.$$

Solving the equation:
$$7E - 3 = E + 75$$
$$7E - E = 75 + 3$$
$$6E = 78$$
$$E = 13$$

expressed in an equation by using letters, symbols, and constant terms. For example, a formula in electricity states that the voltage across any part of a circuit is equal to the product of the current and resistance of that part of the circuit. In formula form, this is expressed as $E = IR$, where E is the *voltage or difference in potential* expressed in *volts*, I is the *current* expressed in *amperes*, and R is the *resistance* expressed in *ohms*.

b. Solving the Formula. To solve a formula, perform the same operations on both members of an equation until the desired unknown can be isolated in one member of the equation. If the numerical values for some variables are given, substitute in the formula and solve for the unknown as in any other equation.

Example 1: Solve the formula $T = \frac{12(D-d)}{l}$ for D.

Multiply both sides by l:
$$Tl = 12D - 12d$$

Transpose and change signs:
$$12D = Tl + 12d$$

Divide both sides by 12:
$$\frac{12D}{12} = \frac{Tl}{12} + \frac{12d}{12}$$

$$D = \frac{Tl}{12} + d$$

Example 2: Given the formula for electrical power, $P = I^2R$, find the value of P in watts when $I = 15.4$ amperes and $R = 25.7$ ohms.

Substituting the given numerical values for I and R:
$$P = I^2R$$
$$P = (15.4)^2 \times 25.7$$
$$= 237.16 \times 25.7$$
$$= 6{,}095 \text{ watts}$$

Example 3: Given the formula for the total resistance of two resistors in parallel,
$$R_T = \frac{R_1 R_2}{R_1 + R_2},$$
solve for R_2 in ohms when

$$3x + 3y = 51$$
$$-3x + 2y = -6$$
$$5y = 45$$
$$y = 9$$

Substitute $y = 9$ in the first equation and solve for x: Refer to (1) and (2) above.

c. Additional Examples. If the coefficients of the unknowns differ (for example, $3x$ and x and $2y$ and $4y$), multiply one or both equations to establish equal coefficients for one of the unknowns (x or y).

Example 1: Solve for x and y if $3x + 2y = 7$ and $x + 4y = 9$.

Multiply the first equation by 2 so that $2y$ will become $4y$:
$$6x + 4y = 14$$
$$x + 4y = 9$$

Subtract the second equation from the first equation:
$$6x + 4y = 14$$
$$-x - 4y = -9$$
$$5x = 5$$
$$x = 1$$

Solve for y by substituting $x = 1$ in either equation.

Example 2: Solve for x and y if $2x + 3y = 24$ and $3x - 4y = 2$.
$$2x + 3y = 24$$
$$3x - 4y = 2$$

Multiply the first equation by 4 to change $3y$ to $12y$; multiply the second equation by 3 to change $4y$ to $12y$; then add the two equations:
$$8x + 12y = 96$$
$$9x - 12y = 6$$
$$17x = 102$$
$$x = 6$$

Solve for y by substituting $x = 6$ in either equation.

85. Solving Formulas

a. The Formula. A formula is a rule or law that states a scientific relationship. It can be

---

Check: $7(13) - 3 = 13 + 75$
$91 - 3 = 13 + 75$
$88 = 88$

Example 2: A triangle has a perimeter of 30 inches. The longest side is 7 inches longer than the shortest side, and the third side is 5 inches longer than the shortest side. Find the length of the three sides.

Let $x = $ length of shortest side.
$x + 7 = $ length of longest side.
$x + 5 = $ length of third side.
$x + (x + 5) + (x + 7) = 30$

Solving the equation:
$$x + x + 5 + x + 7 = 30$$
$$3x + 12 = 30$$
$$3x = 30 - 12$$
$$3x = 18$$
$$x = 6 = \text{shortest side.}$$
$$6 + 5 = 11 = \text{third side.}$$
$$6 + 7 = 13 = \text{longest side.}$$

84. Simultaneous Equations

a. Definition. Simultaneous equations are two or more equations satisfied by the same sets of values of the unknown quantities. They are used to solve a problem with two or more unknown quantities.

b. Example. Assume that the sum of two numbers is 17, and that three times the first number less two times the second number is equal to 6. What are the numbers? In setting up equations for this problem, let x equal the first number and y equal the second number. The first equation is $x + y = 17$, and the second equation is $3x - 2y = 6$. This problem can be solved in three ways: by substitution, by addition, or by subtraction. All three methods are explained below.

(1) *Substitution.*
$$x + y = 17 \text{ or } x = 17 - y$$

Substitute $x = 17 - y$ in the second equation:
$$3x - 2y = 6$$
$$3(17 - y) - 2y = 6$$

Remove the parentheses:
$$51 - 3y - 2y = 6$$

Transpose:
$$-5y = 6 - 51$$
$$-5y = -45$$
$$5y = 45$$
$$y = 9$$

Substitute $y = 9$ in the first equation and solve for x:
$$x + y = 17 \text{ or } x + 9 = 17$$

Transpose:
$$x = 17 - 9$$
$$x = 8$$

(2) *Addition.*
$$x + y = 17$$
$$3x - 2y = 6$$

Before adding, change the y in the first equation to $2y$ so that the y terms drop out when added; thus, the first equation must be multiplied by 2.
$$2x + 2y = 34$$
$$3x - 2y = 6$$
$$5x = 40$$
$$x = 8$$

Substitute $x = 8$ in the first equation and solve for y:
$$x + y = 17 \text{ or } 8 + y = 17$$
$$y = 17 - 8$$
$$y = 9$$

(3) *Subtraction.*

Before subtracting, multiply the first equation by 3 so that the x terms drop out when subtracted.
$$3x + 3y = 51$$
$$3x - 2y = 6$$

Subtract the second equation from the first equation:

$R_1 = 40$ ohms and $R_2 = 60$ ohms.

$$R_T = \frac{R_1 R_2}{R_1 + R_2}$$

Substitute the given numerical values for R_1 and R_2:

$$R_T = \frac{40 \times 60}{40 + 60}$$
$$= \frac{2,400}{100}$$
$$= 24 \text{ ohms}$$

86. Review Problems—Equations

a. Solve for the unknown quantity in each of the following:

(1) $y + 12 = 15$

(2) $\frac{n}{8} = \frac{1}{4}$

(3) $0.63s = 53.55$

(4) $47x - 17 = 235 - 37x$

(5) $(10m + 6) - (11 - 15m) = 14m + 6m$

(6) $x + y = 3$
    $3x + 2y = 1$

(7) $a - 3b = 0$
    $5a - 4b = 11$

(8) $7x - 5y = 1$
    $5x + y = 19$

(9) $4m - 2n = 2$
    $3m + n = 14$

(10) $3r - 9s = 15$
     $6r - 7s = 41$

b. Solve the following formulas for the quantity indicated:

(1) $Fd = Wh$ for d

(2) $v^2 = v_0^2 + 2gh$ for g

(3) $F = \frac{w}{y}a$ for a

(4) $H = \frac{D^2N}{2.534}$ for N

(5) $F = \frac{22.5 \, BIl}{10^8}$ for l

c. Solve the following linear equations for the unknown quantity:

(1) $7(2x - 6) - 8 = 10x + 10$

(2) $10(x - 2) - 10(2 - x) = 4x - 40$

(3) $9.8a - 9.4 = 6.8a + .6$

(4) $2x + 3 + \frac{11x - 11}{3} = 22$

(5) $3R + 2(R - 4) = 6R - 10(R - 2)$

(6) $\frac{5Z}{4} + 2Z = \frac{3}{3} + \frac{Z}{3} - 7Z$

(7) $-(5x + 15) = 5x + 21 - \frac{5(2 - x)}{2}$

(8) $\frac{11y - 13}{25} + \frac{17y + 4}{21} + \frac{19y}{7} + \frac{3}{7} = 28\frac{1}{7} + \frac{5y - 25\frac{1}{2}}{4}$

(9) $\frac{4X_L}{5} - 6X_L + 2 = \frac{X_L}{4}$

(10) $(x - 1)(x + 1) + x(1 - x) = 4x(2x + 1) - 8x(x - 2)$

d. Solve the following sets of simultaneous linear equations:

(1) $5x - 2y = 10$
    $3x - y = 7$

(2) $6a + 15b = 69$
    $6a - 6b = 14$

(3) $x - 3y = -17$
    $2x + 6y = 50$

(4) $6x - 8y = 20$
    $3x + 2y = -14$

(5) $-4x + y = 13$
    $8x - 5y = -29$

(6) $2I - \frac{2T - 22}{3} = 30$
    $\frac{3I - 15}{4} + 6Z = 108$

(7) $\frac{2}{x} + y = 1$
    $\frac{1}{x} + 2y = 1\frac{1}{4}$

(8) $\frac{a}{3} + \frac{b}{4} = 1$
    $\frac{a}{5} + \frac{b}{2} = -\frac{4}{5}$

(9) $\frac{5}{x} + \frac{2}{y} = -1$
    $\frac{3}{x} + \frac{1}{y} = 1\frac{2}{3}$

(10) Solve for r and s:
     $(a - b)r + (a + b)s = a^2 - b^2$
     $(a + b)r - (a - b)s = 2ab$

e. Solve the following problems:

(1) Three times a voltage (E) diminished by 2 is equal to that voltage. What is the voltage?

(2) The sum of two resistances in series is 20 ohms. One resistance is 20 ohms. Give the algebraic expression for the other.

(3) If a certain voltage (E) is tripled and the result is diminished by 220 volts, the remainder is equal to the original voltage. What is the voltage?

(4) When two resistors are connected in series, the total resistance (R) is the sum of the two resistances. If one resistor is 25 ohms and the total resistance is 100 ohms, what is the value of the other resistor?

(5) The current (I) from a battery is divided among three circuits. The first circuit draws 20 milliamperes more than the second circuit, and the second circuit draws 20 milliamperes more than the third circuit. If the total current drawn is 240 milliamperes, what is the current in each circuit?

(6) Solving by the formula $I = \frac{E}{R}$, how much current (I) does an electric circuit having a resistance (R) of 20 ohms take if the voltage (E) is 110 volts?

Section IX. QUADRATIC EQUATIONS

87. General

A quadratic equation is one which can be reduced to the form $ax^2 + bx + c = 0$ where a, b, and c are known and x is the unknown quantity. In other words, a quadratic equation contains the square of the unknown quantity, such as x^2, but no higher power. For example, $3x^2 + 5x - 2 = 0$ and $x^2 - 4x + 3 = 0$ are quadratic equations. The form $ax^2 + bx + c = 0$ is called the *general quadratic equation*.

88. Pure Quadratic Equations

A pure quadratic equation is obtained from the general quadratic equation when b is equal to zero and the middle term (bx) does not appear. The equation then becomes $ax^2 + c = 0$. The pure quadratic equation has two roots that are equal in absolute value but have opposite signs. As discussed in paragraph 49, all numbers have two square roots. The equation $x^2 - 36 = 0$ is a pure quadratic equation since there are two numbers which, when substituted for x, will satisfy the equation. Thus $(+6)^2 - 36 = 0$ since $36 - 36 = 0$; also, $(-6)^2 - 36 = 0$ since $36 - 36 = 0$. Therefore, $x = \pm 6$.

Example: Solve the equation $x^2 - 5 = 20$ for x.

$$x^2 - 5 = 20$$
$$x^2 = 25$$
$$x = \pm 5$$

Check:

$$(\pm 5)^2 - 5 = 20$$
$$25 - 5 = 20$$
$$20 = 20$$

89. Solution by Factoring

a. Quadratic equations are found in many applications of even the simplest nature. For example, suppose that a sheet of metal is to be cut so that it has an area of 30 square inches, and that the length of the piece will be 1 inch longer than the width. With x representing the unknown width and $x + 1$ the unknown length, $x(x + 1)$ equals the area; therefore, the equation that must be satisfied is $x(x + 1) = 30$. By performing the indicated multiplication and subtracting 30 from each side, the equation now can be written in the form of a quadratic equation, as $x^2 + x - 30 = 0$.

b. To solve this equation, factor the left-hand side into the equivalent equation: $(x - 5)(x + 6) = 0$. The product of two factors is zero if either of the factors is zero (par. 53). Thus, each factor is set equal to zero and solved for the unknown. The equation is satisfied if $x - 5 = 0$ or $x = 5$. Note that the equation also is satisfied if $x + 6 = 0$. This illustrates an important fact concerning quadratic equations: *Every quadratic equation has two solutions.* Only one solution, however, may be appropriate when quadratic equations are used to solve actual problems. The quadratic equation only gives two *possible* solutions—the *actual* solution must be determined by referring to the facts in the original problem.

Example 1: Solve the equation $x^2 - 2x = 0$ for x.

$$x^2 - 2x = 0$$

Factoring:

$$x(x-2) = 0$$

so $x = 0$

or $x - 2 = 0$
$x = 2$

Thus, 0 or 2 are the roots of the equation $x^2 - 2x = 0$.

Example 2: Solve the equation $2x^2 - 3x - 5 = 0$ for x.

$$2x^2 - 3x - 5 = 0$$

Factoring:

$$(2x - 5)(x + 1) = 0$$

so $x + 1 = 0$
and $x = -1$

or $2x - 5 = 0$
$2x = 5$
$x = \frac{5}{2}$ or $2\frac{1}{2}$

Thus, -1 and $2\frac{1}{2}$ are the roots of the equation $2x^2 - 3x - 5 = 0$.

90. Solution by Completing the Square

In solving quadratic equations, the method of factoring described in paragraph 89 usually is best if the factors are immediately apparent by inspection. When the values of the unknown are not whole numbers or rational fractions, a quadratic equation can be solved more easily by the method of *completing the square*. This method also is used to derive the quadratic formula (par. 91). For example, to solve the equation $2x^2 - x - 2 = 0$ by completing the square, proceed as follows:

a. Transpose all terms involving x to the left-hand side of the equation and all other terms to the right-hand side. The equation is now in the form $2x^2 - x = 2$, or $x^2 - \frac{1}{2}x = 1$. When using this method, the coefficient of the squared term must be unity (one).

b. Add a number to both sides of the equation so that the left-hand side will be a perfect trinomial square. To determine this number, divide the coefficient of the middle term $(-\frac{1}{2})$ by 2 and square the resulting number.

$$x^2 - \frac{1}{2}x = 1$$

$$x^2 - \frac{1}{2}x + \frac{1}{16} = 1 + \frac{1}{16}$$

c. Replace the trinomial square on the left-hand side of the equation with the square of a binomial.

$$(x - \frac{1}{4})^2 = \frac{17}{16}$$

d. Extract the square root of both sides of the equation.

$$x - \frac{1}{4} = \pm \frac{\sqrt{17}}{4}$$

Thus, $x = \frac{1 \pm \sqrt{17}}{4}$

91. The General Quadratic Equation

a. General. Another method of solving quadratic equations consists of substitution in a formula derived from the general quadratic equation (*b* below). The general quadratic equation is in the form $ax^2 + bx + c = 0$, and any quadratic equation can be written in this form (par. 87). Thus, in the equation $2x^2 + 5x - 3 = 0$, $a = 2$, $b = 5$, and $c = -3$. Similarly, in the equation $9x^2 - 25 = 0$, $a = 9$, $b = 0$, and $c = -25$.

b. Deriving Formula for Solving any Quadratic Equation. Since the general quadratic equation, $ax^2 + bx + c = 0$, represents any quadratic equation, the roots of this equation will represent the roots of any quadratic equation; then, if the general quadratic equation is solved for the unknown values, the roots obtained will serve as a formula for finding the roots of any quadratic equation. The formula is derived from the general form by the method of completing the square; thus, given the general equation $ax^2 + bx + c = 0$, proceed as follows:

(1) Divide through by the coefficient a.

$$x^2 + \frac{bx}{a} + \frac{c}{a} = 0$$

(2) Subtract the term $\frac{c}{a}$ from both sides of the equation.

$$x^2 + \frac{bx}{a} = -\frac{c}{a}$$

This operation prepares the equation for the addition of a quantity to both sides of the equation that will make the left-hand side a perfect square. This quantity is obtained by dividing the coefficient of the x term by 2, and squaring the quotient. Since the coefficient of the x term is $\frac{b}{a}$, the quantity to be added to both sides of the equation is $(\frac{b}{2a})^2$, or $\frac{b^2}{4a^2}$.

(3) Add $\frac{b^2}{4a^2}$ to both sides of the equation.

$$x^2 + \frac{bx}{a} + \frac{b^2}{4a^2} = \frac{b^2}{4a^2} - \frac{c}{a}$$

(4) Factor the left-hand side of the equation, and add the fraction on the right-hand side.

$$(x + \frac{b}{2a})^2 = \frac{b^2 - 4ac}{4a^2}$$

(5) Take the square root of both sides of the equation.

$$x + \frac{b}{2a} = \pm \frac{\sqrt{b^2 - 4ac}}{2a}$$

(6) Subtract $\frac{b}{2a}$ from both sides of the equation.

$$x = -\frac{b}{2a} \pm \frac{\sqrt{b^2 - 4ac}}{2a}$$

(7) Collect the terms on the right-hand side of the equation.

$$x = \frac{-b \pm \sqrt{b^2 - 4ac}}{2a}$$

This equation is known as the *quadratic formula*. The two roots of any quadratic equation can be obtained by substituting in the formula the particular values of a, b, and c.

92. Solution by the Quadratic Formula

In practical problems, pure quadratic equations (par. 88) are seldom found, and solution by factoring (par. 89) can be used only occasionally. However, any quadratic equation can be solved by the method of completing the square (par. 90)—the method used to derive the quadratic formula (par. 91). This method is unnecessary, however, when the values for a, b, and c for any quadratic equation can be substituted in the formula $x = \frac{-b \pm \sqrt{b^2 - 4ac}}{2a}$.

Example 1: Solve the equation $2x^2 - 6x + 3 = 0$ by using the quadratic formula.

$$2x^2 - 6x + 3 = 0$$
$$a = 2; b = -6; c = 3$$

Substituting in the formula:

$$x = \frac{-b \pm \sqrt{b^2 - 4ac}}{2a}$$

$$x = \frac{-(-6) \pm \sqrt{36 - (4)(2)(3)}}{4}$$

$$= \frac{6 \pm \sqrt{12}}{4}$$

$$= \frac{3 \pm \sqrt{3}}{2}$$

Thus, $x = \frac{3 + \sqrt{3}}{2}$ or $x = \frac{3 - \sqrt{3}}{2}$

Check: $x = \frac{3 + \sqrt{3}}{2}$

$$x = \frac{3 + 1.732}{2} = 2.366$$

$$x = \frac{3 - \sqrt{3}}{2}$$

$$x = \frac{3 - 1.732}{2} = .634$$

Substituting in the equation:

$2(2.366)^2 - 6(2.366) + 3 = 0$
$11.20 - 14.20 + 3 = 0$
$14.20 - 14.20 = 0$

Substituting in the equation:

$2(.634)^2 - 6(.634) + 3 = 0$
$2(.40) - 3.80 + 3 = 0$
$3.80 - 3.80 = 0$

$3x^2 + 5x - 2 = 0$
$a = 3; b = 5; c = -2$

Substituting in the formula:
$$x = \frac{-b \pm \sqrt{b^2 - 4ac}}{2a}$$
$$x = \frac{-5 \pm \sqrt{25 - (4)(3)(-2)}}{(2)(3)}$$
$$= \frac{-5 \pm 7}{6}$$

Thus, $x = \frac{1}{3}$ or $x = -2$.

Check: $x = \frac{1}{3}$

Substituting in the equation:
$$3\left(\frac{1}{3}\right)^2 + 5\left(\frac{1}{3}\right) - 2 = 0$$
$$\frac{3}{9} + \frac{5}{3} - 2 = 0$$
$$\frac{1}{3} + \frac{5}{3} - 2 = 0$$
$$\frac{1}{3} + \frac{5}{3} - \frac{6}{3} = 0$$
$$\frac{6}{3} - \frac{6}{3} = 0$$

$x = -2$

Substituting in the equation:
$$3(-2)^2 + 5(-2) - 2 = 0$$
$$12 - 10 - 2 = 0$$
$$12 - 12 = 0$$

93. Character of the Roots

a. The values for unknowns that are not *which can be expressed as the ratio of two integers. For example, 9, $\frac{7}{3}$, $\frac{1}{8}$, and $\sqrt{16}$ are rational numbers. Any whole number is rational since it is the quotient of itself and unity; thus, $9 = \frac{9}{1}$. Numbers such as $\frac{7}{3}$ and $\frac{1}{8}$ are often referred to as rational fractions. A radical is rational if it can be expressed as the quotient of two whole numbers. Thus $\sqrt{16}$ is rational since $\sqrt{16} = 4 = \frac{4}{1}$. A number such as $\sqrt{3}$ which cannot be written as the ratio of two whole numbers is called irrational. Rational and irrational numbers, taken together, make up the system of real numbers. Any number, such as $3 + \sqrt{3}$, which contains a radical sign that cannot be removed also is considered irrational. Roots of quadratic equations are real if a minus sign does not occur under a radical. For example, $x = 5$ is a real root—roots such as $x = \frac{3 + \sqrt{3}}{2}$ or $x = \frac{3 - \sqrt{3}}{2}$ are real, but irrational.*

b. One important fact to be remembered when using the quadratic formula is that the expression under the radical sign, $b^2 - 4ac$, must be regarded as a whole before the square root can be taken. The quantity $b^2 - 4ac$ is called the *discriminant* of the quadratic equation. Many things can be learned about a quadratic equation merely by inspecting the discriminant. If the value of the discriminant is positive, real roots will be obtained when the equation is solved. These roots are either rational or irrational—rational when the discriminant is a perfect square, irrational when it is not. The roots are equal only when the value of $b^2 - 4ac$ is zero. When $b^2 - 4ac$ is negative, the square root will be that of a negative number and the roots will be imaginary.

c. In summary, *a quadratic equation always has two solutions.* The solutions will be:

Real and equal......... if $b^2 - 4ac$ equals 0.
Unequal but real...... if $b^2 - 4ac$ is positive.
Real and rational..... if $b^2 - 4ac$ is a perfect square.
Imaginary.............. if $b^2 - 4ac$ is negative.

94. Review Problems—Quadratic Equations

a. Solve by factoring.

(1) $2x^2 + 3x = 0$
(2) $(x - 4)x = 0$
(3) $(x + 3)\frac{x}{3} = 0$
(4) $\frac{1}{4}x^2 + \frac{1}{4}x = 0$
(5) $2x^2 - 128 = 0$
(6) $\frac{3}{4}x^2 - 2 = 1$
(7) $3x^2 - 25 = 2$
(8) $3x(x - 2) + 2x(3 - x) = 16$
(9) $x^2 - x - 42 = 0$
(10) $x^2 - 13x + 12 = 0$

b. Solve by completing the square.

(1) $x^2 + 3x - 1 = 0$
(2) $y^2 + 6y - 10 = 0$
(3) $E^2 - 4E + 1 = 0$

CHAPTER 6
GRAPHS

Section I. BASIC CHARACTERISTICS OF GRAPHS

95. General

A graph is a pictorial representation of the relation between two or more quantities. In many instances, problems are more clearly understood when solved graphically than when solved by other methods. Numerical data taken from an experiment or calculations derived from a formula require interpretation, and a curve on a graph depicting such data will provide a picture that shows at a glance how one factor or function depends on another.

96. The Number Line

a. In figure 15, on a straight line of indeterminate length, a point 0 has been chosen from which to measure distances. The point 0 is called the origin. A unit of measurement also has been chosen, and positive and negative integers have been marked off and labeled. The usual choice of two numbers is shown by the arrow. On the number line, Z_1 corresponds to -4, Z_2 corresponds to $3\frac{1}{2}$, and Z_3 corresponds to 5.2.

b. Consider a number z as corresponding to a point a distance of z units from 0. If z is positive, the point will be in the direction of the arrow from 0; if z is negative, the point will be in the opposite direction from 0. The relative size of two numbers is indicated graphically by the relative positions on the number

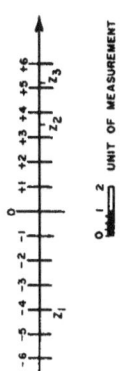

Figure 15. The number line.

line of points corresponding to the two numbers. For example, if z is greater than w, the point corresponding to z will be to the right of the point corresponding to w; if z is less than w, the point corresponding to z will be to the left of the point corresponding to w. The number of units from the origin to the point representing a certain number, regardless of direction, is the absolute value (par. 35) of the number.

97. Rectangular Coordinates

a. In the preceding paragraph, a relationship was given between numbers and points on a straight line. A similar relationship can be established between a pair of numbers and a point on a plane. In figure 16, two other lines are drawn perpendicular to each other at their origins for form a set of axes. The horizontal axis is commonly called the x axis;

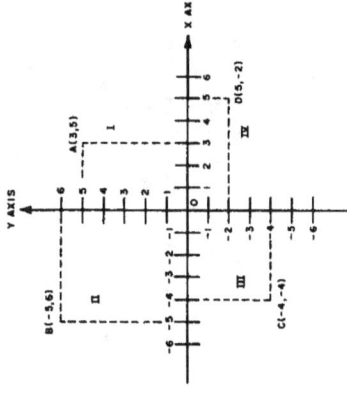

Figure 16. Rectangular coordinates.

c. Solve by using the quadratic formula.

(1) $a^2 + 2a + 1 = 0$
(2) $12y^2 - 6y + y = 0$
(3) $0 = 1 + 5E + 3E^2$
(4) $6I^2 + I - 12 = 0$
(5) $2c^2 + 4c - 6 = 0$
(6) $15R^2 = 22R + 5$
(7) $\frac{Z}{3} - \frac{2}{2} = 1 - Z$
(8) $\frac{3}{r - 2} = 1 + \frac{2}{r + 3}$
(9) $\frac{3x + 2}{2x + 4} = \frac{x + 2}{2x}$
(10) $0 = 6 - \frac{b - 2}{b + 2} + \frac{b - 1}{b + 1}$

(4) $2E^2 + 8E - 3 = 0$
(5) $8H^2 - 8H = 5$
(6) $5L^2 - 5 = 2L^2 - 10L$
(7) $14r^2 - 28r - 42 = 0$
(8) $\frac{1}{v^2} - \frac{4}{v} = 2$
(9) $y^2 - 5 = 2y$
(10) $8x^2 - 8x = 8$

the vertical axis is commonly called the *y axis*. Any point on the plane can be located with reference to the two axes: It must lie a certain number of units to the right (positive) or to the left (negative) of the *y* axis; and it must lie a certain number of units above (positive) or below (negative) the *x*-axis. To locate a point with reference to the set of axes, it is necessary only to know the *x* value and the *y* value of the point. These two values are known as the *coordinates* of the point. The *x* value, called the *abscissa*, is written first; the *y* value, called the *ordinate*, follows. The two numbers are separated by a comma and are usually inclosed in parentheses. Thus, in figure 16, the correct notation for the coordinates at point A is (3,5), because the *x* value is 3 and the *y* value 5.

b. The axes divide the graph into four sections, or *quadrants*, identified by the Roman numerals I, II, III, and IV in figure 16. The signs of the abscissa and the ordinate in each of the quadrants are given in the chart below.

Quadrant	Abscissa	Ordinate
I	+	+
II	−	+
III	−	−
IV	+	−

98. Plotting Points

The procedure for locating points by their coordinates is called *plotting* the points. To plot the point D (5,−2) in figure 16, for example, on the *x* axis five units to the right of the *y* axis; then erect a perpendicular to the *y* axis two units below the *x* axis; the point of intersection of these two perpendiculars is the point D (5,−2).

99. Review Problems—Plotting Points

a. Plot each of the following points and state the quadrant, if any, in which each lies:

(1) (4,2)
(2) (4,−2)
(3) (−1,3)
(4) (6,−1)
(5) (3,0)
(6) (0,−3)
(7) (−15,−27)
(8) (3¼,4¾)
(9) (5.6,−6.5)

b. Plot the points in the following chart and connect them by straight segments in the order of increasing values of *x*:

x	−3	−2	−1	0	1	2	3	4
y	18	8	2	0	2	8	18	32

c. Plot the points in the following chart and sketch a smooth curve passing through them in the order of increasing values of *x*:

x	−3	−2	−1	0	1	2	3
y	−37	−8	5	8	7	7	17

d. If $y = 2x − 3$, plot the points for which $x = 4, 2, 1, 0, −1, −2,$ and $−4$ after finding the corresponding values of *y*.

e. Draw the triangle of which the vertices are (−2,6), (3,2), and (0,−3).

f. Draw the quadrilateral of which the vertices, connected in the order given, are (1,3), (−3,4), (−2,−5), and (3,−2).

Section II. GRAPHING EQUATIONS

100. Graphing Linear Equations

a. General. An equation in the first degree in two unknowns is called a *linear equation* since its graph is a straight line. For example, $x + y = 5$, $2x + y = 12$, and $x − 6y = 6$ are linear equations. An equation is said to be of the first degree in two unknowns if only the first power of either unknown is involved and if neither of the unknowns appears in a denominator.

b. Plotting Graphs of Linear Equations.

(1) The first step in plotting the graph of a linear equation (or of any other equation or formula) is to set up a table of values for both unknowns that will satisfy the equation. In the equation $x + y = 5$, for example, it is apparent that there are a number of values for *x* and *y* that will satisfy the equation. For any number assigned to *x*, there is a corresponding number for *y* which will satisfy the equation. Consider that 4 and −4 will be the maximum plus and minus values for *x*. Using the values 4, 3, 2, 1, 0, −1, −2, −3, and −4 for *x*, the equation is solved for *y* at each value of *x*. These are arranged in tabular form as shown on figure 17.

(2) Each of these pairs of values gives a point on a graph. Consider each of the corresponding points as coordinates—the value of *x* the abscissa and the value of *y* the ordinate. The line joining these points (fig. 17) is the graph of the equation $x + y = 5$. Note that the coordinates for any two points are sufficient to determine its graph. Therefore, plotting the coordinates for any two points is sufficient to determine the graph of a first degree equation. Plotting a third point, however, will serve as a check, for if the three points are not on the same straight line, one of them is in error.

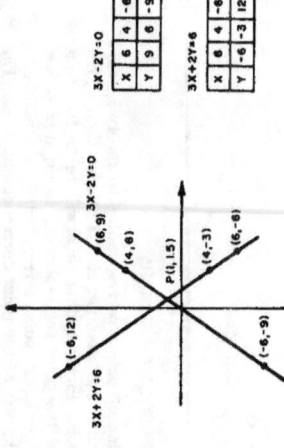

Figure 17. Graph of linear equation.

101. Graphical Solution of Simultaneous Linear Equations

a. When two *independent* linear equations contain the same two related unknowns, there will be an unlimited number of solutions for each equation. However, *there can be only one set of values that will satisfy both equations*. Determining the one set of values is known as the simultaneous solution of the two independent equations.

b. Graphically, the two equations can be solved simultaneously by plotting them on the same graph and locating their point of intersection (if there is one). For example, consider the graphical solution of the equations $3x − 2y = 0$ and $3x + 2y = 6$. Selecting 6 and −6 as the maximum plus and minus values for *x* and using $x = 4$ as a checkpoint, the coordinates for both equations are determined. For the equation $3x − 2y = 0$, these coordinates are (6,9), (4,6), and (−6,−9); for the equation $3x + 2y = 6$, (6,−6), (4,−3), and (−6,12). These coordinates are plotted on an axis and a line is drawn joining the plotted points of each equation (fig. 18). The graphs of the two independent linear equation cross at point P, where $x = 1$ and $y = 1.5$. To check the graphical solution of the equations, substitute these values for *x* and *y* in the original equations. Since they satisfy both equation, the graphical solution is correct.

c. If two *dependent* equations are plotted on a graph, their lines will coincide. For example, the equations $x + y = 4$ and $2x + 2y = 8$

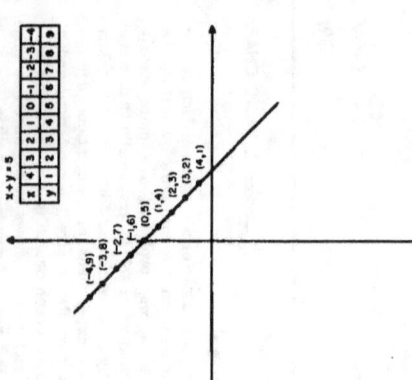

Figure 18. Graphical solution of simultaneous linear equations.

are dependent, since they can be reduced to identical forms. Selecting the same plus and minus values for x and the same checkpoint as in b above, the coordinates for both equations are found to be $(6,-2)$, $(4,0)$, and $(-6,10)$. Plotted on a graph, both equations form a single line (fig. 19).

d. Simultaneous equations that have no common solution are called *inconsistent*. No solution is possible for the equations $x + y = 3$ and $x + y = 5$, because there are no values for x and y which, when added together to make 3, will also equal 5. Using 6 and -6 as maximum plus and minus values for x, and using $x = 4$ as a checkpoint, the coordinates for equation $x + y = 3$ are found to be $(6,-3)$, $(4,-1)$, and $(-6,9)$; the coordinates for $x + y = 5$ are $(6,-1)$, $(4,1)$, and $(-6,11)$. Plotted on a graph, these equations form parallel lines (fig. 20).

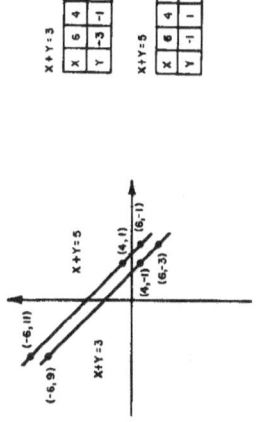

Figure 19. Graph of dependent simultaneous linear equations.

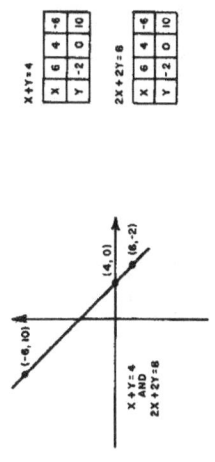

Figure 20. Graph of inconsistent simultaneous linear equations.

102. Graphing Quadratic Equations

a. The Dependent Variable. In graphing a quadratic equation, only two values, or points, for plotting the equation can be obtained by finding the roots of the equation (par. 88). These values do not give a complete picture of the equation. To get a continuous graph, a *dependent variable* is introduced. This variable, usually identified by the letter y, gets its name from the fact that it depends on another quantity for its value. For example, in the equation $y = x^2 - 6x + 5$, the value of y depends on the value of x; therefore, y is a dependent variable. The quantity on which y depends is called the *independent variable*. A more accurate designation for the dependent variable is $f(x)$, meaning *function of x*. Using this designation, the equation given above would be written $f(x) = x^2 - 6x + 5$. If the independent variable in the equation were z, the equation would be written $f(z) = z^2 - 6z + 5$.

b. Graphical Solution of Quadratic Equations. In the original equation $f(x) = x^2 - 6x + 5$, different values are substituted for the unknown to find the corresponding values of the function; thus if x equals -1, the equation becomes $f(-1) = (-1)^2 - 6(-1) + 5 = 12$; if x equals zero, the equation becomes $f(0) = 0 - 0 + 5 = 5$; if x equals 1, the equations becomes $f(1) = (1)^2 - 6(1) + 5 = 0$, etc. Compile a table of enough values to make it possible to plot the equation, as shown in figure 21. The graph of the function crosses the x-axis at two points, 1 and 5, which give a graphical solution of the equation $x^2 - 6x + 5 = 0$. The equation also may be solved by factoring, as follows:

$$(x-1)(x-5) = 0$$
$$x - 1 = 0 \text{ and } x - 5 = 0$$
$$x = 1 \text{ and } x = 5$$

Thus, the solutions or the roots of the equation are obtained when $f(x) = 0$. These roots represent the points where the graph of $f(x) = x^2 - 6x + 5$ crosses the x-axis.

c. Properties of Functions. In addition to the original equation, $f(x) = x^2 - 6x + 5$, consider three equations that differ in one respect—their constant terms are not the same. For example:

$$f(x) = x^2 - 6x + 8$$
$$f(x) = x^2 - 6x + 9$$
$$f(x) = x^2 - 6x + 12$$

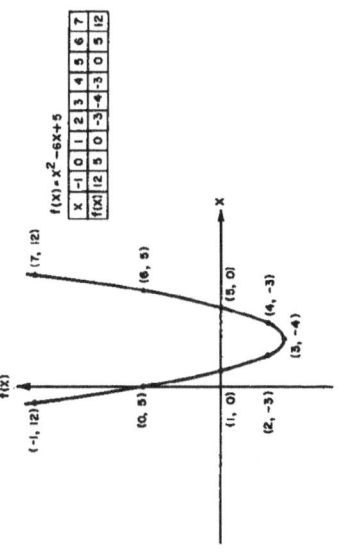

Figure 21. Graph of function of quadratic equation.

The graphs of the four corresponding functions have interesting properties and can be studied more advantageously when plotted on the same graph, as shown in figure 22.

(1) The function of $x^2 - 6x + 5$ crosses the horizontal or x-axis at two points, 1 and 5. These points indicate that the roots of the equation are $x = 1$ and $x = 5$. To compare this information with the discussion on quadratic equations in chapter 5, the discriminant of the equation must be investigated. The discriminate of $x^2 - 6x + 5$ is $(b^2 - 4ac) = (36 - 4 \cdot 1 \cdot 5) = 36 - 20 = 16$. Referring to the summary of the character of roots in paragraph 93, the roots are real and rational. To prove this, substitute the value of the discriminant in the quadratic formula.

$$x = \frac{-b \pm \sqrt{b^2 - 4ac}}{2a}$$

$$x = \frac{-(-6) \pm \sqrt{16}}{2}$$

$$x = \frac{6+4}{2} = 5 \text{ or } \frac{6-4}{2} = 1$$

Thus, the discriminant is a perfect square and the roots are real and rational.

(2) The function of $x^2 - 6x + 8$ crosses the horizontal axis at 2 and 4, indicating that the roots are $x = 2$ and $x = 4$. Calculating the discriminant, $(b^2 - 4ac) = (36 - 4 \cdot 2 \cdot 2) = 36 - 32 = 4$. Thus, the discriminant is a perfect square and will give real and rational roots.

(3) The function of $x^2 - 6x + 9$ touches the x-axis at only one point, 3. Thus, both roots of the equation are $x = 3$. Calculating the discriminant, $(b^2 - 4ac) = (36 - 4 \cdot 9) = 0$, which indicates that the roots are real and equal. Check the graph of this equation (fig. 22); it will be seen that the curve just touches the x-axis at one point. Thus, the root $x = 3$ must be counted twice and may be called a double root.

(4) The equation $f(x) = x^2 - 6x + 12$ has a discriminant equal to $(36 - 4 \cdot 12)$ or -12. Solving for the roots of this equation,

$$x = \frac{6 \pm \sqrt{-12}}{2} = 3 \pm \sqrt{-3}.$$

This is imaginary, but the meaning becomes apparent when the graph of the function of the equation is inspected. The plot does not cross the x-axis and, therefore, both roots must be imaginary.

d. Minimum Value of a Quadratic.

(1) The minimum value of a quadratic function will occur at $x = \frac{-b}{2a}$ when

the general quadratic equation $ax^2 + bx + c = y$ (par. 91) defines the coefficients a and b. This relation can be checked by calculating the value of x at which the minimum value of the function $x^2 - 6x + 5$ occurs and comparing this calculated value with the plot of the equation (fig. 21 or 22). Thus,

$$x = -\frac{b}{2a} = -\frac{(-6)}{2(1)} = \frac{6}{2} = 3,$$

and the minimum value of the function $x^2 - 6x + 5$ occurs at $x = 3$. Checking the graph verifies this statement. The minimum value of the functions $x^2 - 6x + 8$, $x^2 - 6x + 9$, and $x^2 - 6x + 12$ also occurs at $x = 3$.

(2) To find the value of the function at the minimum point, substitute for x. The minimum occurs at $x = -\frac{b}{2a}$; therefore, substitute $-\frac{b}{2a}$ for x in the function of the general quadratic equation.

$$f(x) = ax^2 + bx + c$$
$$= a\left(-\frac{b}{2a}\right)^2 + b\left(-\frac{b}{2a}\right) + c$$
$$= \frac{b^2}{4a} - \frac{b^2}{2a} + c = \frac{b^2}{4a} - \frac{2b^2}{4a} + c$$
$$= -\frac{b^2}{4a} + c$$

Thus, to find the value of the function $f(x) = x^2 - 6x + 5$ at the minimum point:

$$f(x) = -\frac{b^2}{4a} + c = -\frac{36}{4} + 5 =$$
$$-9 + 5 = -4$$

This method can be used to find the minimum value of the function if the value of x at which the minimum occurs is *not* known. However if it is known that the minimum value occurs at $x = 3$, merely substitute this value

$$f(x) = x^2 - 6x + 5$$
$$= 9 - 6 \cdot 3 + 5$$
$$= 14 - 18$$
$$f(x)\min = -4$$

(3) Note that in all cases where the word *minimum* is used, the word *maximum* is applicable if the equation $y = f(x)$ is such that its graph has a maximum instead of a minimum. If the equation were $f(x) = 3 + 6x - x^2$, the minus sign preceding the term x^2 would indicate that the curve has a maximum.

e. Practical Application. The methods of analysis presented in c and d above can be used for some very important relationships in applied electricity and electronics. It may be used, for example, to find the load resistance of a circuit in terms of the circuit components necessary to obtain maximum power transfer.

103. Review Problems—Graphs

a. Plot the graphs of the following linear equations:

(1) $2x - 5 = y$
(2) $5 - 2x = y$
(3) $y = 5x$
(4) $3x + 2y = 18$
(5) $5x - 5y = 20$
(6) $3x + y + 14 = 0$

b. Plot the graphs of the following sets of simultaneous equations:

(1) $2x + 3y = 12$
    $3x - y = 7$
(2) $x + y = 9$
    $5x + y = 17$
(3) $x + 5y = 22$
    $3x - 2y = -2$
(4) $3x - 2y = 0$
    $x - 5y = 13$
(5) $6x + 2y = 12$
    $4y + 2y = 10$
(6) $x - 2y = 0$
    $y = 1 + x$

c. Find the roots of the following quadratic equations to the nearest tenth by plotting their graphs:

(1) $y^2 - 2y - 2 = 0$
(2) $x^2 - 1 + x = 0$
(3) $9 - y^2$
(4) $x^2 - 2x + 2 = 0$
(5) $x^2 - 5x + 3 = 0$
(6) $10 - 3x - x^2 = 0$

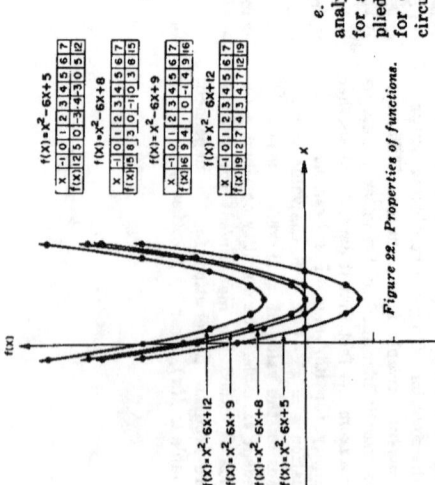

Figure 22. Properties of functions.

CHAPTER 7
POWERS OF 10

104. General

The technique of using powers of 10 can greatly simplify mathematical calculations. A number containing many zeros to the right or to the left of the decimal point can be dealt with much more readily when put in the form of powers of 10. For example, .0000037 × .0000021 can be handled more easily when put in the form $3.7 \times 10^{-6} \times 2.1 \times 10^{-5}$.

105. Table of Powers of 10

The table below gives some of the values of the powers of 10. In a whole number, the exponent is positive and equals the number of zeros following the 1; in decimals, the exponent is negative and equals one more than the number of zeros immediately following the decimal point.

Number	Power of 10	Number	Power of 10
.000001	10^{-6}	1	10^0
.00001	10^{-5}	10	10^1
.0001	10^{-4}	100	10^2
.001	10^{-3}	1,000	10^3
.01	10^{-2}	10,000	10^4
.1	10^{-1}	100,000	10^5
		1,000,000	10^6

106. Expressing Numbers in Scientific Notation

Any number written as the product of an integral power of 10 and a number between 1 and 10 is said to be expressed in *scientific notation*.

Example 1: $81,000,000 = 8.1 \times 10,000,000 = 8.1 \times 10^7$

Example 2: $600,000,000 = 6 \times 100,000,000 = 6 \times 10^8$

Example 3: $.000,000,000,9 = 9 \times .000,000,000,1 = 9 \times 10^{-10}$

107. Addition and Subtraction of Numbers in Scientific Notation

Numbers expressed in scientific notation can only be added or subtracted if the powers of 10 are the same. For example, 3×10^5 can be added to 2×10^5 to get 5×10^5; however, 3×10^4 cannot be added to 2×10^5 because the powers of 10 are not the same. The number 3×10^4 can be changed to 30×10^5, however, and it can then be added to 2×10^5 to obtain 32×10^5. The answers to problems solved by using scientific notation can be left in the exponential form. In the examples below, however, the answers are converted to the decimal form to aid in understanding this technique.

Example 1: Add 450,000 and 763,000.

$$450,000 + 763,000 = 45 \times 10^4 + 76.3 \times 10^4$$
$$= 121.3 \times 10^4$$
$$= 1,213,000$$

Example 2: Add .000,068,25 and .000,007,54.

$$.000,068,25 + .000,007,54 = 6825 \times 10^{-8} + 754 \times 10^{-8}$$
$$= 7579 \times 10^{-8}$$
$$= .000,075,79$$

Example 3: Subtract .000,004,33 from .000,05.

$$.000,05 - .000,004,33 = 5000 \times 10^{-8} - 433 \times 10^{-8}$$
$$= 4567 \times 10^{-8}$$
$$= .000,045,67$$

108. Multiplication of Numbers in Scientific Notation

The general rules covering the multiplication of radicals (par. 74) also apply in the multiplication of numbers that are expressed in scientific notation.

Example 1: Multiply 100,000 by 1,000.
$$100,000 \times 1,000 = 10^5 \times 10^3 = 10^{5+3} = 10^8 = 100,000,000$$

Example 2: Multiply 25,000 by 5,000.
$$25,000 \times 5,000 = 2.5 \times 10^4 \times 5 \times 10^3 = 2.5 \times 5 \times 10^{4+3}$$
$$= 12.5 \times 10^7$$
$$= 125,000,000$$

Example 3: Multiply 1,800, .000015, 300, and .0048.
$$1,800 \times .000015 \times 300 \times .0048$$
$$= 1.8 \times 10^3 \times 1.5 \times 10^{-5} \times 3 \times 10^2 \times 4.8 \times 10^{-3}$$
$$= 1.8 \times 1.5 \times 3 \times 4.8 \times 10^{3-5+2-3}$$
$$= 38.88 \times 10^{-3}$$
$$= .03888$$

109. Division of Numbers in Scientific Notation

The general rules covering the division of radicals (par. 75) also apply in the division of numbers that are expressed in scientific notation.

Example 1: Divide 75,000 by .0005.
$$\frac{75,000}{.0005} = \frac{75 \times 10^3}{5 \times 10^{-4}} = \frac{75}{5} \times 10^{3+4} = 15 \times 10^7 = 150,000,000$$

Example 2: Divide 14,400,000 by 1,200,000.
$$\frac{14,400,000}{1,200,000} = \frac{144 \times 10^5}{12 \times 10^5} = \frac{144}{12} = 12$$

Example 3: Divide 98,100 by .0025, 180, and 1,090,000.
$$\frac{98,100}{.0025 \times 180 \times 1,090,000} = \frac{9.81 \times 10^4}{2.5 \times 10^{-3} \times 1.8 \times 10^2 \times 1.09 \times 10^6}$$
$$= \frac{9.81 \times 10^4}{2.5 \times 1.8 \times 1.09 \times 10^{-3+2+6}}$$
$$= \frac{9.81 \times 10^4}{4.905 \times 10^5}$$
$$= 2 \times 10^{-1}$$
$$= .2$$

110. Finding the Power or Root of a Number in Scientific Notation

The general rules covering powers and roots (pars. 71 and 72) also apply to numbers expressed in scientific notation.

Example 1: Find the square root of 144,000,000.
$$\sqrt{144,000,000} = \sqrt{144 \times 10^6}$$
$$= 12 \times 10^3$$
$$= 12,000$$

Example 2: Find the cube root of .000,008.
$$\sqrt[3]{.000,008} = \sqrt[3]{8 \times 10^{-6}}$$
$$= 2 \times 10^{-2}$$
$$= .02$$

Example 3: Square 15,000.
$$(15,000)^2 = (15 \times 10^3)^2$$
$$= 225 \times 10^6$$
$$= 225,000,000$$

Example 4: Find the square root of $(160,000)^3$.
$$\sqrt{160,000^3} = (160,000)^{3/2}$$
$$= (16 \times 10^4)^{3/2}$$
$$= 64 \times 10^6$$
$$= 64,000,000$$

Example 5: Find the square root of $\frac{86,900}{3,560,000}$.
$$\sqrt{\frac{86,900}{3,560,000}} = \sqrt{\frac{8.69 \times 10^4}{3.56 \times 10^6}}$$
$$= \sqrt{2.44 \times 10^{-2}}$$
$$= .156$$

111. Review Problems—Powers of 10

In the following problems, leave the answer in powers of ten:

  a. Convert the following numbers to powers of 10 and add:
    (1) 1,245,000 + 368,000
    (2) 79,000 + 421,000
    (3) .000,007,66 + .000,054

  b. Convert the following numbers to powers of 10 and subtract:
    (1) 333,400 — 22,500
    (2) .000,068 — .000,049
    (3) .000,004,89 — .000,000,398

  c. Convert the following numbers to powers of 10 and multiply:
    (1) 446,000 × 200
    (2) 7,700 × .003,2
    (3) .000,096 × .000,33
    (4) .003,66 × 4,000,000

  d. Convert the following numbers to powers of 10 and divide:
    (1) 668,000 ÷ 4,000
    (2) 88,445,000 ÷ .000,55
    (3) .000,963 ÷ .000,009
    (4) .006,93 ÷ 21

  e. Convert the following numbers to powers of 10 and perform the indicated operations:
    (1) $\sqrt{64,000,000}$
    (2) $\sqrt[3]{.000,169}$
    (3) $.003^3$
    (4) $27,000^{2/3}$

CHAPTER 8
LOGARITHMS

112. General

Many lengthy mathematical operations may be accomplished more easily through the use of logarithms. With logarithms (also called logs), multiplication of numbers is reduced to a simple process of addition, division becomes a process of subtraction, raising a number to a power becomes simple multiplication, and extraction of roots is done by simple division.

113. Definition

The logarithm of a given number is the power to which another number (called the base) must be raised to equal the given number. The word "logarithm" has the same meaning as the word "exponent."

Example: Find the logarithm of 1,000 to the base 10.

From the definition, the logarithm of a number (1,000) is the power (x) to which another number called the base (10) must be raised to equal the given number (1,000).

Thus, $10^x = 1,000$. Since $10^3 = 1,000$, then:

$$10^x = 10^3 \text{ and by inspection:}$$

$$x = 3$$

Therefore, the logarithm of 1,000 to the base 10 equals 3 or $\log_{10} 1,000 = 3$.

114. Types of Logarithms

a. Common Logarithms. Common logarithms use the number 10 as a base. They are so universally used that the 10 usually is omitted; the answer in paragraph 113 could be $\log 1,000 = 3$. Some values of common logarithms are included in the table below. The common logarithm of any number between these values consists of the logarithm of the smaller number plus a decimal. For example, the log of a number between 100 and 1,000, such as 157, consists of the log of the smaller number (10) plus a decimal. The log of 157 is 2.1959.

$\log 1 = 0$	$\log .1 = -1$
$\log 10 = 1$	$\log .01 = -2$
$\log 100 = 2$	$\log .001 = -3$
$\log 1,000 = 3$	$\log .0001 = -4$
$\log 10,000 = 4$	

b. Natural Logarithms. Natural logarithms are based upon the irrational number *e*, and are written both as log, and ln. Natural logarithms are used in special applications and as such are not explained further in this text.

115. Parts of Logarithms

a. Logarithms are divided into two parts, the integral and the decimal. The integral part is known as the *characteristic*, and the decimal part is called the *mantissa.*

(1) *The characteristic of any number is one less than the number of digits to the left of the decimal point.* Thus, the characteristic for the number 3 is 1 — 1 or zero, since there is one number to the left of the decimal point. The characteristic for 30, with two numbers to the left of the decimal point, is 2 — 1 or 1. Similarly, the characteristic for 300 is 2, and the characteristic of 3,000 is 3. The characteristic of the log of a decimal is negative and is based upon the position of the first rational number to the right of the decimal point. *If there are no numbers to the left of the decimal point, the characteristic is negative.* In the number .327, for example, the first rational number is in the first decimal place and the characteristic is -1; in the number .03, the first rational number is in the second decimal place and the characteristic is -2. Similarly, the characteristic for .003 is -3, and the characteristic for .0003 is -4.

(2) The mantissa is always the same for a given sequence of integers, regardless of where the decimal point appears among them. Thus, the *mantissa* is the same for 1570, 157, 15.7, 1.57, .157, and .0157, and the logs of these numbers differ only in respect to their characteristics. Their logarithms, respectively, are 3.1959, 2.1959, 1.1959, 0.1959, -1.1959 and -2.1959.

b. The mantissa is always positive—even when the characteristic is negative. This fact poses a problem of notation, and also complicates the addition and subtraction of logarithms.

(1) In the notation of logarithms, to say that $\log .157$ is -1.1959 is not strictly true, for what we mean to say is -1 plus .1959. To overcome this problem, the minus sign is generally written above the characteristic, and is made long enough to cover the entire negative portion of the logarithm. More properly, therefore, $\log .157$ is written $\bar{1}.1959$.

(2) In the addition and subtraction of logarithms, the complication can be removed by expressing the negative characteristic in a positive manner; more precisely, by adding a large enough number to the characteristic and by subtracting the same number from the entire logarithm. Thus, the log of .157 is written 9.1959-10, and the log of .0157 is written 8.1959—10.

116. Finding a Logarithm

The characteristic must be obtained, in each instance, by following the rules given in paragraph 115a(1).

Example 1: Find the logarithm of 333.

Determine the characteristic of 333. The characteristic is 3 — 1, or 2.

Determine the mantissa of 333. In the table of common logarithms, look down the N column for the number 33. The mantissa for 333 is in the horizontal row headed by the number 3. The mantissa is .5224.

$\log 333 = 2.5224.$

Example 2: Find the logarithm of .127.

Determine the characteristic of .127. The characteristic is -1 or 9. $----10$.

Determine the mantissa of .127. In the table of common logarithms, look down the N column for 12. The mantissa for 127 is in this horizontal row in the column headed by the number 7. The mantissa is .1038.

$\text{Log} .127 = 9.1038{-}10.$

117. Logarithmic Interpolation

The table of common logarithms given in appendix is adequate if the given number has three or less integers. If it has four or more integers, however, it is necessary to interpolate—that is, to find the proportional part of the difference between the logarithms shown in the table.

Example 1: Find the logarithm of 2.369.
Step 1.

The characteristic of 2.369 is 0. Since the mantissa of 2.369 for this number cannot be found in the table, it is necessary to interpolate. Look for the mantissas of the numbers next lower and higher than 2369. The mantissa of the number 2360 is .3729 and the mantissa of the number 2370 is .3747. Since 2369 lies between 2360 and 2370, the mantissa of

2369 must lie between .3729 and .3747. This may be written:

$$\log 2360 = .3729$$
$$\log 2369 = .3729 + x$$
$$\log 2370 = .3747$$

Step 2. Set up the proportions. The difference between 2369 and 2360 is 9. The difference between 2370 and 2360 is 10. Therefore, the desired mantissa is $\frac{9}{10}$ of the difference between these two. Let the difference between the mantissa of 2369 and 2360 equal x. The difference between .3747 and .3729 is .0018. The proportion is $\frac{x}{.0018}$.

Step 3. Solve the problem.

$$\frac{9}{10} = \frac{x}{.0018}$$
$$10x = .0162$$
$$x = .0016$$

Step 4. Since the value of x is .0016, the mantissa of 2369 is .3729 + .0016 or .3745. Therefore, log 2.369 = 0.3745.

Example 2: Find the logarithm of .017234.

Step 1. The characteristic of .017234 is —2 or 8. ———— —10. The numbers in the table lower and higher than 17234 are 17200 and 17300. The mantissa of 17200 is .2355; the mantissa of 17300 is .2380. The difference between 17234 and 17200 is 34; the difference between 17200 and 17300 is 100; the difference between .2380 and .2355 is .0025. This may be written:

$$\log 17200 = .2355$$
$$\log 17234 = .2355 + x$$
$$\log 17300 = .2380$$

Step 2. Let the difference between the mantissas of 17234 and 17200 equal x. The equation is as follows:

$$\frac{34}{100} = \frac{x}{.0025}$$
$$100x = .0850$$
$$x = .00085 = .0009$$

Step 3. Since the value of x is .0009, the mantissa of 17234 is .2355 + .0009 or .2364. Therefore, log .017234 = 8.2364—10.

118. Reading Antilogarithms

The process of finding the antilogarithm (also called antilog), consists of determining the number from which the logarithm was derived. This process is essentially the reverse of finding the logarithm (par. 116). Consequently, the location of the decimal point is determined from the characteristic, and the numerical value of the number is determined from the mantissa.

Example 1: Find the antilog of 1.8954.

Step 1. Since the characteristic of 1.8954 is 1, there will be two digits to the left of the decimal point in the number.

Step 2. Look in the table for the mantissa, .8954. The number given for .8954 is 786.

Step 3. Count off two digits from the left and insert the decimal point. The antilog of 1.8954 is 78.6.

Example 2: Find the antilog of 7.0828—10.

Step 1. Since the characteristic of the logarithm is —3, the first significant figure will be in the third decimal place.

Step 2. Look for the mantissa .0828 in the table. The number given for .0828 is 121.

Step 3. Add two zeros to the right of the decimal point and before the first significant figure. Thus, the antilog of 7.0828—10 is .0021.

119. Antilogarithmic Interpolation

If the mantissa of a logarithm does not appear in the table, it is necessary to interpolate.

Example 1: Find the antilog of 2.7654.

Step 1. Since the characteristic of the logarithm is 2, there will be three digits to the left of the decimal point in the number.

Step 2. The mantissa in the table lower than .7654 is .7649. The num-

ber with .7649 as a mantissa is 582. The mantissa higher than .7654 is .7657. The number with .7657 as a mantissa is 583.

Step 3. Set up the proportions. The difference between .7654 and .7649 is .0005; the difference between .7657 and .7649 is .0008. The proportional difference is $\frac{.0005}{.0008}$.

Step 4. The difference between 583 and 582 is 1. This can be written:

$$\text{antilog } .7649 = 582$$
$$\text{antilog } .7654 = 582 + x$$
$$\text{antilog } .7657 = 583$$

Step 5. Let x equal the difference between the number represented by the mantissa .7654 and the number 582. The equation is as follows:

$$\frac{5}{8} = \frac{x}{1}$$
$$8x = 5$$
$$x = .625$$

Step 6. The number is 582 + .625. Since there are three digits to the left of the decimal point, the antilog of 2.7654 is 582.625.

Example 2: Find the antilog of 6.7166—10.

Step 1. Since the characteristic of the logarithm is —4, the first rational number will be in the fourth decimal place.

Step 2. The mantissa in the table lower than .8166 is .8162; the number with .8162 as a mnatissa is 655. The mantissa in the table higher than .8166 is .8169; the number with .8169 as a mantissa is 656.

Step 3. The difference between .8162 and .8166 is .0004; the difference between .8169 and .8162 is .0007. The proportional difference is $\frac{.0004}{.0007}$ or $\frac{4}{7}$. The difference between 656 and 655 is 1. This may be written:

$$\text{antilog } .8162 = 655$$
$$\text{antilog } .8166 = 655 + x$$
$$\text{antilog } .8169 = 656$$

Step 5. Let x equal the difference between the number represented by the mantissa .8166 and the number 655. The equation is as follows:

$$\frac{4}{7} = \frac{x}{1}$$
$$7x = 4$$
$$x = .57$$

Step 6. The number is 655 + .57. Since the first rational figure is in the fourth decimal place, the antilog of 6.7166—10 is .00065557.

120. Addition and Subtraction of Logarithms

Logarithms are added and subtracted arithmetically. Since every negative characteristic is positive (par. 115b), however, every negative characteristic should be expressed as a positive (par. 115b).

Example 1: Add the logarithms 3.7493 and 2.4036.

$$\begin{array}{r} 3.7493 \\ +2.4036 \\ \hline 6.1529 \end{array}$$

Example 2: Add the logarithms 3.4287 and 6.3982.

$$\begin{array}{r} 3.4287 \\ +4.3982-10 \\ \hline 7.8269-10 \end{array}$$

Example 3: Add the logarithms 8.9324—10, 7.2812—10, 5.4138—10, and 9.9918—10.

$$\begin{array}{r} 8.9324-10 \\ 7.2812-10 \\ 5.4138-10 \\ +9.9918-10 \\ \hline 31.6192-40 \\ (-30) \quad (-30) \\ \hline 1.6192-10 \end{array}$$

Example 4: Subtract the logarithm 9.1245 from the logarithm 6.3058.

To subtract a larger logarithm from a smaller logarithm, add 10 or a multiple of 10 to the smaller logarithm, and subtract the same number from the logarithm by writing that number with a minus sign to the right of the logarithm. The number chosen for this purpose should be the least that will cause the smaller logarithm to exceed the larger.

$$16.3058-10$$
$$\underline{9.1245}$$
$$7.1813-10$$

Example 5: Subtract the logarithm 3.7980—10 from 2.8686. When subtracting a negative logarithm from a positive logarithm, where that part of the characteristic of the negative logarithm to the left of the mantissa is larger than the characteristic of the positive logarithm, add 10 or a multiple of 10 to the characteristic of the positive logarithm, and subtract that same amount from the right of the positive logarithm.

$$12.8686-10$$
$$\underline{3.7980-10}$$
$$9.0706$$

121. Multiplication by Use of Logarithms

The logarithm of the product of two numbers is equal to the sum of the logarithms of the numbers. Thus, $\log(2 \times 6) = \log 2 + \log 6$; and $\log(12 \times 8) = \log 12 + \log 8$.

Example 1: Multiply 68.2 by 40.8 by using logarithms.

$$\log(68.2 \times 40.8) = \log 68.2 + \log 40.8.$$
$$\log 68.2 = 1.8338$$
$$\underline{\log 40.8 = 1.6107}$$
$$\log(68.2 \times 40.8) = 3.4445$$
antilog .4440 = 278
antilog .4445 = 278 + x
antilog .4455 = 279
$$\frac{5}{15} = \frac{x}{1}$$
$$15x = 5$$
$$x = .33$$
antilog .4445 = 2783
$$68.2 \times 40.8 = 2{,}783$$

Example 2: Find the product of 2.11 and 41.3 by using logarithms.

$$\log(2.11 \times 41.3) = \log 2.11 + \log 41.3.$$
$$\log 2.11 = 0.3243$$
$$\underline{\log 41.3 = 1.6160}$$
$$\log(2.11 \times 41.3) = 1.9403$$
antilog .9400 = 871
antilog .9403 = 871 + x
antilog .9405 = 872
$$\frac{3}{5} = \frac{x}{1}$$
$$5x = 3$$
$$x = .6$$
antilog 1.9403 = 87.16
$$2.11 \times 41.3 = 87.16$$

122. Division by Use of Logarithms

The logarithm of the quotient of two numbers is equal to the difference between the logarithms of the numbers. Thus, $\log(75 \div 83) = \log 75 - \log 83$, and $\log(8 \div 2) = \log 8 - \log 2$.

Example 1: Divide 785 by 329 by using logarithms.

$$\log(785 \div 329) = \log 785 - \log 329.$$
$$\log 785 = 2.8949$$
$$\underline{\log 329 = 2.5172}$$
$$\log(785 \div 329) = 0.3777$$
antilog .3766 = 238
antilog .3777 = 238 + x
antilog .3784 = 239
$$\frac{11}{18} = \frac{x}{1}$$
$$18x = 11$$
$$x = .611$$
antilog 0.3777 = 2.386
$$785 \div 329 = 2.386$$

Example 2: Find the value of $\frac{3}{7}$ by using logarithms.

$$\log \frac{3}{7} = \log 3 - \log 7.$$
$$\log 3 = 0.4771$$
$$\log 7 = 0.8451$$

Since the logarithm of 7 is greater than the logarithm of 3, it is necessary to add 10. —10 to the logarithm of 3 before subtracting the logarithm of 7.

$$\log 3 = 10.4771-10$$
$$\underline{\log 7 = 0.8451}$$
$$\log(3 \div 7) = 9.6320-10$$
antilog .6314 = 428
antilog .6320 = 428 + x
antilog .6325 = 429
$$\frac{6}{11} = \frac{x}{1}$$
$$11x = 6$$
$$x = .55$$
antilog 9.6320—10 = .42855
$$3 \div 7 = .42855$$

123. Finding the Power of a Number by Logarithms

The logarithm of a number raised to a power is equal to the logarithm of the number multiplied by the power.

Example 1: Evaluate $(18.7)^3$.
$$\log(18.7)^3 = 3 \log 18.7$$
$$\log 18.7 = 1.2718$$
$$ 3$$
$$ 3.8154$$
antilog .8149 = 653
antilog .8154 = 653 + x
antilog .8156 = 654
$$\frac{5}{7} = \frac{x}{1}$$
$$7x = 5$$
$$x = .7$$
antilog 3.8154 = 6537
$$(18.7)^3 = 6{,}537$$

Example 2: Evaluate $(.03625)^4$.
$$\log(.03625)^4 = 4 \log .03625$$
$$\log 3620 = .5587$$
$$\log 3625 = .5587 + x$$
$$\log 3630 = .5599$$
$$\frac{5}{10} = \frac{x}{.0012}$$
$$x = .0006$$
$$\log(.03625)^4 = 4\,(8.5593-10)$$
$$= 34.2372-40$$
$$\text{(Subtract)} \quad \underline{30.0000-30}$$
$$= 4.2372-10$$
antilog .2355 = 172
antilog .2372 = 172 + x
antilog .2380 = 173
$$\frac{17}{25} = \frac{x}{1}$$
$$25x = 17$$
$$x = .68 = .7$$
antilog 4.2372—10 = .000001727
$$(.03625)^4 = .000001727$$

Example 3: Evaluate $(2.13)^{\frac{2}{3}}$.
$$\log(2.13)^{\frac{2}{3}} = \tfrac{2}{3} \log 2.13$$
$$= \tfrac{2}{3} \times 0.3284$$
$$= 0.2189$$
antilog .2175 = 165
antilog .2189 = 165 + x
antilog .2201 = 166
$$\frac{14}{26} = \frac{x}{1}$$
$$26x = 14$$
$$x = .5$$
antilog 0.2189 = 1.655
$$(2.13)^{\frac{2}{3}} = 1.655$$

124. Finding the Root of a Number by Logarithms

The logarithm of the root of a number is equal to the logarithm of the number divided by the root.

Example 1: Evaluate $\sqrt[4]{34987}$.
$$\log \sqrt[4]{34987} = \frac{\log 34987}{4}$$
$$\log 34900 = .5428$$
$$\log 34987 = .5428 + x$$
$$\log 35000 = .5441$$
$$\frac{87}{100} = \frac{x}{.0013}$$
$$100x = .1131$$
$$x = .0011$$
$$= \frac{4.5439}{4}$$
$$= 1.135975 = 1.1360$$
antilog .1335 = 136
antilog .1360 = 136 + x
antilog .1367 = 137
$$\frac{25}{32} = \frac{x}{1}$$
$$32x = 25$$
$$x = .78$$
antilog 1.1360 = 13.678
$$\sqrt[4]{34987} = 13.678$$

Example 2: Evaluate $\sqrt[3]{76.24}$.
$$\log \sqrt[3]{76.24} = \frac{\log 76.24}{3}$$
$$\log 7620 = .8820$$
$$\log 7624 = .8820 + x$$
$$\log 7630 = .8825$$
$$\frac{4}{10} = \frac{x}{.0005}$$

126. Computation by Logarithms

In performing logarithmic computations, follow the principles given in paragraphs 117 through 125. When negative quantities are involved (in multiplication and division), disregard the minus sign when making logarithmic calculations. After calculating the antilog, the sign is determined in accordance with the algebraic law of signs for multiplication and division.

Example 1: Evaluate $\sqrt[3]{\dfrac{(94.7)^2 \, (.00789)}{(3.71)^3 \, (.345)}}$.

$$\log (94.7)^2 = 2 \log 94.7 = 2 \times 1.9763 = 3.9526$$

$$\log (94.7)^2 + \log (.00789) = \dfrac{7.8971-10}{11.8497-10} = 1.8497$$

$$\log (3.71)^3 = 3 \log 3.71 = 3 \times 0.5694 = 1.7082$$

$$\log (3.71)^3 + \log (.345) = \dfrac{9.5378-10}{11.2460-10} = 1.2460$$

$$\log \dfrac{(94.7)^2 \, (.00789)}{(3.71)^3 \, (.345)} = \dfrac{1.8497}{1.2460} = 0.6037$$

$$\log \sqrt[3]{\dfrac{(94.7)^2 \, (.00789)}{(3.71)^3 \, (.345)}} = \dfrac{0.6037}{3} = .2012$$

antilog .2012 = 1.5892

Example 2: Evaluate $\sqrt[4]{\dfrac{(6.484)^2 \cdot \sqrt[3]{7.667}}{(12.35)^2 \cdot \sqrt[3]{3007}}}$

$$\log (6.484)^2 = 2 \log 6.484 = 2 \times 0.8118 = 1.6236$$

$$\log \sqrt[3]{7.667} = \dfrac{\log 7.667}{3} = \dfrac{0.8846}{3} = 0.2949$$

$$\log (6.484)^2 + \log \sqrt[3]{7.667} = 1.6236 + .2949 = 1.9185$$

$$\log (12.35)^2 = 2 \log 12.35 = 2 \times 1.0917 = 2.1834$$

$$\log \sqrt[3]{3007} = \dfrac{\log 3007}{3} = \dfrac{3.4782}{3} = 1.1594$$

$$\log (12.35)^2 + \log \sqrt[3]{3007} = 2.1834 + 1.1594 = 3.3428$$

$$\log \dfrac{(6.484)^2 \cdot \sqrt[3]{7.667}}{(12.35)^2 \cdot \sqrt[3]{3007}} = \dfrac{11.9185-10}{3.3428} = 8.5757-10$$

$$10x = .0020$$
$$x = .0002$$
$$= 1.8822$$
$$= \dfrac{1.8822}{3} = 0.6274$$

antilog 0.6274 = 4.24

$\sqrt[3]{76.24} = 4.24$

Example 3: Evaluate $\sqrt[3]{.0073573}$.

$$\log \sqrt[3]{.0073573} = \dfrac{\log .0073573}{3}$$

$$\log 73500 = .8663$$
$$\log 73573 = .8663 + x$$
$$\log 73600 = .8669$$

$$\dfrac{73}{100} = \dfrac{x}{.0006}$$
$$100x = .0438$$
$$x = .0004$$

The quotient of 7.8667−10 divided by 3 is 2.6222−3⅓. By adding 20.0000−20 to 7.8667−10, the sum, 27.8667−30, can be divided by 3 and the quotient will be a workable logarithm.

$$\log .0073573 = 7.8667-10$$
$$\text{add } \dfrac{20.0000-20}{27.8667-30}$$

$$\dfrac{27.8667-30}{3} = 9.2889-10$$

antilog .2878 = 194
antilog .2889 = 194 + x
antilog .2900 = 195

$$\dfrac{11}{22} = \dfrac{x}{1}$$
$$22x = 11$$
$$x = .5$$

antilog 9.2889−10 = .1945
$\sqrt[3]{.0073573} = .1945$

125. Cologarithms

The *cologarithms* of a number is the logarithm of the reciprocal of the number. For example, $\operatorname{colog} N = \log \dfrac{1}{N}$. However,

$$\log \dfrac{1}{N} = \log 1 - \log N$$

$$\log \dfrac{1}{N} = 0 - \log N$$

$$\log \dfrac{1}{N} = -\log N$$

Therefore, $\operatorname{colog} N = \log \dfrac{1}{N} = -\log N$. Thus the cologarithm of a number is the logarithm of the number subtracted from the logarithm of 1 (0.0000 or, to avoid a negative mantissa, 10.0000−10).

Example 1: Evaluate the cologarithm of 373.

$$\operatorname{colog} 373 = \log \dfrac{1}{373}$$

$$\log 1 = 10.0000-10$$
$$\log 373 = 2.5717$$
$$\operatorname{colog} 373 = 7.4283-10$$

Example 2: Evaluate $\dfrac{2.37}{3.61}$.

$$\log \dfrac{2.37}{3.61} = \log 2.37 - \log 3.61$$
$$= \log 2.37 + \operatorname{colog} 3.61$$

$$\log 1 = 10.0000-10$$
$$\log 3.61 = 0.5575$$
$$\operatorname{colog} 3.61 = 9.4425-10$$
$$\log 2.37 = 0.3747$$
$$\qquad\qquad 9.8172-10$$

antilog 9.8172−10 = .65643

$$\log \sqrt[4]{\frac{(6.484)^2 \sqrt[3]{7.667}}{(12.35)^2 \sqrt[5]{3007}}} = \frac{38.5757-40}{4}$$
$$= 9.6439-10$$
antilog $9.6439-10 = .4405$

127. Review Problems—Logarithms

a. Find the logarithms of the following numbers to the base 10:

(1) 785
(2) 3.57
(3) .0345
(4) .000476
(5) 49.6
(6) 273.5
(7) 760.1
(8) 7.234
(9) .009875
(10) .00005254

b. Find the antilogs of the following logarithms:

(1) 4.8457
(2) 2.4330
(3) 9.5453—10
(4) 6.8299—10
(5) 0.6010
(6) 2.5690
(7) 5.4343—10
(8) 5.6994
(9) 0.2018
(10) 4.5372—10

c. Using logarithms, find the products of the following to four significant figures:

(1) 6.93×23.7
(2) 186×215
(3) 64.3×21.4
(4) $.089 \times .076$
(5) 135×42.3

d. Using logarithms, find the quotients of the following to four significant figures:

(1) $148 \div 297$
(2) $\frac{251}{648}$
(3) $14.9 \div 37.4$
(4) $47.38 \div 63.29$
(5) $\frac{1.06}{4.35}$

e. Using logarithms, evaluate the following:

(1) $(.0293)^4$
(2) $(1.756)^7$
(3) $(7.953)^{\frac{1}{3}}$
(4) $(69.37)^{.7}$
(5) $(27.98)^2$
(6) $\sqrt[3]{.01325}$
(7) $\sqrt{815}$
(8) $\sqrt[4]{7698}$
(9) $\sqrt[5]{8.942}$
(10) $\sqrt[4]{.00007991}$

f. Using logarithms, compute the following:

(1) $\frac{3.8 \times 2.6}{4.3}$
(2) $\sqrt[3]{\frac{541 \times 47.3}{.0157}}$
(3) $\frac{44.1 \times 1.82}{10.27 \times .32}$
(4) $\frac{85.21 \times \sqrt[3]{4651}}{\sqrt{46.82} \times 6.230}$
(5) $\frac{(31.21)^3}{40.70}$
(6) $\sqrt[3]{\frac{(57.20)^2}{(31.42)^3}}$
(7) $\sqrt{\frac{.08152 \times 1.963}{95.27}}$
(8) $\sqrt{\frac{.8531}{9.327}} \times \sqrt[3]{\frac{518.2}{61.52}}$
(9) $\frac{48.19 \times \sqrt[3]{56.02}}{431.6 \times \sqrt[4]{46.25} \times \sqrt{16.34}}$
(10) $\sqrt{\frac{.008150 \times .08532}{.01234 \times \sqrt[3]{.09156}}}$

CHAPTER 9
PLANE GEOMETRY

128. Introduction

Plane geometry is that part of geometry which deals with plane figures. In electronics, as in many other fields, it is necessary to know how to deal with areas of common plane figures. This chapter presents the formulas for finding the areas of triangles, quadrilaterals (plane figures having four sides and four angles), and circles. No effort has been made to cover the entire field of geometry. Only those principles and proofs are presented that are of value in practical work.

129. Definitions

a. Lines. A line has length, but no width or thickness. What is drawn on paper and called a line has thickness and breadth because of the material used to draw it—however, this mark only *represents* the actual line.

b. Angles. An angle, such as *ABC* in A, figure 23, is formed by the intersection of two lines. An angle, therefore, is the measure of the difference in direction of two straight lines that meet. The lines which form the angle, *AB* or *BC*, are called the *sides* of the angle, and the point of meeting, *B*, the vertex. The symbol ∠ is used to indicate angles. Angles usually are measured in *degrees*. A complete circle or rotation consists of 360 degrees. The symbol ° is used to indicate degrees; it is written to the right and slightly above the number. For example, 30 degrees is written 30°. Each degree consists of 60 *minutes*, and each minute is further broken down into 60 *seconds*. The symbol ′ is used to indicate minutes; the symbol ″ indicates seconds. For example, 20 minutes is written 20′; 15 seconds is written 15″.

(1) When one straight line is *perpendicular* to another straight line, the angle formed is a right angle (90°) (B, fig. 23).

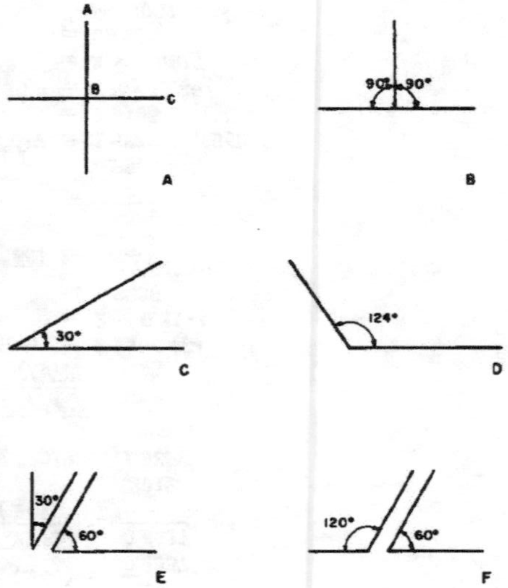

(2) Two right angles, added together, form a *straight angle*. A straight angle, therefore, is an angle of 180°.

(3) Any angle less than a right angle is an *acute angle* (C, fig. 23).

(4) Any angle greater than a right angle and less than 180° is an *obtuse angle* (D, fig. 23).

(5) Two angles whose sum is one right angle are called *complementary angles* (E, fig. 23).

(6) Two angles whose sum is a straight angle are called *supplementary angles* (F, fig. 23).

Figure 23. Angles.

130. Basic Principles of Geometric Construction

a. Reproducing Angles. To draw an angle equal to a given angle *BAC* (fig. 24)—

(1) Draw a line, *A'C'*.

(2) With *A* as the center, use a compass to strike an arc that cuts the sides of the given angle at *X* and *Y*. Using the same radius, strike a similar arc, *X'Y'*, on the line, *A'C'*.

(3) Measure the opening of the given angle by setting one point of the compass at *Y* and the other at *X*. With the compass at this distance and with *Y'* as the center, strike an arc as shown in figure 24. This will cut the first arc at point *X'*.

(4) Draw a line, *A'B'*, through *X'*. The new angle, *B'A'C'*, is the same size as angle *BAC*.

Figure 24. Reproducing an angle.

b. Finding the Midpoint of a Straight Line Segment. To find the midpoint of any straight line segment, such as *AB* in figure 25—

(1) Use a radius greater than half the length of *AB*. Using point *A* as the center, draw arcs *CD* and *C'D'*. With point *B* as the center, and using the same radius, draw arcs *EF* and *E'F'*.

(2) Draw a straight line to connect the points where the arcs intersect. Point *X*, where this line intersects *AB*, is the midpoint of straight line segment *AB*.

c. Constructing a Perpendicular. To construct a perpendicular to a straight line at a given point—

(1) On the straight line, such as *AB* in figure 26, mark point *P* at which the perpendicular is to be constructed.

(2) Set a compass for a radius less than the shorter of the two segments, *AP*

Figure 25. Bisecting a straight line segment.

or *PB*. With *P* as a center, draw arcs cutting line *AB* at points *X* and *Y*.

(3) Set the compass for a radius greater than *PX*. With *X* as a center, draw an arc above point *P* (fig. 26). Keep the compass at the same setting and, with *Y* as a center, draw another arc intersecting the one drawn with *X* as a center. (The two arcs may be drawn to intersect below point *P* instead of above.)

(4) Draw a straight line from the point where the two arcs intersect to point *P*. The line is perpendicular to *AB*.

(5) To construct the perpendicular bisector of a straight line segment, first find the midpoint of the line segment (*b* above), and construct the perpendicular at that point.

Figure 26. Constructing a perpendicular to a straight line at a point on the line.

d. Constructing a Perpendicular to a Straight Line from a Point Not on the Line. To draw a perpendicular to a straight line from a point outside the line, such as point *P* in figure 27—

(1) With point *P* as the center, draw an arc cutting line *AB* at points *X* and *Y*.

(2) Using a radius greater than one-half the distance between *X* and *Y* and, with points *X* and *Y* as centers, draw arcs that intersect.

(3) Draw a straight line from point *P*, through the point where the two arcs intersect, to line *AB*. The line is perpendicular to *AB*.

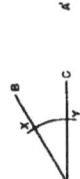

Figure 27. Constructing a perpendicular to a straight line from a point not on the line.

e. Finding the Center of a Circle.

(1) Draw any two chords, such as *AB* and *AC* in figure 28.

(2) Construct the perpendicular bisector of each chord (*c* above). Point *X*, where the two perpendicular bisectors meet, is the center of the circle.

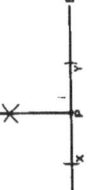

Figure 28. Finding the center of a circle.

f. Bisecting an Angle. Any angle, such as angle *CAB* in figure 29, can be divided into two equal angles. An angle, thus divided, is said to be bisected. To bisect an angle—

(1) Using *A* as a center, draw an arc cutting the sides of angle *CAB* at *X* and *Y*.

(2) With *X* and *Y* as centers, draw intersecting arcs.

(3) Draw a straight line from *A* through the point where the arcs intersect. The line divides angles *CAB* into two

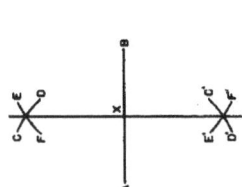

Figure 29. Bisecting an angle.

equal angles and is called the bisector of angle *CAB*.

131. Triangles

a. General. A triangle is a plane figure bounded by three straight lines. There are several different kinds of triangles.

(1) An *equilateral triangle* (A, fig. 30) has three equal sides and three equal angles; each angle equals 60°.

(2) An *isosceles triangle* has two equal

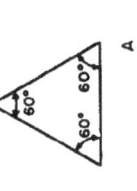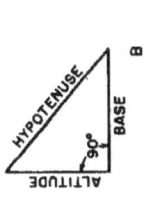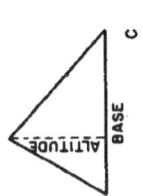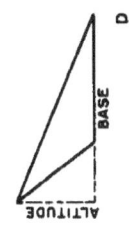

Figure 30. Triangles.

sides and two equal angles. The equal angles are opposite the equal sides.

(3) A *right triangle* (B, fig. 30) has one right angle.

(4) An *oblique triangle* (C and D, fig. 30) is one that does not contain a right angle. Thus, all except right triangles are oblique triangles.

b. Base. The base of a triangle is the side on which the triangle is supposed to stand. However, any side of a triangle may be used as the base.

c. Altitude. The altitude is the perpendicular line distance from the vertex of the triangle to the base or the base extended. In B, figure 30, the altitude of a right triangle is shown, in C, figure 30, the altitude of an acute triangle, and in D, figure 30, the altitude of an obtuse triangle. Note that in an obtuse triangle, it is necessary to extend the base of the triangle to find the altitude.

d. Area. The area of a triangle is the entire surface within the perimeter.

e. Hypotenuse. The side opposite the right angle of any right triangle is the hypotenuse (B, fig. 30).

132. Law of Angles of Any Triangle

The sum of the angles of any triangle is equal to 180°. When given any two of three angles of a triangle, the third angle can be found by subtracting the sum of the given angles from 180°

Example 1:

If two angles of a triangle are 90° and 45°, what is the size of the third angle?

$90° + 45° = 135°$
$180° - 135° = 45°$

Therefore, the third angle is 45°.

Example 2:

Angle A of triangle ABC is 100°; angle B is 30°. What is the size of angle C?

$\angle A + \angle B + \angle C = 180°$
$\angle A = 100°$
$\angle B = 30°$
$\angle A + \angle B = 130°$
$\angle C = 180° - 130°$
$\angle C = 50°$

133. Law of Right Triangles

a. The Pythagorean Theorem. This theorem, which applies to any right triangle, states that *the square of the hypotenuse is equal to the sum of the squares of the other two sides.* The Pythagorean theorem is of prime importance in trigonometry (ch. 10) since the value of one side of a right triangle can be found if the other two sides are known. Thus, in figure 31:

$c^2 = a^2 + b^2$ or $25 = 16 + 9$
$a^2 = c^2 - b^2$ or $16 = 25 - 9$
$b^2 = c^2 - a^2$ or $9 = 25 - 16$

Example 1: Find the hypotenuse of a right triangle if the sides are 3 and 4 inches long, respectively.

$c^2 = a^2 + b^2$
$c^2 = 9 + 16$
$c^2 = 25$
$c = \sqrt{25}$
$c = 5$ inches

Example 2: The hypotenuse of a right triangle is 13 inches long and one side is 5 inches long. Find the length of the other side.

$c^2 = a^2 + b^2$
$13^2 = 5^2 + b^2$
$b^2 = 169 - 25$
$b^2 = 144$
$b = \sqrt{144}$
$b = 12$ inches

Example 3: Given the right triangle ABC (fig. 31), find c if $a = 7$ and $b = 6$.

$c^2 = a^2 + b^2$
$c^2 = 49 + 36$
$c^2 = 85$
$c = \sqrt{85}$
$c = 9.22-$

```
      9. 2 2
    √85.00 00
     81
     ---
    182   400
           364
          ----
    1842  3600
          3684
```

Example 4: Given the right triangle ABC (fig. 31), find b if $a = 9$ and $c = 12$.

$b^2 = c^2 - a^2$
$b^2 = 144 - 81$
$b^2 = 63$
$b = \sqrt{63}$
$b = 7.93+$

```
      7. 9 3
    √63.00 00
     49
     ---
    149   1400
           1341
          ----
    1583  5900
          4749
```

Example 5: Given the right triangle ABC (fig. 31), find a if $b = 6$ and $c = 13$.

$a^2 = c^2 - b^2$
$a^2 = 169 - 36$
$a^2 = 133$
$a = \sqrt{133}$
$a = 11.53+$

```
      1 1. 5 3
    √133.00 00
     1
     ---
    21   33
          21
         ----
    225  1200
         1125
         ----
    2303 7500
         6909
```

b. Special Right Triangles. The two right triangles in examples 1 and 2 of *a* above are special right triangles with sides that have whole numbers. These triangles are called the 3-4-5 right triangle and the 5-12-13 right triangle, although their sides may also be multiples of these numbers. For example, a triangle having sides of 6, 8, and 10 inches is also a 3-4-5 right triangle, because its sides are multiples of 3, 4, and 5. When determining the unknown side of a right triangle, the process is greatly simplified if the triangle is a 3-4-5 or 5-12-13 right triangle. In these cases, the unknown side can often be determined by inspection.

Example 1: The hypotenuse of a right triangle is 15 inches long, and one side is 12 inches long. Find the other side.

Since 15 and 12 can be divided by 3 to give 5 and 4, the triangle is a 3-4-5 right triangle. The third side, therefore, is equal to 3 times 3, or

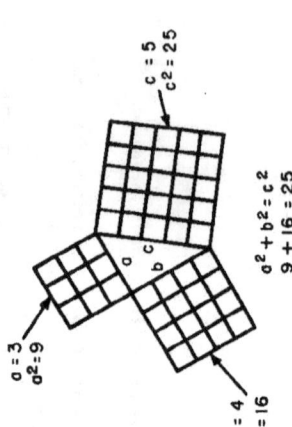

Figure 31. The Pythagorean theorem.

9 inches. The answer can be checked by the Pythagorean theorem.

Example 2: The two sides of a triangle are 10 and 24 feet long. Find the length of the hypotenuse.

Dividing 10 and 24 by 2 gives 5 and 12, the two sides of a 5–12–13 right triangle. Therefore, the hypotenuse is 2 times 13, or 26 inches.

134. Area of Any Triangle

The area of any triangle is equal to one-half the product of its base and altitude. The formula for finding the area is $A = \frac{bh}{2}$ where b is the base of the triangle and h is the altitude.

Example 1:

What is the area of a triangle with a base of 15 inches and an altitude of 10 inches?

$$A = \frac{bh}{2}$$
$$= \frac{15 \times 10}{2}$$
$$= \frac{150}{2}$$
$$= 75 \text{ square inches}$$

Example 2:

Find the area of a right triangle if the base measures 7 feet and the hypotenuse 25 feet.

$$c^2 - b^2 = a^2$$
$$a^2 = 25^2 - 7^2 = 625 - 49$$
$$a^2 = 576$$
$$a = \sqrt{576} = 24 \text{ feet altitude}$$

$$A = \frac{bh}{2}$$
$$= \frac{7 \times 24}{2} = \frac{168}{2}$$
$$= 84 \text{ square feet}$$

135. Quadrilaterals

A quadrilateral is a plane figure bounded by four straight lines.

a. A *parallelogram* (A, fig. 32) is a quadrilateral having both pairs of opposite sides parallel.

b. A *rectangle* (B, fig. 32) is a parallelogram that has four right angles.

c. A *square* (C, fig. 32) is a rectangle, all four sides of which are equal.

d. A *trapezoid* (D, fig. 32) is a quadrilateral with two sides (called bases) parallel and unequal.

136. Area of Any Parallelogram

The area of any parallelogram is equal to the product of the base by the altitude. The formula for finding the area is $A = bh$ where b is the base and h is the height or altitude.

Example 1: Find the area of a square, each side of which is 15 inches.

$$A = bh$$
$$= 15 \times 15$$
$$= 225 \text{ square inches}$$

Example 2: What is the area of a rectangle with a base of 12 inches and an altitude of 7 inches?

$$A = bh$$
$$= 12 \times 7$$
$$= 84 \text{ square inches}$$

137. Area of Trapezoid

The area of a trapezoid is determined by multiplying one-half the sum of the bases by the altitude of the trapezoid.

Thus, $A = \left(\frac{B+b}{2}\right)h$.

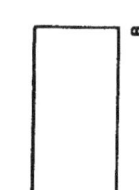
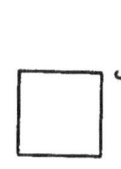
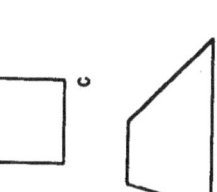

Figure 32. Quadrilaterals.

Example: Find the area of a trapezoid the bases of which are 16 and 10 inches long and the altitude is 8 inches.

$$A = \left(\frac{B+b}{2}\right)h$$
$$= \left(\frac{16+10}{2}\right)8$$
$$= \frac{26}{2} \times \overset{4}{\underset{1}{8}}$$
$$= 104 \text{ square inches}$$

138. Circles

a. General. A circle is a plane figure bounded by a closed curve, every point of which is equidistant from the center.

b. Circumference. The circumference is the curved line that bounds a circle (A, fig. 33).

c. Chord. A chord is a straight line drawn through a circle and terminated at its intersections with the circumference (B, fig. 33).

d. Diameter. The diameter of a circle is a chord that passes through the center of the circle (A, fig. 33).

e. Radius. The radius of a circle is a straight line from the center to a point on the circumference (A, fig. 33). All radii of the same circle are of equal length, one-half of the diameter.

f. Arc. An arc is any part of the circumference of a circle.

g. Segment. A segment is that area of a circle bounded by a chord and the arc subtended by that chord (C, fig. 33).

h. Sector. A sector is the area between an arc and two radii drawn to the ends of the arc (C, fig. 33).

i. Tangent. A tangent is a straight line that touches the circumference of a circle at only one point and is perpendicular to the radius drawn to the point of contact (B, fig. 33). This

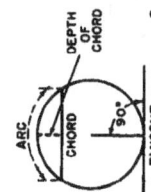
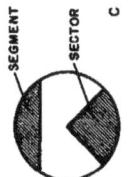

Figure 33. Circles.

point is called the *point of tangency* or the *point of contact*.

j. Concentric Circles. Concentric circles are circles having a common center (D, fig. 33).

k. Pi (π). The Greek letter π is used to represent the relationship of the circumference of any circle to its diameter. Roughly, it equals $\frac{22}{7}$. More approximately, it equals 3.1416. In many applications, it is rounded off to 3.14.

139. Circumference of Any Circle

The circumference of any circle is π times the diameter; therefore, $C = \pi D$.

Example 1: Find the circumference of a circle if the diameter is $6\frac{1}{2}$ inches.

$C = \pi D$
$= 3.14 \times 6.5$
$= 20.42$ inches

Example 2: Find the diameter of a circular tank having a circumference of $31\frac{1}{2}$ inches.

When the circumference of a circle is given, the diameter is calculated by dividing the circumference by $\pi - D = \frac{C}{\pi}$.

$D = \frac{C}{\pi}$
$= \frac{31.5}{3.1416}$
$= 10.03$ inches

140. Area of Any Circle

a. The area of any circle is equal to π multiplied by the radius squared; therefore, $a = \pi r^2$.

Example 1: Find the area of a circle having a diameter of 5 feet 6 inches.

$A = \pi r^2$
$= \pi \left(\frac{5.5}{2}\right)^2$
$= \pi (2.75)^2$
$= 3.14 \times 7.56$
$= 23.76$ square feet

Example 2: What is the diameter of a circle the area of which is 78.54 square rods?

$A = \pi r^2$ and $r = \frac{D}{2}$
$A = \pi \left(\frac{D}{2}\right)^2$
$A = \frac{\pi D^2}{4}$

Transposing:
$D^2 = \frac{4A}{\pi}$
$D = \sqrt{\frac{4A}{\pi}}$
$D = 2\sqrt{\frac{A}{\pi}}$

Substituting and solving for D:
$D = 2\sqrt{\frac{78.54}{3.1416}}$
$D = 2\sqrt{25}$
$D = 2 \times 5$
$D = 10$ rods

b. The area of any circle also is equal to one-half the product of the circumference and the radius.

Example: If the diameter of a circle is 10 inches, and the circumference of the circle is 31.416 inches, what is the area of the circle?

$A = \frac{1}{2}Cr$
$r = \frac{1}{2}D$ or $r = 5$
$A = \frac{1}{2}(31.416 \times 5)$
$= \frac{157.08}{2}$
$= 78.54$ square inches

141. Area of Ring

A ring is the area between the circumferences of two concentric circles. The area of a ring may be found by subtracting the area of the small circle from the area of the large circle. If R is the radius of the large circle and r is the radius of the small circle, a simplified formula for the area of the ring can be developed as follows:

Area of ring = area of large circle — area of small circle
$= \pi R^2 - \pi r^2$
$= \pi(R^2 - r^2)$

By factoring $(R^2 - r^2)$ into $(R + r)(R - r)$, the formula also can be written:
$A = \pi(R + r)(R - r)$

Example: Find the area of a ring having an inside diameter of 8 inches and an outside diameter of 12 inches.

$A = \pi(R + r)(R - r)$
$= 3.14(6 + 4)(6 - 4)$
$= 3.14 \times 10 \times 2$
$= 62.8$ square inches

142. Review Problems—Plane Geometry

a. Find the area of a rectangle having a base of 12 inches and an altitude of 8 inches.

b. What is the area of a square, each side of which is 6 inches?

c. Find the area of a triangle of which the altitude is 5 inches and the base is 10 inches.

d. Find the area of a triangle having an altitude of 15 inches and a base of 2 inches.

e. What is the hypotenuse of a right triangle the sides of which are 12 and 8 inches?

f. Find the third side of a right triangle if one side is 7 inches and the hypotenuse is 9 inches.

g. Identify the following figures, give the formulas, and solve for the required quantity.

(1) FIND AREA

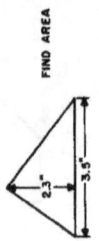
(2) FIND AREA

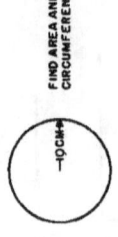
(3) FIND AREA AND CIRCUMFERENCE

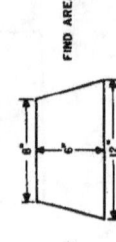
(4) FIND AREA

h. What are the perimeters of the following figures?

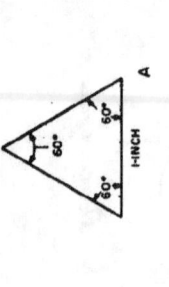
A

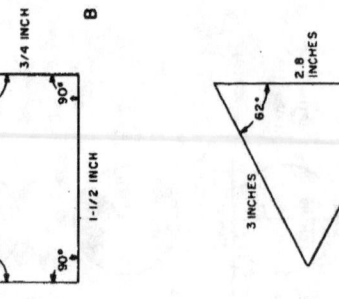
B

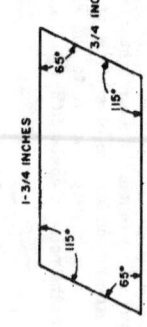
C

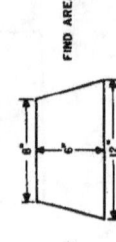
D

i. Find the area of the largest circle that can be cut from a square piece of sheet metal with sides of 10 inches.

j. If the height of an antenna is 80 feet, how far from its top is an object on the ground 60 feet from the base of the pole?

k. How many square feet of lumber are needed to build 10 boxes 18 inches by 16 inches by 9 inches?

l. A metal plate is in the shape of an equilateral triangle. If the altitude is 14 inches, what is the perimeter?

CHAPTER 10
TRIGONOMETRY

Section I. BASIC TRIGONOMETRIC THEORY

143. Introduction

a. Definition. Trigonometry deals with the relationships between the sides and angles of triangles. It uses the theories of basic mathematics—the numbers of arithmetic, the equations of algebra, and the theorems of geometry—to aid in the measurement of the sides and angles of triangles.

b. Application. The ability to use angles and their trigonometric relationships in electrical calculations is especially important in the study of alternating current (ac). Most effects of ac circuit components can be studied or described only in terms of the part of a cycle by which a current lags behind a corresponding voltage, or vice versa. A large percentage of the problems relating to the analysis of ac circuits and communication networks involves the solution of the right triangle in some form. Certain facts about right triangles are familiar (ch 9)—namely, that the square of the hypotenuse is equal to the sum of the squares of the other two sides ($c^2 = a^2 + b^2$), that the sum of the acute angles of a right triangle is 90°, and that the sum of the interior angles of any triangle is 180°. However, it would be impossible to solve certain problems with only this information. After learning other relationships between the sides and angles of triangles, it will be found that trigonometry is an easy and accurate method of solving many problems in ac electricity.

144. Trigonometric Functions

a. General. Trigonometry is based on the six trigonometric functions involved in the study of the right angle. If the value of one quantity depends on the value of a second quantity, the first quantity is said to be a function of the second. The six trigonometric functions —sine (sin), cosine (cos), tangent (tan), cotangent (cot), secant (sec), and cosecant (csc) —are derived from the ratios of the sides of a right triangle to each other.

b. The Right Triangle. Figure 34 shows a right triangle, with the angles labeled A, B, and C; C is the right angle. The sides of the triangle are labeled a, b, and c, with the side opposite each angle given the same letter as the angle. The following are the trigonometric ratios of the sides of a triangle:

$$\sin = \frac{\text{opposite side}}{\text{hypotenuse}}$$

$$\cos = \frac{\text{adjacent side}}{\text{hypotenuse}}$$

$$\tan = \frac{\text{opposite side}}{\text{adjacent side}}$$

$$\cot = \frac{\text{adjacent side}}{\text{opposite side}}$$

$$\sec = \frac{\text{hypotenuse}}{\text{adjacent side}}$$

$$\csc = \frac{\text{hypotenuse}}{\text{opposite side}}$$

c. Angle A. Refer again to figure 34. Using the acute angle A, a is the opposite side, b is the adjacent side, and c, which is the hypotenuse. Therefore,

$$\sin A = \frac{a}{c}$$

$$\cos A = \frac{b}{c}$$

$$\tan A = \frac{a}{b}$$

$$\cot A = \frac{b}{a}$$

$$\sec A = \frac{c}{b}$$

$$\csc A = \frac{c}{a}$$

d. Angle B. Using the acute angle B in figure 34, b is the opposite side, a is the adjacent side, and c is the hypotenuse. Therefore,

$$\sin B = \frac{b}{c}$$

$$\cos B = \frac{a}{c}$$

$$\tan B = \frac{b}{a}$$

$$\cot B = \frac{a}{b}$$

$$\sec B = \frac{c}{a}$$

$$\csc B = \frac{c}{b}$$

e. Angle C. Right angle C is the angle which establishes the relationship between the other sides and other angles and thus may be called a constant. Although it is possible to obtain functions for angle C, they are not covered here because they are not needed in solving problems of this type.

Example:

Determine the values of the trigonometric functions of a right triangle with sides as follows: $a = 3, b = 4, c = 5$ (fig. 35).

Functions of angle A:

$$\sin A = \frac{a}{c} = \frac{3}{5}$$

$$\cos A = \frac{b}{c} = \frac{4}{5}$$

$$\tan A = \frac{a}{b} = \frac{3}{4}$$

$$\cot A = \frac{b}{a} = \frac{4}{3}$$

$$\sec A = \frac{c}{b} = \frac{5}{4}$$

$$\csc A = \frac{c}{a} = \frac{5}{3}$$

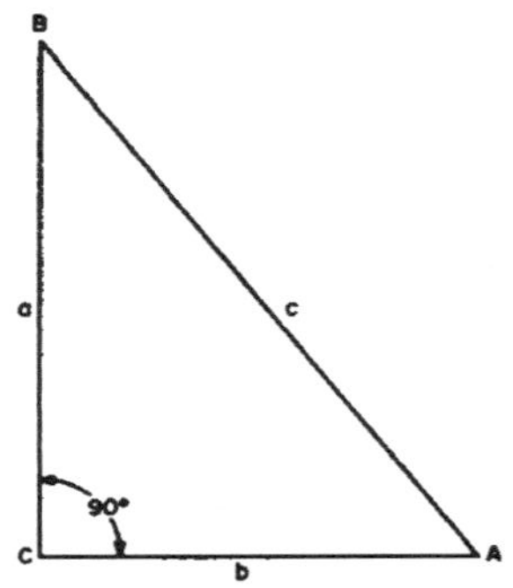

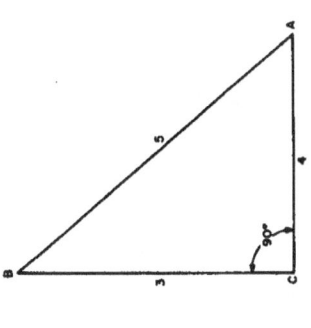

Figure 34. Trigonometric functions of the right triangle.

Figure 35. Right triangle with sides known.

Functions of angle B:

$$\sin B = \frac{b}{c} = \frac{4}{5}$$

$$\cos B = \frac{a}{c} = \frac{3}{5}$$

$$\tan B = \frac{b}{a} = \frac{4}{3}$$

$$\cot B = \frac{a}{b} = \frac{3}{4}$$

$$\sec B = \frac{c}{a} = \frac{5}{3}$$

$$\csc B = \frac{c}{b} = \frac{5}{4}$$

145. Reciprocal Relations of Trigonometric Functions

From the definitions of the six trigonometric functions (par. 144), the reciprocal relations (listed below) can be determined. The cosecant, secant, and cotangent should always be thought of as the reciprocals of the sine, cosine, and tangent, respectively.

$$\sin A = \frac{a}{c} = \frac{1}{\frac{c}{a}} = \frac{1}{\csc A}$$

$$\cos A = \frac{b}{c} = \frac{1}{\frac{c}{b}} = \frac{1}{\sec A}$$

$$\tan A = \frac{a}{b} = \frac{1}{\frac{b}{a}} = \frac{1}{\cot A}$$

$$\csc A = \frac{c}{a} = \frac{1}{\frac{a}{c}} = \frac{1}{\sin A}$$

$$\sec A = \frac{c}{b} = \frac{1}{\frac{b}{c}} = \frac{1}{\cos A}$$

$$\cot A = \frac{b}{a} = \frac{1}{\frac{a}{b}} = \frac{1}{\tan A}$$

147. Solving for Unknown Functions

If one trigonometric function of a right triangle is known, the other trigonometric functions can be determined. This is done by using the Pythagorean theorem (par. 133).

Example 1: Given the right triangle ABC (fig. 23): side a is 4; side C is 9. Since $\sin A = \frac{4}{9}$, find the other trigonometric functions of angle A.

$$\sin A = \frac{a}{c}; \text{ also, } \sin A = \frac{4}{9}.$$

Therefore, $a = 4, c = 9$

$$b^2 = c^2 - a^2$$
$$b^2 = 81 - 16$$
$$b^2 = 65$$
$$b = \sqrt{65}$$
$$b = 8.06$$

```
        8. 0 6
√65.00 00
    64
1606  10000
      9636
```

$$\sin A = \frac{4}{9}$$
$$\cos A = \frac{8.06}{9}$$
$$\tan A = \frac{4}{8.06}$$
$$\cot A = \frac{8.06}{4}$$
$$\sec A = \frac{9}{8.06}$$
$$\csc A = \frac{9}{4}$$

146. Functions of Complementary Angles

a. The function of an acute angle is equal to the cofunction of its complementary angle. Apply the definitions of the trigonometric functions (par. 144) to angles A and B to obtain the following relations:

$$\sin B = \frac{b}{c} = \cos A$$
$$\tan B = \frac{b}{a} = \cot A$$
$$\sec B = \frac{c}{a} = \csc A$$
$$\cos B = \frac{a}{c} = \sin A$$
$$\cot B = \frac{a}{b} = \tan A$$
$$\csc B = \frac{c}{b} = \sec A$$

b. With angle B equal to $90° - A$, these relations may be written:

$$\sin (90° - A) = \cos A$$
$$\tan (90° - A) = \cot A$$
$$\sec (90° - A) = \csc A$$
$$\cos (90° - A) = \sin A$$
$$\cot (90° - A) = \tan A$$
$$\csc (90° - A) = \sec A$$

Example 2: Given the right triangle ABC (fig. 23): side A is $\sqrt{3}$; side b is 7. Since $\tan A = \frac{\sqrt{3}}{7}$ or $\frac{1}{7}\sqrt{3}$, find the other trigonometric functions of angle A.

$\tan A = \frac{a}{b}$; also, $\tan A = \frac{1}{7}\sqrt{3} = \frac{\sqrt{3}}{7}$.

Therefore,

$$a = \sqrt{3}, b = 7$$
$$c^2 = a^2 + b^2$$
$$c^2 = 3 + 49$$
$$c^2 = 52$$
$$c = \sqrt{52}$$
$$c = \sqrt{4} \cdot \sqrt{13}$$
$$c = 2\sqrt{13}$$

$$\sin A = \frac{\sqrt{3}}{2\sqrt{13}}$$
$$\cos A = \frac{7}{2\sqrt{13}}$$
$$\tan A = \frac{\sqrt{3}}{7}$$
$$\cot A = \frac{7}{\sqrt{3}}$$
$$\sec A = \frac{2\sqrt{13}}{7}$$
$$\csc A = \frac{2\sqrt{13}}{\sqrt{3}}$$

148. Solving for Sides and Trigonometric Functions When One Side and One Function Are Given

When one side and one function of an angle of a right triangle are given, the two other sides and the remaining trigonometric functions of the given angle can be found. These are determined by use of the Pythagorean theorem.

Example 1: Given the right triangle ABC (fig. 34): if the hypotenuse is 30 inches and sec $A = 5$, solve for sides a and b and the trigonometric functions of angle A.

$\sec A = \frac{c}{b}$; also, $\sec A = \frac{30}{b}$; but $\sec A = 5$ or $\frac{5}{1}$

Therefore, $\frac{30}{b} = \frac{5}{1}$
$$5b = 30$$
$$b = 6 \text{ inches}$$

$$a^2 = c^2 - b^2$$
$$a^2 = 900 - 36$$
$$a^2 = 864$$
$$a = \sqrt{864}$$
$$a = \sqrt{144}\sqrt{6}$$
$$a = 12\sqrt{6} \text{ inches}, b = 6 \text{ inches}, c = 30 \text{ inches}$$

be an angle of approximately 14°.

150. Common Trigonometric Functions

a. General. There are two special-case right triangles that are commonly used in solving mathematical problems. These are the right isosceles triangle (par. 131a) with equal acute angles of 45° (fig. 37) and the right triangle with acute angles of 30° and 60°. The functions of these angles are tabulated in appendix III.

b. Trigonometric Functions of 45°. Draw the right triangle ABC (fig. 37) with angle A equal to 45°. Because the acute angles of a right triangle are complementary, angle A plus angle B equals 90°. Thus, angle B is also 45°. Since sides opposite equal angles are equal, side a is equal to side b.

Let $a = 1$ and $b = 1$.

$c^2 = a^2 + b^2$
$c^2 = 1 + 1$
$c^2 = 2$
$c = \sqrt{2}$

$\sin 45° = \frac{1}{\sqrt{2}} \cdot \frac{\sqrt{2}}{\sqrt{2}} = \frac{\sqrt{2}}{2} = \frac{1}{2}\sqrt{2}$

$\cos 45° = \frac{1}{\sqrt{2}} \cdot \frac{\sqrt{2}}{\sqrt{2}} = \frac{\sqrt{2}}{2} = \frac{1}{2}\sqrt{2}$

$\tan 45° = \frac{1}{1} = 1$

$\cot 45° = \frac{1}{1} = 1$

$\sec 45° = \frac{\sqrt{2}}{1} = \sqrt{2}$

$\csc 45° = \frac{\sqrt{2}}{1} = \sqrt{2}$

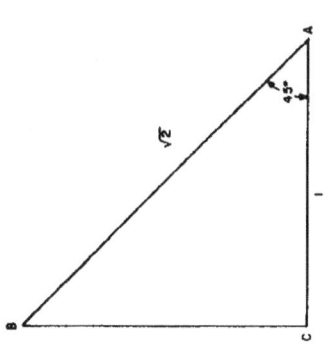

Figure 37. Right isosceles triangle—trigonometric functions of 45°.

c. Trigonometric Functions of 30° and 60°. Draw the equilateral triangle ABX (fig. 38). The angles of any equilateral triangle are 60° and the sides are equal (par. 131a). Drop a perpendicular BC to the center of the base AX. Right angles ACB and BCX are formed by the perpendicular and the base. The angles ABC and XBC are 30° angles. Since the sides of the equilateral triangle are equal, the perpendicular bisecting the base makes the base AC of the right triangle ABC one-half the length of the base AX of the equilateral triangle. Thus, the side opposite the right angle in a right triangle is twice the length of the side opposite the 30° angle.

Let $b = 1$ and $c = 2$.

$a^2 = c^2 - b^2$
$a^2 = 4 - 1$
$a^2 = 3$
$a = \sqrt{3}$

$\sin 60° = \frac{\sqrt{3}}{2} = \frac{1}{2}\sqrt{3}$

$\cos 60° = \frac{1}{2}$

$\tan 60° = \frac{\sqrt{3}}{1} = \sqrt{3}$

$\cot 60° = \frac{1}{\sqrt{3}} \cdot \frac{\sqrt{3}}{\sqrt{3}} = \frac{\sqrt{3}}{3} = \frac{1}{3}\sqrt{3}$

$\sec 60° = \frac{2}{1} = 2$

$\csc 60° = \frac{2}{\sqrt{3}} = \frac{2\sqrt{3}}{3} = \frac{2}{3}\sqrt{3}$

$\sin 30° = \frac{1}{2}$

$\cos 30° = \frac{\sqrt{3}}{2} = \frac{1}{2}\sqrt{3}$

$\tan 30° = \frac{1}{\sqrt{3}} \cdot \frac{\sqrt{3}}{\sqrt{3}} = \frac{\sqrt{3}}{3} = \frac{1}{3}\sqrt{3}$

$\cot 30° = \frac{\sqrt{3}}{1} = \sqrt{3}$

$\sec 30° = \frac{2}{\sqrt{3}} \cdot \frac{\sqrt{3}}{\sqrt{3}} = \frac{2\sqrt{3}}{3} = \frac{2}{3}\sqrt{3}$

$\csc 30° = \frac{2}{1} = 2$

Example 2: Given the right triangle ABC (fig. 34): solve for sides b and c and the trigonometric functions of angle A when side a is 21.2 inches and $\sin A = \frac{4}{7}$.

$\sin A = \frac{a}{c}$; also, $\sin a = \frac{21.2}{c}$, but $\sin A = \frac{4}{7}$.

Therefore, $\frac{21.2}{c} = \frac{4}{7}$
$4c = 148.4$
$c = 37.1$ inches

$b^2 = c^2 - a^2$
$b^2 = 1376.41 - 449.44$
$b^2 = 926.97$
$b = \sqrt{926.97}$
$b = 30.4$ inches, $a = 21.2$ inches, $c = 37.1$ inches

$\sin A = \frac{21.2}{37.1} = \frac{4}{7}$

$\cos A = \frac{30.4}{37.1}$

$\tan A = \frac{21.2}{30.4} = \frac{5.3}{7.6}$

$\cot A = \frac{30.4}{21.2} = \frac{7.6}{5.3}$

$\sec A = \frac{37.1}{30.4}$

$\csc A = \frac{37.1}{21.2} = \frac{7}{4}$

Step 4. Join A and B, thus forming the right triangle ABC (B, fig. 36).

Step 5. $\tan A = \frac{1}{4}$; therefore, A is the required angle. Measuring angle A with a protractor shows it to

149. Constructing an Acute Angle of Right Triangle When One Trigonometric Function Is Known

When the trigonometric function of an acute angle is given, the angle may be constructed geometrically. Use the definition given for the given function.

Example: Construct the acute angle A of right triangle ABC if $\tan A = \frac{1}{4}$.

Step 1. Let $a = 1$ and $b = 4$ units.

Step 2. Erect perpendicular lines AC and BC. Use cross-sectional paper if available.

Step 3. Measure off 1 unit along BC and 4 units along AC (A, fig. 36).

Figure 36. Constructing an angle when one function is known.

152. Calculations Involving Angles

a. Addition. To add angles, arrange the degrees, minutes, and seconds in separate columns and add each column separately. If the sum of the seconds column is 60 or more, subtract 60 or a multiple of 60 from that column, and add 1 minute or the same multiple of 1 minute to the minutes column. If the sum of the minutes column is 60 or more, subtract 60 from that column and add 1° to the degree column.

Example 1: Add 20° 40′ 25″, 8° 35′ 5″, and 30° 58′ 51″.

```
 20°  40′  25″
  8°  35′   5″
 30°  58′  51″
 58° 133′  81″
```

Subtract 60″ from 81″ and add 1′ to 133′.

```
 58° 133′   81″
    +  1′  −60″
 58° 134′   21″
```

Subtract 120′ from 134′ and add 2° to 58°.

```
  58°  134′  21″
  + 2° −120′
  60°   14′  21″
```

Example 2: Add 15° 44′ 36″ and 12° 38′ 35″.

```
 15° 44′ 36″
 12° 38′ 35″
 27° 82′ 71″ = 27° 83′ 11″ = 28° 23′ 11″.
```

b. Subtraction. To subtract angles, arrange the degrees, minutes, and seconds in separate columns with the larger angle on top. Then, subtract the individual columns. If the upper number in a column is too small to allow subtraction, one unit must be taken away from the preceding column and 60 units added to the insufficient number to make subtraction possible.

Example 1: Subtract 14° 51′ 30″ from 86° 45′ 10″.

```
  86° 45′ 10″
 −14° 51′ 30″
```

Subtraction cannot be performed in either the seconds or minutes columns. Subtract 1′ from 45′ leaving 44′, and add 60″ to 10″ for a total of 70″.

```
  86° 44′ 70″
 −14° 51′ 30″
```

Subtraction still cannot be performed in the minutes column. Subtract 1° from 86°, leaving 85°, and add 60′ to 44′ for a total of 104′.

```
  85° 104′ 70″
 −14°  51′ 30″
  71°  53′ 40″
```

Example 2: Subtract 10° 35′ 42″ from 19° 20′ 20″.

```
  19° 20′ 20″
 −10° 35′ 42″
```

151. Solving for Sides of 45°–45°–90° or 30°–60°–90° Triangles When One Side Is Given

In special cases, right triangles can be solved when only one side is given. These are the 45°–45°–90° isosceles triangle and the 30°–60°–90° triangle.

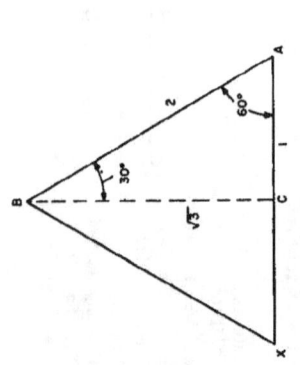

Figure 38. Equilateral right triangle—trigonometric functions of a right triangle with angles of 30° and 60°.

Example 1: Solve for the unknown sides of right triangle ABC if angle $A = 60°$ and $b = 4$ inches.

$\tan 60° = \dfrac{a}{b} = \dfrac{a}{4}$; however, $\tan 60° = \sqrt{3}$.

Therefore,

$\dfrac{a}{4} = \dfrac{\sqrt{3}}{1}$

$a = 4\sqrt{3}$ inches

$\cos 60° = \dfrac{b}{c} = \dfrac{4}{c}$; however, $\cos 60° = \dfrac{1}{2}$.

Therefore,

$\dfrac{4}{c} = \dfrac{1}{2}$

$c = 8$ inches

Thus, $a = 4\sqrt{3}$ inches, $b = 4$ inches, $c = 8$ inches.

Example 2: Solve for the unknown sides of right triangle ABC if angle $A = 45°$ and $c = 6$ inches.

$\sin 45° = \dfrac{a}{c} = \dfrac{a}{6}$; however, $\sin 45° = \dfrac{\sqrt{2}}{2}$.

Therefore,

$\dfrac{a}{6} = \dfrac{\sqrt{2}}{2}$

$2a = 6\sqrt{2}$

$a = 3\sqrt{2}$

$\cos 45° = \dfrac{b}{c} = \dfrac{b}{6}$; however, $\cos 45° = \dfrac{\sqrt{2}}{2}$.

Therefore,

$\dfrac{b}{6} = \dfrac{\sqrt{2}}{2}$

$2b = 6\sqrt{2}$

$b = 3\sqrt{2}$ inches

Thus, $a = 3\sqrt{2}$ inches, $b = 3\sqrt{2}$ inches, $c = 6$ inches.

Subtraction cannot be performed in either the minutes or seconds columns. Therefore, change 19° 20′ 20″ to 18° 79′ 80″ and subtract.

```
  18° 79′ 80″
 −10° 35′ 42″
   8° 44′ 38″
```

c. *Multiplication.* To multiply an angle by a given number, multiply each column by the number. If the answer in the seconds or minutes column is greater than 60, reduce as in the addition of angles (*a* above).

Example 1: Multiply 15° 21′ 40″ by 3:

```
15° 21′ 40″
        3
45° 63′ 120″ = 45° 65′ 0″ = 46° 5′
```

Example 2: Multiply 12° 14′ 36″ by 5.

```
12° 14′ 36″
        5
60° 70′ 180″ = 60° 73′ = 61° 13′
```

d. *Division.* To divide an angle by a given number, divide each column by the number (beginning with the degrees column). Change the remainder in degrees, if any, into minutes and add it to the minutes column; then, perform division on the numbers in the minutes column. Change the remainder in minutes, if any, to seconds and add it to the seconds column; then, perform division on the numbers in the seconds column.

Example 1: Divide 71° 22′ 21″ by 3.

```
     23°   47′   27″
   3)71°   22′   21″
     69                
      2° = 120′
           142′
           141′
             1′ = 60″
                  81″
                  81″
```

Example 2: Divide 166° 17′ 36″ by 6.

```
     27°   42′   56″
   6)166°  17′   36″
     162                
       4° = 240′
            257′
            252′
              5′ = 300″
                   336″
                   336″
```

153. Review Problems—Basic Trigonometry

Note. In the following problems, angle C is the right angle and equals 90°.

a. Find the third side of each of the following right triangles ABC, if two sides are:

(1) $a = 5, b = 7$
(2) $b = 18, c = 19$
(3) $a = 17, c = 43$
(4) $a = 3b$
(5) $a = 2m, c = m^2 + 1$

b. Given the right triangle ABC, solve for the trigonometric functions of angle A in each of the following cases:

(1) $\sin A = \dfrac{4}{7}$

(2) $\tan A = \dfrac{2}{3}$

(3) $\cos A = \dfrac{\sqrt{3}}{2}$

(4) $\csc A = 2.4$

(5) $\cot A = \dfrac{1}{y}$

(6) $\sec A = 2\dfrac{2}{3}$

c. Solve each of the right triangles (ABC) for the two unknown sides:

(1) $\sin A = \dfrac{1}{2}, a = 17$

(2) $\tan A = \dfrac{3}{4}, b = 12$

(3) $\cos A = \dfrac{4}{5}, c = 20$

(4) $\csc A = \dfrac{15}{7}, c = 37.5$

(5) $\cot A = \dfrac{3}{5}, a = 10$

(6) $\sec A = \dfrac{9}{4}, b = 18.4$

d. Solve each of the following right triangles (ABC) for the unknown sides:

(1) $A = 30°, a = 10$
(2) $B = 45°, b = 7$
(3) $A = 60°, c = 8$
(4) $B = 30°, a = 9$
(5) $B = 60°, c = 25$

Section II. NATURAL TRIGONOMETRIC FUNCTIONS

154. Tables and Their Uses

For convenience in computing, trigonometric functions are arranged in tables similar to the tables of logarithms. The ratios themselves are called *natural* sines, cosines, tangents, cotangents, etc. The tables give the sines and cosines, the tangents and cotangents, and the secants and cosecants of the angles from 0° to 90°. Angles less than 45° are read down the page; the degrees are at the top of the page and the minutes are on the left. Angles greater than 45° are read up the page; the degrees are at the bottom of the page and the minutes are on the right. As with logarithms, it is necessary to interpolate to find the function of an angle which does not reduce to an integral number of minutes. When working with the sine and tangent, which are increasing in size from 0° to 90°, it is necessary to add in interpolation. When working with the cosine and cotangent, which are decreasing in size from 0° to 90°, it is necessary to subtract.

155. Finding the Function of an Angle From the Table

To find the function of an angle from the table, proceed much the same as with the table of logarithms. This is illustrated by the following examples:

a. *When an Angle Is Given in the Table.*

Example 1: Find the cosine of 44° 27′.

Step 1. Turn to the table of sines and cosines.
Step 2. Locate the 44° column at the top of the page.
Step 3. Locate the 27′ at the left of the page.
Step 4. Read .71386 in the column headed Cosin.
Step 5. Cos 44° 27′ = .71386.

Example 2: Fine the tangent of 86° 18′.

Step 1. Turn to the table of tangents and cotangents.
Step 2. Locate the 86° column at the bottom of the page.
Step 3. Locate the 18′ at the right of the page.
Step 4. Read 15.4638 in the column headed Tang.
Step 5. Tan 86° 18′ = 15.4638.

b. *When an Angle Is Not Given in the Table.*

Example 1: Find the sine of 32° 46′ 36″.

sin 32° 46′ = .54122
sin 32° 46′ 36″ = .54122 + x
sin 32° 47′ = .54146

$$\begin{array}{ll} \sin 32^\circ\ 46'\ 36'' & 32'\ 47' \\ \underline{-32^\circ\ 46'} & \underline{-32^\circ\ 46'} \\ \quad 36'' & \quad 1' = 60'' \end{array}$$

$$\text{ratio} = \frac{36}{60} = \frac{6}{10} = \frac{3}{5}$$

$$.54146 - .54122 = .00024$$

$$\text{ratio} = \frac{x}{.00024}$$

$$\frac{3}{5} = \frac{x}{.00024}$$

$$5x = .00072$$

$$x = .000144$$

$$\sin 32^\circ\ 46'\ 36'' = .54122 + .000144 = .54136$$

Example 2: Find the tangent of 56° 43′ 27″.

$$\tan 56^\circ\ 43' = 1.52332$$

$$\tan 56^\circ\ 43'\ 27'' = 1.52332 + x$$

$$\tan 56^\circ\ 44' = 1.52429$$

$$\frac{27}{60} \text{ or } \frac{9}{20} = \frac{x}{.00097}$$

$$20x = .00873$$

$$x = .000436 \text{ or } .00044$$

$$\tan 56^\circ\ 43'\ 27'' = 1.52332 + .00044 = 1.52376$$

156. Finding an Angle When the Trigonometric Function Is Given

The procedure for using the table to find an angle corresponding to a function is similar to that of logarithms. This is illustrated in the examples in *a* and *b* below.

a. When the Function Is Given in the Table.

Example: Find the value of angle *A* if sine $A = .27284$.

Step 1. Find .27284 in the Sine column of the Sines and Cosines table.

Step 2. Reading 15° at the top of the column and 50′ in the minutes column on the left, angle $A = 15^\circ\ 50'$.

b. When the Function Is Not Given in the Table.

Example 1: Find the value of angle *A* when sine $A = .78112$.

$$.78098 = \sin 51^\circ\ 21'$$

$$.78112 = \sin 51^\circ\ 21' + x$$

$$.78116 = \sin 51^\circ\ 22'$$

$$\begin{array}{ll} .78112 & .78116 \\ \underline{-.78098} & \underline{-.78098} \\ .00014 & .00018 \end{array}$$

$$\text{ratio} = \frac{.00014}{.00018} = \frac{14}{18} = \frac{7}{9}$$

$$51^\circ\ 22' - 51^\circ\ 21' = 1' = 60''$$

$$\text{ratio} = \frac{x}{60}$$

$$\frac{7}{9} = \frac{x}{60}$$

$$9x = 420$$

$$x = 47$$

$$\text{angle } A = 51^\circ\ 21'\ 47''$$

Example 2: Find the value of angle *A* when cot $A = .33820$.

$$.33848 = \cot 71^\circ\ 18'$$

$$.33820 = \cot 71^\circ\ 18' + x$$

$$.33816 = \cot 71^\circ\ 19'$$

$$\frac{28}{32} \text{ or } \frac{7}{8} = \frac{x}{60}$$

$$8x = 420$$

$$x = 53$$

$$\text{angle } A = 71^\circ\ 18'\ 53''$$

157. Solving a Right Triangle When an Acute Angle and the Hypotenuse Are Given

To solve for the unknowns in a right triangle when an acute angle and the hypotenuse are given. proceed as in *a* and *b* below. In both examples, angle *C* is the right angle; therefore, angle $C = 90^\circ$.

Example 1: Find the unknown sides *a* and *b*, and the value of angle *B* in right triangle *ABC* (fig. 39) if angle *A* is 33° 15′ and the hypotenuse, *c* is 9 inches.

$$\angle A + \angle B + \angle C = 180^\circ$$

$$\angle B = 180^\circ - \angle A - \angle C$$

$$\angle B = 180^\circ - 33^\circ\ 15' - 90^\circ$$

$$\angle B = 56^\circ\ 45'$$

$$\sin A = \frac{a}{c}$$

$$\sin 33^\circ\ 15' = \frac{a}{9}$$

$$a = 9 \sin 33^\circ\ 15'$$

$$a = 9 \times .54829 = 4.93461$$

$$a = 4.93461$$

$$\text{Cos } A = \frac{b}{c}$$

$$\cos 33^\circ\ 15' = \frac{b}{9}$$

$$b = 9 \cos 33^\circ\ 15'$$

$$b = 9 \times .83629$$

$$b = 7.52661$$

Therefore, $\angle A = 33^\circ\ 15'$ $\quad a = 4.93461$ inches

$\angle B = 56^\circ\ 45'$ $\quad b = 7.52661$ inches

$\angle C = 90^\circ$ $\quad c = 9$ inches

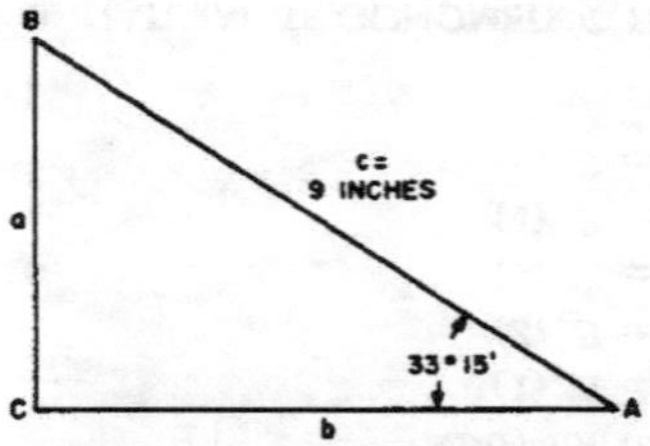

Figure 39. Solving a right triangle when an acute angle (33° 15′) and the hypotenuse are given.

Example 2: Solve for the unknown sides a and b, and the value of angle B in right triangle ABC (fig. 40) if angle A is 24° 35′ 36″ and the hypotenuse, c, is 12 inches.

$\angle B = 180° - \angle A - \angle C$
$\angle B = 180° - 24° 35′ 36″ - 90°$
$\angle B = 65° 24′ 24″$

$\sin A = \dfrac{a}{c}$

$\sin 24° 35′ 36″ = \dfrac{a}{12}$

$a = 12 \sin 24° 35′ 36″$

$\sin 24° 35′ = .41602$
$\sin 24° 35′ 36″ = .41602 + x$
$\sin 24° 36′ = .41628$

$\dfrac{36}{60}$ or $\dfrac{3}{5} = \dfrac{x}{.00026}$

$5x = .00078$
$x = .00016$

$\sin 24° 35′ 36″ = .41602 + .00016 = .41618$

$a = 12 \times .41618$
$a = 4.99416$

$\cos A = \dfrac{b}{c}$

$\cos 24° 35′ 36″ = \dfrac{b}{12}$

$b = 12 \cos 24° 35′ 36″$

$\cos 24° 35′ = .90936$
$\cos 24° 35′ 36″ = .90936 - x$
$\cos 24° 36′ = .90924$

$\dfrac{36}{60}$ or $\dfrac{3}{5} = \dfrac{x}{.00012}$

$5x = .00036$
$x = .00007$

$\cos 24° 35′ 36″ = .90936 - .00007 = .90929$

$b = 12 \times .90929$
$b = 10.91148$

Therefore, $\angle A = 24° 35′ 36″$ $a = 4.99416$ inches
$\angle B = 65° 24′ 24″$ $b = 10.91148$ inches
$\angle C = 90°$ $c = 12$ inches

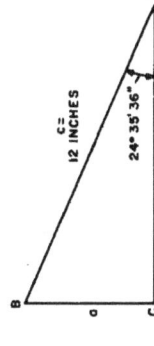

Figure 40. Solving a right triangle when an acute angle (24°35′36″) and the hypotenuse are given.

158. Solving a Right Triangle When an Acute Angle and the Adjacent Side Are Given

To solve a right triangle when an acute angle and the adjacent side are given, proceed as shown in the example below. Angle C is the right angle.

Example: Find the unknown sides a and c and the value of angle B in the right triangle ABC (fig. 41) if angle A is 37° 42′ 42″ and the side adjacent to angle A is 8 inches.

$\angle B = 180° - 90° - 37° 42′ 42″$
$\angle B = 52° 17′ 18″$

$\cos A = \dfrac{b}{c}$

$\cos 37° 42′ 42″ = \dfrac{8}{c}$

$c (\cos 37° 42′ 42″) = 8$

$\cos 37° 42′ = .79122$
$\cos 37° 42′ 42″ = .79122 - x$
$\cos 37° 43′ = .79105$

$\dfrac{42}{60}$ or $\dfrac{7}{10} = \dfrac{x}{.00017}$

$10x = .00119$
$x = .00012$

$\cos 37° 42′ 42″ = .79122 - .00012 = .79110$

$.79110c = 8$

$c = \dfrac{8}{.79110}$

$c = 10.11$

$\tan A = \dfrac{a}{b}$

$\tan 37° 42′ 42″ = \dfrac{a}{8}$

$a = 8 \tan 37° 42′ 42″$

$\tan 37° 42′ = .77289$
$\tan 37° 42′ 42″ = .77289 + x$
$\tan 37° 43′ = .77335$

$\dfrac{42}{60}$ or $\dfrac{7}{10} = \dfrac{x}{.00046}$

$10x = .00322$
$x = .00032$

$\tan 37° 42′ 42″ = .77289 + .00032 = .77321$

$a = 8 \times .77321$
$a = 6.18568$

Therefore, $\angle A = 37° 42′ 42″$ $a = 6.18568$ inches
$\angle B = 52° 17′ 18″$ $b = 8$ inches
$\angle C = 90°$ $c = 10.11$ inches

159. Solving a Right Triangle When Hypotenuse and One Side Are Given

Given the hypotenuse and one other side of a right triangle, solve for the unknown angles and side as illustrated in the example below.

Example: Find the unknown angles A and B, and side c of right triangle ABC (fig. 42) if the hypotenuse is 12 inches and the side opposite angle A is 8 inches.

$$b^2 = c^2 - a^2$$
$$b^2 = 12^2 - 8^2$$
$$b^2 = 144 - 64$$
$$b^2 = 80$$
$$b = \sqrt{80}$$
$$b = 8.94$$

$$\sin A = \frac{a}{c}$$
$$\sin A = \frac{8}{12} = \frac{2}{3}$$
$$\sin A = .66667$$

$$.66653 = \sin 41° 48'$$
$$.66667 = \sin 41° 48' + x$$
$$.66675 = \sin 41° 49'$$

$$\frac{14}{22} = \frac{x}{60}$$
$$22x = 840$$
$$x = \frac{840}{22} = 38$$

$$.66667 = \sin 41° 48' 38''$$

angle $A = 41° 48' 38''$
$\angle B = 180° - \angle C - \angle A$
$\angle B = 180° - 90° - 41° 48' 38''$
$\angle B = 48° 11' 22''$

Therefore, $\angle A = 41° 48' 38''$ $a = 8$ inches
$\angle B = 48° 11' 22''$ $b = 8.94$ inches
$\angle C = 90°$ $c = 12$ inches

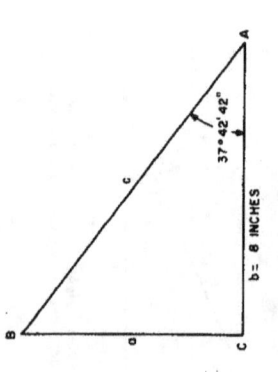

Figure 41. Solving a right triangle when an acute angle and the adjacent side are given.

160. Solving a Right Triangle When Two Sides Are Given

When two sides of a right triangle are given, solve for the unknown angles and the hypotenuse as shown in the example below.

Example: Find the unknown angles A and B and side c in right triangle ABC (fig. 43) if side a is 8 inches and side b is 10 inches.

$$c^2 = a^2 + b^2$$
$$c^2 = 64 + 100$$
$$c^2 = 164$$
$$c = \sqrt{164}$$
$$c = 12.8$$

$$\tan A = \frac{a}{b}$$
$$\tan A = \frac{8}{10}$$
$$\tan A = .80000$$

$$.79972 = \tan 38° 39'$$
$$.80000 = \tan 38° 39' + x$$
$$.80020 = \tan 38° 40'$$

$$\frac{28}{48} \text{ or } \frac{7}{12} = \frac{x}{60}$$
$$12x = 420$$
$$x = 35$$

$$.80000 = \tan 38° 39' 35''$$

angle $A = 38° 39' 35''$
$\angle B = 180° - \angle C - \angle A$
$\angle B = 180° - 90° - 38° 39' 35''$
$\angle B = 51° 20' 25''$

Therefore, $\angle A = 38° 39' 35''$ $a = 8$ inches
$\angle B = 51° 20' 25''$ $b = 10$ inches
$\angle C = 90°$ $c = 12.8$ inches

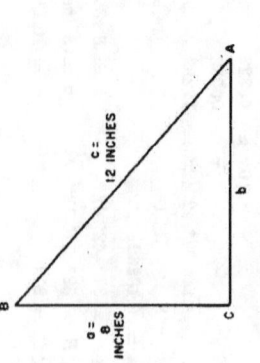

Figure 42. Solving a right triangle, when the hypotenuse and one side are given.

161. Solving a 30°–60°–90° Triangle When One Side Is Given

In a 30°–60°–90° triangle, the side opposite the 30° angle is equal to one-half the hypotenuse. Refer to paragraph 150c for the derivation of the trigonometric functions. Solve for the unknown sides as shown in the example below.

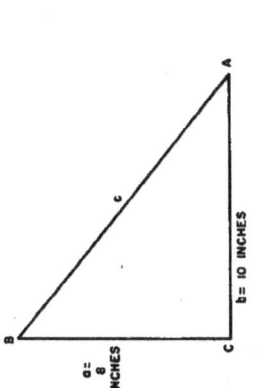

Figure 43. Solving a right triangle when two sides are given.

Example: Find the unknown sides b and c of 30°–60°–90° triangle ABC (fig. 44) if the side opposite the 60° angle is 6 inches.

$$\sin 60° = \frac{\sqrt{3}}{2}; \text{ also, } \sin 60° = \frac{a}{c} = \frac{6}{c}$$

$$\frac{\sqrt{3}}{2} = \frac{6}{c}$$

$$\sqrt{3}c = 12$$

$$c = \frac{12}{\sqrt{3}}$$

Eliminate $\sqrt{3}$ in the denominator by multiplying $\frac{12}{\sqrt{3}}$ by $\frac{\sqrt{3}}{\sqrt{3}}$:

$$c = \frac{12}{\sqrt{3}} \cdot \frac{\sqrt{3}}{\sqrt{3}} = \frac{12\sqrt{3}}{\sqrt{9}} = \frac{12\sqrt{3}}{3} = 4\sqrt{3}$$

$$c = 4\sqrt{3} = 4 \times 1.7321 = 6.9284$$

$$\tan 60° = \frac{\sqrt{3}}{1}; \text{ also, } \tan 60° = \frac{a}{b} = \frac{6}{b}$$

$$\frac{\sqrt{3}}{1} = \frac{6}{b}$$

$$\sqrt{3}b = 6$$

$$b = \frac{6}{\sqrt{3}} \cdot \frac{\sqrt{3}}{\sqrt{3}} = \frac{6\sqrt{3}}{\sqrt{9}} = \frac{6\sqrt{3}}{3} = 2\sqrt{3}$$

$$b = 2\sqrt{3} = 2 \times 1.7321 = 3.4642$$

Therefore, $a = 6$ inches

$b = 3.4642$ inches

$c = 6.9284$ inches

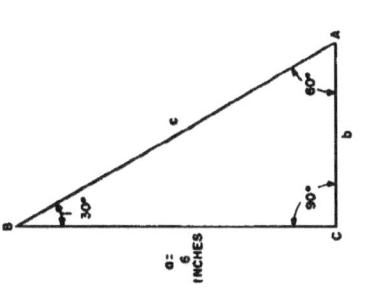

Figure 44. Solving a 30°–60°–90° triangle when one side is given.

162. Solving a 45°–45°–90° Triangle When One Side Is Given

In a 45°–45°–90° triangle, the sides opposite the equal angles are equal. Refer to paragraph 150b for the derivation of the trigonometric functions. Solve for the unknown sides as shown in the example below.

Example: Find the unknown sides a, b, and c of 45°–45°–90° triangle ABC (fig. 45) if the side opposite acute angle A is 5 inches.

$$\sin 45° = \frac{1}{\sqrt{2}}; \text{ also, } \sin A = \frac{a}{c} = \frac{5}{c}$$

$$\frac{1}{\sqrt{2}} = \frac{5}{c}$$

$$c = 5\sqrt{2}$$

$$c = 5 \times 1.4142 = 7.0710$$

$$\tan 45° = \frac{1}{1}; \text{ also, } \tan A = \frac{a}{b} = \frac{5}{b}$$

$$\frac{1}{1} = \frac{5}{b}$$

$$[b = 5]$$

Therefore, $a = 5$ inches

$b = 5$ inches

$c = 7.071$ inches

163. Angles of Elevation and Depression

When an object is higher than the observer's eye, the angle between the horizontal and the line of sight to the object is called the *angle of elevation* (A, fig. 46). When an object is lower than the observer's eye, the angle between the line of sight to the object and the horizontal is called the *angle of depression* (B, fig. 46).

Example:

A television antenna mast is 450 feet high (fig. 47). Find to the nearest second the angle of elevation to its top at a point 200 feet from the base of the mast.

$$\tan A = \frac{a}{b}$$

$$\tan A = \frac{450}{200}$$

$$\tan A = 2.2500$$

$$2.2496 = \tan 66° 2'$$

$$2.2500 = \tan 66° 2' + x$$

$$2.2513 = \tan 66° 3'$$

$$\frac{4}{17} = \frac{x}{60}$$

$$17x = 240$$

$$x = 14$$

$$2.2500 = \tan 66° 2' 14''$$

$$A = 66° 2' 14''$$

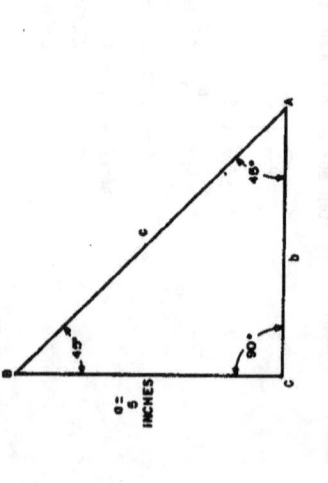

Figure 45. Solving a 45°–45°–90° triangle when one side is given.

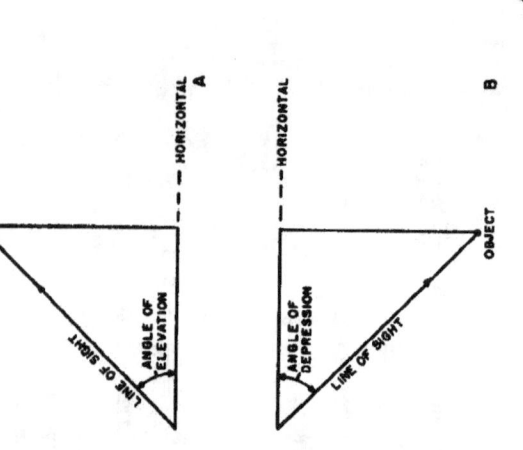

Figure 46. Angles of elevation and depression.

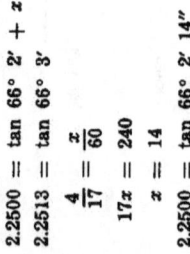

Figure 47. Finding the angle of elevation to top of an antenna mast.

164. Review Problems—Natural Trigonometric Functions

a. Find the sine, cosine, tangent, and cotangent of the following angles:

(1) 1° 30'
(2) 15° 25'
(3) 32° 10'
(4) 36° 39'
(5) 44° 59'
(6) 44° 59' 45''
(7) 35° 12' 15''
(8) 54° 27' 32''
(9) 48° 25' 37''
(10) 67° 33' 42''

b. Solve for the values of the following angles in degrees, minutes and seconds:

(1) $\sin A = .25737$
(2) $\cot A = .43279$
(3) $\cos A = .94000$
(4) $\tan A = .47237$
(5) $\cot A = 1.17529$
(6) $\cos A = .36243$
(7) $\sin A = .37778$
(8) $\tan A = .67676$
(9) $\tan A = 1.29000$
(10) $\cot A = .79653$

c. Solve for the following (angle $C = 90°$):

(1) Angle A in right triangle ABC when $a = 19$ and $c = 27$.
(2) Side a in right triangle ABC when $A = 37° 15'$ and $c = 17$.
(3) Side c in right triangle ABC when $A = 42° 37' 15''$ and $a = 22$.
(4) Side B in right triangle ABC when $A = 37° 45' 42''$ and $c = 25$.
(5) Side c in right triangle ABC when $A = 14° 35'$ and $b = 12$.
(6) Angle A in right triangle ABC when $b = 7$ and $c = 12$.
(7) Side a in right triangle ABC when $A = 47° 22' 52''$ and $b = 31$.
(8) Side b in right triangle ABC when $A = 56° 31' 25''$ and $a = 25$.
(9) Angle A in right triangle ABC when $a = 17$ and $b = 23$.
(10) Side b in right triangle ABC when $A = 7° 32' 54''$ and $a = 17$.
(11) Side c in right triangle ABC when $a = 15$ and $b = 27$.
(12) Angle A in right triangle ABC when $a = 15$ and $b = 27$.

d. Solve the following problems:

(1) Over a distance of 300 feet, the angle of elevation of a road is 8° 24' 30''. What is the rise in feet?

(2) The angle of elevation to the top of an antenna mast is 34° 17' 50''. If the distance from the transit to the center of the mast is 110 feet, how high is the mast? The transit is 5 feet high.

(3) If a ladder 15 feet long just touches the top of a wall and subtends an angle of 35° 24' 16'' with the ground, how far is the lower end of the ladder from the wall and how high is the wall?

(4) A captive balloon is anchored by 950 feet of cable. A man observes that the angle of elevation from his point of observation to the bottom of the balloon is 16° 47' 12''. How far is he from the balloon anchor?

(5) An excavation is 33 feet wide. The angle of depression from the top of one side to the bottom of the other side is 19° 34' 24''. How deep is the excavation?

(6) The angle of elevation from a given

point to the top of a tower is 17° 37' 15". Moving back 40 feet in a direct line, the angle of elevation from this point to the top of the tower is 15° 35' 20". Find the height of the tower.

(7) To determine the height of a tower, two sights are taken on a straight line perpendicular to the tower. If the distance between the points of observation is 60 feet and the angles of elevation are 32° 30' 15" and 28° 15' 30", respectively, what is the height of the tower?

(8) From a point in an open field a man sights on two mileposts along the side of a highway. The angles formed by an imaginary line perpendicular to the highway and the sights on the mileposts are 33° 20' and 39° 17' 30". How far is the man from the closest point on the highway?

(9) An airplane is flying between two towns at an altitude of 5,000 feet. The angle of depression to the outskirts of one town is 50° 26' 14", while the angle to the outskirts of the other town is 64° 44' 12". How far apart, in a direct line, are the two towns?

(10) A radio antenna on top of a building is 10 feet high. The angle of elevation to the base of the pole is 37° 17' 20"; the angle of elevation to the top of the antenna is 40° 30' 15". How high is the building?

(11) In a 45°–45°–90° right triangle the hypotenuse is 2 inches long. Find the length of the other two sides.

(12) In a 30°–60°–90° right triangle the hypotenuse is 6 inches long. Find the length of the other two sides.

Section III. TRIGONOMETRIC LAWS

165. Solving Oblique Triangles

An oblique triangle is one in which one of the angles is a right angle. The formulas in this section are used primarily to solve oblique triangles, but may also be used to solve right triangles. In the solution of triangles by trigonometric laws, the four following cases arise:

a. When any side and any two angles are given.

b. When any two sides and the angle opposite one of them are given.

c. When any two sides and the angle included between them are given.

d. When the three sides are given.

166. Law of Sines

In any triangle, the sides are proportional to the sines of the opposite angles.

Thus, $\dfrac{a}{\sin A} = \dfrac{b}{\sin B} = \dfrac{c}{\sin C}$.

b. Two Angles and One Side Given.

Example: Solve for the unknowns in oblique triangle ABC (fig. 48) when angle $A = 35°\ 47'\ 36''$, angle $B = 68°\ 42'\ 27''$, and the side opposite angle A is 15 inches.

$$\angle C = 180° - \angle A - \angle B$$
$$\angle C = 180° - 35°\ 47'\ 36'' - 68°\ 42'\ 27''$$
$$\angle C = 75°\ 29'\ 57''$$

$$\frac{a}{\sin A} = \frac{b}{\sin B}$$
$$b \sin A = a \sin B$$
$$b = \frac{a \sin B}{\sin A}$$
$$b = \frac{15 \sin 68°\ 42'\ 27''}{\sin 35°\ 47'\ 36''}$$

$\sin 68°\ 42'$	$= .93169$
$\sin 68°\ 42'\ 27''$	$= .93169 + x$
$\sin 68°\ 43'$	$= .93180$

$$\frac{27}{60} \text{ or } \frac{9}{20} = \frac{x}{.00011}$$
$$20x = .00099$$
$$x = .000049 = .00005$$
$$\sin 68°\ 42'\ 27'' = .93169 + .00005 = .93174$$

$\sin 35°\ 47'$	$= .58472$
$\sin 35°\ 47'\ 36''$	$= .58472 + x$
$\sin 35°\ 48'$	$= .58496$

$$\frac{36}{60} \text{ or } \frac{3}{5} = \frac{x}{.00024}$$
$$5x = .00072$$
$$x = .00014$$
$$\sin 35°\ 47'\ 36'' = .58472 + .00014 = .58486$$

$$b = \frac{15 \times .93174}{.58486}$$
$$b = \frac{13.97610}{.58486}$$
$$b = 23.89$$

$$\frac{a}{\sin A} = \frac{c}{\sin C}$$
$$c \sin A = a \sin C$$
$$c = \frac{a \sin C}{\sin A}$$
$$c = \frac{15 \sin 75°\ 29'\ 57''}{\sin 35°\ 47'\ 36''}$$

$\sin 75°\ 29'$	$= .96807$
$\sin 75°\ 29'\ 57''$	$= .96807 + x$
$\sin 75°\ 30'$	$= .96815$

$$\frac{57}{60} \text{ or } \frac{19}{20} = \frac{x}{.00008}$$
$$20x = .00152$$
$$x = .000076 = .00008$$
$$\sin 75°\ 29'\ 57'' = .96807 + .00008 = .96815$$

$$c = \frac{15 \times .96815}{.58486}$$
$$c = \frac{14.52225}{.58486}$$
$$c = 24.83$$

Therefore, $\angle A = 35°\ 47'\ 36''\quad a = 15$ inches
$\angle B = 68°\ 42'\ 27''\quad b = 23.89$ inches
$\angle C = 75°\ 29'\ 57''\quad c = 24.83$ inches

b. Two Sides and One Angle Given.

Example: Find the unknowns in oblique triangle ABC (fig. 49) when angle $A = 53°\ 35'\ 40''$, the side opposite angle A is 10 inches, and the side opposite angle B is 12 inches.

$$\frac{a}{\sin A} = \frac{b}{\sin B}$$

$$a \sin B = b \sin A$$

$$\sin B = \frac{b \sin A}{a}$$

$$\sin B = \frac{12 \sin 53°\ 35'\ 40''}{10}$$

$$\sin 53°\ 35' = .80472$$
$$\sin 53°\ 35'\ 40'' = .80472 + x$$
$$\sin 53°\ 36' = .80489$$

$$\frac{40}{60} \text{ or } \frac{2}{3} = \frac{x}{.00017}$$
$$3x = .00034$$
$$x = .00011$$

$$\sin 53°\ 35'\ 40'' = .80472 + .00011 = .80483$$

$$\sin B = \frac{12 \times .80483}{10}$$

$$\sin B = \frac{4.82898}{5}$$

$$\sin B = .96579\underline{6} = .96580$$

$$.96578 = \sin 74°\ 58'$$
$$.96580 = \sin 74°\ 58' + x$$
$$.96585 = \sin 74°\ 59'$$

$$\frac{2}{7} = \frac{x}{60}$$
$$7x = 120$$
$$x = 17$$

$$.96580 = \sin 74°\ 58'\ 17''$$

$$\angle B = 74°\ 58'\ 17''$$
$$\angle C = 180° - \angle A - \angle B$$

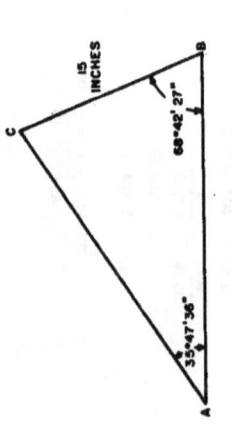

Figure 48. Solving an oblique triangle by the law of sines when two angles and a side are given.

$$\angle C = 180° - 53°\ 35'\ 40'' - 74°\ 58'\ 17''$$
$$\angle C = 51°\ 26'\ 3''$$

$$\frac{a}{\sin A} = \frac{c}{\sin C}$$
$$c \sin A = a \sin C$$
$$c = \frac{a \sin C}{\sin A}$$
$$c = \frac{10 \sin 51°\ 26'\ 3''}{\sin 53°\ 35'\ 40''}$$

$$\sin 51°\ 26' = .78188$$
$$\sin 51°\ 26'\ 3'' = .78188 + x$$
$$\sin 51°\ 27' = .78206$$

$$\frac{3}{60} \text{ or } \frac{1}{20} = \frac{x}{.00018}$$
$$20x = .00018$$
$$x = .000009 = .00001$$

$$\sin 51°\ 26'\ 3'' = .78188 + .00001 = .78189$$

$$c = \frac{10 \times .78189}{.80483}$$
$$c = \frac{7.8189}{.80483}$$
$$c = 9.71$$

Therefore, $\angle A = 53°\ 35'\ 40''$ $a = 10$ inches
$\angle B = 74°\ 58'\ 17''$ $b = 12$ inches
$\angle C = 51°\ 26'\ 3''$ $c = 9.71$ inches

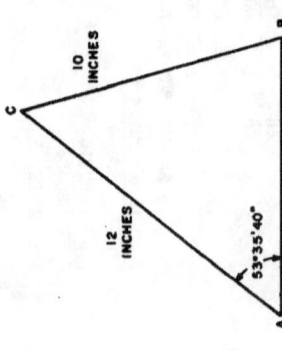

Figure 49. Solving an oblique triangle by the law of sines when two sides and an angle are given.

167. Law of Cosines

In any triangle, the square of any side equals the sum of the squares of the other two sides minus twice the product of these two sides times the cosine of the angle between them.

Thus, $a^2 = b^2 + c^2 - 2bc \cos A$
$b^2 = a^2 + c^2 - 2ac \cos B$
$c^2 = a^2 + b^2 - 2ab \cos C$

Example: Find the unknowns in oblique triangle ABC (fig. 50) when angle $C = 56°\ 45'\ 24''$, the side opposite angle A is 6 inches, and the side opposite angle B is 8 inches.

$$c^2 = a^2 + b^2 - 2ab \cos C$$
$$c^2 = 6^2 + 8^2 - 2(6)(8) \cos 56°\ 45'\ 24''$$
$$c^2 = 36 + 64 - 96 \cos 56°\ 45'\ 24''$$
$$c^2 = 100 - 96 \cos 56°\ 45'\ 24''$$

$$\cos 56°\ 45' = .54829$$
$$\cos 56°\ 45'\ 24'' = .54829 - x$$
$$\cos 56°\ 46' = .54805$$

$$\frac{24}{60} \text{ or } \frac{2}{5} = \frac{x}{.00024}$$
$$5x = .00048$$
$$x = .000096 \text{ or } .00010$$

$$\cos 56°\ 45'\ 24'' = .54829 - .00010 = .54819$$
$$c^2 = 100 - 96(.54819)$$
$$c^2 = 100 - 52.62624$$
$$c^2 = 47.37376$$
$$c = \sqrt{47.37376}$$
$$c = 6.882$$

$$\frac{a}{\sin A} = \frac{c}{\sin C}$$
$$c \sin A = a \sin C$$
$$\sin A = \frac{a \sin C}{c}$$
$$\sin A = \frac{6 \sin 56°\ 45'\ 24''}{6.882}$$

$$\sin 56°\ 45' = .83629$$
$$\sin 56°\ 45'\ 24'' = .83629 + x$$
$$\sin 56°\ 46' = .83645$$

$$\frac{24}{60} \text{ or } \frac{2}{5} = \frac{x}{.00016}$$
$$5x = .00032$$
$$x = .000064 = .00006$$

$$\sin 56°\ 45'\ 24'' = .83629 + .00006 = .83635$$

$$\sin A = \frac{6(.83635)}{6.882}$$
$$\sin A = \frac{5.01810}{6.882}$$
$$\sin A = .72916$$

$$.72897 = \sin 46°\ 48'$$
$$.72916 = \sin 46°\ 48' + x$$
$$.72917 = \sin 46°\ 49'$$

$$\frac{19}{20} = \frac{x}{60}$$
$$20x = 1140$$
$$x = 57$$

$$.72917 = \sin 46°\ 48'\ 57''$$
$$\angle A = 46°\ 48'\ 57''$$
$$\angle B = 180° - \angle C - \angle A$$
$$\angle B = 180° - 56°\ 45'\ 24'' - 46°\ 48'\ 57''$$
$$\angle B = 76°\ 25'\ 39''$$

Therefore, $\angle A = 46°\ 48'\ 57''$ $a = 6$ inches
$\angle B = 76°\ 25'\ 39''$ $b = 8$ inches
$\angle C = 56°\ 45'\ 24''$ $c = 6.882$ inches

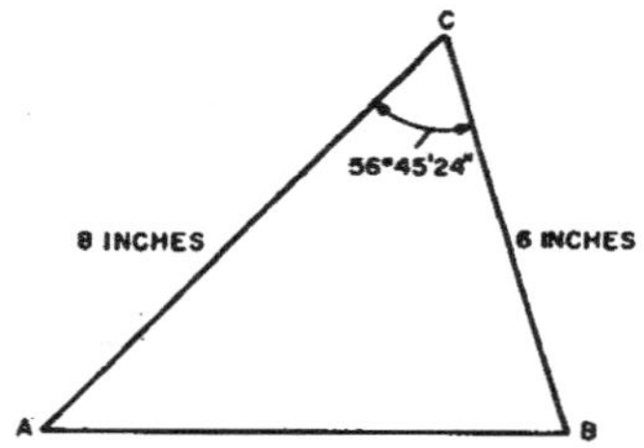

Figure 50. Solving an oblique triangle by the law of cosines when an angle and two sides are given.

168. Law of Tangents

The law of tangents is expressed by the formula $\dfrac{a-b}{a+b} = \dfrac{\tan \frac{1}{2}(A-B)}{\tan \frac{1}{2}(A+B)}$, where a and b are any two sides and A and B are the angles opposite these sides.

Example: Find the unknowns in oblique triangle ABC (fig. 51) when two sides of the triangle are 9 and 11 inches, respectively, and angle C, the angle included between these two sides, is $40°\ 40'\ 40''$.

$$\angle A + \angle B + \angle C = 180°$$
$$\angle A + \angle B + 40°\ 40'\ 40'' = 180°$$
$$\angle A + \angle B = 180° - 40°\ 40'\ 40''$$
$$\angle A + \angle B = 139°\ 19'\ 20''$$

$$\tfrac{1}{2}(A+B) = \frac{139°\ 19'\ 20''}{2}$$
$$\tfrac{1}{2}(A+B) = 69°\ 39'\ 40''$$

$$\frac{a-b}{a+b} = \frac{\tan \frac{1}{2}(A-B)}{\tan \frac{1}{2}(A+B)}$$

$$\frac{11-9}{11+9} \text{ or } \frac{2}{20} = \frac{\tan \frac{1}{2}(A-B)}{\tan \frac{1}{2}(A+B)}$$

$$20 \tan \tfrac{1}{2}(A-B) = 2 \tan 69°\ 39'\ 40''$$
$$10 \tan \tfrac{1}{2}(A-B) = \tan 69°\ 39'\ 40''$$
$$\tan \tfrac{1}{2}(A-B) = \frac{\tan 69°\ 39'\ 40''}{10}$$

$$\tan 69°\ 39' = 2.69612$$
$$\tan 69°\ 39'\ 40'' = 2.69612 + x$$
$$\tan 69°\ 40' = 2.69853$$

$$\frac{40}{60} \text{ or } \frac{2}{3} = \frac{x}{.00241}$$
$$3x = .00482$$
$$x = .00161$$

$$\tan 69°\ 39'\ 40'' = 2.69612 + .00161 = 2.69773$$

$$\tan \tfrac{1}{2}(A - B) = \frac{2.69773}{10}$$
$$\tan \tfrac{1}{2}(A - B) = .26977$$

.26951 = tan 15° 5'
.26977 = tan 15° 5' + x
.26982 = tan 15° 6'

$$\frac{26}{31} = \frac{x}{60}$$
$$31x = 1560$$
$$x = 50$$

.26977 = tan 15° 5' 50"

$$\tfrac{1}{2}(A - B) = 15° 5' 50''$$

$\tfrac{1}{2}(A + B) = \tfrac{1}{2}A + \tfrac{1}{2}B = 69° 39' 40''$
$\tfrac{1}{2}(A - B) = \tfrac{1}{2}A - \tfrac{1}{2}B = 15° 5' 50''$
(add) $A = 84° 44' 90''$

$\angle A = 84° 45' 30''$

$\tfrac{1}{2}(A + B) = \tfrac{1}{2}A + \tfrac{1}{2}B = 69° 38' 100''$
$\tfrac{1}{2}(A - B) = \tfrac{1}{2}A - \tfrac{1}{2}B = 15° 5' 50''$
(subtract) $B = 54° 33' 50''$

$\angle B = 54° 33' 50''$

$$\frac{a}{\sin A} = \frac{c}{\sin c}$$
$$c \sin A = a \sin C$$
$$c = \frac{a \sin C}{\sin A}$$
$$c = \frac{11 \sin 40° 40' 40''}{\sin 84° 45' 30''}$$

sin 40° 40'   = .65166
sin 40° 40' 40'' = .65166 + x
sin 40° 41''   = .65188

$$\frac{40}{60} \text{ or } \frac{2}{3} = \frac{x}{.00022}$$
$$3x = .00044$$
$$x = .000146 = .00015$$
sin 40° 40' 40'' = .65166 + .00015 = .65181

sin 84° 45'   = .99580
sin 84° 45' 30'' = .99580 + x
sin 84° 46'   = .99583

$$\frac{30}{60} \text{ or } \frac{1}{2} = \frac{x}{.00003}$$
$$2x = .00003$$
$$x = .000015 = .00002$$
sin 84° 45' 30'' = .99580 + .00002 = .99582

$$c = \frac{11 \sin 40° 40' 40''}{\sin 84° 45' 30''}$$
$$c = \frac{11 \times .65181}{.99582}$$
$$c = \frac{7.16991}{.99582}$$
$$c = 7.2$$

Therefore, $\angle A = 84° 45' 30''$ $a = 11$ inches
          $\angle B = 54° 33' 50''$ $b = 9$ inches
          $\angle C = 40° 40' 40''$ $c = 7.2$ inches

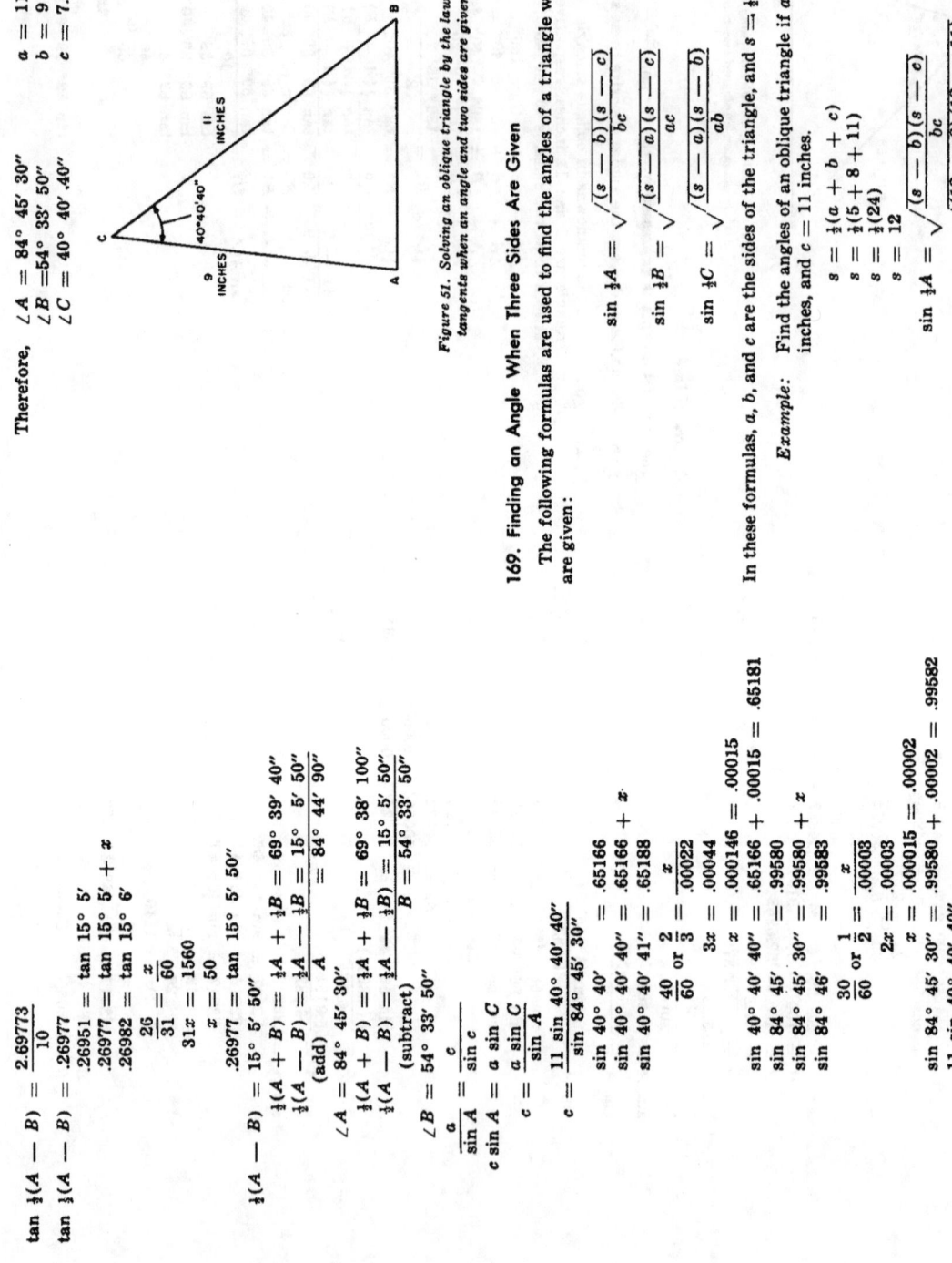

Figure 51. Solving an oblique triangle by the law of tangents when an angle and two sides are given.

169. Finding an Angle When Three Sides Are Given

The following formulas are used to find the angles of a triangle when three sides of the triangle are given:

$$\sin \tfrac{1}{2}A = \sqrt{\frac{(s-b)(s-c)}{bc}}$$

$$\sin \tfrac{1}{2}B = \sqrt{\frac{(s-a)(s-c)}{ac}}$$

$$\sin \tfrac{1}{2}C = \sqrt{\frac{(s-a)(s-b)}{ab}}$$

In these formulas, a, b, and c are the sides of the triangle, and $s = \tfrac{1}{2}(a + b + c)$.

Example: Find the angles of an oblique triangle if $a = 5$ inches, $b = 8$ inches, and $c = 11$ inches.

$s = \tfrac{1}{2}(a + b + c)$
$s = \tfrac{1}{2}(5 + 8 + 11)$
$s = \tfrac{1}{2}(24)$
$s = 12$

$$\sin \tfrac{1}{2}A = \sqrt{\frac{(s-b)(s-c)}{bc}}$$
$$\sin \tfrac{1}{2}A = \sqrt{\frac{(12-8)(12-11)}{(8)(11)}}$$
$$\sin \tfrac{1}{2}A = \sqrt{\frac{(4)(1)}{88}}$$
$$\sin \tfrac{1}{2}A = \sqrt{\frac{4}{88}} = \sqrt{\frac{1}{22}}$$
$$\sin \tfrac{1}{2}A = \sqrt{.0454545}$$

$$\sin \tfrac{1}{2}A = .21319$$
$$.21303 = \sin 12° \ 18'$$
$$.21319 = \sin 12° \ 18' + x$$
$$.21331 = \sin 12° \ 19'$$
$$\frac{16}{28} \text{ or } \frac{4}{7} = \frac{x}{60}$$
$$7x = 240$$
$$x = 34$$
$$.21319 = \sin 12° \ 18' \ 34''$$
$$\tfrac{1}{2}A = 12° \ 18' \ 34''$$
$$\angle A = 24° \ 36' \ 68'' \text{ or } 24° \ 37' \ 8''$$
$$\sin \tfrac{1}{2}B = \sqrt{\frac{(s-a)(s-c)}{ac}}$$
$$\sin \tfrac{1}{2}B = \sqrt{\frac{(12-5)(12-11)}{(5)(11)}}$$
$$\sin \tfrac{1}{2}B = \sqrt{\frac{(7)(1)}{55}}$$
$$\sin \tfrac{1}{2}B = \sqrt{\frac{7}{55}}$$
$$\sin \tfrac{1}{2}B = \sqrt{.1272727}$$
$$\sin \tfrac{1}{2}B = .35675$$
$$.35674 = \sin 20° \ 54'$$
$$.35675 = \sin 20° \ 54' + x$$
$$.35701 = \sin 20° \ 55'$$
$$\frac{1}{27} = \frac{x}{60}$$
$$27x = 60$$
$$x = 2$$
$$.35675 = \sin 20° \ 54' \ 2''$$
$$\tfrac{1}{2}B = 20° \ 54' \ 2''$$
$$\angle B = 40° \ 108' \ 4'' \text{ or } 41° \ 48' \ 4''$$
$$\angle C = 180° - \angle A - \angle B$$
$$\angle C = 180° - 24° \ 37' \ 8'' - 41° \ 48' \ 4''$$
$$\angle C = 180° - 66° \ 25' \ 12''$$
$$\angle C = 113° \ 34' \ 48''$$

Therefore, $\angle A = 24° \ 37' \ 8''$
$\angle B = 41° \ 48' \ 4''$
$\angle C = 113° \ 34' \ 48''$

170. Finding the Area of a Triangle When Two Sides and the Included Angle Are Given

The formula for finding the area of a triangle when two sides and the included angle are given is $S = \frac{1}{2} ab \sin C$ where S is the area of the triangle, a and b are the given sides, and C is the included angle.

Example: Find the area of oblique triangle ABC (fig. 52) when two sides are 7 and 8 inches, respectively, and the included angle is 50° 50′ 50″.

$$S = \tfrac{1}{2}ab \sin C$$
$$S = \tfrac{1}{2} \times 7 \times 8 \times \sin 50° \ 50' \ 50''$$
$$\sin 50° \ 50' = .77531$$
$$\sin 50° \ 50' \ 50'' = .77531 + x$$
$$\sin 50° \ 51' = .77550$$
$$\frac{50}{60} \text{ or } \frac{5}{6} = \frac{x}{.00019}$$
$$6x = .00095$$
$$x = .00016$$
$$\sin 50° \ 50' \ 50'' = .77531 + .00016 = .77547$$
$$S = \tfrac{1}{2} \times 7 \times 8 \times .77547 = 21.71316$$
$$S = 21.71316 \text{ square inches}$$

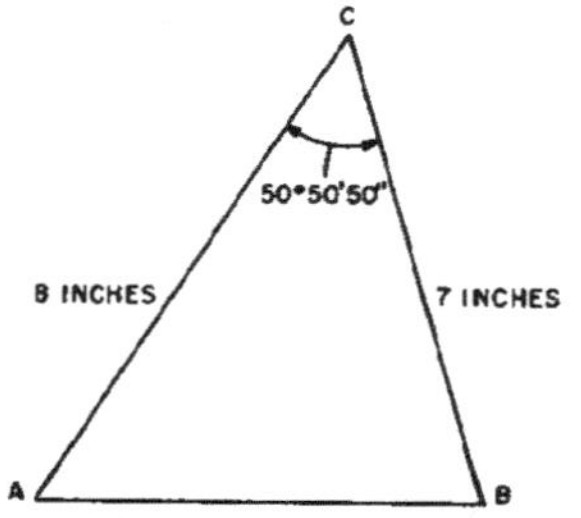

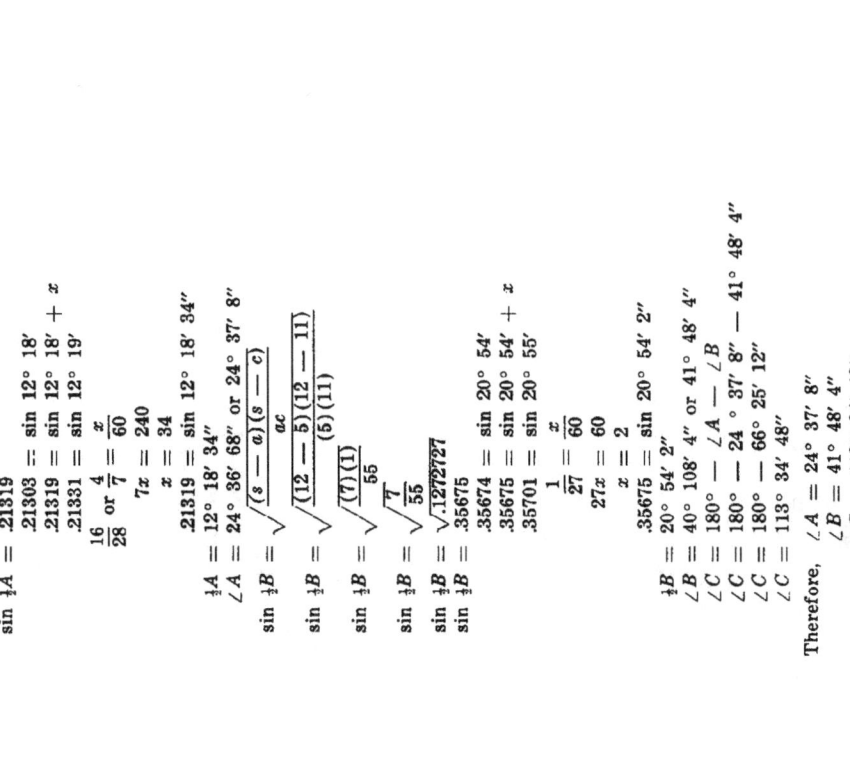

Figure 52. Solving for the area of an oblique triangle when two sides and the included angle are given.

171. Finding the Area of a Triangle When Two Angles and a Side Are Given

The formula for finding the area of a triangle when two angles and a side are given is $S = \frac{a^2 \sin B \sin C}{2 \sin A}$ where S is the area of the triangle, B and C are the given angles, and a is the given side.

Example: Find the area of oblique triangle ABC (fig. 53) when the two angles are 38° 42′ 48″ and 68° 52′ 42″ and the side is 10 inches.

$$\angle A = 180° - \angle B - \angle C$$
$$\angle A = 180° - 38° \ 42' \ 48'' - 68° \ 52' \ 42''$$
$$\angle A = 180° - 107° \ 35' \ 30''$$
$$\angle A = 72° \ 24' \ 30''$$
$$S = \frac{a^2 \sin B \sin C}{2 \sin A}$$
$$S = \frac{10^2 \sin 38° \ 42' \ 48'' \sin 68° \ 52' \ 42''}{2 \sin 72° \ 24' \ 30''}$$
$$\sin 38° \ 42' = .62524$$
$$\sin 38° \ 42' \ 48'' = .62524 + x$$
$$\sin 38° \ 43' = .62547$$
$$\frac{48}{60} \text{ or } \frac{4}{5} = \frac{x}{.00023}$$
$$5x = .00092$$
$$x = .00018$$
$$\sin 38° \ 42' \ 48'' = .62524 + .00018 = .62542$$
$$\sin 68° \ 52' = .93274$$
$$\sin 68° \ 52' \ 42'' = .93274 + x$$

antilog 1.4857 = 30.6
antilog 1.4858 = 30.6 + x
antilog 1.4871 = 30.7

$$\frac{1}{14} = \frac{x}{.1}$$

$14x = .1$

$x = .007$

antilog 1.4858 = 30.6 + .007 = 30.607

$S = 30.607$ square inches

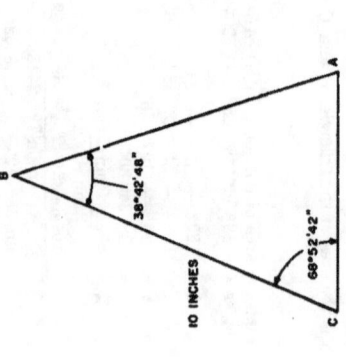

Figure 53. Solving for the area of an oblique triangle when two angles and a side are given.

172. Finding the Area of Triangle When Three Sides Are Given

To find the area of triangle when three sides are given, use the formula

$$S = \sqrt{s(s-a)(s-b)(s-c)}$$

where a, b, and c are the sides of the triangle and $s = \frac{1}{2}(a+b+c)$.

Example: Find the area of an oblique triangle when the sides are 8, 11, and 15 inches, respectively.

$s = \frac{1}{2}(a+b+c)$
$s = \frac{1}{2}(8+11+15)$
$s = \frac{1}{2}(34)$
$s = 17$
$S = \sqrt{s(s-a)(s-b)(s-c)}$
$S = \sqrt{17(17-8)(17-11)(17-15)}$
$S = \sqrt{17(9)(6)(2)}$
$S = \sqrt{1836}$
$S = 42.84$ square inches

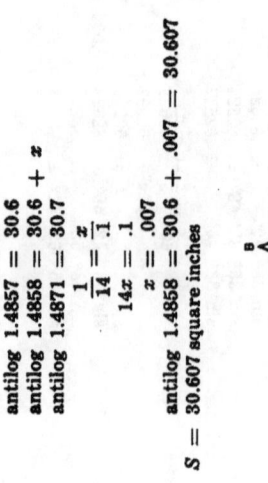

sin 68° 53' = .93285

$\frac{42}{60}$ or $\frac{7}{10} = \frac{x}{.00011}$

$10x = .00077$

$x = .000077$ or .00008

sin 68° 53' 42'' = .93274 + .00008 = .93282
sin 72° 24' = .95319
sin 72° 24' 30'' = .95319 + x
sin 72° 25' = .95328

$\frac{30}{60}$ or $\frac{1}{2} = \frac{x}{.00009}$

$2x = .00009$

$x = .000045$ or .00005

sin 72° 24' 30'' = .95319 + .00005 = .95324

$S = \frac{100 \times .62542 \times .93282}{2 \times .95324}$

$S = \frac{50 \times .62542 \times .93282}{.95324}$

$S = \log 50 + \log .62542 + \log .93282 - \log .95324$

log 50 = 1.6990
log .62500 = 9.7959—10
log .62542 = 9.7959—10 + x
log .62600 = 9.7966—10

$\frac{42}{100} = \frac{x}{.0007}$

$100x = .0294$

$x = .000294$ or .0003

log .62542 = 9.7959—10 + .0003 = 9.7962—10
log .93200 = 9.9694—10
log .93282 = 9.9694—10 + x
log .93300 = 9.9699—10

$\frac{82}{100} = \frac{x}{.0006}$

$100x = .0410$

$x = .00041$ or .0004

log .93282 = 9.9694—10 + .0004 = 9.9698—10
log .95300 = 9.9791—10
log .95324 = 9.9791—10 + x
log .95400 = 9.9795—10

$\frac{24}{100} = \frac{x}{.0004}$

$100x = .0096$

$x = .000096$ or .0001

log .95324 = 9.9791—10 + .0001 = 9.9792—10

$S = 1.6990 + 9.7962-10 + 9.9698-10 - 9.9792-10$

  1.6990
  9.7962—10
+ 9.9698—10
  ─────────
  21.4650—20
— 9.9792—10
  ─────────
  11.4858—10 or 1.4858

173. Review Problems—Trigonometric Laws

a. In an oblique triangle *ABC*, angle $A = 42°\ 15'\ 12''$, angle $B = 75°\ 28'\ 10''$, and side *b* measures 21 inches. Solve the triangle for angle *C* and side *a*.

b. In an oblique triangle *ABC*, angle $C = 52°\ 30'$, side $b = 45$ inches, and side $c = 38$ inches. Solve for angle *B*.

c. In an oblique triangle *ABC*, sides *a*, *b*, and *c* opposite angles *A*, *B*, and *C* have lengths of 9, 16, and 21 inches, respectively. Find the three angles of the triangle.

d. In an oblique triangle where *a* and *b* are any two sides and *A* and *B* are the angles opposite these sides, angle $C = 57°\ 20'\ 45''$, $a = 9.73$ inches, and $b = 6.47$ inches. Find angles *A* and *B*.

e. The three sides of a triangle are 40, 37, and 13 inches, respectively. Find the area of the triangle.

f. Two sides of an oblique triangle measure 12 and 18 feet, respectively. The angle between the two sides is 115°. Find the area of the triangle.

g. In a triangle *ABC*, angle $A = 30°$ and angle $B = 60°$. The side opposite angle $C = 16$ inches. Find the area of the triangle.

h. In an oblique triangle *ABC*, angle $C = 62°\ 50'$. The side opposite angle *A* measures 9.65 inches, and the side opposite angle *B* measures 17.85 inches. Find angles *A* and *B* and the length of the side opposite angle *C*.

CHAPTER 11
RADIANS

extensively in electrical formulas (part II).

174. Angular Measurement Using Radians

a. Definition. A radian is a unit of angular measurement equal to that angle which, when its vertex is upon the center of a circle, intercepts an arc that is equal in length to the radius of the circle. Thus, in figure 54, central angle *AOB* is equal to 1 radian because arc *AB* is equal to radius *OA*.

(1) The system that makes use of the radian is called the *natural system of angular measurement* because it has no arbitrary unit, such as the degree, but is founded upon the observation that the absolute size of any angle is the ratio of its arc to the radius of that arc. Where the arc and radius are equal, the ratio is 1, and this unit is the radian.

(2) The natural system of angular measurement—also called the circular system and the radian system—is used

b. Finding Any Angle. To find any angle, such as angle *AOC* in figure 54, determine the number of times that radius *r* will go into arc length *ABC*, thus determining the number of radians in the angle. Thus,

$$\text{Angle} = \frac{\text{arc}}{\text{radius}}$$

or, if angle *AOC* is denoted by the Greek letter θ (Theta) and arc *ABC* by *s*,

$$\theta = \frac{s}{r} \text{ radians}$$

Example: A circle has a radius of 6 inches. Find the angle subtended at the center of the circle by an arc 9 inches in length.

$$\theta = \frac{s}{r}$$
$$= \frac{9}{6}$$
$$= 1.5 \text{ radians}$$

c. Finding Length of Arc. To find the length of an arc intercepted by a central angle when the radius of the circle and the number of radians in the angle are known, use the formula in *b* above in the form—

$$s = r\theta$$

Example: A circle has a radius of 5 feet. How long is the arc intercepted by a central angle of 1.5 radians?

$$s = r\theta$$
$$= 5 \times 1.5$$
$$= 7.5 \text{ feet}$$

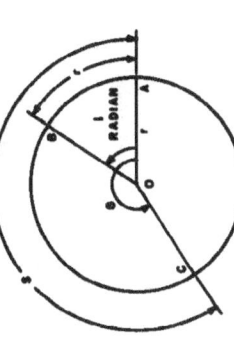

Figure 54. The radian or circular system of measurement.

175. The Relation Between Degrees and Radians

a. General. It is often necessary to convert an angle from degrees to radians or from radians to degrees. If the angle is one complete revolution, the arc is one complete circumference of a circle; thus, it is 2π times the radius. Therefore, the angle is equal to $2\pi r$ divided by r—that is, 2π radians ($\pi = 3.1416$).

Therefore,   1 revolution = 2π radians
also   1 revolution = 360°
Thus, 2π radians = 360°

$$1 \text{ radian} = \frac{360°}{2\pi} = \frac{180°}{\pi} = 57.29578°$$

and since   360° = 2π radians

$$1° = \frac{2\pi}{360} = \frac{\pi}{180} = 0.017453 \text{ radians}$$

To change radians to degrees, accurate to seconds, use figures accurate to at least five decimal places.

b. Changing Degrees to Radians and Radians to Degrees.

Example 1: Change 2.74 radians to degrees, minutes, and seconds.

1 radian = 57.29578°
2.74 radians = 2.74(57.29578)
             = 156.99044°
1° = 60'
.99044° = .99044(60)'
        = 59.4264'
.4264' = .4264(60)"
       = 25.5"
2.74 radians = 156° 59' 25.5"

Example 2: Change 57° 15' 18" to radians.

Step 1. Change the minutes and seconds to decimals of a degree:

1' = 60"
18" = $\frac{18}{60}$
    = .3'
15.3' = $\frac{15.3}{60}$
      = .255°
57° 15' 18" = 57.255°

Step 2. Change to radians:

1° = .017453 radian
57.255° = 57.255(.017453)
        = .99927 radian

c. Expressing Angles in Radians as Multiples of π. It is often convenient to express angles in radians as multiples of π. Since 360° = 2π radians, 90° = $\frac{1}{2}\pi$ radians, 40° = $\frac{1}{4}\pi$ radians, etc. It is necessary only to multiply the degrees by $\frac{\pi}{180}$ to change to radians.

Example: Express 135° in radians as a multiple of π.

$$135° = 135\left(\frac{\pi}{180}\right)$$
$$= \tfrac{3}{4}\pi \text{ radians}$$

176. Review Problems—Radians

a. Find the angle θ for the following arc lengths and radii:

(1) $r = 5$ inches, $s = 2$ inches.
(2) $r = 3$ feet, $s = 12$ feet.
(3) $r = .8$ miles, $s = 6.4$ miles.
(4) $r = 27$ meters, $s = 75$ meters

b. Find the arc lengths for the following angles and radii:

(1) $\theta = 5$ radians, $r = 7$ inches
(2) $\theta = 8$ radians, $r = 2.2$ feet
(3) $\theta = 2.1$ radians, $r = 9$ miles
(4) $\theta = .03$ radians, $r = .066$ inch

c. Express the following angles in radians:

(1) 30°
(2) 263° 12'
(3) 158° 33'
(4) 336° 24' 22"

d. Express the following angles in degrees:

(1) .8 radians
(2) 25 radians
(3) 3.45 radians
(4) 3π radians

e. Express the following angles as multiples of π:

(1) 30°
(2) 60°
(3) 225°
(4) 720°

CHAPTER 12
VECTORS

177. Plane Vectors

a. A line segment used to represent a quantity that has direction as well as magnitude is called a vector. The length of a vector is proportionate to the magnitude, and the arrow, or head, of the vector indicates the direction of the quantity represented.

b. The quantity represented by a vector is called a vector quantity. This is the directed magnitude itself. Electrical quantities, such as current and voltage, are vector quantities in ac circuits.

Example: An airplane is flying northeast at 120 miles per hour. Its speed is represented on figure 55 by line *OA*. The direction in which the airplane is traveling is represented by the direction of the line.

178. Vector Notation

Because a vector quantity has direction as well as magnitude, the methods of denoting a vector are different from the methods of denoting a scaler quantity. A vector may be denoted by two letters, the first indicating the origin, or initial point, and the other indicating the head or terminal point. For example, a vector may be represented by the letters *AB*, indicating that the quantity went from *A* to *B*. A small arrow sometimes is placed over the letters for emphasis; for example, $\overrightarrow{AB}$. Another method of notation is $A\underline{/\theta}$, where *A* represents the magnitude of the quantity, and $\underline{/\theta}$ represents the angle the vector makes with some reference line. For example, if line *OE* in figure 55 were used as the reference line, vector *OA* could be represented by the notation $120\underline{/45°}$, where 120 represents the magnitude of the quantity, and $\underline{/45°}$ represents the direction with respect to line *OE*. With respect to line *ON*, vector *OA*, would be represented by the notation $120\underline{/-45°}$.

179. Addition of Vectors, Parallelogram Method

The addition of vectors by the parallelogram method is shown in figure 56. To add vector *OA* to *OC*, draw a vector *OC* with its initial point located at the initial point of vector *OA*, and complete the parallelogram with these vectors forming two sides. The diagonal vector *OB*, with its initial point at the same initial point of *OA* and *OC* and its terminal point at the opposite vertex of the parallelogram, is the sum of *OA* and *OC*. Thus, two vectors (*OA* and *OC*) acting simultaneously on a point or object may be replaced by a single vector called the *resultant* (*OB*). The resultant vector will pro-

Figure 55. The velocity of an airplane described by a vector.

duce the same effect on the object as the joint action of the two vectors.

180. Addition of More Than Two Vectors

a. In determining the resultant (par. 179) of vectors when more than two quantities are represented, proceed as follows:

(1) Find the resultant of two of the vector quantities.

(2) Determine the final resultant between the third quantity and the resultant obtained from (1), above.

b. Assume three forces U, V, and W are acting on point O as shown in A, figure 57. Force U exerts 150 pounds at an angle of 60°, V exerts 100 pounds at an angle of 135°, and W exerts 150 pounds at an angle of 260°. Find the resultant of forces on point O.

(1) The resultant of any two vectors, such as U and W, are determined graphically by the line R_1 (B, fig. 57). To solve this problem first draw the vectors to scale at the designated angles; then construct the parallelogram OUTW with adjacent sides WT and UT. The resultant R_1 of OW and OU will be the diagonal OT.

(2) Combine the resultant R_1 with force V, then construct another parallelogram to scale as in (1), above. The final resultant R_2 is similarly determined by the line SO (C, fig. 57).

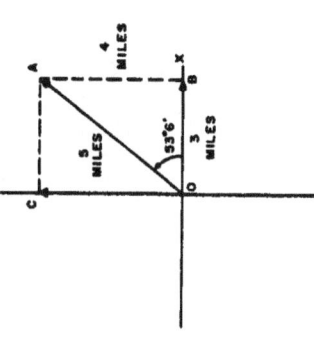

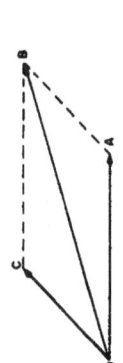

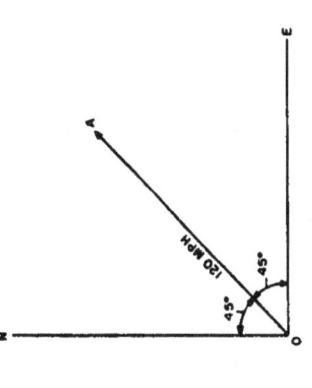

Figure 58. Horizontal and vertical components of vector.

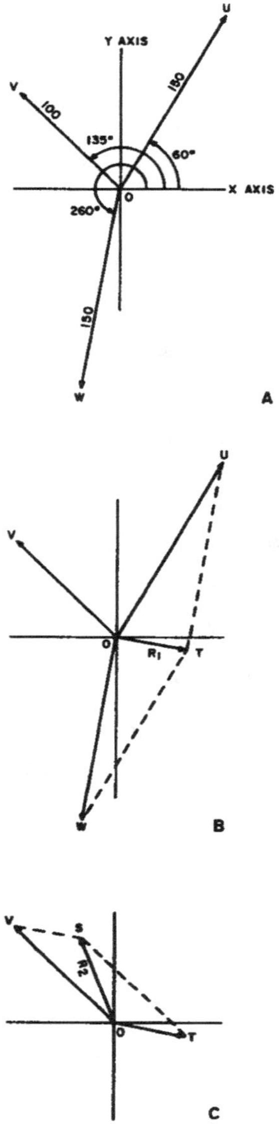

Figure 57. Resolution of three vectors.

Figure 56. Adding vectors, parallelogram method.

This, then, is the resolution of all three forces U, V, and W acting on point O.

nent of 3 and a vertical component of 4. This is done by using the sine and cosine function as follows:

$$\sin 53° 6' = \frac{BA}{5}$$

$$.79968 = \frac{BA}{5}$$

$$BA = 5 \times .79968$$
$$= 4 \text{ (approx)}$$

$$\cos 53° 6' = \frac{OB}{5}$$

$$.60042 = \frac{OB}{5}$$

$$OB = 5 \times .60042$$
$$= 3 \text{ (approx)}$$

181. Components of a Vector

a. A vector may be resolved into components along any two specified directions. If the directions of the components are chosen so that they are at right angles to each other, the components are called *rectangular components*.

b. By placing the initial point of a vector at the origin of the X and Y axes, the rectangular components are readily obtained either graphically or by computation. In figure 58, a vector with a magnitude of 5 and a direction of 53° 6' is shown broken down into a horizontal compo-

ANSWERS TO PROBLEMS

Paragraph 12.

$a(1) \frac{3}{5}; .6; 60\%.$ (2) $\frac{1}{2}; .5; 50\%.$ (3) $\frac{3}{8}; .375; 37\frac{1}{2}\%.$ (4) $\frac{1}{4}; .25; 25\%.$ (5) $\frac{5}{8}; .625; 62\frac{1}{2}\%.$ (6) $\frac{3}{5}; .6; 60\%.$ (7) $\frac{3}{10}; .3; 30\%.$ (8) $\frac{7}{10}; .7; 70\%.$ (9) $2\frac{1}{4}; 2.25; 225\%.$ (10) $\frac{7}{8}; 1.875; 187\frac{1}{2}\%.$ (11) $\frac{2}{25}; .08; 8\%.$ (12) $\frac{3}{50}; .06; 6\%.$ (13) $\frac{9}{50}; .18; 18\%.$ (14) $\frac{1}{400}; .0025.$ (15) $\frac{1}{40}; .025; 2\frac{1}{2}\%.$ (16) $\frac{1}{20}; .05; 5\%.$ (17) $\frac{1}{12}; .08\frac{1}{3}$ (See note below.) $8\frac{1}{3}\%.$ (18) $\frac{3}{8}; .375; 37\frac{1}{2}\%.$ (19) $1\frac{1}{20}; 1.05; 105\%.$ (20) $\frac{1}{25}; .04; 4\%.$

Note. This mixed decimal and fractional form is often used when an unending decimal would result.

$b(1) 150;$ (2) 50; (3) 4; (4) 900.
$c(1) 150\%;$ (2) $275\%;$ (3) $150\%;$ (4) $550\%.$
$d(1) 1.64;$ (2) 2,496; (3) .34; (4) 4.42.
$e(1) .207\%;$ (2) .028%.
$f(1) 433\frac{1}{3};$ (2) 2,500; (3) 520; (4) 200; (5) 200.

Paragraph 21.

a 336.6 pounds. b $3\frac{3}{7}$ days. c \$5.00. d \$1400.00. e .372 ohm. $.298$ ohm; $.459$ ohm; .893 ohm. f 2.820 pounds; 3.776 pounds; 4.119 pounds; 2,567 pounds. g 300 rpm. h 157.5 rpm.

Paragraph 25.

$a(1) 21;$ (2) 33; (3) 50; (4) 2.90; (5) 50.1; (6) 70.01; (7) 86.5; (8) 75.89.
$b(1) 2.236;$ (2) 2.646; (3) 3.317; 3.606; (5) 3.873; (6) 4.123.
$c(1) .158$ ampere; (2) .085 ampere; (3) .283 ampere; (4) 1.118 amperes.

Paragraph 42.

$a(1) 17;$ (2) 58; (3) $-21;$ (4) $-139°;$ (5) -252 volts.
$b(1) 251$ amperes; (2) -8 volts; (3) $-.6375cy;$ (4) $-31.99az^2;$ (5) $1.810x^2y.$
$c(1) -17.92;$ (2) $-72;$ (3) $-\frac{8}{35}.$ (4) .075852; (5) .0028125; (6) 120.
$d(1) 9;$ (2) $-\frac{20}{21};$ (3) 700; (4) 250; (5) $+\frac{2}{3}$ ampere; (6) $-.0025.$
$e(1) -4;$ (2) 14; (3) $-25;$ (4) 19; (5) 11; (6) 16; (7) 44; (8) 66; (9) $+2;$ (10) 18.

Paragraph 50.

$a(1) 6a^4 - 4a^2b^2 + 4b^4.$ (2) $E + 3RI + 20ZI.$ (3) $w + x + 9y + 8z.$
$b(1) 19ax + 17by - 9cz.$ (2) $-25w - 3z + 8y + 2z.$ (3) $4a^2 - 34ab + 6b^2.$
$c(1) 7.$ (2) 1. (3) 1.
$d(1) f^{10}.$ (2) $y^{a+b}.$ (3) $y^{2m}.$ (4) $r^4.$ (5) $R^{2m}.$ (6) $r^{m+1}.$
$e(1) \frac{4}{x^4}.$ (2) $\frac{1}{r^3}x^6.$ (3) $\frac{1}{36^2a^{20}}.$ (4) $\frac{1}{I^2R}.$ (5) $\frac{a^2}{8b^3}.$ (6) $\frac{3E}{4I^2R}.$
$f(1) 10a^2b - 15a^2b^2 + 35ab^3.$ (2) $4a^3 + 12a^2 + 4a.$ (3) $t^3 - 27.$ (4) $2x^4 + 5x^3y + 4x^2y^2 + 2xy^3 - y^4.$ (5) $9x^4 - 34x^2y^2$

$+ 25y^4$. (6) $\dfrac{a-c}{ca}$. (7) $\dfrac{3L-R^2}{R}$.

(8) $1 - 2a^2b + 3a^4b^5$. (9) $2z^2 + z - 1 + \dfrac{3z+4}{z^2+3}$. (10) $4b^2 - b$.

Paragraph 61.

a(1) $5(5+1-6)$; (2) $4(2+1-8)$; (3) $3(3-6+7)$; (4) $7r(1-3+5)$; (5) $2(5x+4y+3z)$.

b(1) $49z^2y^6$; (2) $4w^{10}$; (3) $64a^{10}b^8$; (4) $729a^6z^3$; (5) $-27b^3z^{12}$.

c(1) 5; (2) $+8$; (3) $\pm ab^3$; (4) $\pm 6yz^2$; (5) $\pm 10ab^5$; (6) $\pm 20a$; (7) -3; (8) $-x^3$; (9) 4; (10) $5x^4y^5z^2$.

d(1) $3(x+2)$; (2) $5a(a+3)$; (3) $2x(5x^2 - 7z^2 - 1)$; (4) $3z(2ay + 3bz - 4c)$; (5) $m(m^2 + m - 5x)$; (6) $3a^3(a^2 - 2ab - b^2)$; (7) $7ry^3(1 - 2 + 8m)$; (9) $r(r_1^2 + r_2^2)$; $2xam(6x + 7a + 8m)$; (8) $14^{3}ry$; (10) $\dfrac{1}{16}cd(4c^2 - 2cd + d^2)$.

Paragraph 69.

a(1) $z = 5\dfrac{2}{5}$; (2) $z = 4$; (3) $r = 2$; (4) $x = \dfrac{-13}{16}$; (5) $t = 1$; (6) $x = 7\dfrac{3}{4}$; (7) $r = 4$; (8) $z = 1$.

b(1) 8; (2) z; (3) $3(r + s)$; (4) $3(a - s)$; (5) $(I - 6)(I - 9)$; (6) $\dfrac{8E^2I^2}{2I^2R}$; (7) $\dfrac{2f}{6+F^2c}$.

c(1) $\dfrac{rR}{rR^2}$, $\dfrac{r}{rR^2}$, $\dfrac{R^2}{rR^2}$; (2) $\dfrac{a-1}{a^2-1}$, $\dfrac{x(a+1)}{a^2-1}$; (3) $\dfrac{3b}{6x}$, $\dfrac{2c}{6x}$; (4) $\dfrac{y(y+3)}{2(y+3)}$, $\dfrac{y}{2(y+3)}$; (5) $\dfrac{2(c+1)}{c(c+1)}$, $\dfrac{3c}{c(c+1)}$; (6) $\dfrac{2i}{2e-10}$, $\dfrac{i}{2e-10}$; (7) $\dfrac{y}{C^2-d^2}$, $\dfrac{z(c+d)}{C^2-d^2}$.

d(1) $\dfrac{12}{a}$; (2) $\dfrac{7s+11}{4t}$; (3) $\dfrac{9y^2a + 10xb}{12x^2y^3}$; (4) $\dfrac{6(z^2-2)}{z^4 - 5z^2 + 4}$; (5) $\dfrac{9c^2 + 2cd - 12d^2}{12c^2d^2}$; (6) $\dfrac{2r^2 + r - 13}{r^2 + 2r - 15}$;

(7) $\dfrac{12y-1}{4}$; (8) $\dfrac{4ab}{a^2-b^2}$; (9) $\dfrac{16(2-5q)}{25q^2}$; (10) $\dfrac{3t+4v}{12tv^3}$.

e(1) $\dfrac{3y^2}{8}$; (2) $\dfrac{a^9}{b^6}$; (3) $\dfrac{xz}{21my}$;

(4) $\dfrac{(s-r)^2}{s^2}$; (5) $\dfrac{3}{5x}$; (6) $\dfrac{1}{a^3}$;

(7) $15z$; (8) $\dfrac{a^3}{6cd}$; (9) $\dfrac{4su}{5}$;

(10) $\dfrac{e+3}{e+2}$.

f(1) 10; (2) $14\sqrt{5}$; (3) $x - \dfrac{x\sqrt{3}}{2}$; (4) $\dfrac{3a\sqrt{2}+a}{2}$; (5) $(r+1)\sqrt{rsi}$; (6) $\dfrac{2y\sqrt{x^2-y^2}}{x^2-y^2}$; (7) $\sqrt[3]{5} + 8\sqrt{x}$; (8) $7\sqrt{a} - 6\sqrt{b}$; (9) $3\sqrt{x} + y - 4\sqrt{x} - y$; (10) $7ab\sqrt{5a}$.

g(1) $12\sqrt{10}$; (2) 18; (3) $8ab^2$; (4) $2z^5\sqrt{3z}$; (5) $2xy\sqrt{xy}$; (6) $24pq^2\sqrt[3]{qr^2}$; (7) $a+b+c+2(\sqrt{ab} + \sqrt{ac} + \sqrt{bc})$; (8) $ax\sqrt{a}(a+x+1)$; (9) 8; (10) $2axy^2\sqrt[3]{2a}$.

h(1) 2; (2) 5; (3) $2\sqrt[3]{x}$; (4) $3\sqrt{zy}$; (5) $\sqrt{6}+2$; (6) $12a^{12}\sqrt{25} \cdot 3^5 \cdot 5^4 \cdot a^2$; (7) $\dfrac{c-\sqrt{2c}-4}{c-8}$; (8) $\sqrt{15}$; (9) $\dfrac{e^2+f^2+2\sqrt{e^2+f^2}}{e^2}$; (10) $\dfrac{4b\sqrt{1-4b^2}+1}{8b^2-1}$.

Paragraph 76.

a(1) 2; (2) 16; (3) $5\sqrt{2}$; (4) $\sqrt[3]{\dfrac{4}{4}}$;

(5) $3\sqrt{2x-1}$; (6) $\dfrac{x^{\frac{1}{4}} \sqrt[n]{6}}{y}$; (7) x^2y;

(8) $\sqrt[9]{d^2e^3}$; (9) $\dfrac{4r^2}{s}$; (10) $a^{3}b$.

b(1) $\sqrt[3]{4}$; (2) $\sqrt[5]{a^9b^4}$; (3) $\sqrt[12]{6^7}$; (4) $2 \cdot \sqrt{2f}$; (5) $5\sqrt{x}$; (6) $\sqrt{a^3c^2}$; (7) $6\sqrt[3]{r}$; (8) $2b \cdot \sqrt[3]{a^2}$; (9) $\sqrt{2r_1} + 3r_2$; (10) $3y\sqrt[5]{x}$.

c(1) $a^{\frac{3}{5}}$; (2) $(5x)^{\frac{1}{4}}$; (3) $6xd^{\frac{1}{4}}$; (4) $z^{\frac{1}{4}}$; (5) $(3a^3b^5)^{\frac{1}{3}}$; (6) $y^2a^{\frac{1}{2}}$; (7) $8(3e)^{\frac{1}{4}}$; (8) $9gi$; (9) $3bcd^{\frac{1}{4}}$; (10) $(x-y)^{\frac{1}{2}}$.

d(1) $2\sqrt{3}$; (2) $3\sqrt{7}$; (3) $3x\sqrt{7}$; (4) $12ab^2\sqrt{2}$; (5) $2bd\sqrt{15}$; (6) $2I\sqrt{2R}$; (7) $9pz\sqrt{7p}$; (8) $12dr^4\sqrt{3ds}$; (9) $45a^2\sqrt{5}$; (10) $112w^4z^4y\sqrt{2zx}$.

e(1) $\dfrac{\sqrt{2}}{10}$; (2) $\dfrac{\sqrt{z}}{2x}$; (3) $\dfrac{2\sqrt{3a}}{3}$; (4) $\dfrac{\sqrt[3]{x^2}}{x}$;

(5) $\dfrac{\sqrt[4]{27a^3x^4}}{3ax}$; (6) $\dfrac{\sqrt[3]{(3-2x)^2}}{3-2x}$;

(7) $\dfrac{\sqrt[3]{a}(a+b)}{a}$; (8) $\dfrac{\sqrt[3]{ab^2c^2}}{bc}$;

(9) $\dfrac{\sqrt[3]{s+1}}{s+1}$; (10) $\sqrt[5]{(i+3)^3}$.

Paragraph 79.

a(1) $j5\sqrt{3}$; (2) $j\sqrt{23}$; (3) $\dfrac{j}{3}$;

(4) $-j10z^2y\sqrt{z}$; (5) $\dfrac{1}{2}$;

(6) $-4xy\sqrt[3]{2x^4y^2}$.

b(1) $16 + j109$; (2) $41 - j22$; (3) $61 - j251$; (4) $44 + j10$; (5) $6 + j11$; (6) $-2 - j47$.

c(1) $779 - j371$; (2) $59 + j114$; (3) $-22 + j15$; (4) $155 - j61$; (5) $169 + j23$; (6) $9 - j8$.

d(1) $-55 + j46$; (2) $6 - 6\sqrt{6} + j(6\sqrt{2} + 6\sqrt{3})$; (3) 13; (4) $-5 - j12$; (5) $-j8$; (6) $46 - j48$; (7) $f^2 + j2fg - g^2$; (8) $I^2 + E^2$; (9) $-68 - j239$; (10) $71 - j17$.

e(1) $\dfrac{3}{13} - j\dfrac{2}{13}$; (2) $1 - j6$; (3) $-\dfrac{6}{25}$

$+ j\dfrac{17}{25}$; (4) $1 + j2$; (5) $\dfrac{(x^2 + j2xy - y^2)}{(x^2 + y^2)}$;

(6) $2(1 - j2)$; (7) $\dfrac{3(1+j)}{2}$; (8) $\dfrac{1 + j13}{10}$;

(9) $\dfrac{38 + j34}{65}$; (10) $\dfrac{I^2 + j2IE - E^2}{I^2 + E^2}$.

Paragraph 86.

a(1) 3; (2) 2; (3) 85; (4) 3; (5) 1; (6) $z = -5, y = 8$; (7) $a = 3, b = 1$; (8) $x = 3, y = 4$; (9) $m = 3, n = 5$; (10) $r = 8, s = 1$.

b(1) $d = \dfrac{Wh}{F}$. (2) $g = \dfrac{v^2 - v_0^2}{2h}$.

(3) $a = \dfrac{Fg}{w}$. (4) $N = \dfrac{2.534H}{D^2}$. (5) $l = \dfrac{10F}{22.5BI}$.

c(1) 15; (2) 0; (3) $\dfrac{10}{3}$; (4) 4; (5) $\dfrac{28}{9}$;

(6) $\dfrac{12}{119}$; (7) $-2\dfrac{12}{25}$; (8) 8; (9) $\dfrac{40}{109}$;

(10) $-\dfrac{1}{19}$.

d(1) $x = 4, y = 5$; (2) $a = 4.95, b = 2.62$; (3) $x = 4, y = 7$; (4) $z = -2, y = -4$; (5) $x = -3, y = 1$; (6) $I = 13, Z = 17$;

(7) $x = 4, y = \dfrac{1}{2}$; (8) $a = 6, b = -4$;

(9) $x = 5, y = -1$; (10) $r = \dfrac{(a+b)}{2}$,

$s = \dfrac{(a-b)}{2}$.

e(1) 1 volt; (2) $R = 20$ ohms; (3) 110 volts; (4) 75 ohms; (5) 100 milliamperes, 80 milliamperes, 60 milliamperes; (6) 5.5 amperes.

Paragraph 94.

a(1) $0, -\dfrac{3}{2}$; (2) $0, 4$; (3) $0, -3$; (4) $0, -2, \pm 5$; (5) ± 8; (6) ± 3; (7) ± 3; (8) ± 4; (9) $7, -6$; (10) $1, 12$.

b(1) $\dfrac{-3 \pm \sqrt{13}}{2}$; (2) $-3 \pm \sqrt{19}$; (5) $\dfrac{1}{2} \pm \dfrac{\sqrt{14}}{4}$; (6) $-\dfrac{5}{3} \pm \dfrac{2\sqrt{10}}{3}$; (7) $-1, 3$;

$2 \pm \sqrt{3}$; (4) $-2 \pm \dfrac{\sqrt{22}}{2}$

(8) $-1 \pm \dfrac{\sqrt{6}}{2}$; (9) $1 \pm \sqrt{6}$; (10) $\dfrac{1}{2} \pm \dfrac{\sqrt{5}}{2}$

$c(1) -1; (2) -\frac{3}{4}, \frac{2}{3}; (3) \frac{-5 \pm \sqrt{13}}{6};$
$(4) -\frac{3}{2}, \frac{4}{3}; (5) -3, 1; (6) -\frac{1}{5}, \frac{5}{3};$
$(7) \pm \sqrt{2}; (8) \pm \sqrt{19}; (9) -1, 2;$
$(10) \frac{-5 \pm \sqrt{7}}{3}$

Paragraph 111.

$a(1)$ $1,613 \times 10^5$; (2) 500×10^3, or 5×10^5; (3) $6,166 \times 10^{-8}$.
$b(1)$ $3,109 \times 10^2$; (2) 19×10^{-4}; (3) $4,492 \times 10^{-9}$.
$c(1)$ 892×10^6; (2) $2,464 \times 10^{-2}$, or 24.64; (3) $3,168 \times 10^{-11}$; (4) $14,640$.
$d(1)$ 167; (2) $1,608 \times 10^8$ 107; (4) 33×10^{-5}.
$e(1)$ 4×10^2, or 400; (2) 13×10^{-3}; (3) 27×10^{-9}; (4) 9×10^2, or 900.

Paragraph 127.

$a(1)$ 2.8949; (2) 0.5527; (3) $8.5378-10$; (4) $6.6776-10$; (5) 1.6955; (6) 2.4570; (7) 2.8809; (8) 0.8593; (9) $7.9946-10$; (10) $5.7205-10$.
$b(1)$ $70,097$ (2) 271; (3) $.351$; (4) $.000676$; (5) 3.99; (6) 370.67; (7) $.00002718$; (8) $500,500$; (9) 1.5915; (10) $.000003445$.
$c(1)$ 164.2; (2) $39,990(3)$ $1,376$; (4) $.006764$; (5) $5,710$.
$d(1)$ $.4983$; (2) $.3874$; (3) $.3984$; (4) $.7487$; (5) $.2437$.
$e(1)$ $.0000007372$; (2) 51.46; (3) 3.47; (4) 19.43; (5) 783; (6) $.2367$; (7) 5.343; (8) 87.74; (9) 1.55; (10) $.09456$.
$f(1)$ 2.298; (2) 11.77; (3) 24.43; (4) 33.37 (5) $.4509$; (6) $.4725$; (7) $.04088$; (8) $.6153$; (9) $.0576$; (10) $.35367$.

Paragraph 142.

a 96 square inches. b 36 square inches. c 25 square inches. d 15 square inches. e 14.422 square inches. f 5.657 square inches. $g(1)$ Parallelogram, $A = bh$, 120 square inches; (2) Triangle, $A = \frac{bh}{2}$ 4.025 square inches; (3) Circle, $A = \pi r^2$, 314 square centimeters; $C = \pi D$, 62.8 centimeters; (4) Trapezoid, $A = \frac{B+b}{2} h$, $A = 60$ square inches. $h(1)$ 3 inches. (2) $4\frac{1}{2}$ inches; (3) 8.8 inches; (4) 5 inches. i 78.5 square inches. j 100 feet. k 82.5 square feet. l 48.496 inches.

Paragraph 153.

$a(1)$ $c = 8.603$. (2) $a = 6.08$. (3) $b = 39.5$. (4) $c = b\sqrt{10}$. (5) $b = m^2 - 1$.
$b(1)$ $\sin A = \frac{4}{7}$, $\cos A = \frac{\sqrt{33}}{7}$, $\tan A = \frac{4}{\sqrt{33}}$, $\cot A = \frac{\sqrt{33}}{4}$, $\sec A = \frac{7}{\sqrt{33}}$, $\csc A = \frac{7}{4}$.
(2) $\sin A = \frac{2}{\sqrt{13}}$, $\cos A = \frac{3}{\sqrt{13}}$, $\tan A = \frac{2}{3}$, $\cot A = \frac{3}{2}$, $\sec A = \frac{\sqrt{13}}{3}$, $\csc A = \frac{\sqrt{13}}{2}$
(3) $\sin A = \frac{1}{2}$, $\cos A = \frac{\sqrt{3}}{2}$, $\tan A = \frac{\sqrt{3}}{3}$, $\cot A = \sqrt{3}$, $\sec A = \frac{2}{3}\sqrt{3}$, $\csc A = 2$.
(4) $\sin A = \frac{1}{2.4}$, $\cos A = \frac{1.09}{1.2}$, $\tan A = \frac{1}{2.18}$, $\cot A = 2.18$, $\sec A = \frac{1.2}{1.09}$, $\csc A = 2.4$.
(5) $\sin A = \frac{y\sqrt{y^2+1}}{y^2+1}$, $\cos A = \frac{\sqrt{y^2+1}}{y^2+1}$,
$\tan A = y$, $\cot A = \frac{1}{y}$, $\sec A = \sqrt{y^2+1}$,
$\csc = \frac{\sqrt{y^2+1}}{y}$.

(6) $\sin A = \frac{\sqrt{55}}{8}$, $\cos A = \frac{3}{8}$, $\tan A = \frac{\sqrt{55}}{3}$, $\cot A = \frac{3\sqrt{55}}{55}$, $\sec A = 2\frac{2}{3}$, $\csc A = \frac{8\sqrt{55}}{55}$

$c(1)$ $a = 17$, $b = 29.4$, $c = 34$. (2) $a = 9$, $b = 12$, $c = 15$. (3) $a = 12$, $b = 16$, $c = 20$. (4) $a = 17.5$, $b = 10\sqrt{11}$, $c = 37.5$. (5) $a = 10$, $b = 6$, $c = 2\sqrt{34}$. (6) $a = 37.08$, $b = 18.4$, $c = 41.4$.
$d(1)$ $b = 10\sqrt{3}$, $c = 20$. (2) $a = 7$, $c = 7\sqrt{2}$. (3) $a = 4\sqrt{3}$, $b = 4$. (4) $b = 3\sqrt{3}$, $c = 6\sqrt{3}$. (5) $a = 12.5$, $b = 12.5\sqrt{3}$.

Paragraph 164.

$a(1)$ $.02618$, $.99966$, $.02619$, 38.1885. (2) $.26584$, $.96402$, $.27576$, 3.62636. (3) $.53238$, $.84650$, $.62892$, (4) 1.59002. (4) $.59693$, $.80230$, $.74402$, 1.34405. (5) $.70690$, $.70731$, $.99942$, 1.00058. (6) $.70706$, $.70716$, $.99986$, 1.00014. (7) $.57649$, $.81710$, $.70553$, 1.41737. (8) $.81370$, $.58129$, 1.39982, $.71438$. (9) $.74811$, $.66357$, 1.12740, $.88700$. (10) $.92429$, $.38169$, 2.42158, $.41295$.
$b(1)$ $14°$ $54'$ $51''$; (2) $66°$ $35'$ $51''$; (3) $19°$ $56'$ $54''$; (4) $25°$ $17'$ $5''$; (5) $40°$ $23'$ $35''$; (6) $68°$ $45'$ $2''$; (7) $22°$ $11'$ $47''$; (8) $34°$ $5'$ $19''$; (9) $52°$ $13'$ $2''$; (10) $51°$ $29'$ $49''$
$c(1)$ $44°$ $43'$ $29''$; (2) 10.29; (3) $32.5(4)$ 19.76; (5) 12.4; (6) $54°$ $18'$ $52.5''$; (7) 33.69; (8) 16.5; (9) $36°$ $28'$ $9''$; (10) 128.3; (11) $30 \angle 9(12)$ $29°$ $3'$ $15''$
$d(1)$ 52.28 feet; (2) 80.027 feet; (3) 47.63 feet, 8.69 feet high; (4) $3,149$ feet; (5) 11.734 feet; (6) 91.77 feet; (7) 206 feet; (8) $3,578$ feet; (9) $16,647$ feet (3.153 miles); (10) 82.12 feet; (11) 1.414 inches each; (12) side opposite $60° \angle 5.196$ inches, side opposite $30° \angle 3$ inches.

Paragraph 173.

a $C = 62°$ $16'$ $38''$, $a = 14.59$. b $B = 69°$ $58'$, c $A = 23°$ $33'$ $22''$, $B = 45°$ $16'$ $31''$, $C = 111°$ $10'$ $7''$, d $A = 81°$ $31'$ $41''$, $B = 41°$ $7'$ $29''$. e 240 square inches. f 97.880 square feet. g 55.424 square inches. h $A = 32°$ $33'$ $45''$, $B = 84°$ $36'$ $15''$, $c = 15.95$ inches.

Paragraph 176.

$a(1)$ $.4$ radian; (2) 4 radians; (3) 8 radians; (4) 2.78 radians.
$b(1)$ 35 inches; (2) 17.6 feet; (3) 18.9 miles; (4) $.00198$ inch.
$c(1)$ $.52$ radian; (2) 4.6 radians; (3) 2.77 radians; (4) 5.89 radians.
$d(1)$ $45°$ $50'$ $11.8''$; (2) $1432°$ $23'$ $40.2''$; (3) $197°$ $40'$ $13.44''$; (4) $540°$.
$e(1)$ $\pi/6$; (2) $\pi/3$; (3) $5\pi/4$; (4) 4π.

www.ingramcontent.com/pod-product-compliance
Lightning Source LLC
Chambersburg PA
CBHW082035300426
44117CB00015B/2489